新时代英汉翻译教程

A Textbook of English-Chinese Translation in the New Era

罗 天 编著

人民交通出版社股份有限公司
北 京

内 容 提 要

本书主要内容包括英汉对比知识、翻译方法、翻译专题和语篇翻译,为英语专业高年级学生或者其他英汉翻译的初学者,提供了一本系统全面、具体深入、循序渐进而紧跟时代的翻译教程。

本书可供高校英语专业、翻译专业、商务英语专业等高年级学生学习,也可供相关专业硕士研究生和其他翻译爱好者等参考。

图书在版编目(CIP)数据

新时代英汉翻译教程 / 罗天编著. —北京:人民交通出版社股份有限公司,2019.8
ISBN 978-7-114-15818-6

Ⅰ.①新… Ⅱ.①罗… Ⅲ.①英语—翻译—高等学校—教材 Ⅳ.①H315.9

中国版本图书馆 CIP 数据核字(2019)第 196119 号

Xinshidai Ying-Han Fanyi Jiaocheng

书　　名:	新时代英汉翻译教程
著 作 者:	罗　天
责任编辑:	闫吉维
责任校对:	孙国靖　魏佳宁
责任印制:	张　凯
出版发行:	人民交通出版社股份有限公司
地　　址:	(100011)北京市朝阳区安定门外外馆斜街3号
网　　址:	http://www.ccpress.com.cn
销售电话:	(010)59757973
总 经 销:	人民交通出版社股份有限公司发行部
经　　销:	各地新华书店
印　　刷:	北京市密东印刷有限公司
开　　本:	787×1092　1/16
印　　张:	16.5
字　　数:	419 千
版　　次:	2019年8月　第1版
印　　次:	2019年8月　第1次印刷
书　　号:	ISBN 978-7-114-15818-6
定　　价:	48.00 元

(有印刷、装订质量问题的图书由本公司负责调换)

作者简介

罗天,男,重庆交通大学教授,硕士生导师,澳门大学英语语言学翻译方向博士毕业。先后教授"英汉互译""文学翻译""翻译实践"等本科课程和"翻译史研究""翻译研究方法论"等硕士研究生课程。曾获得《中国翻译》韩素音翻译奖;指导学生参加国内外翻译大赛,共有30余名学生获奖。在Perspectives,LANS-TTS,Babel,《中国翻译》《翻译季刊》《外国语文》等国内外学术期刊发表论文近30篇;其中SSCI和A&HCI收录论文3篇。出版学术专著2部、译著2部;参与编写翻译教材2部,主编1部;主持国家社科基金项目和教育部人文社科项目各1项,完成其他省级科研项目4项。

前　言

在长期的翻译教学、实践以及研究过程中，我们越来越期待这样一种英汉翻译教程的出现：它应该能够为初学者提供较为系统的英汉对比知识；在此基础上让初学者能够较为轻松地熟悉基本翻译理论知识；它能够循序渐进地培养初学者的翻译能力；它应该以语篇为基本单位；它有助于培养学生分析、思辨、逻辑等方面的能力；它应该紧跟时代步伐；它应该是初学者随时可以参考的良师益友。

然而，环顾四周，我们心目中的教材难觅芳踪。苦等之下，不如自己动手，丰衣足食。于是，经过多年的构思，这本教程逐渐成形。

首先，本书系统全面地介绍了翻译基础知识，包括英汉对比知识、翻译方法、翻译专题、语篇翻译等内容；在附录部分，还提供了英汉译音表、中英标点符号对照表、语料库与翻译等等内容。教材内容几乎涵盖了当代翻译初学者所需掌握的主要知识结构和体系，让初学者对翻译有一个全面、客观的了解。比如，本书从9个方面对英汉两种语言进行了对比；介绍了20种翻译方法，方法之多，远超绝大多数的教材。其中回译法、形译法等是翻译知识体系中不可缺少的一环，一般翻译教科书并未谈及，而本书专设章节介绍。

其次，本教程对一些翻译专题的讨论比较具体深入。专题讨论涉及专有名词的翻译、修辞与翻译、文化与翻译、译文校改等方面。探讨专有名词的翻译时，又分为人名、地名、术语的翻译来讲解。讲解人名翻译时，又分为英美人名来源、外国人名的翻译原则与方法、华人华裔人名的回译、文学作品中人名的翻译四个方面。讲解外国人名的翻译原则与方法时，又细分为先名后姓、音译为主、名从主人、约定俗成、符合标准、同名同译六个方面来论述。这些深入细致的探讨无疑会为译者提供极具价值的参考，以应对纷繁复杂的翻译实践。

再次，本教程在编排体例上循序渐进。从整体内容编排来看，先介绍英汉对比知识，再讨论翻译方法，接着讨论翻译专题，然后进入语篇翻译。这样有助于学习者由浅入深，由易到难，由局部到整体，由词到句到文体再到语篇，循序渐进地学习翻译知识。从每章内容的编排来看，每章有一个中心议题，所有的练习材料和理论讲解都围绕中心议题展开。每章开始是400词以内的热身翻译练习，学生先获得一定的感性认识；然后通过双语阅读或者佳译赏析，模仿学习；再到认知升级部分，讲解翻译理论知识；最后落实到较长语篇的翻译，长度500~2000词。利用教材，学习者可以体验一个从实践到理论再到实践、从感性认识到理性认识再到感性认识的螺旋式上升过程。

最后，本书在内容上紧扣时代特色。在翻译理论部分，博采众长，集中汇集、体现了当代最新翻译研究方面的成果，如摘译、编译等方法，异化归化等策略，目的功能论、翻译的语篇分析途径，最新诗歌翻译策略等。在佳译赏析和翻译实践材料的选择上，既有文艺复兴时期培根的散文，也有18世纪的独立宣言；更有最近发生的事件，如阿富汗的重重危机、第一张黑洞照片、巴黎圣母院大火等。应该说，在照顾历史与经典的同时，本教程更加贴近现实，保持与时代同步。

本书的练习分为热身练习和翻译实践两部分。前者短小，可供每一位初学者练习；后者有短有长，短者可供单人练习，长者可供小组讨论，集体练习，以丰富练习的样式，调节课堂氛围。

本书的适用对象包括各类高校英语专业、翻译专业、商务英语专业等高年级学生，部分硕士研究生和其他翻译爱好者等。

在教程编写过程中，参考引用了国内外大量专家学者的教材、专著和期刊论文等。虽然尽力注明，但由于篇幅限制，部分文献在书中并未得以一一注明，在此致以诚挚的谢意和歉意。同时也恳请广大读者，对本书的不足和错漏之处，批评指正。

本教材是重庆交通大学规划教材立项建设项目的成果。编写者为重庆交通大学外国语学院罗天老师。编写期间，得到了重庆交通大学各部门以及人民交通出版社股份有限公司各位编辑的热心帮助和支持，在此表示衷心感谢。

编　者
2019年5月

目　　录

第一章　认识翻译 ……………………………………………………（ 1 ）
　热身练习 ………………………………………………………………（ 1 ）
　　'Oh, so you're a translator-That's interesting!' ……………………（ 1 ）
　双语阅读 ………………………………………………………………（ 2 ）
　　1. China: Importing Knowledge through Translation ………………（ 2 ）
　　2.《译学英华》总序 …………………………………………………（ 5 ）
　认知升级 ………………………………………………………………（ 6 ）
　　一、翻译的概念 ………………………………………………………（ 6 ）
　　二、翻译的标准 ………………………………………………………（ 8 ）
　　三、翻译的步骤 ………………………………………………………（ 9 ）
　　四、译者的素质 ………………………………………………………（ 11 ）
　翻译实践 ………………………………………………………………（ 13 ）
　　A Textbook of Translation (Excerpt) ……………………………（ 13 ）

第二章　英汉对比(1) ………………………………………………（ 15 ）
　热身练习 ………………………………………………………………（ 15 ）
　　Sea Gulls …………………………………………………………（ 15 ）
　双语阅读 ………………………………………………………………（ 15 ）
　　1. Missing: 100,000 Children a Year ……………………………（ 15 ）
　　2. 盲人挑灯 …………………………………………………………（ 16 ）
　认知升级 ………………………………………………………………（ 16 ）
　　一、英语多变化，汉语多重复 ………………………………………（ 16 ）
　　二、英语多名介，汉语多动词 ………………………………………（ 19 ）
　　三、英语多抽象，汉语多具体 ………………………………………（ 21 ）
　　四、英语多屈折，汉语少形变 ………………………………………（ 24 ）
　翻译实践 ………………………………………………………………（ 26 ）
　　Downsizing in Vogue ………………………………………………（ 26 ）

第三章　英汉对比(2) ………………………………………………（ 28 ）
　热身练习 ………………………………………………………………（ 28 ）
　　A Young Fisherman ………………………………………………（ 28 ）
　双语阅读 ………………………………………………………………（ 28 ）
　　1. Nature's Resurrection ……………………………………………（ 28 ）
　　2. 春 …………………………………………………………………（ 29 ）

认知升级 …… （29）
    一、英语重形合，汉语重意合 …… （29）
    二、英语多长句，汉语多短句 …… （33）
    三、英语多物称，汉语多人称 …… （34）
    四、英语多被动，汉语多主动 …… （36）
    五、英语前重心，汉语后重心 …… （38）
  翻译实践 …… （41）
    Pollution in India …… （41）

第四章　翻译技巧（1） …… （43）
  热身练习 …… （43）
    The Making of Ashenden（Excerpt） …… （43）
  佳译赏析 …… （44）
    Genius Sacrificed for Failure …… （44）
  认知升级 …… （45）
    一、直译与意译 …… （45）
    二、音译与形译 …… （48）
    三、增译与省译 …… （50）
    四、回译与转类 …… （52）
    五、具体与抽象 …… （58）
  翻译实践 …… （60）
    Columbine at 20：How School Shootings Became 'Part of the American Psyche' …… （60）

第五章　翻译技巧（2） …… （64）
  热身练习 …… （64）
    Beyond Life …… （64）
  佳译赏析 …… （64）
    On Growing Old Gracefully …… （64）
  认知升级 …… （66）
    一、替换与加注 …… （66）
    二、分译与合译 …… （67）
    三、正译与反译 …… （70）
    四、转态与重组 …… （71）
    五、摘译与编译 …… （75）
  翻译实践 …… （79）
    Moment in Peking（Excerpt） …… （79）

第六章　专有名词的翻译 …… （81）
  热身练习 …… （81）
    The First Black Hole Image：What Can We Really See? …… （81）
  佳译赏析 …… （82）
    Brain-Computer Interfaces …… （82）
  认知升级 …… （85）

  一、人名的翻译 ………………………………………………………（85）
  二、地名的翻译 ………………………………………………………（92）
  三、术语的翻译 ………………………………………………………（98）
 翻译实践 …………………………………………………………………（103）
  Demography and Automation ………………………………………（103）

第七章 修辞、文化与翻译 …………………………………………（107）
 热身练习 …………………………………………………………………（107）
  Notre Dame: The Human Spark ……………………………………（107）
 佳译赏析 …………………………………………………………………（108）
  Beauty(Excerpt) ……………………………………………………（108）
 认知升级 …………………………………………………………………（110）
  一、修辞与翻译 ……………………………………………………（110）
  二、文化与翻译 ……………………………………………………（114）
 翻译实践 …………………………………………………………………（120）
  A Hero Reborn: "China's Tolkien" Aims to Conquer Western Readers …（120）

第八章 语篇分析与翻译 ……………………………………………（122）
 热身练习 …………………………………………………………………（122）
  Cuban Missile Crisis Address to the Nation(Excerpt) ……………（122）
 佳译赏析 …………………………………………………………………（123）
  The Declaration of Independence …………………………………（123）
 认知升级 …………………………………………………………………（126）
  一、语篇特征与翻译 ………………………………………………（126）
  二、文本类型与翻译 ………………………………………………（129）
  三、功能目的与翻译 ………………………………………………（131）
 翻译实践 …………………………………………………………………（133）
  Afghan's Time of Endless Crisis ……………………………………（133）

第九章 译文校改 ……………………………………………………（137）
 热身练习 …………………………………………………………………（137）
  Of Virtue ……………………………………………………………（137）
 佳译赏析 …………………………………………………………………（138）
  Of Great Place ………………………………………………………（138）
 认知升级 …………………………………………………………………（140）
  一、词义的推敲 ……………………………………………………（140）
  二、逻辑的判断 ……………………………………………………（148）
  三、风格的统一 ……………………………………………………（153）
  四、译文的美化 ……………………………………………………（159）
 翻译实践 …………………………………………………………………（168）
  The Sounds of Manhattan …………………………………………（168）

第十章 文学语篇的翻译（1） ………………………………………（170）
 热身练习 …………………………………………………………………（170）

  The Adventures of Huckleberry Finn(Excerpt) ……………………… (170)
 佳译赏析 ………………………………………………………………… (171)
  Seeing the Wind ………………………………………………………… (171)
  Vanity Fair (Excerpt) …………………………………………………… (172)
 认知升级 ………………………………………………………………… (174)
  一、散文的翻译 ………………………………………………………… (174)
  二、小说的翻译 ………………………………………………………… (179)
 翻译实践 ………………………………………………………………… (184)
  Celebrated Jumping Frog of Calaveras County ………………………… (184)

第十一章　文学语篇的翻译(2) ……………………………………… (188)
 热身练习 ………………………………………………………………… (188)
  The Charge of the Light Brigade ……………………………………… (188)
 佳译赏析 ………………………………………………………………… (190)
  The Diverting History of John Gilpin ………………………………… (190)
  The Merchant of Venice(Excerpt) …………………………………… (191)
 认知升级 ………………………………………………………………… (193)
  一、诗歌的翻译 ………………………………………………………… (193)
  二、戏剧的翻译 ………………………………………………………… (204)
 翻译实践 ………………………………………………………………… (210)
  Lord Ullin's Daughter …………………………………………………… (210)

第十二章　应用语篇的翻译 …………………………………………… (212)
 热身练习 ………………………………………………………………… (212)
  Agreement ……………………………………………………………… (212)
 佳译赏析 ………………………………………………………………… (213)
  The United Nations Charter(Excerpt) ………………………………… (213)
 认知升级 ………………………………………………………………… (215)
  一、商务语篇的翻译 …………………………………………………… (215)
  二、科技语篇的翻译 …………………………………………………… (219)
  三、法律语篇的翻译 …………………………………………………… (225)
 翻译实践 ………………………………………………………………… (235)
  The BMW 7 Series ……………………………………………………… (235)

参考文献 ………………………………………………………………… (238)
附录1　英汉译音表 …………………………………………………… (240)
附录2　英汉标点符号对照表 ………………………………………… (242)
附录3　语料库与翻译 ………………………………………………… (243)
附录4　计算机辅助翻译 ……………………………………………… (249)
附录5　全国翻译专业资格(水平)考试 ……………………………… (252)
附录6　翻译竞赛简介 ………………………………………………… (253)

第一章
认识翻译

倘若拿河流来作比,中华文化这一条长河,有水满的时候,也有水少的时候,但却从未枯竭。原因就是有新水注入。注入的次数大大小小是颇多的。最大的有两次,一次是从印度来的水,一次是从西方来的水。而这两次的大注入依靠的都是翻译。中华文化之所以能长葆青春,万应灵药就是翻译。翻译之为用大矣哉!

——季羡林《中国翻译词典》序《中国翻译》1995年第3期

The history of the different civilizations is the history of their translations. Each civilization, as each soul, is different, unique. Translation is our way to face this otherness of the universe and history.

——Octavio Paz (1914—1998)
Mexican writer, poet, and diplomat, winner of the 1990 Nobel Prize for Literature

热身练习

请将下列段落翻译为汉语,并思考当今社会对翻译职业的要求。

'Oh, so you're a translator-That's interesting!'
Geoffrey Samuelsson-Brown

An opening gambit at a social or business gathering is for the person next to you to ask what you do. When the person finds out your profession the inevitable response is, 'Oh so you're a translator-that's interesting' and before you have a chance to say anything, the next rejoinder is, 'suppose you translate things like books and letters into foreign languages, do you?' Without giving you a chance to utter a further word you are hit by the fatal catch-all, 'Still, computers will be taking over soon, won't they?' When faced with such a verbal attack you hardly have the inclination to respond.

The skills clusters that the translator needs at his fingertips are shown in Figure 1.

Regrettably, an overwhelming number of people-and these include clients-harbour many misconceptions of what is required to be a skilled translator. Such misconceptions include the following:

- As a translator you can translate all subjects.
- If you speak a foreign language ipso facto, you can automatically translate into it. If you can hold a conversation in a foreign language, then you are bilingual.

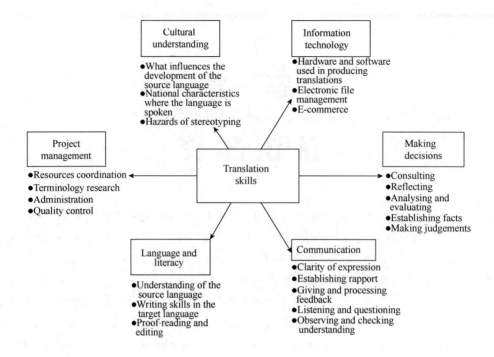

Figure 1 *Translation skills clusters*

- Translators are mind-readers and can produce a perfect translation without having to consult the author of the original text, irrespective of whether it is ambiguous, vague or badly written.
- No matter how many versions of the original were made before final copy was approved or how long the process took, the translator needs only one stab at the task, and very little time, since he gets it right first time without the need for checking or proofreading. After all, the computer does all that for you.

(286 words)

请阅读以下英文和中文段落,思考翻译在中国历史中扮演的作用。

1. China: Importing Knowledge through Translation❶
Jean Delisle & Judith Woodsworth

From the Yuan (1280—1368) to the Ming (1368—1644) dynasties, the translation of sutras took on less importance. As Yuan rulers directed their attention westwards, Arabs began to settle in China, becoming mandarins or merchants. Having learned Chinese, some erudite high officials translated scientific works from Arabic or European languages. The Arab Al-Tusi Nasir Al-Din (1201—

---

❶Delisle, Jean & Woodsworth, Judith. Translators through History (Revised edition). John Benjamins Publishing. 2012:98-101.

74) translated Euclid's *Elements* some works of astronomy including Ptolemy's *Almagest* and Plato's Logic. An Arabic pharmacopoeia Al-Jamic fi-al-Adwiya al-Mufradah (Dictionary of Elementary Medicines), made up of thirty-six volumes listing some 1,400 different medicines, was translated toward the end of the Yuan dynasty. This was published during the following dynasty as Hui Hui Yao Fang. Later the Ming Emperor Zhu Yuanzhang ordered two mandarins of Arab origin, Ma Hama and Ma Sayihei, to translate two Arabic books on astronomy with the help of two officials, Li Chong and Wu Bozhong. Beyond satisfying the curiosity of a few scholars, these works are alleged to have had minimal scientific merit, given the already advanced state of knowledge in China.

The situation was to change toward the end of the sixteenth century. With the arrival of Christian missionaries, the Jesuits in particular, China came into contact with Europe, which had begun to overtake China in some scientific and technological fields. To facilitate their relations with Chinese officials and intellectuals, the missionaries translated works of Western science as well as Christian texts. From 1582, the year when Jesuits initiated work in China, until 1773, when the Society of Jesus was dissolved and the Jesuits left, seventy-one missionaries of various nationalities undertook this kind of work. They were Italian: Matteo Ricci (1552—1610), Nicolaus Longobardi (1559—1654), Sabbathinus de Ursis (1575—1620), Julius Aleni (1582—1649) and Jacobus Rho (1593—1638), whose Chinese names were Li Madou, Long Huamin, Xiong Sanba, Ai Rueno and Luo Yagu, respectively; Portuguese: Franciscus Furtado (1587—1652), whose Chinese name was Fu Fanji; Swiss: Jean Terrenz (1576—1630), known as Deng Yuhan; Belgian: Ferdinand Verbiest (1623—1688), known as Nan Huairen; with a contingent from France, Germany and other places (Ma 1995:377-78). The missionaries were often assisted by Chinese collaborators such as Xu Guangqi, a distinguished scientist and prime minister during the last years of the Ming dynasty, a period of intense scholarship and intellectual activity; Li Zhizao, a scientist and government official; Wang Zheng, an engineer and government official; and xue Fengzuo, a scientist. Matteo Ricci was assisted by Xu Guangqi when he translated Euclid's *Elements* in 1607 and by Li Zhizao when he translated the *Astrolabium* by German Jesuit and mathematician Christophorus Clavius. For these scholars, translation was not confined to passive reproduction; instead, the translated text served as a basis for further research. Li Zhizao, for example, uses his preface to *Astrolabiuniy* the first work to set out the foundations of Western astronomy in Chinese, to make the point that the Earth is round and in motion.

With their translation of Clavius's *Trattato della figura isoperimetre* (Treatise on Isoperimetric Figures), published in 1608, Ricci and Li Dang introduced the concept of equilateral polygons inside the circle. In 1612, a six-volume translation by De Ursis and Xu was the first Chinese work on hydrology and reservoirs; it also dealt with physiology and described some of the techniques used in the distillation of medicines. As he translated, Xu performed experiments. Thus, he used the book he was in the process of translating as a kind of textbook, and translation was in turn a catalyst leading to new discoveries.

Translations were carried out in the fields of mathematics, astronomy, medicine, law, literature and religion. A 1613 translation by Ricci and Li showed how to perform written arithmetic operations: addition, subtraction, multiplication and division. They also introduced the Chinese to classical logic via a Portuguese university-level textbook brought in by a missionary in 1625.

In 1644, the Qing (Ching) dynasty replaced the earlier, more scholarly Ming Dynasty. Conflicts between the missionary order and the Pope, as well as between the Christians and the Manchu court, diminished the influence of the Church. Translation into Chinese all but stopped for roughly a hundred years with the expulsion of foreign missionaries by the Yongzheng Emperor in the eighteenth century. It resumed following the British invasion (1840—42) and the subsequent arrival of American, British, French and German missionaries. Foreign missionaries dominated scientific and technical translation initially, but Chinese translators, trained in China or at foreign universities, gradually took over the transmission of Western knowledge.

A leading figure during this period was the Chinese mathematician Li Shanlan (1811—82), who collaborated with the British missionary Alexander Wylie (1815—77) on a translation of a work on differential and integral calculus. The Chinese mathematician Hua Hengfang (1833—1902) and the British missionary John Fryer (1839—1928) translated a text on probability taken from the *Encyclopedia Britan-nica*. In 1877 Hua and Fryer translated Hymers's *Treatise on Plane and Spherical Trigonometry* (1858). This translation is a good example of how knowledge is both transmitted and generated through the translation process. It contributed to the dissemination of modern mathematical theory and, at the same time, stimulated the personal research carried out by the translators. Fryer and his collaborators also translated approximately one hundred chemistry treatises and textbooks. Many of these were published by the Jiangnan Ordnance Factory, where Fryer and Xu were the official translators.

The earth sciences, too, were introduced to China through translation. During the Opium War, Lin Zexu, a Chinese official, translated part of the *Cyclopaedia of Geography* by Murray Hugh. Published in 1836, it was the most up-to-date work on world geography at the time. Wei Yuan (1794—1857) and Xu Jishe (1795—1873) made extensive use of this translation to compile their own book on world geography. By the end of the Qing dynasty, many medical books were available in Chinese. Ding Dubao (1874—1952), a physician and translator, was responsible for over fifty medical translations. He was awarded national and international prizes for his role in translating and disseminating works of medicine and pharmacology.

Just as translators helped open China to Western knowledge, they brought China to the attention of the West by reproducing classical Chinese works in foreign languages. These works of philosophy, politics, education and military science enabled Europeans to become acquainted with the long history and rich civilization of China. The translators, European sinologists living in China and working in close collaboration with Chinese scholars, included missionaries Martin Martini (1614—61), Antoine Gaubille (1689—1759), Jean Joseph Amiot (1728—93), Pierre Marchal Cibot (1727—80), and Ernst Faber (1839—99). Published in bilingual editions and accompanied by copious explanatory notes, these translations helped make the rest of the world more familiar with Chinese culture.

The missionary and sinologist James Legge (1815—91) was particularly distinguished. While abroad, primarily in Hong Kong, he applied himself to the study of the Chinese language and traditional writings. He translated and published a substantial body of work from Chinese into English, notably in collaboration with the scholar Wang Tao (1828—97). He believed it was his duty to be a "Missionary to his own people and race [...] to translate and explain the learning of the East to the scholars and missionaries of the West" (Ride 1970:10). Ultimately, he dedicated more of his career to his translations from Chinese than he did to his missionary work, leaving Hong Kong and going on to become the first professor of Chinese at Oxford University.

After a series of sporadic periods of translation activity over its long history, China is currently experiencing what has been called a new "wave of translation". Dating from the opening to the outside world in the late 1970s, it is a comprehensive and intense movement encompassing all areas of knowledge (Lin 2002:168). Connected with this surge in practical translation is a growing body of research by Chinese scholars working in the field of translation studies. (1300 words)

2.《译学英华》总序❶
孔慧怡

在人类文明史上,有不少进展都源于外来知识的冲击,令社会、文化和知识系统产生巨大变化,终于使整个文化面貌一新。由于知识的传递主要依赖语言为工具,外来的知识明显地牵涉到外语,所以翻译一直是传播外来知识的重要管道。我们甚至可以说,世界上各主要文化系统的发展都和翻译活动脱离不了关系。

公元8世纪,信奉伊斯兰教的阿拉伯国家大量翻译古希腊的哲学和自然科学文献,同时也引进源于印度的知识,因此在很短的时间内,阿拉伯文化有了突飞猛进的发展,在公元8世纪到13世纪这几百年里,阿拉伯世界在数学、医学和自然科学等方面取得的成就,可以说执全球科学文明的牛耳;同时,伊斯兰教在教义和理论方面,也因为受到古希腊学术的冲击,而建立起更完备的体系和规条。

公元12世纪,欧洲以西班牙、北意大利等地为中心,大量翻译阿拉伯学者的著作,并且通过阿拉伯文的译本,重新认识古希腊的哲学和科学思想。这些在欧洲早已成为"绝学"的文献,从阿拉伯文再翻译成拉丁文,直接带动中世纪欧洲文明的重大革新。假如我们说,西方现代文明的缘起就在这一次基于翻译和重译的文化承传,也绝不是夸大之言。

以上两个例子,正好说明翻译活动可以产生多么巨大的促进文化发展的力量。但是假如我们再思考阿拉伯文明和欧洲文明在这段时间之后的发展方向,我们会发现它们虽然都以古希腊学术成果为基础,后来却走上了完全不同的道路。为什么同样的文献以翻译的方式介绍到两个地区,到最后会演变出截然不同的结果呢?既然外来知识是相同的,那么最终的分别肯定在于阿拉伯和欧洲文化环境的差异了。因此,这两个例子也告诉我们:翻译所造成的长远文化影响并不取决于原著或译作本身,而是取决于一时一地的文化环境会把外来知识引上什么道路。

中国历史上也有过和阿拉伯、欧洲类似的经验,通过翻译引进外来知识,达到文化上的飞跃发展和重大革新。其中最瞩目的例子,莫过于历时超过10个世纪的佛经翻译活动。始于公元2世纪中叶而大盛于公元4世纪至8世纪的佛经翻译活动,可以说对中国文化的每一个层面都造成深远影响。中国的语言、文学、民间艺术、本土信仰、宗教组织、社会风尚等方面,都因为佛学通过翻译在中国传播而有了新的发展;更值得注意的是,源于本土的哲学

---

❶孔慧怡.总序.译学英华.香港中文大学翻译研究中心.2005:5-7.

思想在佛经翻译的高潮已经过去之后,因为得到佛学思想的启示,完成了极富历史意义的自我更新——宋明理学就是这个过程的产物。

同样,明末清初欧洲耶稣会教士到中国传教,他们通过翻译引进中国的天文、地理和自然科学知识,不但在当时的先进士大夫群中造成影响,也间接对清末力求国家自强革新的知识分子起了启发作用——通过翻译而得以传播的外来知识,在朝廷禁教之后,并没有完全烟消云散。从历史和文化意义来看,清末改革派希望从"西学"入手,达到富国强兵的目标,可以说与明末士大夫对"西学"或"天学"的探讨是一脉相承的。

中国翻译传统源远流长,我们可以列举更多的例子,证明翻译活动引起的主体文化(host culture)反响是深远而又持久的;但中国本土文化所提供的环境,在上述不同的翻译活跃期,到底如何有选择性地把外来知识引上某些轨道,也许更值得我们关注,因为这样的研究才会充分显示翻译活动作为跨文化沟通的枢纽,其可能性和局限性在什么地方。综合上面所列举的种种情况,我们可以清楚地看到,要从事深入的翻译研究,应该考虑两大范畴:第一是主体文化的规范和环境,第二是翻译活动与主体文化在很长一段时间里产生的相互影响。

认知升级

Translation "may very probably be the most complex type of event yet produced in the evolution of the cosmos".

——I.A.Richards❶

一、翻译的概念

1.翻译的定义

对翻译的定义,可以有不同的角度,从不同的层次进行。

首先,翻译是一种语言实践。例如,纽马克(Peter Newmark)在 *A Textbook of Translation* 中将翻译看作"Often, though not by any means always, it is rendering the meaning of a text into another language in the way that the author intended the text"❷。又如,张培基认为,"翻译是运用一种语言把另一种语言所表达的思维内容准确而完整地重新表达出来的语言活动"❸。冯庆华认为,"翻译是许多语言活动中的一种,它是用一种语言形式把另一种语言形式里的内容重新表现出来的语言实践活动"❹。

其次,翻译是一种高级思维过程,例如毛荣贵将翻译描述为,"一种更换语言形式和转移信息内容(包括思想、意义、情感、修辞、文体、风格、文化乃至口吻等)的复杂的思维及表达过程"❺。

再次,翻译还是一种社会、文化交际活动。例如,孙致礼给翻译的界定是,"翻译是把一

---

❶Richards, I.A.. "Toward a Theory of Translating", in Arthur F. Wright (Ed.).*Studies in Chinese Thought*.Chicago: University of Chicago Press, 1953:246-262.
❷Newmark, Peter.*A Textbook of Translation*.Shanghai: Shanghai Foreign Language Education Press, 2001:5.
❸张培基,等.英汉翻译教程.上海:上海外语教育出版社,1980/2000:绪论.
❹冯庆华.实用翻译教程:英汉互译(第三版).上海:上海外语教育出版社,2010:3.
❺毛荣贵.新世纪大学英汉翻译教程.上海:上海交通大学出版社,2002:11.

种语言表达的意义用另一种语言传达出来,以达到沟通思想情感、传播文化知识、促进社会文明,特别是推动译语文化兴旺昌盛的目的"❶。陈宏薇认为,"翻译是跨语言、跨文化、跨社会的交际活动"❷。

在英文中,translation("翻译")作为一个名词使用时,通常包含如下几层含义:

Translation can refer to:(1) translating:the **process**(to translate;the activity rather than the tangible object);(2) a translation:the **product** of the process of translating(i.e.the translated text);(3) translation:the abstract **concept** which encompasses both the process of translating and the product of that process.❸

The term translation itself has several meanings:it can refer to the general subject **field**, the **product**(the text that has been translated) or the **process**(the act of producing the translation, otherwise known as translating).❹

在汉语中,"翻译"一词的意义更为丰富。它既可以代表笔译,也可以代表口译;既可以指从事翻译的人,也可以指翻译职业或者产业;既可以用作动词,也可以用作名词。在具体的语境之中,需要辨别"翻译"的具体含义。

2.翻译的分类

根据设定的标准,可以对翻译进行不同的分类。例如,雅各布森以符号代码为依据,在其《翻译研究的语言学方面》(*On Linguistic Aspects of Translation*)一文中,提出了著名的翻译的三分法:语内、语际和符际翻译。

1.**Intralingual translation** or *rewording* is an interpretation of verbal signs by means of other signs of the same language.

2.**Interlingual translation** or *translation proper* is an interpretation of verbal signs by means of some other language.

3.**Intersemiotic translation** or *transmutation* is an interpretation of verbal signs by means of signs of nonverbal sign systems.❺

在雅各布森的分类体系中,语内翻译(intralingual translation)指某种语言内部不同符号之间的转换,比如将古汉语翻译成现代汉语、将四川话翻译成广东话;语际翻译(interlingual translation)指两种不同语言符号系统之间的转换,比如将汉语翻译成英语、将日语翻译成法语等,这是严格意义上的翻译(translation proper),它也是今天被人们最为广泛讨论的翻译类型;符际翻译(intersemiotic translation)则指语言与非语言符号系统之间的转换,比如将手势语翻译成书面语、将图片翻译成文字等。

又如,从翻译媒介入手,又可以将翻译划分为口译(interpreting)、笔译(translating)、机辅翻译(computer-aided translation)和机器翻译(machine translating)等。

以翻译题材为分类标准,可以将翻译划分为文学翻译(literary translation)、科技翻译

---

❶孙致礼.新编英汉翻译教程.上海:上海外语教育出版社,2003:6.
❷陈宏薇,等.汉英翻译基础.上海:上海外语教育出版社,1998:10.
❸Bell,Roger T..*Translation and Translating:Theory and Practice*.New York:Longman Inc.,1991:13.此段引文中的黑体为编者所加.
❹Munday,Jeremy.*Introducing Translation Studies:Theories and Applications*.London & New York:Routledge,2001:4-5.此段引文中的黑体为编者所加.
❺Jakobson,Roman."On Linguistic Aspects of Translation",in Lawrence Venuti(Ed.).*The Translation Studies Reader*.London & New York:Routledge,2004:114.此段引文中的黑体为编者所加.

(technical translation)、经贸翻译(business translation)、法律文本翻译(legal translation)、宗教翻译(religious translation)和政治文献翻译(translation of political texts)等。

从翻译方式上来看,翻译还有全译(complete translation)、节译(selective translation)、编译(editing translation, trans-editing)、改译(rewriting)以及译写(transcreation)等类别。

根据翻译的不同类别,我们可以从不同层面和维度更加深入、细致地描写、理解和研究翻译活动。

二、翻译的标准

翻译的标准也是一个众说纷纭的问题。例如,1790年,英国爱丁堡大学的历史学教授泰特勒(Alexander Fraser Tytler,1747—1813)提出了其影响深远的翻译三原则,即:

I would therefore describe a good translation to be, *That, in which the merit of the original work is so completely transfused into another language, as to be as distinctly apprehended, and as strongly felt, by a native of the country to which that language belongs, as it is by those who speak the language of the original work.*

Now, supposing this description to be a just one, which I think it is, let us examine what are the laws of translation which may be deduced from it.

It will follow,

Ⅰ.That the Translation should give a complete transcript of the ideas of the original work.

Ⅱ. That the style and manner of writing should be of the same character with that of the original.

Ⅲ.That the Translation should have all the ease of original composition.❶

从泰特勒的翻译三原则看来,翻译首先应当把原作的意思全部转移到译文中,其次译文应当具备原作的风格和文体,再次译文应当和原作同样地通顺自然。

美国语言学家、翻译家尤金·奈达(Eugene A. Nida, 1914—2011)认为:

Translating consists in **reproducing** in the receptor language the **closest natural equivalent** of the source-language message, first in terms of **meaning** and secondly in terms of **style**.❷

翻译的首要目的,在于对源语信息的复制(reproducing…the source-language message)。其次,在这一"复制"的过程当中,应当遵循对等原则(equivalent)。而对等又可以进一步细化为两个层面,即语义层面(meaning)与文体层面(style)。首要的对等在于语义层面,力求复制出与源语信息最为接近的意义(closest meaning);其次追求文体层面的对等,力求以最为接近于源语文体特色的方式复制源语信息(natural style)。

中国学者也提出过翻译标准。例如,1894年,《马氏文通》的作者马建忠(1845—1900)在其《拟设翻译书院议》一文当中提出了"善译"的翻译原则。他在文中指出:

夫如是则一书到手,经营反复,确知其意旨之所在,而又摹写其神情、仿佛其语气,然后心悟神解,振笔而书,译成之文,适如其所译而止,而曾无毫发出入于其间。夫而后

---

❶Tytler, Alexander Fraser. *Essay on the Principles of Translation*. London: Dent & New York: Dutton, 1907: 8-9.

❷Nida, Eugene A. & Charles R. Taber. *The Theory and Practice of Translation*. Leiden: E. J. Brill, 1969/1982: 12. 此段引文中的黑体为编者所加。

能使阅者所得之益与观原文无异,则为善译也已。❶

马建忠的"善译"大体包含了三方面的要求:第一,译者需要真正理解原作的"意旨""神情"和"语气";第二,译文要能够传达原作的意义(意旨)、精神(神情)和风格(语气);第三,译文要与原作毫无出入,"适如其所译",而"无毫发出入于其间"。

1898年,严复(1854—1921)在其翻译的英国生物学家赫胥黎(Thomas Henry Huxley, 1825—1895)的《天演论》(*Evolution And Ethics*)一书的"译例言"中,提出了著名的"信、达、雅"的翻译三原则。严复在其"译例言"的开篇即指出:

> 译事三难:信、达、雅。求其信已大难矣,顾信矣不达,虽译犹不译也,则达尚焉。海通已来,象寄之才,随地多有,而任取一书,则其能与于斯二者,则以寡矣。其故在浅尝,一也;偏至,二也;辨之者少,三也。今是书所言,本五十年来西人新得之学,又为作者晚出之书。译文取明深义,故词句之间,时有所颠倒附益,不斤斤于字比句次,而意义则不倍本文。题曰达旨,不云笔译,取便发挥,实非正法。什法师又云:学我者病。来者方多,幸勿以是书为口实也。❷

在严复看来,"信"指忠实于原文,"达"强调译文的通顺,"信、达而外,求其尔雅"❸,即强调译文也要适当重视其修辞与文采。严复的信、达、雅三原则,在今天看来虽然不尽完美,但是在很长一段时期内,"信、达、雅三字,是翻译界的金科玉律,尽人皆知"❹。

1932年,林语堂(1895—1976)在《论翻译》一文当中提出,"翻译的标准问题,大概包括三方面。我们可依三方面的次序讨论。第一是忠实标准,第二是通顺标准,第三是美的标准"❺。此三原则与严复的"信、达、雅"三原则大体相符。

1963年,钱锺书(1910—1998)先生在《林纾的翻译》一文中指出,"文学翻译的最高理想可以说是'化'。把作品从一国文字转变成另一国文字,既能不因语文习惯的差异而露出生硬牵强的痕迹,又能完全保存原作的风味,那就算得入于'化境'"❻。

对于本科阶段的翻译初学者而言,我们不妨将"忠实""通顺"和"优美"作为译文质量的基本追求。

三、翻译的步骤

翻译是一个包含了语言技巧与艺术的复杂过程,掌握科学的翻译程序,可以帮助我们高效优质地完成翻译任务。奈达在《翻译理论与实践》(*The Theory and Practice of Translation*)一书中,将翻译的过程分为四个步骤:分析(analysis)、转换(transfer)、重组(restructuring)、校验(testing),即:

---

❶ 张岱年.采西学议:冯桂芬 马建忠集.沈阳:辽宁人民出版社,1994:225.
❷ 严复.天演论.北京:商务印书馆,1981:xi.
❸ 严复.天演论.北京:商务印书馆,1981:xi.
❹ 郁达夫.读丁珰生的译诗而论及于翻译.郁达夫文集(第五卷·文论)(国内版).广州:花城出版社 & 香港:生活·读书·新知 三联书店香港分店,1982:189.
❺ 林语堂.论翻译.林语堂名著全集(第十九卷·语言学论丛).长春:东北师范大学出版社,1994:306.
❻ 钱锺书.林纾的翻译.七缀集.北京:生活·读书·新知 三联书店,2002/2008:77.

(1) analysis, in which the surface structure (*i.e.*, the message as given in language A) is analyzed in terms of (a) the grammatical relationships and (b) the meanings of the words and combinations of words, (2) transfer, in which the analyzed material is transferred in the mind of the translator from language A to language B, and (3) restructuring, in which the transferred material is restructured in order to make the final message fully acceptable in the receptor language.❶ (4) testing of the translation, this should cover the entire range of possible problems: accuracy of rendering, intelligibility, stylistic equivalence, etc...testing the translation does not consist in merely comparing texts to see the extent of verbal consistency or conformity (translators can be consistently wrong as well as consistently right), but in determining how the potential receptors of a translation react to it.❷

实际上,有多位学者对翻译过程做出过思考与描述。经过综合考虑,本教材将翻译的过程归纳为下述三个步骤。

1.阅读分析

对原文进行阅读分析是做好翻译的第一步。阅读分析包括四个层面:

首先,从词汇层面上分析原文。(1)对不熟悉或者生僻的字词短语,要借助字典、词典、百科全书等工具类书籍查明其出处及用法意义。(2)注意区分原文中的普通名词、专业术语、文化专有项等。(3)分析原文在用词上的特点,是使用了高频词还是低频词?(4)这些词语的语体色彩如何?是正式还是非正式?(5)这些词语的感情色彩如何,是褒义、贬义还是中性?(6)这些词语是单义词还是多义词?如果是多义词,在本文中的最贴切的含义是什么?

其次,从句子层面上分析原文。(1)分析原文的句式结构,使用了哪些句型(陈述句、祈使句、疑问句还是感叹句)。(2)句式的简单与繁复、短小与冗长等。(3)对于疑难长句,最好分析句子的主语、谓语、宾语、定语、状语、补语、表语等成分,以准确理解长句的意思。(4)对段落内部各个句子之间的逻辑关系,也可以进行梳理,以便找出每一段落的主题句或者大意。

再次,从语篇层面上分析原文。在字词理解的基础之上,分析原文的篇章结构、衔接、连贯、互文性(引用、典故等)、文体、修辞方法、语言风格以及创作意图等,厘清文本类型。

最后,从语境层面上分析原文,把握原文的基本大意,作者的目的、意图、功能、接受情况等;将原文放在大背景下进行考察,分析原文所受到的社会、历史、文化等外部因素的影响。

2.转换表达

"表达的好坏主要取决于对原文理解的深度以及对译文语言的修养程度。表达是理解的结果,但理解正确并不意味着必然能表达得正确"❸。在转换表达的阶段,需要重点考虑以下问题:

首先,要充分认识英语和汉语之间的差异。(1)注意体会原文的隐含意义,避免机械照搬原文的字面意义,避免"假朋友"等错误。(2)要意识到英汉语在词汇搭配方面的显著差异,避免译文生硬。

---

❶ Nida, Eugene A. & Charles R. Taber. *The Theory and Practice of Translation*. Leiden: E.J.Brill, 1969/1982: 21.
❷ Nida, Eugene A. & Charles R. Taber. *The Theory and Practice of Translation*. Leiden: E.J.Brill, 1969/1982: 163.
❸ 张培基.英汉翻译教程.上海:上海外语教育出版社,1980/2000:12.

其次,要注意整体翻译策略和技巧的选用。根据翻译单位、翻译目的等因素,从直译、意译、音译、切分、合并等翻译方法中选取最为恰当者,进行语言转换。这些翻译方法要有利于译文在总体上保持统一的表述风格与文体风格。

最后,要考虑忠实与通顺的统一。尽量避免出现忠实而不通顺,或者通顺而不忠实的文体。既要努力传达原文信息,又要使译文具有一定的可读性。在满足忠实、通顺的基础上,努力追求译文的美感,尽量给读者带来美的感受。

3. 审校修正

根据纽马克的建议,"按照翻译文本的难易程度,用在审校与修正译文上的时间应当达到翻译用时的50%~70%"❶,可见审校与修正在翻译过程中的重要性。结合翻译实践,我们认为审校与修正应当大致包括如下几个步骤:

第一遍,对照原文审校,保证对原文信息的忠实。主要从字词的角度修正名称、日期、地点、数字、专有名词、标点符号、语法等方面的错误,同时从整体的角度调整句式并处理段落的漏译等。

第二遍,抛开原文,单独审校译本,提高译文的可读性。在这一过程中,主要着眼于译文风格的修正,消除不通顺的文字以及不符合汉语表达习惯的文字,使整个译本读起来自然流畅。

第三遍,往往需要将译本放置一周左右的时间再进行通读审校。诚如钱歌川(1903—1990)先生所言,"凡是翻译出来的一字一句,一事一物,都必须要合乎逻辑,合乎情理,否则必然有误"❷。因此,这一遍的审校主要着力于译文的逻辑性,修正译文当中前后矛盾、不符合语言表达习惯以及社会文化风俗的地方。

四、译者的素质

翻译需要译者不仅具备精深的双语语言,还需要有一定的专业知识、文化知识等,也需要具备良好的职业道德。

例如,林语堂在《论翻译》一文中指出,译者应当在三个方面着力,即:

翻译的艺术所倚赖的:第一是译者对于原文文字上及内容上透彻的了解;第二是译者有相当的国文程度,能写清顺畅达的中文;第三是译事上的训练,译者对于翻译标准及手术的问题有正当的见解。❸

PACTE Group❹则认为,翻译技能包括:双语技能、语言外技能、工具技能、翻译知识、身体精神能力以及策略技能。

综合众多学者的观点,我们认为译者应当具备以下几方面的素质:

第一,扎实的英汉双语功底。英汉译者要不断提升自己在字词、语法、句法以及篇章结构方面的英文造诣,要能够充分理解、深入分析原文的意义。欠缺相应的英文水准,翻译也就无从谈起。其次,以汉语为母语的译者,必须对自己的母语有充分的了解与把握。母语所学不精,便会出现只可意会不能言传的现象。好的汉语修养能够帮助我们精确表达原文中的思想。

---

❶ Newmark, Peter. *A Textbook of Translation*. Shanghai: Shanghai Foreign Language Education Press, 2001/2005: 37.
❷ 钱歌川. 翻译的基本知识. 长沙: 湖南科学技术出版社, 1981: 9.
❸ 林语堂. 论翻译. 林语堂名著全集(第十九卷·语言学论丛). 长春: 东北师范大学出版社, 1994: 305.
❹ PACTE. Investigating translation competence. Meta, 2005, 50(2): 609-19.

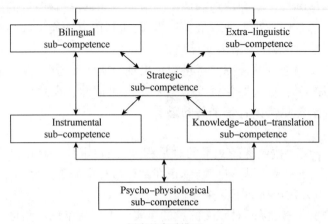

译者的素质模型

第二，基本的翻译理论知识，以便指导实践。结合自己多年的翻译实践与理论研究，许钧教授指出，"研究翻译理论对于提高并指导翻译实践有百利而无一害。作为一名译者，如果同时具有正确的翻译观、敏锐的理论意识，能够通过理论研究不断地反省、总结、设法解决自己翻译实践中出现的种种问题，就能够更快地进步，翻译得更好"❶。翻译理论可以帮助译者全面而充分、高屋建瓴地分析解决所遇到的翻译实践问题，指导译者更好地把握整个翻译过程，评估自己的翻译质量。

第三，广博的百科知识。吕叔湘（1904—1998）先生在《翻译工作和"杂学"》一文当中指出，"要做好翻译工作……必得对于原文有彻底的了解。……了解原文的第一步，不用说，是获得足够的词汇和文法知识。……第二道关是熟语。……第三道关，就是字典不能帮忙的那些个东西：上自天文，下至地理，人情风俗，俚语方言，历史上的事件，小说里的人物，五花八门，无以名之，名之曰'杂学'"❷。当然，一个人的时间精力毕竟有限，要做到真正意义上的"杂家"并不十分容易，需要译者博览群书，日积月累，善于查证工具书。

第四，某个专业领域的特长。所谓"术业有专攻"，每位译者都会因为自身的爱好以及生活阅历等的不同而擅长于某个领域的翻译，因此译者可以充分了解自身的翻译潜质，尽量集中精力从事自己擅长的专业领域，才更有可能产生优秀的译本。

第五，深厚的东西文化修养。翻译离不开对文化背景知识的掌握，文化背景知识不仅包括相关国家的历史、地理、风土人情、自然风貌、文学艺术、文化传统、宗教信仰等方面，还包括对中西文化差异的认识。王佐良（1916—1995）先生曾经在《翻译中的文化比较》一文中提出，"翻译者必须是一个真正意义的文化人。人们常说：他必须掌握两种语言，确实如此；但是，不了解语言当中的社会文化，谁也无法真正掌握语言"❸。一名合格的英汉译者，不仅要对本民族文化有深厚的了解，还必须不断加深对英语国家文化的了解，对比和把握两种文化的异同，如此才可能深入理解原文中的文化内涵，并创造出好的译品。例如以下词汇的理解和翻译，就涉及许多文化知识：Hellen of Troy（红颜祸水），Melapu's herb（灵丹妙药，来自古希腊罗马神话传说），honey moon（蜜月，来自民族风俗），bell the cat（自告奋勇），sour grape

---

❶穆雷，许钧.关于翻译实践与翻译研究的互动关系——许钧教授访谈录.外语与外语教学，2006(202:1):57.

❷吕叔湘.翻译工作和"杂学".中国对外翻译出版公司选编.翻译理论与翻译技巧论文集.北京：中国对外翻译出版公司，1983:218-219.

❸王佐良.翻译中的文化比较.翻译通讯，1984(1):2.

(酸葡萄,来自寓言故事)等。

第六,严谨的逻辑。诚如钱歌川先生所言,"自然物的名词是很少被人误译的,人为物的名词被人误译的机会也不太多,最容易出纰漏的,就是抽象名词和行动词乃至修饰语之类。所以有时单是语言的知识还不够用,最后非得乞灵于逻辑不可。逻辑是翻译者的最后一张王牌,是他必须具有的基本要素"❶。有些初学者,常常因为忽略逻辑问题,犯下可笑的翻译错误。

第七,高度的责任感与职业道德。所谓职业道德,刘士聪说:"就是责任心,对自己负责,对他人负责,对艺术负责。换言之,也就是要真实,对自己真实,对他人真实,对艺术真实。"科技发展和经济全球化使对外交流与合作日益频繁。在文化传播方面,翻译的桥梁作用越来越明显。随着我国改革开放的进一步深化、加入世贸组织和综合国力的日渐增强,我国在国际事务中的作用越来越重要。作为翻译人员,不仅要把国外先进的文明成果介绍到国内,还要把我国的优秀文化、科技成果推向全世界,所以翻译人员肩负着不可取代的历史使命。

请将下列段落翻译为汉语。

A Textbook of Translation(Excerpt)
Peter Newmark

Translation has its own excitement, its own interest. A satisfactory translation is always possible, but a good translator is never satisfied with it. It can usually be improved. There is no such thing as a perfect, ideal or 'correct' translation. A translator is always trying to extend his knowledge and improve his means of expression; he is always pursuing facts and words. He works on four levels: translation is first a science, which entails the knowledge and verification of the facts and the language that describes them-here, what is wrong, mistakes of truth, can be identified; secondly, it is a skill, which calls for appropriate language and acceptable usage; thirdly, an art, which distinguishes good from undistinguished writing and is the creative, the intuitive, sometimes the inspired, level of the translation; lastly, a matter of taste, where argument ceases, preferences are expressed, and the variety of meritorious translations is the reflection of individual differences.

As a means of communication, translation is used for multilingual notices, which have at last appeared increasingly conspicuously in public places; for instructions issued by exporting companies; for tourist publicity, where it is too often produced from the native into the foreign' language by natives as a matter of national pride; for official documents, such as treaties and contracts; for reports, papers, articles, correspondence, textbooks to convey information, advice and recommendations for every branch of knowledge. Its volume has increased with the rise of the mass media, the increase in the number of independent countries, and the growing recognition of the importance of linguistic minorities in all the countries of the world. Its importance is highlighted by the mistransla-

---

❶ 钱歌川.翻译的基本知识.长沙:湖南科学技术出版社,1981:9.

tion of the Japanese telegram sent to Washington just before the bomb was dropped on Hiroshima, when mokasutu was allegedly translated as 'ignored' instead of 'considered', and by the ambiguity in UN Resolution 242, where 'the withdrawal from occupied territories' was translated as 'le retrait des territoires occupes' and therefore as a reference to all of the occupied territory to be evacuated by the Israelis.

Translation has been instrumental in transmitting culture, sometimes under unequal conditions responsible for distorted and biased translations, ever since countries and languages have been in contact with each other. Thus the Romans 'pillaged' Greek culture; the Toledo School transferred Arabic and Greek learning to Europe; and up to the nineteenth century European culture was drawing heavily on Latin and Greek translations. In the nineteenth century German culture was absorbing Shakespeare. In this century a centrifugal world literature has appeared, consisting of the work of a small number of international 5 writers (Greene, Bellow, Solzhenitsyn, Boll, Grass, Moravia, Murdoch, Lessing, amongst those still living, succeeding Mann, Brecht, Kafka, Mauriac, Valery, etc.), which is translated into most national and many regional languages. Unfortunately there is no corresponding centripetal cultural movement from Regional or peripheral authors.

That translation is not merely a transmitter of culture, but also of the truth, a force for progress, could be instanced by following the course of resistance to Bible translation and the preservation of Latin as a superior language of the elect, with a consequent disincention to translation between other languages.

(553 words)

第二章

英汉对比（1）

热身练习

请将下面的段落译为汉语，注意其中名词、介词的用法。

Sea Gulls

Sea gulls are excellent flyers. They can fly many miles without stopping. With a short rest here and there, they can fly form one end of a country to the other. They are good gliders, too. When they slide, they seem to be sliding invisible slides way up in the air. Sea gulls are good swimmer, too. Their feet are webbed—the little stretches of skin between their toes make paddles. Gulls are floaters. They stay on top of the water like a piece of wood. It's a good thing they do because on long trips over the ocean they drop down onto the water and float while they take a nap. (112 words)

双语阅读

阅读以下两篇文章，比较分析英汉在用词方面的不同特点。

1. Missing: 100,000 Children a Year
Gary Turbak

These are not isolated cases. The best estimates are that about a million American youngsters leave home each year, with 90 percent returning in two weeks. Approximately, 100,000 are thus unaccounted for. Add another 25,000 to 100,000 stolen by divorced or separated parents, and the total becomes significant. "Kids who just disappear present a big problem that people had better start opening their eyes to," says Dick Ruffinne of Bergen County, New Jersey sheriff's office.

……

"The first time disappearance of a minor should be prima facieevidence that a kidnapping has taken place," says John Clinkscales whose son disappeared six years ago. "The FBI could then become immediately involved, and there might be a chance of finding some of these children. We need help."

2.盲人挑灯

一个漆黑的夜晚,一个苦行僧走到一个荒僻的村落中,他看见有一盏昏黄的灯正从巷道的深处静静地亮过来,身旁的一位村民说:"孙瞎子过来了。"苦行僧百思不得其解,一个双目失明的人,挑起一盏灯笼岂不可笑?僧人于是问:"敢问施主,既然你什么也看不见,那你为何挑一盏灯笼呢?"盲人说:"现在是黑夜吗?我听说黑夜里如果没有灯光的映照,那么满世界的人都和我一样是盲人,所以,我就点燃了盏灯。"僧人若有所悟地说:"原来您是为别人照明呀?"但那盲人却说:"不,我是为自己!"盲人问僧人:"你是否因为夜色漆黑而被其他行人碰撞过?但我就没有。虽说我是盲人,但我挑了这盏灯笼,既为别人照亮了路,也让别人看到了我而不会碰撞我了。"

认知升级

我相信,对于中国学生最有用的帮助是让他认识英语和汉语的差别。在每一个具体问题——词形、词义、语法 范畴、句子结构上都尽可能用汉语的情况来跟英语作比较,让他通过这种比较得到更深刻的领会。

——吕叔湘 1947《中国人学英语》

一句中国话,翻成英语怎么说;一句英语,中国话里如何表达,这又是一种比较。只有比较才能看出各种语文表现法的共同之点和特殊之点。

——吕叔湘 1942《中国人学英语》

一、英语多变化,汉语多重复

英语与汉语在用词方面的一个重要差异就是:英语多变化,汉语多重复。英语中除了有意强调或出于修辞的需要,很少在句子中随意重复相同的音节、词语或句式。Hodges & Whitten 指出:"Never use the same word or write the same thing twice in a sentence unless you are repeating intentionally for emphasis or for clarity."[1]

总之,除了有特殊意图或者修辞需要的重复以外,在能明确表达意思的前提下,英语宜尽量避免重复,采用的主要方法有:同义词、上义词、替代等。

1.同义词(synonym)

英语词汇的来源较多,包括拉丁语、法语和本族语等,所以英语的同义词和近义词较为丰富,数量多于汉语。在表达相近的词义时,英语可供选词的余地较大,可以通过同义词、近义词替换来变换表达方式。英语同义词替代的现象常见于用不同的名称来表示同一人或事物。在阅读分析英文时,读者要根据上下文或特定的背景知识,判断所指是哪一件事物,以免产生误解。

例如在上文 *Missing*:100,000 *Children a Year* 中,表达"儿童"这个概念,就使用了"children""youngster""kids""minor"等同义词。

例如在一篇英文报道中,"电视机"这一名词,可以用 the television set, the TV, telly, the

---

[1] Hodges, J. and M. Whitten. *Harbrace College Handbook*. New York: Henry Holt and Co. Inc., 1967: 244.

tube, the goggle-box, the idiot box 等代替。

又如，表达"我认为"，第一次可以用 I think，第二次再用 I think 显然就很乏味，可以换成 I believe, I imagine 之类的表达，第三次可以用 I hold, I assume 等，第四次可以用 in my view, in my opinion 等表达方式。

2. 上义词（superordinate）

英语常常用上义词替代某个名词来进行变换，以回避重复。汉语则一般较少采用英语的这类变称，而较多重复同一名称。以下例句可以说明汉语习惯于同词重复而英语常常易词变换的特点：

例 1 I've just read John Smith's essay. The whole thing is very well-thought out.（上义词 the thing 指代 essay）

我刚读了约翰·史密斯的文章，整篇文章考虑得十分周详。

例 2 I want to thank my partner in this journey, a man who campaigned from his heart and spoke for the men and women he grew up with on the streets of Scranton and rode with on the train home to Delaware, the Vice President-elect of the United States, Joe Biden. (Obama's Victory Speech in 2008)（上义词 a man 指代 Joe Biden）

我要感谢我的竞选伙伴——新当选的美国副总统拜登。他全心参与竞选活动，为普通民众代言，他们是他在斯克兰顿从小到大的伙伴，也是在他回故乡特拉华州的火车上遇到的男男女女。

例 3 John has bought himself a new Ford. He practically lives in the car.（概括词 the car 替代上文 a new Ford）

约翰买了一部新的福特牌汽车，他几乎就住在车里。

例 4 The monkey's most extraordinary accomplishment was learning to operate a tractor. By the age of nine, it had learned to solo on the vehicle.

这只猴子最了不起的技能是学会驾驶拖拉机。到了九岁的时候，它已经学会单独表演驾驶拖拉机了。

3. 替代（substitution）

用替代的形式来代替句中或上文已出现过的词语或内容，以避免重复并衔接上下文，这是英语的一项重要原则。替代的形式主要有以下几种：

（1）名词替代（nominal substitution）

用代词或某些名词来取代名词或名词词组，这类词如：第三人称代词、指示代词（this, that, these, those）、关系代词（who, whom, whose, that, which）、连接代词（who, whom, whose, what, which）、不定代词（all, each, either, neither, one/ones, none, little, several, many, other, some, any）以及名词（enough, half, the same, the kind, the former, the latter）等。英语常用这类替代词来避免重复，汉语则较常重复其所代替的名词或词组。

例 1 Flattery is more dangerous than hatred because it covers the stain which the other causes to be wiped.

奉承远比仇恨危险，因为奉承掩饰人的污点，而仇恨却促使人们抹掉污点。

例 2 Big powers have their strategies while small countries also have their own lines.

强国有强国的策略，小国也有小国的路线。

例 3 For years my father soothed my little sister and me to sleep with his delightfully fantastic tales. <u>They</u> were inexhaustible; each night there was a new <u>one</u>, told in the darkness against the evening throb of the tenement.

多少年来，我父亲用他那些美妙离奇的故事把妹妹和我送入梦乡。他的故事讲也讲不完，在黑暗中伴着<u>经济公寓夜间的搏动</u>，每天晚上都有一个新的故事展开❶。

(2) 动词替代(verbal substitution)

用动词的替代词来取代动词或动词词组，这类替代词主要有：代动词 do，复合代动词 do so, do it, do that, do this, do the same，以及替代句型 so + do +主语, so +主语+ do, so + be+主语, so +主语+be, so+ will+主语, so+主语+will 等。汉语也有替代的方式，但也常常重复其所代替的动词(词组)，如：

例 1　If he is allowed to leave, <u>so should I be</u>.
要是准许他走，也该准许我走。

例 2　He never really succeeded in his ambitions. He might have <u>done</u>, one felt, had it not been for the restlessness of his nature.
他雄心勃勃，但从未如愿以偿。人们觉得，要不是他那贪得无厌的本性，他也许会有所作为。

例 3　革命是<u>解放生产力</u>，改革也是<u>解放生产力</u>。
Revolution means the emancipation of the productive forces, and so does reform.

(3) 分句替代(clausal substitution)

用替代词 so 或 not 来取代充当宾语的 that 从句，用 if so 或 if not 来取代条件从句，用 as 来取代分句的一部分等。汉语也有替代的方式，但为了使表达正确清楚，也常常重复其所代替的词语。如：

例 1　He might be wrong. <u>If not</u>, why was he in such low spirits?
他可能错了。如果没有错，他为什么那么消沉呢？

例 2　Would you open an e-mail from a stranger requesting a lunch date? <u>If so</u>, you are a prime target for a computer virus.
有陌生人给你发来电子邮件，邀你共进午餐，你会打开吗？如果打开，你的电脑很可能就会染上病毒。

例 3　她个子很<u>高</u>，她母亲个子也<u>高</u>。
She's very tall, as is her mother.

英语常常喜欢变化，而汉语多用重复形式，连续使用某个词语是常见的事(庄绎传, 2002)。这种重复现象有时不止出现在一句话里，还时不时出现在几句话里。汉语中重复现象比比皆是，可能与中国文化讲究平衡与对称的美学心理有关。

首先，汉语中，四字成语的使用比例很高，这些四字成语中，大量存在着重复现象，如：三心二意、奇形怪状、奇思妙想、半斤八两、生离死别、翻天覆地、争先恐后、伶牙俐齿、称心如意、发号施令、惊天动地、唉声叹气、步步为营、刺刺不休、楚楚动人、草草收兵、死气沉沉、喜气洋洋、风尘仆仆、大名鼎鼎、人才济济、千里迢迢、安安稳稳、朝朝暮暮、抽抽噎噎、偷偷摸摸、吞吞吐吐、红红火火、星星点点、隐隐约约、轰轰烈烈等。

---

❶张春柏.英汉汉英翻译教程.北京：高等教育出版社,2003:181.

其次，汉语则不太习惯于名称替换，因而较常重复同一名称。例如，在双语阅读"盲人挑灯"一文中，"盲人"就重复使用了5次，僧人使用了3次。动词重复的情况也比较多见。在下例中，"偷"字重复了3次，"打"字重复了6次。

例1 一个喝酒的人说道，"他怎么会来？……他打折了腿了。"掌柜说，"哦！""他总仍旧是偷。这一回，是自己发昏，竟偷到丁举人家里去了。他家的东西，偷得的吗？""后来怎么样？""怎么样？先写服辩，后来是打，打了大半夜，再打折了腿。""后来呢？""后来打折了腿了。""打折了怎样呢？""怎样？……谁晓得？许是死了。"掌柜也不再问，仍然慢慢地算他的账。

再次，在汉语中，某些句子结构也倾向于重复。

例1 这几双鞋，大的大，小的小，我都不能穿。
Some of these shoes are too big and others too small. None of them fits me.

例2 我们一些旧衣服和旧家具，当的当了，卖的卖了。（吴敬梓：《儒林外史》）
Our old clothes and few sticks of furniture have been pawned or sold.

例3 我书架上的小说你最爱哪一本，你就可以借哪一本。
You may borrow whichever novel in my bookcase you like best.

例4 就火腿和牛肉而言，眼下牛肉比较便宜。
Of ham and beef, the latter is cheaper today.

例5 一定的文化反映一定社会的政治和经济，又深刻地作用和影响一定社会的政治和经济。
Any given culture is a reflection of the politics and economics of a given society, and the former in turn has a tremendous effect and influence on the latter.

二、英语多名介，汉语多动词

从词类的运用来看，英语和汉语有一个显著差异：英语多用名词和介词，呈静态(static)；而汉语多用动词，呈动态(dynamic)。

在他的 Factual Writing (1985:40) 中，Martin 举例说明了英语多用名词的倾向：

There is little **doubt** that television **coverage** of a domestic slaughtering **operation**, conducted in a government approved abattoir, which involved the **slaughter** of lambs, calves and swine, would generate a good deal of public **revulsion and protest**. (37 words)

Martin 评价说：

In this extract most of the specific actions appear in noun form, and some have been nominalized; that is, turned into nouns from prior full clausal forms ("doubt", "coverage", "slaughtering operation", "slaughter", "revulsion", "protest"). In a text of thirty-seven words, there are only two main verbs ("is" and "generate"), both very general. Doings and happenings have been turned into things. The dynamics of action has been changed into a static of relations.

英语是综合—分析语，具有词缀丰富的特点。这些丰富的词缀使一些动词和形容词很容易派生为名词，这种现象称为名词化(nominalization)。名词化是现代英语发展的自然趋势。在许多情况下，用名词代替动词可以使行文和表意都更为简洁。

由于英语多用名词，必然也要多用介词，因而产生了介词优势。介词优势与名词优势相结合，使英语的静态倾向更明显。

例1 He's a chain smoker.
他一根接一根地抽烟。

例2 This novel defies easy classification.
这部小说很难分类。

例3 The computer is a far more careful and industrious inspector than human beings.
计算机比人检查得更细心、更勤快。

例4 Rebecca's wit, cleverness, and flippancy made her speedily the vogue in London among a certain class.
丽贝卡人又机智,口角又俏皮,喜欢油嘴滑舌地讲笑话,在伦敦自有一等人捧她,立刻就在这群人中走俏。

例5 …that we here highly resolve…, that this nation under God, shall have a new birth of freedom, and that government of the people, by the people, for the people, shall not perish from the earth.
所以我们要在这里表示最大的决心……;这个国家在上帝的保佑下,一定要获得自由的新生;民有、民治、民享的政府绝不会从地球上消失。

例6 Northrop Frye's criticism is richly textured, so dense with insight, and so wide-ranging in its references.
诺思罗普·弗莱德批评肌理丰盈、创见良多、涉猎广泛、旁征博引。

例7 Studies serve for delight, for ornament and, for ability. Their chief use for delight is in privateness and retiring; for ornament, is in discourse; and for ability, is in the judgment and disposition of business. For expert men can execute, and perhaps judge of particulars, one by one; but the general counsels, and the plots and marshalling of affairs, come best from those that are learned. (Francis Bacon: Of Studies)
读书足以怡情、足以博采、足以长才。其怡情也,最见于独处幽居之时;其博采也,最见于高谈阔论之中;其长才也,最见于处世判事之际。练达之士虽能分别处理细事或一一判别枝节,然纵观统筹、全局策划,则舍好学深思者莫属。(王佐良译《论读书》)

与英语动词不同,汉语的动词十分丰富,应用广泛而自由,并无人称与数的限制,没有严格意义上的时态、语态、语气的变化,没有谓语动词与非谓语动词的区别,因而使用频率较高,常常大量采用连动式或兼语式的说法。相对而言,汉语的动词由于无形态变化,也缺少同源名词及同源形容词,因此若要表示动作意义,往往只能采用动词本身。

例1 我所认识的人中数她最会记仇。
She is the best hater I've ever known.

例2 现在急需想出新法子来补救。
There is a crying need for a new remedy.

例3 要不是我能干重活,早就给辞退了。
It was only my capacity for hard work that saved me from early dismissal.

例4 我虽然交游广泛,却只愿与少数几人亲密往来。
Though fond of many acquaintances, I desire an intimacy only with a few.

例5 种种时代迹象表明,必须改进行政管理体系。

The signs of times point to the necessity of the modification of the system of administration.

例6 由于通货膨胀，社会的不满情绪不断加剧，在此情况下，政府只得放慢改革。
Amid mounting social discontents over inflation, the government had to slow its reforms.

三、英语多抽象，汉语多具体

抽象表达法(method of abstract diction)在英语里使用得相当普遍,尤其常用于社会科学论著、官方文章、报刊评论、法律文书、商业信件等文体。英语的抽象表达法主要见于大量使用抽象名词。这类名词语意概括,指称笼统,覆盖面广,往往有一种"虚泛""曲折""隐晦"的特点,便于用来表达复杂的思想和微妙的情绪。

抽象表达法得以流行,还有以下几个主要原因。首先,英语在用词方面常常有一种名词化(nominalization)的倾向。英语常常使用-ness,-tion,-ty,-ism,-ment,-ence,-ship 等后缀,将表示具体动作、过程、特征、环境成分的动词、形容词、副词甚至介词等转换成为名词,从而使得词义虚化。英语名词化的主要功能有增大词汇密度、扩展句子的信息容量、增强客观性、提升正式程度。它的优点是有简洁、凝练、信息量大点。当然,名词化也有一些缺点,其中一个就是名词化转换而来的名词多为抽象名词,而非具体名词,这样就使得英语显得较为抽象,语义模糊难辨,理解难度较大。M.Young 曾指出:"an excessive reliance on the noun at the expense of the verb will, in the end, detach the mind of the writer from the realities of here and now, from when and how and in what mood the thing was done, and insensibly induce a habit of abstraction, generalization and vagueness."

英语的名词化现象,在英语里到处可见。以下两例引自美国的一家教育杂志,其抽象名词可谓泛滥成灾。

例1 Merely to enumerate these five outstanding characteristics of an urban community, namely, chaotic stimulation, mechanization, impersonalization, commercialization and complexity of organization, suggests many implications for the city education.

例2 For most Americans, irrespective of party affiliation and predisposition, isolationism is defunct and participation and cooperation commonsensed and essential, in international relations.

其次,随着科学技术的发达和文明社会的进步,原有的感性表达方式已经不足以表达复杂的理性概念,因而需要借助于抽象、概括的方法。

例1 The signs of the times point to the necessity of the modification of the system of administration.(It is becoming clear that the administrative system must be modified)

例2 No year passes now without evidence of the truth of the statement that the work government is becoming increasingly difficult.("Spectator")(Every year shows again how true it is that…)

例3 There seems to have been an absence of attempt at conciliation between rival sects.(Daily Telegraph)(=The sects seem never even to have tried mutual conciliation)

此外,许多作者为了显耀其思想深奥而故弄玄虚、追随时尚,也喜欢采用抽象表达法。例如:

例1 The absence of intelligence is an indication of satisfactory developments. (= No news is good news)

例2 Was this the realization of an anticipated liability? (= Did you expect you would have to do this?)

例3 The actual date of the completion of the purchase should coincide wilt the availability of the new facilities. (= The purchase should not be completed until the new facilities are available)

例4 A high degree of carelessness, pre-operative and post-operative, on the part of some of the hospital staff, took place. (= Some of the hospital staff were very careless both before and after the operation)

例5 The lack of figures may prove to be an obstacle to the efficiency of the whole of the proposed statistical content of the exercise. (Lack of figures may make it difficult to produce accurate statistics.)

再次,抽象词语意义模糊,便于掩饰作者真实的思想,以迎合其某种表达的需要,因而也得以流行。滥用抽象词语在公文里已是司空见惯。

例1 Strangeness of samples has been shown to lead to relative rejection of products in the comparative absence of clues to a frame of reference with which judgement may take place. Variation in clues selected by judges as a basis for evaluation lead to greater inter-judge disagreement. Addition of a functional (utilitarian) basis for judgement tends to reduce relative importance of product physical characteristics as a basis for judgement. In the absence of any judgmental frame of reference reduction in the number of product physical attributes apparent to the judge appears to reduce operation of bases for rejection and increase homogeneity of judgment between subjects; inter-sample discrimination is also reduced.

例2 The object of this visit is a pooling of knowledge to explore further the possibility of a joint research effort to discover the practicability of making use of this principle to meet a possible future NATO requirement and should be viewed in the general context of interdependence.

这段冗长的话无非是想说:

This visit is to find out whether we can, together, develop the folding-wing plane for NATO. 此次访问是为了探讨我们两国是否能够为北约组织合作研制一种可折翼的飞机。

最后,英语词义内涵一般比较广泛,词的用法比较灵活,一词多义、一词多用的现象非常普遍,这也有助于表达比较概括、笼统的意义。如 service 一词,可以作服务、上菜、服务机构、部门人员、军种、设施、维修、发球、送达、仪式等多种解释;power 一词,可以作能力、体力、动力、权力、势力、电力、强国、有权力的人、有影响的机构等多种解释。

总之,英语有过分使用抽象表达法的倾向。不少文体学家提倡具体与抽象相结合的选词法,即"a mixture of long abstract Latin words with short concrete Anglo-Saxon words"。

与英语相比,汉语由于更多地使用动词,因而显得较为具体。汉语常常以实的形式表达虚的概念,以具体的形象表达抽象的内容。这主要是因为汉语缺乏像英语那样的词缀虚化手段。汉语没有形态变化,形式相同的词,可以是名词,也可以是动词,还可以是形容词或其他词。名词从形式上很难辨别出"具体"或"抽象"。

汉语是意象性语言,文字符号具有象形、会意和形声的特点,许多汉字模拟自然现象和客观事物(如日、月、山、凹、凸),许多事物通过"观物取象""立意于象"而得以命名(如 X 光透视、电脑),不少外来词通过形象性的意译或模拟拼音加形象而得以译名(如:Coca-Cola 可口可乐、Worldwide Web 万维网、mini-skirt 迷你裙),大量词语通过直觉领悟便可获知其意。

汉语表达形象、意象、象征、联想、想象的词语(如比喻、成语、谚语、歇后语等)相当丰富,用词倾向于具体,常常以实的形式表达虚的概念。汉语喜好"实""明""直""显""形""象"的表达法,即措辞具体、含义明确,叙述直接。常常借助生动具体的形象性词语表达抽象笼统的意义(如:土崩瓦解;水乳交融;三天打鱼,两天晒网)。

汉语语篇常采用取象类比、设象喻理、以喻代议的表达方式,让读者领悟深奥的道理。汉语喜欢用动词化表达法(verbal style),常用或连用重复、重叠动词,采用"连动式""兼语式",词语的意义生动活泼,丰富多彩,有利于表达动态的情感和形象性、直觉性的行为。

例1 故其疾如风,其徐如林,侵掠如火,不动如山,难知如阴,动如雷震。(孙武《孙子兵法》)

这是孙子《军争》篇中的一句,意思是按照战场形势的需要,部队行动迅速时,如狂风飞旋;行进从容时,如森林徐徐展开;攻城略地时,如烈火迅猛;驻守防御时,如大山岿然;军情隐蔽时,如乌云蔽日;大军出动时,如雷霆万钧。此处用较为生动具体的形象比喻来表达较为抽象的军事行动原则。

当然,汉语表达抽象意义的词语也不乏其例,但抽象名词的比例没有英语那么多。如旧时流行的蒙学课本《三字经》,就有一些抽象名词,如"性相近,习相远""教五子,名俱扬""养不教,父之过""人不学,不知义"等。

现代汉语的一些抽象词尾(如"性""化""度""品""主义"等)大多来自外语。例如,"性"译自英语的-ness,-ty,-ance 等(如 necessity 必要性,correctness 正确性,dependence 依赖性);"化"译自英语的-zation,-tion 等(modernization 现代化,abstraction 抽象化),"度"略等于英语的-ty,ty 等(如 length 长度,intensity 强度);"主义"译自英语的-ism,-ness 等(patriotism 爱国主义,slavishness 奴隶主义);"品"则相当于英语的某些含义较广的名词(如 commodity 商品,narcotics 毒品,daily necessities 日用品)。

现代汉语虽然可以从外文中引进这类抽象的记号,但其应用的范围仍然相当有限,如 Americanism 就不能译为"美国主义",而应译为具体的词,如"美国用语""美国发音""美国腔""美国习俗""美国方式""对美国的信仰或效忠"等;realization 也不能译为"实现化",而应译为具体的动词或名词,如"实现""认识""认清""体会""变卖""换取"等。

由于汉语缺乏像英语那样的虚化手段,因而常常用比较具体的方式来表达抽象的意义。Rudolf Flesch 对汉语用词具体(concrete)、表达清晰(clear)、语言形象(picturesque)大加赞扬,并以此来批评英语那种措辞抽象(abstract)、含义晦涩(obscure)、词句冗长(long-winded)的不良文风。他曾作如下生动的比较:

Chinese does more to you than just simplify your constructions. It simplifies your ideas. In other languages, the affixes are a splendid means of getting away from reality into vague generalities and abstractions. For instance, in English you have the simple word *sign*, meaning "a mark". Now you add an affix to that word and you get *signify*, "to make a mark." Next you add another affix, and you arrive at "significant" "making a mark." Now you add a prefix for a change, and you have significant, "making no mark." Finally, you add another suffix, and you come out with insignificance the making of no mark. "What did you do? You took a simple noun, and made it successively into a verb, an adjective, another adjective, and again a noun. You have added no meaning but just some empty syllables. Now you can be serious and philosophic and talk about the insignificance of man. A Chinese would say something about *Man no mark*. So while you give in to the temptations of English affixes and fill your talk with masses of empty syllables and words, he keeps his feet on the ground and says everything in the most concrete, specific words. He has to; there are no other words in Chinese.

If you think, however, that Chinese has no way of expressing abstract ideas, you are wrong. Remember, the Chinese were talking and writing about religion and philosophy long before our own civilization started. If they had no exact word for an abstraction, they used the concrete word, or words, that came nearest to the idea. So, naturally, instead of using words like *antiprogressivism*, as our thinkers do, they formed the habit of expressing ideas by metaphors, similes, and allegories, in short, by every known device for waking a thing plain by comparing it with something else.

四、英语多屈折，汉语少形变

英语是一种屈折变化语言，通过屈折变化来表示语法关系。屈折变化共有8种，分别用来表示名词、动词和形容词与副词的形态上的变化。汉语没有严格意义上的构形形态变化。正如张春柏所言："由于英语是有形态变化的语言，所以往往同一个汉语词汇，可以有几个不同词性或形态的英语单词与之对应。"❶

具体来说，英语动词都有人称、单复数、时态、语态、语气等变化形式，汉语动词往往没有这些形式变化。因此，英译汉时，需要增加词汇体现英语动词体现出的时体意义。

英语名词、代词的主格与宾格有形态上的区分，如 I 对应的宾格为 me，they 对应的宾格是 them；汉语中的主格与宾格没有区分；所有格方面，英语的属格可以通过's 或者介词 of 体现（China's population, the population of China），而且有名词性物主代词与形容词性物主代词的区分；汉语的属格基本上由"的"体现，"你的、我的、他们的"，很多情况下还可以把结构助词"的"去掉，如"上我家聊天吧！"。

英语名词的数量关系是显性的，必须通过形态体现。也就是说，大多数可数名词表达复数名词必须做出相应的形态变化。如复数加-s, -es。例如单数 one car, 复数 five cars。汉语名词大多数情况下将复数概念融入句子语境，单复数不作明确标识；少数情况下以加"们"等标志予以明示。例如，汉语中常说"他去年买了五台电脑"，而不说"五台电脑们"；汉语中可以说"屋里有五个人"，也可以说"随着时代的变迁，人们的社会生活也在发生着变化"。

例1 Men sometimes say: "We are better and cleverer than women. Women never invent things. We do." It is true that men have invented a lot of useful things: the alphabet, machines, rockets, and guns, too. But scientist and archeologists now agree that women

---

❶ 张春柏.英汉汉英翻译教程.北京：高等教育出版社，2003:42.

invented one important thing.It has changed history.They invented agriculture.(Vivienne Gill)

在该例中,英语可数名词有单数(alphabet,thing)、复数(men,women,machines,rockets,archeologists)之分,标识分明。动词共使用了一般现在时(say)、现在完成时(have invented)、一般过去时(invented)三种时态,也是一目了然。形容词有原级(important),也有比较级(better and cleverer than),也容易区分。

例2 While I, wrap from him in a confused mist of time, was wondering what he would think, could he know that at this actual moment he would have been dead thirty years, and that his memory would be thus preserved and honored in the beloved school, where his delicate spirit had been so strangely troubled.

同时我在寻思着,因为与他之间相隔一段宛若迷雾的年月,假如他知道在这一刻他已经死了三十年,他可爱的母校在以这样的方式纪念他,给他这样高的荣誉,而他上学时,他脆弱的心灵曾经莫名其妙地烦恼过,他会有怎样的感想呢?

英语的非谓语动词包括分词、动名词和不定式三种,这种结构通过变换动词的形态,表达分句间的多重逻辑关系,比如时间、目的、伴随、结果、因果等。汉语没有相应的语法结构。

英语通过动词的屈折变化形式体现时态,汉语的时态则以词汇形式体现。汉语用"着""了""过""正在""已经"和"持续"等词汇表达时态,而英语通过动词的词形变化体现时态。

例1 英语因屈折变化而导致句型的多样。如下例:

He moved astonishingly rapidly.

He moved with astonishing rapidity.

He astonished us by moving rapidly.

He astonished us by his rapid movements.

He astonished us by the rapidity of his movements.

His movements were astonishingly rapid.

His rapid movements astonished us.

His movements astonished us by their rapidity.

The rapidity of his movements was astonishing.

The rapidity with which he moved astonished us.

例2 他们又故意地高声嚷道,"你一定又偷了人家的东西了!"孔乙己睁大眼睛说,"你怎么这样凭空污人清白……""什么清白?我前天亲眼见你偷了何家的书,吊着打。"孔乙己便涨红了脸,额上的青筋条条绽出,争辩道,"窃书不能算偷……窃书!……读书人的事,能算偷么?"(鲁迅《孔乙己》)

在本例中,动词"嚷""说""涨红""绽出""争辩"等均指过去发生的动作;而"偷了""吊着打"则是指过去之前发生的动作,孔乙己所讲"窃书不能算偷"中的"偷"则指普遍发生的动作,相当于英语中的一般现在时。值得注意的是,这些动作大都一一列举,不像英语那样明确划分主次,没有区分主要动词和分词。

例3 扫街的在树影下一阵扫后,灰土上留下来的一条条扫帚的丝纹,看起来既觉得细腻,又觉得清闲,潜意识下并且还觉得有点儿落寞,古人所说的梧桐一叶而天下知秋的遥想,大约也就在这些深沉的地方。(郁达夫《故都的秋》)

本例中,"扫后""留下来"等均比较明确地表达了过去的时间,而"看起来""觉得"则表示现在发生的动作,"说"所指当为过去的动作,时间标识不够清楚,需要区分。

例 4 故校之以计,而索其情,曰:主孰有道?将孰有能?天地孰得?法令孰行?兵众孰强?士卒孰练?赏罚孰明?吾以此知胜负矣。(孙武《孙子兵法》)

此例中,从"主孰有道?"到"赏罚孰明?"共 7 个小句,均表示敌我双方在各个方面的对比,当为隐含的比较级,但是文中并未出现"比""更"此类比较级的标识。

请将下面的段落翻译为汉语。

Downsizing in Vogue

In recent years corporate downsizing has been on the rise throughout the world.

Downsizing is reducing costs by dismissing employees and reassigning their duties to the employees who remain. They usually call it restructuring, rightsizing, reallocating resources, or job separation. They sometimes use dieting metaphors like "trimming the fat," "getting lean and mean," or "shedding weight." Whatever the euphemism, employees affected by these practices know what the words mean to them: layoff. And no "kinder, gentler" words can do much to alleviate the anxiety and distress that come with losing a job.

In their quest to lower costs to stay competitive, companies often wield the ax with little or no regard for the well-being of the people involved. For example, in the past years AT&T have dismissed thousands of managers and employees through downsizing, though many of these people have twenty or more years of loyal employment with the firm. Industry analysts assert that if organizations wish to consider themselves responsible, ethical corporate citizens, they must demonstrate concern for their employees, even when they have to tell them they are no longer employed. Organizations concerned about easing their employees' shock and stress at being laid off can do so through careful planning and preparation. Effective, honest and timely communication is always important, but when staff reductions are imminent, it becomes critical. Employees who know what is going on can prepare themselves for the inevitable and are much better able to cope when the ax finally does fall.

It is sometimes difficult to determine the right thing to do, but many firms are trying. IBM for instance, offers early retirement. AT&T offers job search help and career counseling to displaced employees. Organizations can also support employees whose positions have been eliminated by providing retraining or outplacement assistance and a reasonable severance package. Those being laid off are not, however, the only ones affected by the downsizing. By addressing the needs and concerns of remaining staff, showing sensitivity to their feeling of loss, and dealing with their anxieties about additional layoffs, an organization increases its chances of retaining their loyalty and trust.

Questions about the ethics of downsizing are sure to continue. Do responsible companies lay people off? Is it ethical to close factories? Must employers guarantee workers jobs for life? What are the ethical issues involved when organizations become so downsized they are no longer able to attain their goals a situation known as "corporate anorexia"? What happens, for example, to patients in a hospital that has eliminated so many positions it is no longer able to provide the necessary level of care? If, as most experts agree, downsizing is here to stay, perhaps the real question is not "Is it ethical to downsize?" but "How can companies downsize ethically?"

(428 words)

第三章
英汉对比（2）

1. ...so far as English and Chinese are concerned, the most important difference linguistically is the contrast between hypotaxis and parataxis.

——Eugene Nida

2. 西洋语的结构好象连环，虽则环与环都联络起来，毕竟有联络的痕迹。中国语的结构好象天衣无缝，只是一块一块的硬凑，凑起来还不让它有痕迹。西洋语法是硬的，没有弹性的；中国语法是软的，富于弹性的。惟其是硬的，所以西洋语法有许多呆板的要求，如每一个 clause 里必须有一个主语；惟其是软的，所以中国语法只以达意为主，如初系的目的位可兼次系的主语，又如相关的两件事可以硬凑在一起，不用任何的 connective。

——王力❷

热身练习

请将以下段落译为汉语，注意句式的转换。

A Young Fisherman

He was, now, a huge, strong fellow of six feet high, brood in proportion, and round-shouldered; but with a simpering boy'sface and curly light hair that give him quite a sheepish look. He was dressed in a canvas jacket, and a pair of such very stiff trousers that they would have stood quite as well alone, without any legs in them. And you couldn't so properly have said he wore a hat, as that he was covered in atop, like an old building, with something pitchy.（Charles Dickens, *David Copperfield*）（87 words）

双语阅读

阅读下列段落，比较英汉两种语言在句式方面的差异。

1. Nature's Resurrection

It was beautiful spring weather, but neither dogs nor humans were aware of it. Each day the

---

❶ Nida, Eugene A. *Translating Meaning*. San Dimas California: English Language Institute, 1982:50-75.
❷ 王力.中国语法理论.王力文集(第1卷).济南：山东教育出版社,1984:141.

sun rose earlier and set later.It was dawn by three in the morning,and twilight lingered till nine at night.His whole long day was a blaze of sunshine.The Mostly winter silence had given way to the great spring murmur of awakening life.This murmur arose from all the land,fraught with the joy of living.It came from the things that lived and moved again,things which had been as dead and which had moved during the long months of frost.The sap was rising in the pines.The willows and aspens were bursting out in young buds.Shrubs and vines were putting on fresh garbs of green. Crickets sang in the nights,and in the days all manner of creeping,crawling things rustled forth into the sun.Partridges and woodpeckers were booming and knocking in the forest.Squirrels were chattering,birds singing,and overhead honked the wildfowl driving up from the South in cunning wedges that split the air.(Jack London,*The Call of the Wild*)(259 words)

2.春

盼望着,盼望着,东风来了,春天的脚步近了。

一切都像刚睡醒的样子,欣欣然张开了眼。山朗润起来了,水涨起来了,太阳的脸红起来了。

小草偷偷地从土里钻出来,嫩嫩的,绿绿的。园子里,田野里,瞧去,一大片一大片满是的。坐着,躺着,打两个滚,踢几脚球,赛几趟跑,捉几回迷藏。风轻悄悄的,草软绵绵的。

桃树、杏树、梨树,你不让我,我不让你,都开满了花赶趟儿。红的像火,粉的像霞,白的像雪。花里带着甜味儿;闭了眼,树上仿佛已经满是桃儿、杏儿、梨儿。花下成千成百的蜜蜂嗡嗡地闹着,大小的蝴蝶飞来飞去。野花遍地是:杂样儿,有名字的,没名字的,散在草丛里,像眼睛,像星星,还眨呀眨的。

"吹面不寒杨柳风",不错的,像母亲的手抚摸着你。风里带来些新翻的泥土的气息,混着青草味儿,还有各种花的香,都在微微润湿的空气里酝酿。鸟儿将巢安在繁花嫩叶当中,高兴起来了,呼朋引伴地卖弄清脆的喉咙,唱出宛转的曲子,与轻风流水应和着。牛背上牧童的短笛,这时候也成天嘹亮地响着。(朱自清《春》)(423字)

认知升级

一、英语重形合,汉语重意合

句子是较为理想的汉英互译单位。因此,了解英汉句子的主要差别对学习翻译至关重要。由于思维方式的差异,英汉两种语言中句子组合的机制也不同。一般来说,英语句子重形合(hypotaxis),汉语句子重意合(parataxis)。

英语句子的特点是强调形式和功能,因而英语的句法特征是形合。根据 *The American Heritage Dictionary*, Hypotaxis 指:The dependent or subordinate construction or relationship of clauses arranged with connectives;E.g.I shall despair if you Don't come,即:句中的词语或分句之间用语言形式手段(如关联词)连接起来,表达语法意义和逻辑关系。可以看出,英语的语法呈现外显性(overtness),这体现了英美人重个体、重分析的思维方式。

汉语的意合,指的是词语或分句之间不用语言形式手段连接,句中的语法意义和逻辑关系通过词语或分句的含义表达。根据 *The World Book Dictionary*, Parataxis 指:The arranging of clauses one after the other without connectives showing the relation between them。汉语造句主要采用意合法。可以看出，汉语不重视形式的衔接，而重视语义的连贯，这是汉语语法隐含性（covertness）的一种表现，也是汉人重整体、重综合的思维方式的一种体现。

在这里，英语的形合和汉语的意合所指范围稍广，主要体现在以下四个方面：主谓提挈机制；名词的性、数、格；动词的时态、语态和语气；句子之间的关联。

首先，英语句子遵循严谨的主谓提挈机制：主语由名词、代词或者名词词组构成，必须使用主格；谓语由动词或动词词组构成；有严格的主谓一致的要求；此外，英语句子强调句首第一个字母大写，句末用句号或者问号。

英语句子有主谓结构，主语名词（词组），谓语动词（词组），两者协调一致。句子主次分明，层次清楚，严密规范。这种严谨的主谓提挈机制是英语重形合的一个重要体现。基于这种主谓提挈机制，英语可以组成七种基本句型及其扩展、组合、省略或倒装。

例1 主语（subject）+谓语（verb）：
The small dog is running fast.

例2 主语（subject）+谓语（verb）+状语（adverbial）：
The toilet is out of service.

例3 主语（subject）+谓语（verb）+补足语（complement）：
They have become well-off.

例4 主语（subject）+谓语（verb）+宾语（object）：
He loves Chinese food.

例5 主语（subject）+谓语（verb）+宾语（object）+状语（adverbial）：
He hung the hat on the wall.

例6 主语（subject）+谓语（verb）+间宾（indirect object）+直宾（direct object）：
Paul has mailed me 30 books.

例7 主语（subject）+谓语（verb）+宾语（object）+补足语（complement）：
The students elected him the monitor.

从结构上看，英语句子可分为简单句（simple sentence）和复杂句（multiple sentence）。简单句由一个独立的小句构成。复杂句又分为并列句（compound sentence）和复合句（complex sentence）。并列句由两个以上有并列关系的小句构成；复合句由两个以上有主从关系的小句构成，一个小句为主句，另一个小句为从句，如宾语从句、定语从句、状语从句等。无论简单句还是复杂句，无论并列句、主句还是从句，均需要遵循主谓提挈机制。

汉语主谓结构相当复杂。主语形式多样，可用名词、动词，也可用形容词、数量词；可以表示施事、受事，也可表示时间、地点；主语还经常省略、隐含。汉语主语提挈全句的功能较弱。

例1 我们造了一艘轮船。（施事主语）

例2 轮船我们已经造了一大半。（受事主语）

例3 哭哭啼啼败坏我们的心情。（动词作主语）

例4 很勤快是一大优点。（形容词作主语）

例5 我一个人干就可以了。（复合主语）

例6 早溜掉了。（主语省略）

汉语句子的谓语复杂多样。可以是动词、名词、形容词；可以是多个动词，还可以没有动词,可以是一个单词,也可以是多个词组。主谓之间只要求在语义上一致,没有形式上对应的限制。

1.月<u>明</u>星<u>稀</u>。(形容词作谓语)
2.他<u>离开成都参加会议去了</u>。(连动式谓语)
3.我<u>劝说他接受邀请</u>。(兼语式谓语)
4.这份文件<u>经理要签名</u>。(主谓词组作谓语)
5.一只螃蟹八只脚。(缺少谓语)

其次,英语句子中的名词存在着阴性、阳性之分,单数、复数之分,主格、宾格之分等词形变化。汉语句子中的名词几乎没有阴性、阳性之分,单数、复数之分,主格、宾格之分等词形变化。

例1 For example, intelligence quotient (IQ) test scores vary considerably with illness and disease, educational, social and economic levels—even the skin color of the examiner conducting the IQ test may have a significant effect! There is also difficulty in deciding what intelligence should be applied to. Is it the ability to learn?

Consequently comparisons between an IQ test given to a university student and to an aborigine in Australia will give meaningless results, since the test is most likely to measure the same behavior. Not only are the genotype and the environments of these two individuals totally different, but their motivation for achievement in particular activities will be different.

例2 智力测验就是对智力的科学测试,它主要测验一个人的思维能力、学习能力和适应环境的能力。现代心理学界对智力有不同的看法。所谓智力就是指人类学习和适应环境的能力。智力包括观察能力、记忆能力、想象能力、思维能力等。

一般来说,智商比较高的人,学习能力比较强,但这两者之间不一定完全正相关。因为智商还包括社会适应能力,有些人学习能力强,他的社会适应能力并不强。

再次,英语谓语动词存在着严格区分的时态、语态、语气的变化形式;汉语谓语动词少有严格的时态和语态标志。试比较以下例子中的动词形态变化。

例1 Economic growth cannot continue forever. Even if we can increase the efficiency with which we use resources and transform energy, continued expansion and the taking of the world's primary and secondary biological production will reach limits dictated by food, space, or some other secondary resource. During the last few hundred years science has helped to devise effective hypotheses about ourselves and our environment in the expansionist mode. Now it must help to guide us through an orderly transition from a growing to a dynamically stable economy, a transition that will cause far-reaching social changes. Not least among these changes will be shifts in how, to what ends, and by whom new knowledge will be gained and applied.

例2 二是扎实打好三大攻坚战,重点任务取得积极进展。制定并有序实施三大攻坚战三年行动方案。稳步推进结构性去杠杆,稳妥处置金融领域风险,防控地方政府债务风险,改革完善房地产市场调控机制。深入推进精准脱贫,加强扶贫力量,加大资金投入,强化社会帮扶,贫困地区自我发展能力稳步提高。全面开展蓝天、碧水、净土保卫战。优化能源和运输结构。稳妥推进北方地区"煤改气"

"煤改电"。全面建立河长制、湖长制。化肥农药使用量实现双下降。加强生态环保督察执法。积极应对气候变化。

最后，英文句子与句子之间，主句与从句之间的关系大多是用关系代词、关系副词和连词表示，如 and, if, although, as soon as, as long as, because, when, in order…that, whatever, so 及 so that 等。

汉语句子之间的内部逻辑关系少用或不用关系词和连词，介词也常省略；常使用排比、对偶、对照等；常见紧缩句、四字格等。中国语言学家王力教授在其《中国语法论》中谈到英汉句子的差别时说："西洋语法是硬的，没有弹性；中国的语法是软的，富于弹性。惟其软的，所以中国语法以达意为主。"

例1 One can never see too many summer sunrises on the Mississippi. They are enchanting. First, there is the eloquence of silence; for a deep hush broods everywhere. Next, there is the haunting sense of loneliness, isolation, remoteness from the worry and bustle of the world. The dawn creeps in stealthily; the solid walls of the black forest soften to grey, and vast stretches of the river open up and reveal themselves; the water is smooth, gives off spectral little wreaths of white-mist, there is not the faintest breath of wind, nor stir of leaf; the tranquility is profound and infinitely satisfying. Then a bird pipes up, another follows, and soon the pipings develop into a jubilant riot of music. You see none of the birds, you simply move through an atmosphere of song which seems to sing itself. (Mark Twain, Summer Sunrises on the Mississippi)

例2 雨是最寻常的，一下就是三两天。可别恼。看，像牛毛，像花针，像细丝，密密地斜织着，人家屋顶上全笼着一层薄烟。树叶儿却绿得发亮，小草儿也青得逼你的眼。傍晚时候，上灯了，一点点黄晕的光，烘托出一片安静而和平的夜。乡下去，小路上，石桥边，撑起伞慢慢走着的人；还有地里工作的农夫，披着蓑，戴着笠的。他们的草屋，稀稀疏疏的在雨里静默着。（朱自清《春》）

例3 有一个老村子叫格兰骞斯德，有一个果子园，你可以躺在累累的桃李树荫下吃茶，花果会掉入你的茶杯，小雀子会到你桌上来啄食，那真是别有一番天地。（徐志摩《我所知道的康桥》）

例4 阿Q没有家，住在未庄的土谷祠里；也没有固定的职业，只给人家做短工，割麦便割麦，舂米便舂米，撑船便撑船。（鲁迅《阿Q正传》）

掌握了上述英汉语的差异，我们在英译汉时，不妨选择具有意合特点的汉语句式来翻译英文句子，这样符合汉语习惯，读来流畅自然，简洁明白。

例1 A high mountain stands in the east **and** a large river flows in the west.
译文1. 一座高山矗立在东方，并且一条大河向西边流去。
译文2. 东有高山矗立，西有大江奔流。
译文1亦步亦趋，将英文中的冠词和连词一一译出。特别是"并且"这一连词，在汉语中显得啰唆别扭。相比而言，译文2简洁自然。

例2 **As** we topped the hill, the clouds lifted **and** the harbor looked most beautiful in its semi-circle of hills and half lights.
译文1. 当我们爬到山顶的时候，云散了，**还有**海港在围成半圆形的小山中和中等的光线中，看起来非常漂亮。

译文 2. 我们攀上山顶,云消雾散,只见海港在围成半圆形的小山中,朦朦胧胧,风景秀丽。

译文 2 未将英文的连词"as"明示出来,使用"云消雾散"翻译"the clouds lifted",用"朦朦胧胧"翻译"in half lights",贴切自然,符合汉语表达习惯。而译文 1 虽然表面上忠实于原文的表达方式,将"As we topped the hill"译为"当我们爬到山顶的时候",但却显得不够简明。

例3 He was wearing a loose, long slushy overcoat that hung down to his ankles, looking like a rug draped over his bony shoulders, and a soggy old brown hat, as battered as the shoes he had brought in.

译文 1. 他穿了一件沾满了雪水的宽松的一直拖到脚踝骨的看上去像是披在他的瘦削的肩上的破布长大衣,而且戴了一顶湿漉漉的像他手提的那双破鞋那样的棕色旧帽子。

译文 2. 他身穿大衣,松松垮垮,沾满泥土,一直拖到脚踝骨,像是破布披在瘦骨嶙峋的肩头,头戴一顶湿漉漉的棕色旧帽,手里提着一双破鞋。

英语原文充分体现了形合的特点。主句是 He was wearing an overcoat and a hat,其中修饰 overcoat 的有定语从句 that hung down to his ankles 和现在分词短语 looking like a rug draped over his bony shoulders。短语 as battered as the shoes 修饰 hat,而 shoes 由定语从句 he had brought in 修饰。译文 1 亦步亦趋,按照英文的形式和顺序翻译,显得冗长不堪,难以卒读。译文 2 打破英文形式的束缚,按照汉语讲究意合的特点,重新排列句子,读来自然贴切。

二、英语多长句,汉语多短句

英语书面句子常常繁复冗长,有的长达 200 个单词,甚至整个大段。据统计,专业作者写的句子平均长度为 20 个词,受过教育的人写的句子平均长度为 25 个词。总的看来,英语句子比汉语句子长得多❶。

英语长句较多的原因之一是其形合手段。英语具有各种连接手段,结构十分清晰,句子总是以主谓结构为轴心,通过非谓语动词结构、名词结构、介词结构和从句等从属结构来进行扩展。英语长句较多的另一原因是从属结构(subordination)。F.Crews 认为:"Subordination, the placing of certain elements in modifying roles, is a fundamental principle of writing."在英语中,从句和短语可以充当句子的修饰成分,有时间、地点、方式等从句,从句可以层层叠加,短语可以不断延长。

例1 He had flown in just the day before from Georgia, where he had spent his vacation basking in the sun after the completion of the construction job he had been engaged in the South.

例2 One of the most heartwarming aspects of people who are born with a facial disfigurement, whether minor or major, is the number of them who do not allow it to upset their lives, even reaching out to help others with the same problem.

例3 This century has witnessed dramatic changes in two key factors that define the physical reality of our relationship to the earth: a sudden and startling surge in human popula-

---

❶ 连淑能.英汉对比研究.北京:高等教育出版社,1993/2007:64.

tion, with the addition of one China's worth of people every ten years, and a sudden acceleration of the scientific and technological revolution, which has allowed an almost unimaginable magnification of our power to affect the world around us by burning, cutting, digging, moving, and transforming the physical matter that makes up the earth.

与英语相比较,汉语以中短句居多,最佳长度为7~12字,常用散句、松句、紧缩句、省略句、流水句或并列形式的复句❶。主要原因是汉语少用形合手段,较少使用英语那种从属结构。

在某些情况下,例如表达一些较复杂的思想时,汉语也采用长句。但句子内部,分句与分句之间无须关系连词,往往频繁使用动词,按动作发生的顺序,或逻辑顺序,逐步交代,层层展开,给人以舒缓明快之感。

汉语长句往往以流水句方式出现。长句中有整句,也有大量的零句。整句有主谓结构;零句没有主谓结构,由词或词组构成。整句与零句混合交错,组成了流水句。一口气说几件事,中间似断似连,一逗到底,有一个句号,其中往往转换几个主语或话题。然而,类似汉语的零句,在英语属语法错误,称为破句(fragments),很少使用。

吕叔湘曾指出,"汉语口语里特多流水句,一个小句接一个小句,很多地方可断可连。这些句式流泻铺排,主谓难分,主从难辨,形散神聚,富有节奏,不仅常见于口语,书面语也不乏其例"❷。汉语句子以"意尽为界",句子的信息容量没有语法形式上的限制,弹性很大,一句接着一句,恰似流水,可以无限制地扩展下去❸。

例1　这种床垫工艺先进,结构新颖,造型美观,款式多样,舒适大方,携带方便。

例2　青岛坐落在山东半岛南部,依山临海,天姿秀美,气候凉爽,人称"东方瑞士"。

例3　他这时已是将近六旬的人,一表人才,高个儿,眉目清秀,头发又多又黑,略带花白,恰好衬出他那堂堂的仪表。

例4　自上了轿,进入城中,从纱窗向外瞧了一瞧,其街市之繁华,人烟之阜盛,自与别处不同。(曹雪芹《红楼梦》)

例5　牟尼沟自然风光独特、山川瑰丽多姿,奇险灵秀,令人叹为观止,民族风情浓郁,天宇飞瀑、梦幻花海堪称中国一绝!这里山峦葱绿欲滴,海子安详清亮,山花四季盛开,百鸟欢快歌唱。二道海、扎嘎瀑布、百花湖、翡翠湖、人参湖、柳荫池、明镜湖……在你和大自然的亲近中,处处湖光,幕幕山色,像串串珠玉般,华丽而又静谧地登场,你只需漫步于开满小黄花的湖面栈道,在沁人心脾的芬芳中,享受这不含丝毫尘世喧嚣的眼睛和心灵之约。

在翻译的时候,我们必须考虑到英汉语在繁复与简短方面的差异。如果遇到英文比较繁复的长句,需要将其改写成较为简洁的短句,甚至是汉语的流水句式。处理英语长句和主从句的方法参看本书第五章。

三、英语多物称,汉语多人称

无灵主语(inanimate subject),是指用抽象名词或无生命的事物(如时间、地点等)作主语,它也叫物称(Impersonal subject)。有灵主语(animate subject),是指用有生命的人或动物

---

❶ 连淑能.英汉对比研究.北京:高等教育出版社,1993/2007:64.
❷ 吕叔湘.汉语语法分析问题.北京:商务印书馆,1979:27.
❸ 申小龙.中国句型文化.沈阳:东北师范大学出版社,1988.

作主语,也可谓之人称(personal subject)。

英语多用物称,常用"无灵主语+有灵动词"的形式表达客观事物如何作用于人的感知,使事物以客观口气呈现出来。正如 Leech & Svartvik 所指出的那样:

Formal written language often goes with an impersonal style, i.e. one in which the speaker does not refer directly to himself or his readers, but avoids the pronouns I, you, we. Some of the common features of impersonal language are passives sentences beginning with introductory it, and abstract nouns❶.

同时,英语多用被动语态,这就让所要叙述的客观事物位于句首做主语,使得英语的"物称"更加明显。英语非人称表达法的优点在于,这种句式往往带有隐喻或拟人的修辞色彩,生动形象,有时可使叙述显得客观、冷静,结构趋于严密、紧凑,语气较为委婉、间接。物称表达法作为英语常见的一种文风,尤其常见于书面语,如公文、新闻、科技论著以及散文、小说等文学作品。

例1　The thick carpet killed the sound of my footsteps.
例2　The knowledge of this nuclear fission process has made it possible to use uranium as fuel to obtain nuclear energy.
例3　My hunger and the shadows together tell me that the sun has done much travel since I fell asleep.
例4　The sight of a tailor-shop gave me a sharp longing to shed my rags, and to clothe myself decently once more. (Mark Twain: "The Million Pound Note")
例5　A current search of the files indicates that the letter is no longer in this Bureau's possession. It is noted that the letter was received two months ago, and after study, returned to your office. In view of the foregoing, it is regretted that your office has no record of its receipt. If the letter is found, it would be appreciated if this Bureau was notified at once.

连淑能❷指出:就句法特征而言,英语重物称表达,强调"什么事儿发生在什么人身上",而汉语则重人称表达,突出的是"什么人怎么样了"。

汉语多用人称,常用"有灵主语+有灵动词"的结构,较注重主体思维,以人为中心,更注重"什么人发生了什么事",往往从自我出发来叙述客观事物,或倾向于描述人及其行为或状态,在表达上注重主体性描述。同时,汉语多使用主动,较少使用被动,使得汉语的"人称"更加明显。如果无法确定人称,汉语可以采用"有人""人们""大家""别人"等泛称。如果人称不言自喻,就常常隐含人称或省略人称。

例1　一看到那棵大树,我便想起了童年的情景。
例2　我兴奋得什么话也说不出来。
例3　近来忙于其他事务,未能早些回信,深感抱歉。
例4　这几天心里颇不宁静。今晚在院子里坐着乘凉,忽然想起日日走过的荷塘,在这满月的光里,总该另有一番样子吧。月亮渐渐地升高了,墙外马路上孩子们的欢笑,已经听不见了;妻在屋里拍着闰儿,迷迷糊糊地哼着眠歌。我悄悄地披了大

---

❶ G. Leech and J. Svartvik: A Communicative Grammar of English. New York: Longman, 1974: 25.
❷ 连淑能. 英语的"物称"与汉语的"人称". 山东外语教学, 1993(2): 29-32.

衫,带上门出去。(朱自清《荷塘月色》)

在英汉互译中,进行"人称"和"物称"的转换是非常必要的翻译技巧。英译汉时,常常要将英文的物称主语转换为汉语的人称主语或其他主语,当然,有时还需要对句子的结构做出相应调整。

例1 **The gathering dark** often finds me hastening home in a hurrying crowd.
暮色匆匆的**人群**里,总有我赶路的身影。

例2 **The development** of an economical artificial heart is only a few transient failures away.
只需稍经几次失败,(**我们**)就能研制出廉价的人工心脏了。

例3 **The forty years**, 1840-80, brought almost ten million migrants to America.
在1840—1880年这四十年中,近一千万移民移居美国。

例4 **My conscience** told me that I deserved no extraordinary politeness.
凭良心讲,你待我礼貌有加,我却受之有愧。

例5 Doubts began to creep into people's minds about the likely success of the project.
人们渐渐地对这项计划是否能成功产生怀疑。

例6 The sight of the medical instrument would send shivers down the column of any healthy visitor.
一看到那些医疗器械,即使健康的探视者也会感到毛骨悚然。

例7 **Alarm** began to take entire possession of him.(W.Thackeray)
他开始变得惊恐万状。

四、英语多被动,汉语多主动

著名语言学家 Quirk 指出:

The passive has been found to be as much as ten times more frequent in one text than another. The major stylistic factor determining its frequency seems to be related to the distinction between informative and imaginative prose rather than to a difference of subject matter or of spoken and written English. The passive is generally more commonly used in informative than in imaginative writing, notably in the objective, non-personal style of scientific articles, news items and government communications❶.

在英语的正式文体中,使用被动句几乎成了一种习惯表达(passive habit)。根据统计,英文小说《傲慢与偏见》的前30页中,有135个被动句。而在科技文体中,被动句的使用频率比其他文体要高4倍。英语常在以下几种情况中大量使用被动语态:

(1)行为的实施者未知而难以言明。
(2)行为的实施者从上下文中不言自明。
(3)接受动作的对象是谈话的中心话题,需要强调。
(4)由于特殊原因而不要指明施事者,如为了使叙述显得圆通、得体,或为了表达某种微妙的情绪,如出于礼貌,使措辞得当、语气委婉等。
(5)句法的要求。为了使句子承上启下、前后连贯、便于衔接,或者为了使句子平衡,保持末端重心,以符合主语简短、谓语复杂的表达习惯。

---

❶Quirk, R., S.Greenbaum, G.Leech.and J.Svartvik.*A Grammar of Contemporary English*.Harlow:Longman,1972:807.

(6) 文体的需要。主要指科技文体(technical writing)、新闻文体(newspaperese)、公文文体(bureaucratese)及论述文体中信息性的(informative)文体,更多地使用被动语态。科技文体注重事理和活动的客观叙述,力戒作者的主观臆断,因而常常避免提及动作的发出者。新闻报道注重口气客观、间接、叙事翔实、冷静,行为的实施者有时难以言明。公文则注重叙述公正、无私、口气客观、正式。

例1 The murderer was caught yesterday, and it is said that he will be hanged.(在该句中,抓凶手的人、发出消息的人以及执行绞刑的人都难以说明,所以使用了被动语态。)

例2 She told me that her master had dismissed her. No reason had been assigned; no objection had been made to her conduct. She had been forbidden to appeal to her mistress.(由于首句已经言明实施者master,在后面三个句子中,不必再次指出,因而采用被动语态。)

例3 Her only son was run over by a car.她的独子被汽车轧了。("她的独子"是关注的对象,需要突出强调,放在主语位置,从而产生了被动语态。)

例4 Visitors are requested to show their tickets.(需要游客出示票证,但为了礼貌、语气委婉的需要,采用被动语态。)

例5 Some kinds of plastics can be forced through machines which separate them into long, thin strings, called "fibers", and these fibers can be made into cloth.(第一分句末尾提到fibers,第二分句为保持连贯,也用fibers做主语,从而采用被动语态。)

值得指出的是,对于英语有过分使用被动语态的倾向,一些英美语言学者都主张多用主动语态,不要滥用被动语态。许多学者认为被动语虽有不少用处,但显得冗繁、间接、无力、隐晦、故弄玄虚而深不可测,使交际者之间隔着一层被动的烟幕。

相比而言,汉语中被动语态使用频率较低。著名语言学家王力指出:

> 中国被动式用途之狭,是西洋被动式所比不上的。本来,西洋语言也是主动式多于被动式,尤其在英法语里;有些及物动词竟不能有被动式,例如英语的have,当其用于本义时,罕有用于被动式的。至于中国语呢,就有大部分的及物动词不能用被动式了。……"被"字有"遭受"的意思,因此,被动式所叙述者,对主位而言,必须是不如意或不企望的事。西洋的主动句大多数可转成被动句,中国则恰恰相反,主动句大多数是不能转成被动句的❶。

按照汉语习惯,如句中无须指出行为实施者,主动与被动意义又不致发生混淆,一般就不用被动结构。据统计,在《水浒传》一回中只发现"被"字二三处;而《红楼梦》则二三十回中,才见一处。巴金的《家》初版于1931年,有272处被动句,在1957年做了很大的修订,其中主要的一项就是删改了161处被动句。例如:将"我也许是太自私了,也许是被的别的东西迷住了眼睛"改为"我也许是太自私了,也许是别的东西迷了我的眼睛"。

汉语较少使用被动语态,主要出于以下原因:(1)"五四运动"前,"被字式"曾被称为"不幸语态"(inflictive voice),主要用以表达对主语不利的事,如"被捕""被剥削""身被十二

---

❶王力.中国语法理论.王力文集(第1卷).济南:山东教育出版社,1984:141.

创"等。后来,汉语受西方语言的影响,"被字式"的使用范围有所扩大,频率有所增加,有时也可以用来表达有利的事,如"被选为工会主席""被评为先进工作者"等。(2)汉语的被动式还受到形式的限制。王力指出,"中国正常的被动式是必须把主事者说出来"。这种限制使得许多难以说出动作发出者的句子不能变成被动式。当然,现代汉语有突破这种限制的倾向。

由于汉语的被动式受到意义和形式的限制,大多数被动意义可以采用无主句、主语省略句、主语泛称句(如:人、有人、人们、大家、人家、别人、某人等)、处置式(即"把字式""将字式")或者其他形式的表达。

例1 为什么这些麻烦事总要推给我呢?
例2 风把树刮倒了。
例3 人们常常指责他优柔寡断,虽然这种指责并不总是公正的。
例4 为了确保掩埋的垃圾不污染地下水,消纳场的底部铺设了防水层,并有管道将垃圾腐化后产生的液体抽走。在流经垃圾场的地下水的下游设置了水质抽样井,随时检测地下水质的变化。垃圾产生的沼气被抽到发电机房,发出的电可供附近居民使用。

总之,英语常用被动式,汉语常用主动式。考虑到上述差异,在英汉互译时,句式的转换便成了一种常用的技巧。更多翻译案例请参看本书第五章。

五、英语前重心,汉语后重心[1]

1.英汉句子信息重心的差异

我们知道,英语句子和汉语句子的信息重心一般都落在结果、结论或事实上;但是重心的位置不同:英语句子一般是前重心;汉语句子一般是后重心。

英汉句子在扩展方式上有显著差异。所谓"扩展"是指基本句结构随着思维的发展而呈现的线性延伸。英语句子作从左到右的顺线性延伸,使得句尾呈开放式(close-beginning),句首呈收缩式(open-ending);因此也可以称之为"右分支"结构(right-branching),这样的结构属于"前重心",因为主要信息放在主句中,放在句首,形成前重后轻。例如:

He is singing.

He is singing a song.

He is singing a song composed by a famous musician.

He is singing a song composed by a famous musician in his house.

He is singing a song composed by a famous musician in his house in Beijing.

汉语是从右到左(简称 RL)的逆线性延伸,使得句尾呈收缩式(close-ending),而句首呈开放式(open-beginning),因此也可以称之为"左分支"结构(left-branching),这样的结构也形成了汉语句子"后重心",即把重要信息放在后面的特点。如:

他不理智。

我觉得 他不理智。

我告诉过你我觉得 他不理智。

我清楚地告诉过你我觉得 他不理智。

---

[1] Quirk, et al. *A Comprehensive Grammar of the English Language*. New York: Longman, 1985: 1390.

我见面时清楚地告诉过你我觉得 **他不理智**。

我前天见面时清楚地告诉过你我觉得 **他不理智**。

语序指句子成分排列的次序,它是词语和句子成分之间关系的体现,反映语言使用者的逻辑思维和心理结构模式。汉英两种语言在语序上,既有共性,也有个性。

由于英语十分重视形合手段,英语句子的语序更多地由句子结构确定,比较灵活。例如,英语因果叙述较灵活,表示原因的从句可在主句之前,也可在主句之后。英语表示目的的行为,常是"行为"在前,"目的"在后。在空间上,英语一般是由小到大、由部分到整体排列。

刘宓庆指出:(英语)时序与形态标定相结合,可有后续行为前置式。英语语序的"范围律"是小范围、小范畴事物在前,大范围、大范畴事物在后。……英语中因果安排的可逆性比较突出,特别是带状语的复杂句❶。

例1 It was a seminal moment in American history: the inauguration of the first Transcontinental Railroad on May 10, 1869, in Promontory, Utah.

例2 The 2014 FIFA World Cup is scheduled to take place in Brazil from 12 June to 13 July 2014.

汉语少用形合标识、句子内部顺序以及句间的语序,习惯于遵循由大到小(空间上)、由先到后(时序上)、由因到果(逻辑上)的顺序,这样,汉语句子中的重要信息一般都落在句尾。具体来说,空间上汉语句子习惯从大到小,从整体到局部,从环境到具体,从外围到中心事件。时序上,汉语句子习惯按照事情发生的先后顺序,先发生的事情先讲,后发生的事情后讲。逻辑关系上,汉语句子则一般先讲原因,后讲结果;先说条件,后说结果;先假设,后结果;先叙述事实,后阐述结论或表达评论。

正如刘宓庆所指出的那样:汉语语序有"时序律":先发生的行为在前、后发生的行为在后。汉语语序还有"范围律":大范围、大范畴事物在前,小范围、小范畴事物在后……汉语语序中的"因果律":并扩展为复句语序中的"先次后主""先副后主"式。句子结合中"先因后果"占优势。❷

例1 种瓜得瓜,种豆得豆。

例2 小栓慢慢地从小屋子里走出,两手按了胸口,不住的咳嗽;走到灶下,盛出一碗冷饭,泡上热水,坐下便吃。(鲁迅《药》)

例3 当日地陷东南,这东南一隅有处曰姑苏,有城曰阊门,最是红尘中一二等富贵风流之地。这阊门外有个十里街,街内有个仁清巷,巷内有个古庙,因地方窄狭,皆呼作动葫芦庙。庙旁住着一家乡宦,姓甄,名费,字士隐。(曹雪芹《红楼梦》)

2.英汉定语位置的不同

英汉定语位置也有不同之处。英语的定语基本有两种语序。

第一种是前置。一般来说,英语中单个、少量的形容词、数词、代词、分词、动名词和名词所有格做定语时,放在中心词之前,这一点和汉语基本相同,例如:a red apple(形容词)、hunger strike(名词)、swimming suit(-ing 分词)、coded message(-ed 分词)、his shoes(代词)、the nearby store(副词)、three hundred horses(数词)。

当英语中心词之前出现不同层次的形容词作修饰语时,常常涉及词序问题。一般按下

---

❶刘宓庆.新编汉英对比与翻译.北京:中国对外翻译出版公司,2006:278.
❷刘宓庆.新编汉英对比与翻译.北京:中国对外翻译出版公司,2006:278.

列词序排列：限定词(these,those) + 数量形容词(two) + 描绘性形容词(beautiful) + 大小、长短、高低等形体性形容词(large,long) + 年龄、新旧的形容词(old) + 颜色的形容词(red) + 国籍、来源(Chinese) + 材料(wood) + 用途、目的(writing) + 中心词(desk)。一般来说，和中心词关系越密切，越能说明事物本质的定语，越要靠近它所修饰的名词。如：an interesting old Hollywood film, two attractive large brown Turkish wool carpets。

英语定语位置的第二种情况是后置。动词不定式，分词短语，定语从句，-ible，-able 结尾的形容词与 every, the only 或形容词最高级连用来修饰名词时，some-，any-，every-，no-等构成的复合代词被修饰时，一些固定词组中的定语(如 secretary general)等常常需要后置。值得注意的是，英语中前置定语一般较为简短，而后置定语可以变得十分繁复，甚至可以延长到令人吃惊的地步。

例1 The newly-wedded couple bought a large round green Danish-made bed.

例2 Pollution is a pressing problem which we must deal with.

例3 It was an old woman, tall and shapely still, though withered by time, on whom his eyes fell when he stopped and turned.

例4 But without Adolf Hitler, who was possessed of a demoniac personality, a granite will, uncanny instincts, a cold ruthlessness, a remarkable intellect, a soaring imagination and-until toward the end, when drunk with power and success, he over reached himself-an amazing capacity to size up people and situations, there almost certainly would never have been a Third Reich.

汉语定语的特点是结构前置，即修饰语在前，中心语在后。汉语中的习惯是把最能说明事物本质的放在最前面，而把表示规模大小、力量强弱的定语放在后面。汉语中不同类型词语作定语修饰一个名词时，往往将表明事物本质属性的词语排列在前，将描写性词语排列在后。如果修饰语很多，其排列顺序一般为：时间、地点定语+数量词+表示领属关系的定语+表示数量的定语+限制性定语+描写性定语+表材质、属性的定语。

在汉语中，动词短语，主谓结构短语，介词短语作定语时，也通常前置。如：刚收到的邮件(动词短语)，他写的小说(主谓结构短语)，在四川偏远山区的熊猫(介词短语)。

例1 古代中国现存规模最大，保存最完整的木制建筑群。

例2 中国代表团对南非侵略军袭击一个爱好和平的邻国，残杀和伤害包括妇女、儿童在内的无辜平民，毁坏房屋和汽车的野蛮行径表示极大愤慨。

例3 我们对于国际社会和联合国人权机构在促进和保护人权方面的上述努力表示欢迎。

例4 我们不但要有一个农、林、牧、副、渔布局合理，全面发展，能够满足人民生活和工业发展需要的发达的农业，还要有一个门类齐全、结构合理，能够满足社会消费和整个国民经济发展需要的先进的工业。

3.英汉状语位置的差异

此外，**英汉语状语位置也有显著差异**。在英语中，状语一般出现在句尾宾语之后，呈"主语+谓语+宾语+状语"的模式。如：He watches TV every evening。有时状语位置比较灵活，为了强调，也可出现在句首或句中。如：In a machine a great deal of energy is lost because of the friction between its parts(出现在句首，强调 in a machine 这一事实)；又如：They observed with great care the chemical reaction(出现在句中，对 with great care 有一定强调)。

多个状语同时出现时，英语习惯于从小到大，按照"动词+方式+地点+时间"的顺序排列。

例1 She writes many pages of her novel with great enthusiasm in a seaside hotel every day.

例2 The 2014 FIFA World Cup is scheduled to take place in Brazil from 12 June to 13 July 2014.

例3 Sherman had recently turned down a $50,000-a-year job at a consulting firm, after careful deliberation with his parents, because he hadn't connected well with his potential bosses.

汉语状语一般位于主语和谓语之间，呈"主语+状语+谓语+宾语"的模式。有时为了强调，也可放在主语之前。多个状语同时出现时，汉语习惯于从大到小，按照"时间+地点+方式+动词"的顺序排列。

例1 他每晚都要看电视。

例2 几十年来，我经常想到这一只狗，直到今天，我一想到它，还会不自主地流下眼泪。

例3 1904年巴金出生在中国四川省的一个封建大地主家庭。

例4 1971年7月，人们在得克萨斯州休斯敦附近的宇航中心做了一个有趣的实验。

Pollution in India

Even by the standards of poor countries, India is alarmingly—and unnecessarily—filthy. It needs to clean up.

India stinks. If at this misty time of year its capital, Delhi, smells as if something is burning, that is because many things are: the carcinogenic diesel that supplies three-quarters of the city's motor fuel, the dirty coal that supplies most of its power, the rice stalks that nearby farmers want to clear after the harvest, the rubbish dumps that perpetually smoulder, the 400,000 trees that feed the city's crematoria each year and so on. All this combustion makes Delhi's air the most noxious of any big city. It chokes on roughly twice as much pm 2.5, fine dust that penetrates deep into lungs, as Beijing.

Delhi's deadly air is part of a wider crisis. Seventy percent of surface water is tainted. In the World Health Organisation's rankings of air pollution, Indian cities claim 14 of the top 15 spots. In an index of countries' environmental health from Yale and Columbia universities, India ranks a dismal 177th out of 180.

This does not just make life unpleasant for a lot of Indians. It kills them. Recent estimates put the annual death toll from breathing pm 2.5 alone at 1.2m–2.2m a year. The lifespan of Delhi-dwellers is shortened by more than ten years, says the University of Chicago. Consumption of dirty water directly causes 200,000 deaths a year, a government think-tank reckons, without measuring its contribution to slower killers such as kidney disease. Some 600m Indians, nearly half the country, live in areas where water is in short supply. As pollutants taint groundwater, and global warming makes the vital monsoon rains more erratic, the country is poisoning its own future.

Indian pollution is a danger to the rest of the world, too. Widespread dumping of antibiotics in rivers has made the country a hotspot for anti-microbial resistance. Emissions of carbon dioxide, the most common greenhouse gas, grew by 6% a year between 2000 and 2016, compared with 1.3% a year for the world as a whole (and 3.2% for China). India now belches out as much as the whole of Africa and South America combined.

In the past India has explained its failure to clean up its act by pleading poverty, noting that richer countries were once just as dirty and that its output of filth per person still lags far behind theirs. But India is notably grubby not just in absolute terms, but also relative to its level of development. And it is becoming grubbier. If electricity demand doubles by 2030, as expected, coal consumption stands to rise by 50%.

It is true that some ways of cutting pollution are expensive. But there are also cheap solutions, such as undoing mistakes that Indian bureaucrats have themselves made. By subsidising rice farmers, for instance, the government has in effect cheered on the guzzling of groundwater and the torching of stubble. Rules that encourage the use of coal have not made India more self-reliant, as intended, but instead have led to big imports of foreign coal while blackening India's skies. Much cleaner gas-fired power plants, meanwhile, sit idle.

Reliant on big business for funding and on the poor for votes, politicians have long ignored middle-class complaints about pollution, failing to give officials the backing to enforce rules, or to co-ordinate across jurisdictions. That is a pity, because when India does apply itself to ambitious goals, it often achieves them. Next year it will send its second rocket to the Moon.

Narendra Modi, the prime minister, promised with admirable frankness when he took over to rid the country of open defecation. Four and a half years and some $ 9bn later, his Clean India campaign claims to have sponsored the building of an astonishing 90m toilets. This is impressive, but India is still not clean. Its skies, its streets, its rivers and coasts will remain dangerously dirty until they receive similar attention.

(656 words)

第四章

翻译技巧(1)

The Making of Ashenden (Excerpt)
Stanley Elkin

I've been spared a lot, one of the blessed of the earth, at least one of its lucky, that privileged handful of the dramatically prospering, the sort whose secrets are asked, like the hundred-year-old man. There is no secret, of course; most of what happens to us is simple accident. Highish birth and a smooth network of appropriate connection like a tea service written into the will. But surely something in the blood too, locked into good fortune's dominant genes like a blast ripening in a time bomb. Set to go off, my good looks and intelligence, yet exceptional still, take away my mouthful of silver spoon and lapful of luxury. Something my own, not passed on or handed down, something seized, wrested—my good character, hopefully, my taste perhaps. What's mine, what's mine? Say taste—the soul's harmless appetite.

I've money, I'm rich. The heir to four fortunes. Grandfather on Mother's side was a Newpert. The family held some good real estate in Rhode Island until they sold it for many times what they gave for it. Grandmother on Father's side was a Salts, whose bottled mineral water, once available only through prescription and believed indispensable in the cure of all fevers, was the first product ever to be reviewed by the Food and Drug Administration, a famous and controversial case. The government found it to contain nothing that was actually detrimental to human beings, and it went public, so to speak. Available now over the counter, the Salts made more money from it than ever.

(257 words)

Genius Sacrificed for Failure

英语文本	汉语文本
Genius Sacrificed for Failure William N. Brown	为庸才损英才 威廉·N.布朗
During my youth in America's Appalachian mountains, I learned farmers preferred sons over daughters, largely because boys were better at heavy farm labor (though what boys anywhere could best the tireless Hui′an girls in the fields of Fujian!).	我在美国的阿巴拉契亚山区度过青少年时代时,发现那里的农民重男轻女,多半因为男子更能胜任重体力农活——当然,如果要和福建农田里的惠安妇女相比,她们那份不歇不竭的能耐是任何地方的男子都自叹弗如的!
With only 3% of Americans in agriculture today, brain has supplanted brawn, yet cultural preferences, like bad habits, are easier to make than break. But history warns repeatedly of the tragic cost of dismissing too casually the gifts of the so-called weaker sex.	今天在美国,脑力已经取代了体力,只有3%的美国人在从事农业。但文化上的习俗正如陋规,形成容易冲破难。而对所谓"阴柔"性别,历史再三告诫我们,若对她们的禀赋过于轻率地否认,其代价将会何等惨重!
About 150 years ago, a village church vicar in Yorkshire, England, had three lovely, intelligent daughters but his hopes hinged entirely on the sole male heir, Branwell, a youth with remarkable talent in both art and literature.	约150年前在英国的约克郡有一个乡村教区的牧师,他有三位聪慧可爱的女儿,但是他的希望却独独钉在唯一的继承者儿子布朗维尔身上。这个年轻人在艺术和文学上都有出众的天赋。
Branwell's father and sisters hoarded their pennies to pack him off to London′s Royal Academy of Arts, but if art was his calling, he dialed a wrong number. Within weeks he hightailed it home, a penniless failure.	父亲和姐妹都省吃俭用,帮兄弟打点完备,送他上了伦敦皇家艺术学院。可是尽管他要以艺术为业,但拨错了号。不到几个礼拜,就不名一文,弃甲归家。
Hopes still high, the family landed Branwell a job as a private tutor, hoping this would free him to develop his literary skills and achieve the success and fame that he deserved. Failure again.	然而家人并不就此罢休,他们又想方设法帮布朗维尔捞到一份私人教师的活儿,希望这份差事能够使他自由发展文学才能,走上应得的功成名就的大道。这次又失败了。
For years the selfless sisters squelched their own goals, farming themselves out as teachers and governesses in support of their increasingly indebted brother, convinced the world must eventually recognize his genius. As failures multiplied, Branwell turned to alcohol, then opium, and eventually died as he had lived: a failure. So died hope in the one male—but what of the three anonymous sisters?	几年来,无私的姐妹们压抑着她们自己的目标和志向,受雇于人做管家或家庭教师以支持她们那日益债台高筑的兄弟,她们深信世界总有一天会认识到他的天才。随着接踵而来的失败,布朗维尔开始酗酒,后来又吸上鸦片,最后死时与生前一样,一无所成,于是寄托在这唯一男性身上的指望也随之死去。但,那三位默默无闻的姐妹们又如何了呢?
During Branwell's last years, the girls published a book of poetry at their own expense (under a pseudonym, for fear of reviewers′ bias against females). Even Branwell might have snickered: they sold only 2 copies.	在布朗维尔生前最后几年,姑娘们自己出资出版了一本诗集(用的是假名,以防编辑们对女性的成见)。只卖出两本,就连布朗维尔也哂笑她们。

续上表

英语文本	汉语文本
Undaunted, they continued in their spare time, late at night by candlelight, to pour out their pent-up emotion, writing of what they knew best, of women in conflict with their natural desires and social condition—in reality, less fiction than autobiography! And 19th century literature was transformed by Anne's Agnes Grey, Emily's *Wuthering Heights*, and Charlotte's *Jane Eyre*.	然而她们并不气馁。姐妹们继续利用她们的空余时间,夜深人静时秉烛而书,倾吐她们幽禁的情怀,抒写她们最熟悉的一切。她们描写了那种女性自发的意愿与社会环境之间的冲突。实际上她们所写的与其说是小说不如说是自传!于是,19世纪文学就因安妮的《安格尼斯·格雷》、艾米莉的《呼啸山庄》和夏洛特的《简·爱》而改观了。
But years of sacrifice for Branwell had taken their toll. Emily took ill at her brothers funeral and died within 3 months, aged 29; Anne died 5 months later, aged 30; Charlotte lived only to age 39. If only they had been nurtured instead of sacrificed.	然而,三姐妹为了布朗维尔的多年牺牲,付出了沉重的代价。艾米莉在她兄弟葬礼的那一天便得了病,三个月之后便离世了,年方29岁;五个月后安妮也以30芳龄长逝;夏洛特则只活到39岁。假若她们能早日得到培养而不作牺牲,那该多好啊!
No one remembers Branwell's name, much less his art or literature, but the Bronte sister's tragically short lives teach us even more of life than of literature. Their sacrificed genius cries out to us that in modem society we must value children not by their physical strength or sexual gender, as we would any mere beast of burden, but by their integrity, strength, commitment, courage—spiritual qualities abundant in both boys and girls. China, a nation blessed by more boys and girls than any nation, ignores at her own peril the lesson of the Bronte tragedy.	无人再记得布朗维尔的名字,更不用说他的艺术或文学了。然而从勃朗特三姐妹悲剧性的夭折中我们学到的不仅是文学,更重要的是生命真谛,她们牺牲了的天分向我们大声疾呼:现代社会再不能以体力或性别,把子女当牛马来评估了。它必须就忠诚、能力、责任心、勇敢等男女孩子都富有的精神品质来对他们评价。中国,这个有幸拥有世界上最多的男孩女孩的国家应从勃朗特悲剧中获得认识,免蹈覆辙。
Patrick Bronte fathered Branwell, but more importantly, he fathered Anne, Emily and Charlotte. Were he alive today he would surely urge us to put away our prejudices and avoid his own tragic and irrevocable error of putting all of his eggs in one male basket!	帕特利克·勃朗特养育了布朗维尔,但更重要的,他是安妮、艾米莉和夏洛特的父亲。倘若此人今日仍活着的话,他一定会迫切敦促我们放下我们的古旧偏见,避免他自己的悲剧和抱憾终身的过失:将一切都押在一个男性后裔身上。

认知升级

一、直译与意译

直译和意译是非常重要的翻译方法。由于英汉两种语言的形式结构和用法有相同的一面,汉译时采用"直译"——既忠实原文内容,又保留原文结构形式的翻译方法。但英汉语言之间还有许多差别,如完整照译,常常出现"欧化汉语",这时就需要"意译",即在忠实原文内容的前提下,不保持原文形式,摆脱原文结构的束缚,使译文符合汉语的规范。

1.直译法

直译,在英文中常常称为 literal translation。事实上,它可能用于不同的层面,如词对词翻译(word-for-word Translation)和句对句翻译(sentence-for-sentence Translation)。直译作为一种翻译策略无疑自有其用途,比如,在翻译多种科技文本时,通常就适宜采用直译。在文学翻译中,直译也有其用武之地。纳博科夫(Nabokov)认为,直译是"在另一种语言的相关能力和句法能力所允许的范围内尽可能贴近地翻译原作的确切语境意义"(Nabokov,1964/

1975：viii）。

应当指出，在不违背译文语言规范的条件下，直译有其可取之处，它有助于语言学习者了解目标语结构，有助于保存原作的思想和风格，有助于了解源语文化、民族特色，也可以引进新鲜的表达方法。

但直译必须具有可读性，也就是说，直译最好不要引起读者的误解，也不违反目标语表达方式。直译还适用于含有修辞的句子。在某种程度上，直译不仅能保持原作的特点，而且还可使读者逐步接受原作的文学风格。例如：angel"天使"，dark horse"黑马"，cold war"冷战"等。事实上，许多直译过来的英语词汇已经被广泛地应用于汉语中了。

例1 The operation may not succeed; it's a gamble whether he lives or dies.
手术不一定成功，只能赌一赌看能否保住他的性命。

例2 But after six years of a stormy marriage, Cewe decided to end it.
六载婚姻生活，风雨交加，赛维决定结束这种婚姻。

例3 He walked at the head of the funeral procession, and every now and then wiped his crocodile tears with a big handkerchief.
他走在送葬队伍的前头，还不时用一条大手绢擦一擦他的鳄鱼泪。

2.意译法

当然，每一个民族语言都有它自己的词汇、句法结构和表达方法。当原文的思想内容与译文的表达形式有矛盾而不宜采用直译法处理时，就应采用意译法。意译要求译文能正确表达原文的内容，但可以不拘泥于原文的形式。

意译，常常又称作自由译（Free Translation），或者意对意翻译（Sense-for-Sense Translation），意译的翻译单位也可以大到句子（或更大的单位）。根据卡特福德（Catford）的观点，它们的操作级阶（或层次）应该是不受限的，这是意译的一个先决条件。

比如，由于英、汉两种语言的文化差异，有一些修辞不能采用直译，我们必须求助于意译。

例1 Every dog has his day.
人人皆有得意日。

例2 It's an ill wind that blows nobody good.
对有些人有害的事情可能对另一些人有利。

例3 Nixon was smiling and Kissinger smiling more broadly.
尼克松满面春风，基辛格更是笑容可掬。

例4 He was seized with the despairing sense of his helplessness.
他忽然产生了束手无策的绝望感觉。

例5 Do you see any green in my eye?
你以为我是好骗的吗？

例6 Ruth was upsetting the other children, so I showed her the door.
鲁斯一直在扰乱别的孩子，我把他撵了出去。

在翻译中，几乎都要用到直译和意译。直译与意译相互关联、互为补充，同时，它们又互相协调、互相渗透，不可分割。通过对直译与意译二者关系的正确研究，更多地认识了解到什么时候采用直译、什么时候采用意译，在运用直译与意译的时候所应该掌握的技巧、遵循的原则和应该注意的问题，最终达到提高翻译能力及水平的目的。

例1 It means killing two birds with one stone.

直译法：这意味着一石二鸟。

意译法：这意味着一举两得（一箭双雕）。

例2 Every spirit you take is a nail in your coffin.

直译法：你喝的每一杯酒都是你棺材上的一颗钉子。

意译法：你喝的每一杯酒都在缩短你的性命。

例3 The first time I saw her, half of my life ago, she nearly took my breath away.

直译法：大半生前第一次见到她，她差点儿让我无法呼吸。

意译法：大半生前第一次见到她，我就惊呆了。

例4 He had about as much chance of getting a job as of being chosen mayor of Chicago.

直译：他找到工作的机会和当选芝加哥市长的机会差不多。

意译：他找到工作的机会简直微乎其微。

例5 There is a mixture of the tiger and the ape in the character of a French man.

直译法：法国人的性格混合有老虎和猿的成分。

意译法：法国人的性格既残暴又狡猾。

直译与意译兼顾：虎恶狐狡，兼而有之，这就是法国人的性格。

特别要注意的是："直译"不等于"硬译"，"意译"也不等于"乱译"。英语和汉语在文学形式上也存在着差异，不同文体有各自不同的特点。那么，直译和意译是翻译过程中互不排斥、各有长短的两种方法。

例1 At the door to the restaurant, a stunning, porcelain-faced woman in traditional costume asked me to remove my shoes.

硬译：在通往餐厅的门口，一位迷人的陶瓷般脸蛋的身着和服的妇女叫我脱下鞋子。

乱译：此门通向餐厅，一位美颜如花、衣着传统的妇女让我脱靴。

直译：在通往餐厅的门口有一位妇女，涂脂抹粉、细皮嫩肉、身着和服、十分迷人，她叫我脱下鞋子。

意译：在通往餐厅的门口有一位妇女，她身着和服，仪态优美，面庞陶瓷般光洁白皙，叫我脱去鞋子。

例2 The rather arresting spectacle of little old Japan adrift amid beige concrete skyscrapers is the very symbol of the incessant struggle between the kimono and the miniskirt.

硬译：古老的矮小的日本漂游在灰棕色的钢筋混凝土摩天大楼之间的吸引人的景象是和服与超短裙之间的不断斗争的象征。

乱译：古老迷人的矮小日本漂浮在摩天大楼里，楼里身穿迷你裙和和服的人在不断抗争。

直译：式样古老小巧的日本房屋像小船一般，漂游在灰棕色的钢筋混凝土摩天大楼之间，这引人注目的景象象征着旧传统和新发展之间的不断斗争。

意译：米黄色的混凝土摩天大楼之间，飘荡着小小的古老的日本，构成了一道吸引人的风景，恰恰象征着和服与迷你裙间不断的斗争。

二、音译与形译

1.音译法

音译(transliteration)指用发音近似的汉字将英语词汇翻译过来的方法。音译是吸收外来语的一种主要方式,也叫"借音"(phonetic borrowing)。

音译法大量用于专业术语的翻译,特别是以下4种范畴的"专业术语":(1)新研发的物品,如engine 引擎、nylon 尼龙;(2)新发现的自然现象或物质,如typhoon 台风、gene 基因、hacker 黑客、clone 克隆等;(3)计量单位,此类术语往往由科学家的姓氏转化而来,如Hertz 赫兹(频率单位)、Ohm 欧姆(电阻单位);(4)首字母缩略词构成的术语,如OPEC 欧佩克、TOEFL 托福、PVC(Polyvinyl chloride)聚氯乙烯、SONAR(sound navigation and ranging)声呐(声音导航与测距设备)等。

当然,普通名词也存在音译的现象,例如酷(cool)、迪斯科(disco)、比基尼(bikini)、尤里卡(EURECA)、妈咪(mummy)等。

音译时,还要把握恰当的方法,需要注意以下事项:首先,要注意查证词典等工具书,遵照已有的、约定俗成的音译方法,不能盲目自创。在音译实例中存在着许多常用的、广为人们接受的"音译字",这些字已具备了一定的约定意义。例如,"斯"多与男子名和地名有关(如"罗斯福""斯坦福"),"丝"多与女子名有关(如"爱丽丝"),"司"多与食物有关(如"吐司""寿司")。

其次,要遵照英语或外国文字的汉字译音表(请参见本书附录1英汉译音表)。关于音译选字,音译汉字的选择应遵循汉字的表意性原则,做到"音相似,意相近",即所谓音义兼顾。人名和地名音译选字时,避免将"撕"或"私"等意义负荷量较大或感情色彩比较浓厚的日常用字当作"音译字"。

最后要注意音节的调整。英汉两种语言在语音和音系上存在差异,因而存在对音节进行取舍和选择的问题❶。由于汉语常常使用双音词,英语词音译成汉语时音节数要足以构成一个音步,如果不够,就需要增补。例如,card(卡片)只有一个音节,音译时,再增加一个音节,使其变成两个音节,"卡片",这样既凑足了音步,又表明了意思;gene(基因)也只有一个音节,音译时变成两个音节"基因"。再如,AIDS(艾滋病)也只有一个音节,音译时把不足一个音节的[dz]音译成"滋",再在其后加上一个表示事物种类的汉字"病",用以表意。简言之,增音有两种方法:第一,把源词末尾不足一个音节的辅音音位增补为一个音节;第二,在音译字的前面或后面加上表示事物种类的汉字。增音的理据就是使音译词的音节足以构成一个音步,从而实现一个基本的、稳定的标准韵律词,以达到汉化的目的。

但是,如果英语词汇的音节太多,尤其是四个及以上音节的时候,在音译时就有必要删掉一些轻音或辅音。例如,英文America,有四个音节,但第一个音节是轻音,可以删掉,结果译成一个三音节的基本韵律词"美利坚";Campbell 音译为"坎贝尔",省掉了[m]音,但同时补足了最后一个[l]音,译成汉字"尔";Columbus 音译为"哥伦布",省掉了中间的[m]音和末尾的[s]音。上述这些例子满足了汉语韵律构词对音节数量的要求。也有音义兼顾的例子,如bandage,译为"绷带",省掉了最后一个辅音,选择了两个意义丰富的字作为模拟音,"绷"有"绷紧"之意,"带"有"布带"之意。这里采取了删音和意译结合的方法,既满足了音

---

❶田永弘.音译规范的韵律学视角探究.中国科技术语,2016,18(5):14-18.

节的要求,又便于读者理解意义。

在文学翻译中,有时译者会创造性地发挥,弃用原有的意译,自创音译,使得译文与原词所指称的概念内容、格调语义都有强烈的反差,令人哑然失笑。例如英文"gentleman",有人故意译成"尖头鳗",出人意料,惹人发笑。又如英文"ladies",却有人译成"累得死",不禁让人想到中国妇女的生活状况,会心一笑。鲁迅曾经把 fair play 译为"费厄泼赖",也有讽刺之意。

值得注意的是,有些英语词汇在早期进入汉语时采用音译,后来又改用意译。比如说,英语"democracy",最早中国人将之音译为"德谟克拉西",但后来就改用了日本人以汉字创造的译名"民主";又如英语"science",最早中国人译为"赛因思",后来也改成了日本人的译法"科学";再如英文"telephone",最初中国人译成"德律风",后来也改成了日本人的译法"电话"。"民主""科学""电话"等都是西方世界的概念与事物,是中国所没有的,中国人在迫不得已要引进这些概念时,开始用音译直接"拿来",后来意译的用法就慢慢流行起来,音译弃而不用了。

2. 形译法

形译法(Graphological Translation,或 Pictographic translation),也称"象译",是按照字体的书写形象或物体的形状,再加上中心词的翻译方法。"形译法"主要用于科技英语,特别是科技术语的翻译。

有些科技术语的前半部分是表示该术语形象的字母或单词,翻译这类术语时,应将这一部分译成能表示具体形象的汉字,或保留原来的字母。这样的翻译直接明了,形象生动,较为便捷,容易广大的读者和科技工作者理解和接受。形译法有以下三种类型:

(1)选用近似英文字母形状的汉字翻译:

I-Section 工字形剖面	I-square 丁字尺
I-Steel 工字钢	I-wrench 丁字扳手
Z-iron 乙字铁	cross bit 十字钻头
cross pipe 十字管	cross stitch 十字缝
gable roof 人字屋顶	herringbone gear 人字齿轮

(2)保留英文原字母不译,以字母表达形状,有时在该字母后加"形"字:

A-Frame A 形架	C-clamp C 形夹
S-wrench S 形扳手	T-joint T 形接头
V-gear V 形齿轮	X-ray X 射线
Y-alloy Y 合金	zigzag chain Z 形链
inverted-V engine 倒 V 形发动机	sliding T-handle T 形滑动手柄

(3)按术语英文意思译成相近或相同的汉语形状翻译:

V-belt 三角皮带	X-type 交叉形
Y-pipe 叉形管	Y-curve 叉形曲线
O-ring 环行环(环行圈)	U-bolt 马蹄螺栓
set-square 三角尺	arch dam 拱坝
cross-section 横截面	heart carrier 鸡心夹头
zigzag wave 曲折波	butterfly nut 蝶形螺母

三、增译与省译

1.增译法

按理,译者应该遵循忠实的原则,不得对原文的内容随意增减。可是,由于英汉两种语言文字之间所存在巨大差异,在实际翻译过程中我们很难做到字词句上完全对应。因此,为了准确地传达出原文的信息,往往需要对译文作一些增减。

所谓增译法(addition, or amplification),就是在原文的基础上添加必要的单词、词组、分句或完整句,从而使译文在语法、语言形式上符合汉语的习惯并使译文在文化背景、词语联想方面与原文保持一致,以达到译文与原文在内容、形式和精神方面对等起来的目的。注意:这里的增加不是无中生有、随意地增加,而是确有需要才添加。

增译可以分为词汇增译(Lexical Amplification)、句法增译(Amplification)、修辞增译(Rhetorical Amplification)及文化增译(Cultural Amplification)。也可增加主语、谓语、宾语等;增加的词语可以有动词、名词、概念词、副词、量词、表达复数的词、表达时态的词、语气助词、连词等。

例1 Matter can be changed into energy, and energy into matter.
物质可以转换成能量,能量可以转化为物质。

例2 Histories make men wise; poets witty; the mathematics subtle; natural philosophy deep; moral grave; logic and rhetoric able to contend.
读史使人明智,读诗使人灵秀,数学使人周密,科学使人深刻,伦理使人庄重,逻辑修辞之学使人善辩。

例3 Speed and reliability are the chief advantages of the electronic computers.
速度快、可靠性强是电子计算机的主要优点。

例4 It is really nice and cheap. You will regret for not buying it later.
这真是物美价廉,你不买会后悔的。

例5 She was walking in the street alone, weary and ragged.
她独自一人走在大街上,面容憔悴,衣衫褴褛。

例6 The Americans and Japanese conducted a completely secret exchange of message.
美日双方在完全保密的情况下交换了情报。

例7 The thesis summed up the new achievements made in electronic computers, artificial satellites and rockets.
该论文总结了电子计算机、人造卫星、火箭这三方面的成就。

例8 A red sun rose slowly from the calm sea.
一轮红日从平静的海面冉冉升起。

例9 The mountains began to throw their long blue shadows over the valley.
群山开始向山谷投下一道道蔚蓝色的长影。

句法增译主要用于补充英语省掉的句子成分,表示逻辑关系的连词,增补/重复同位语结构中的先行词。

例1 Better be wise by the defeat of others than by your own.
从别人的失败中吸取教训比从自己的失败中吸取教训更好。

例2 We don't retreat, we never have and never will.

我们不后退,我们从没有后退过,将来也决不后退。

例3 The strongest man cannot alter the law of nature.
即使是最强有力的人也不能改变自然法则。

例4 More thorough testing might have caught the failure initially.
如果测试更为彻底,也许一开始就能找出故障。

例5 Water can be decomposed by energy, a current of electricity.
水可由能量来分解,所谓能量也就是电能。

例6 Day after day he came to his work——sweeping, scrubbing, cleaning.
日复一日,他不断地扫地、擦地板、收拾房间。

修辞增译是为了将隐含意义明示出来,增强表达效果。

例1 After the thunderstorm, the clouds melted away.
雷雨过后,乌云渐渐散去。

例2 Now and then, his boots shone.
他的靴子时时闪闪发光。

例3 As he sat down and began talking, words poured out.
他一坐下来就讲开了,滔滔不绝地讲个没完。

例4 The very earth trembled as with the tramps of horses and murmur of angry men.
地面颤抖,仿佛万马奔腾、千夫怒吼。

例5 With his tardiness, careless and appalling good temper, we had nothing to do with him.
他老是磨磨蹭蹭,马马虎虎,脾气又好得惊人,我们都对他毫无办法。

例6 I had been completely honest in my replies, withholding nothing.
我的回答完全是坦坦荡荡,不藏不掖。

例7 His children, too, were as ragged and wild as if they belonged to nobody.
他的那些孩子,也是穿得破破烂烂,粗野不堪,就像没有父母似的。

英汉文化的巨大差异所造成的文化缺省也促使译者在译文中增加一些解释成分和反映文化背景的信息,以提高其可读性。

例1 Le Monde, the BBC, The New York Times, the entire Arab press, all quote Heikal regularly at length.
法国《世界报》、英国广播公司、《纽约时报》和整个阿拉伯报界,都经常大段引用海卡尔的话。

例2 The death of the Princess of Wales unleashed outpourings of newly-coined honorifics, for instance "a present-day Cinderella whose clock struck midnight all too soon".
威尔士王妃戴安娜之死,导致有关她的新敬语如潮水一般涌流出来,比如有人说她是"当今灰姑娘,只是午夜的钟声过早地敲响"。

2.省译法

省译法(Omission)是指原文中有些词在译文略去不译,因为译文中已有其意,或者译文不言而喻。省译法是删去一些可有可无的,或者有了反而累赘或违背译文习惯表达法的词,并不是把原文的某些思想内容删去。

省译可分为结构省译和修辞省译。所谓结构省译是由于英汉两种语言在句子结构上的差异造成的。在英译汉时经常省略的词有代词、系词、介词、连词、冠词、先行词等。作主语和定语的人称代词以及作定语的物主代词均可省译。

例1 When winter comes, can spring be far away?
冬天来了,春天还会远吗?

例2 Killing two birds with one stone.
一石二鸟。

例3 If you write him, the response would be absolute silence and void.
你写信给他,总是石沉大海。

例4 When the pressure gets low, the boiling point becomes low.
气压低,沸点就低。

例5 He put his hands into his pockets and then shrugged his shoulders.
他双手插进口袋,然后耸了耸肩。

例6 You cannot build a ship, a bridge or a house if you Don't know how to make a design or how to read it.
不会制图或看不懂图纸,就不可能造船、架桥或盖房子。

例7 Liquids have no definite shape, yet they have a definite volume.
液体没有一定的形状,但有一定的体积。

例8 Electrical leakage will cause a fire; hence you must take good care of it.
漏电会引起火灾,因此必须注意。

如果把结构省译看作是强制性的省译手段,那么修辞省译则是可以选择的翻译方法,是为了让语言精练压缩、化繁为简,增强译文表现力。

例1 A wise man will not marry a woman who has attainments but no virtue.
原译:聪明的人是不会娶有才无德的女子为妻的。
改译:智者不娶有才无德之女。

例2 There was no snow, but the leaves were gone from the trees and the grass was dead.
原译:天还没有雪,但是叶子已经从树上落下,草也枯死了。
改译:雪未下,但已叶落草枯。

例3 The more he tried to hide his mistakes, the more he revealed them.
原译:他越是想要掩盖他的错误,就越是容易暴露。
改译:欲盖弥彰。

例4 If you want to kill a snake you must hit it on the head and if you want to catch a band of robbers you must first catch their leader.
原译:如果你想杀死一条蛇,你必须打它的头;如果你想要抓住一帮匪徒,你必须先抓住匪首。
改译:打蛇先打头,擒贼先擒王。

四、回译与转类

1. 回译法

2017年6月,一所"双鸭山大学"成功地吸引了网友注意。微博上出现了这样一段话:"1984年出生在中国广东省广州市,父母是双鸭山大学(Sun Yat-sen University)的老师。五岁那年夏天,随父母去了香港,后来全家移民新加坡。中国清华大学本科和硕士毕业,新加坡南洋理工大学博士毕业,现在香港中文大学任助理教授。"难道这所大学位于黑龙江省东北部双鸭山市?原来,Sun Yat-sen University 是中山大学的英译名,Sun Yat-sen 正是孙中山的英文名字。"双鸭山大学"一时引起人们热议,有中山大学校友戏谑称"可能读了个假大学"。这次事件其实是不懂"回译"惹的祸。

回译(Back Translation)是被翻译成某种语言的文本再被重新翻译成原来语言的过程。也就是说,如果一篇文章用 A 语言书写,被翻译成 B 语言,我们将文本从 B 语言再译为 A 语言,这一过程就是回译。马克·沙特尔沃思(Mark Shuttleworth)和莫伊拉·考伊(Moira Cowie)认为 Back translation is "a process in which a text which has been translated into a given language is retranslated into SL". The procedure of back-translation has been used for various different purposes.

回译绝不是照着原文底本抄录那么简单。有时,回译是恢复庐山真面目、回本溯源的艰难考证活动;有时回译涉及历史文化典故需要考据,有时回译需要照顾原文作者的语言风貌。回译其实复杂困难,稍不留神,就会犯错。甚至会犯一些常识性错误,使读者感到莫名其妙。下面举几个典型的回译错误实例。

1998 年,吉登斯的《民族——国家与暴力》出版了汉译本,其中,有很多译名翻译得不规范,比如:著名的古希腊历史学家希罗多德(Herodotus)译为"黑罗多特思";将孔雀王朝的阿育王(Ashoka)译成"阿肖卡"等。其中最有名的翻译错误是该书中的一段文字:"门修斯(Mencius)的格言'普天之下只有一个太阳,居于民众之上的也只有一个帝王',可以适用于所有大型帝国所建立的界域。"从这句话可以看出译者根本不知 Mencius 指的是中国的思想家孟子。而所谓的格言,即"天无二日,民无二王",也并非孟子所说,而是出自孔子之口。从此"门修斯"就成了一个典故,专门用来指代错误的译名。

2006 年 3 月,法国思想家居伊·德波的名著《景观社会》汉译本正式出版。译文提到"桑卒(Sun Tzu)《战争艺术》"。可是,从描述的内容来看《战争艺术》应该是中国古代著名的兵书《孙子兵法》,其作者"桑卒"应该就是著名的古代军事家孙子。

2008 年 10 月,《中俄国界东段学术史研究:中国、俄国、西方学者视野中的中俄国界东段问题》一本出版。译者将 Chiang Kai-shek 译为"常凯申"。此处 Chiang Kai-shek 为"蒋介石"的威妥玛拼音。威妥玛拼音是 19 世纪后期由英国人 Thomas Francis Wade 制定,被普遍用来拼写中国的人名、地名。新中国成立后开始推行汉语拼音,国内不再使用威妥玛拼音法。可见,译者没有进行深入查证,而将其直接音译,结果出现了错误。

回译过程中,有两种情况需要加以区分。一种是"有本回译",另一种是"无本回译"。

"有本回译"是一个从原文 A 到译文 B 再到原文 A 的过程,要求认真查找核对汉语版本,保持译名准确,以免出错,切忌另起炉灶。例如,如果我们读到英国汉学家大卫·霍克斯(David Hawkes)的《红楼梦》英文版本,要将其中一回的题目回译为中文:

A wordless message meets with silent understanding.

And a groundless imputation leads to undeserved rebukes.

原译:一句无言的话语让人沉默地领会 一番无由的责备酿成无端的叱责。

改译:情中情因情感妹妹 错里错以错劝哥哥。

该例属于有本回译。译文(1)为《红楼梦》原书中没有,译文(2)才是正确的回译。当然,如果我们回译的目的是研究两种语言的异同,译文(1)则可以提供很好的参照。

"无本回译"大多数存在于"异语写作"的情况下。例如,用英文写成的有关中国人物、地理、历史等著作,在翻译成汉语时,首先需要辨认其中的文化名词,这些文化名词要准确回译为汉语的对应词汇;其次在回译时需要尽量采取目标语的表达方式,符合中文的用词构句的习惯,甚至在语体风格上尽量保持与书中所写时代的文风一致。

例1 Tell her You've always thought she'd look beautiful in a cheongsam.
对她说,你原来一直认为,她穿长衫看起来很漂亮。

例2 At Loshan, then as now, a traveller could go up the Polikiang. or Glass River, in a junk to Meishan.(林语堂 The Gay Genius)
在乐山,当年也和现在一样,旅客可以乘一小舟自玻璃江逆流而上直到眉山。

例3 Entering the gate, one faced a green painted screen which shut out the view of the interior from the passers-by.(林语堂 The Gay Genius)
迈步入门,迎面是一座绿漆影壁,阻隔了行人窥探内宅的视线。

例4 Being carefree and well provided, he would often pick up a wine jug and go about with his friends to sit on the grass and enjoy himself. They would laugh and drink and sing, to the amazement of the usually quiet and well-behaved peasants.
东坡的祖父一生衣食无忧,悠闲自在,常携酒一壶,呼伴相游,席地而坐,饮酒畅谈。他们对酒当歌,引得过往拘谨的农人啧啧称奇。

例5 Yang Chun, a high ranking Chinese courtier and former governor based in Chang9 an and recently retired, wrote to the court regarding what he viewed as Xiao Baoyan's unilateral command activities (WS 58.1288). He argued that Xiao Baoyan needed to be placed under surveillance, an argument the court accepted and was in the process of implementing. (Andrew Eisenberg, "Fall of the Northern Wei-Collapse of a Sino-Altaic Regime"北魏的覆亡:一个中原——阿尔泰政权的崩塌)。
刚刚去任的长安守将、汉族重臣杨椿,启奏朝廷,称萧宝寅带兵指挥独断专行(《魏书》58,1288)。杨椿谏劝,当对萧宝寅加以监视。朝廷准奏,并予施行。

例6 The next empress, Shizong's matrilateral cross cousin, Ms. Gao, of Korean descent with a thin family political base at the court, was installed in 508, was forced to enter a convent in 515 after Shizong died, and then was executed in 517 by the reigning Empress Dower Hu (the biological mother of the reigning emperor, Suzong). (Andrew Eisenberg, "Fall of the Northern Wei: Collapse of a Sino-Altaic Regime")。
第二任皇后高氏,为世宗表亲,高丽人,其家族在朝中权卑位低。高氏于公元508年被立为皇后,世宗驾崩后,公元515年被迫出俗为尼,517年为临朝的胡太后(肃宗生母)所杀。(北魏的覆亡:一个中原——阿尔泰政权的崩塌)

2.转类法

"转类"(conversion)是词类转换的简称,意指翻译过程中为了使译文符合目标语的表述方式、方法和习惯,而对原句中的词类等进行转换。具体地说,就是在词性方面,把名词转换为代词、形容词、动词,把动词转换成名词、形容词、副词、介词,把形容词转换成副词和短语等。

转类是一种常见的翻译方法。这是因为英汉对各类词语的使用习惯和频率不一样,例如,英语多用动词、名词,汉语多用动词,在翻译时,如果绝对地按照原语的词性进行翻译,译文会显得晦涩或不符合译语的表达习惯。词性转换有这以下几种情况。

(1) 英语名词转换为汉语动词

英译汉中最重要、最常见的词类转换是根据需要将具有动作性的英语名词转换为汉语动词,或者将可表示概念的动词转换为汉语名词。转换的主要目的是可使译文流畅,符合汉语表达习惯。

英语名词转译成汉语动词主要有以下几种情况:①英语中有些加后缀-er 的名词在句中不指代身份或职业,而是含有较强的动作意味,这是需要转译成汉语动词的;②英语中有许多抽象名词是从动词派生来的,大量出现在政论文体中,可以转译成汉语动词;③作为习语主体的名词转译成动词,如 have a look, take a glance 等。

例 1 I'm no drinker, nor smoker.
我既不喝酒,也不抽烟。

例 2 He is a good eater, good sleeper and talker, but not a good doer.
他能吃能睡能说,就是不能干。

例 3 Indo-China is a drain on French resources.
印度支那战争不断地消耗法国的资源。

例 4 Reluctance among men to retire was associated with anticipated deprivations, mainly of money rather than of attachment to work.
男人不愿退休,与他们预想中将要失去很多东西有关,其中主要是赚钱的机会,而不是对工作的依恋之情。

这里的 deprivations 是从动词 deprive 派生来的,翻译时用动词翻译就顺了。还有些抽象名词是从形容词过来的,也可用动词翻译,此句中的 reluctance 就是一例。

例 5 ... a favourable orientation towards retirement appeared to reflect constraints or resignation rather than choice. Primarily, retirement was associated with awareness of a declining state of health.
他们对退休所表现的赞同倾向,看来并不表明退休是他们自愿选择的,而是反映了他们受到强制或无可奈何的心态。最主要的是,退休使人们联想起健康状况的下降。

例 6 The merits of competition by examination are somewhat questionable, but competition in the certain knowledge of failure is positively harmful.
通过考试来竞争,其好处有点让人怀疑。但是明明知道会失败还是去竞争,这肯定是有害的。

此句,如果翻译成"竞争在失败方面的某些知识肯定是有害的",明显有问题。因为"the certain knowledge of failure"等于"certainly know"。

例 7 The problem of possible genetic damage to human populations from radiation exposures, including those resulting from the fallout from testing of atomic weapons, has quite properly claimed much popular attention in recent years.
人类受到辐射,如原子武器试验放射性尘埃所造成的辐射,基因可能会遭到损伤,近年来这一问题理所当然地引起了广泛重视。

(2) 英语介词转换为汉语动词

在英语中,介词是最活跃的词类之一。英语介词随处可见,并以其形式多样的表达方式,能够具体、准确、简洁、明快地表达出千姿百态的动作概念与含义。英语介词还表达逻辑关系,介词误用则会导致逻辑错误。例如,a book for Peter 表示"一本给彼得的书",a book by Peter 则表示"一本彼得写的书",a book from Peter 是"一本彼得送的书",a book on Peter 为"一本关于彼得的书"。汉语则一般是用动词来表达这些逻辑关系的。因此,在翻译时,往往将介词译为汉语动词。

例 1 He went to the shop for a bottle of sauce.
他到商店去买酱油。

例 2 They have been around for a long time, and it seems likely that they will outlive even the necktie.
牛仔裤已经流行了很长时间,看来其生命力甚至可能超过领带。

例 3 In those years the Republicans were in.
那些年是共和党执政。

例 4 They went on strike in demand of a 40 percent wage increase.
他们举行罢工,要求工资增加40%。

例 5 It is our goal that the people in the undeveloped areas will be finally off poverty.
我们的目标是使不发达地区的人民最终摆脱贫困。

例 6 The company has advertised in the newspaper for electronic experts.
公司在报上登广告招聘电子方面的专家。

(3) 英语形容词转换为汉语动词

英语中某些形容词是由及物动词派生而来的,这类形容词及其短语可以转译为汉语动词。英语中还有一些形容词本身具有动词的含义,如 aware(having knowledge or realization), popular(liked or favored by many people), sure(knowing and believing)等,往往转译成汉语的动词。此外,英语中有许多形容词并不用来修饰名词,而是与系动词组成谓语部分,表示各种意愿、态度、感情和欲望等心理状态,在汉译时通常把此类形容词转换成汉语动词,形成动宾结构。反过来,英语形容词中以-able 和-ible 为后缀的形容词动感明显,使用广泛,汉译英时这类词能较贴切地表达出汉语的动词含义。

例 1 Integrity means you do what you do because it's right and not just fashionable or politically correct.
诚实意味着去做你认为对的事,而不仅仅是为了赶时髦或在政治上不出错。

例 2 They are very much concerned about the future of their country.
他们非常关心国家的前途。

例 3 His whole family were religious.
他全家都信教。

例 4 They were suspicious and resentful of him.
他们不信任他,讨厌他。

例 5 If we were ignorant of the structure of the atom, it would be impossible for us to study nuclear physics.
如果我们不知道原子的结构,我们就不可能研究核子物理学。

(4) 英语副词译为汉语动词

英语中表示状态、方位和方向等意义的副词往往含有动作意味,英译汉时往往译成动词。

例1　What's on tonight?
　　今天晚上演什么剧目?

例2　This textbook will be out pretty soon.
　　这本教材很快就要出版了。

例3　Hopefully, the two sides may come to an agreement on this point.
　　希望双方在这一点上可能达成协议。

例4　A group of men suddenly emerged from a doorway and moved menacingly forward to block her way.
　　一群男子突然出现在门口,向她逼近,堵住了她的去路,来势汹汹。

(5) 英语动词译为汉语名词

在翻译时,虽然英语名词等转换成汉语动词的概率大一些,但是英语动词转换成汉语名词的情况也不罕见。特别是英语中一些由名词派生出来的动词(如 characterize, symbolize, design, figure, impress, behave, witness 等),在汉语中往往找不到相应的动词,在这种情况下,动词便可转换成汉语的名词。

例1　The book did not impress me at all.
　　那本书没留给我什么印象。

例2　Harry aims to become a computer expert.
　　哈里的目标是成为计算机专家。

例3　The electronic computer is chiefly characterized by its accurate and rapid computation.
　　电子计算机的主要特点是计算迅速、准确。

例4　Independent observers have commented favorably on the achievements you have made in this direction.
　　独立观察家们对你们在这方面所取得的成就给予了很高的评价。

(6) 其他词类转译

由于英汉两种语言表达方式不同,还有一些词类可互相转译,如:名词和形容词的互相转译、形容词和副词的互相转译、名词和副词的互相转译等。

例1　Occasionally a drizzle came down, and the intermittent flashes of lightening made us turn apprehensive glances toward Zero.
　　偶尔下一点毛毛雨,断断续续的闪电使得我们不时忧虑地朝着零区方向望去。

例2　It was a clear and unemotional exposition of the President's reasons for willing to begin a Chinese-American dialogue.
　　这篇发言清楚明白、心平气和地说明了总统希望开始中美对话的原因。

例3　He routinely radioed another agent on the ground.
　　跟另一个地勤人员进行了例行的无线电联络。

例4　The President had prepared meticulously for his journey.
　　总统为这次出访作了十分周密的准备。

例5　Buckley was in a clear minority.
　　巴克利显然属于少数。

例6　When he catches a glimpse of a potential antagonist, his instinct is to win him over with charm and humor.

只要一发现有可能反对他的人,他就本能地要用他的魅力和风趣将这人争取过来。

例 7 They have not done so well ideologically, however, as organizationally.
但是,他们的思想工作没有他们的组织工作做得好。

例 8 He is physically weak but mentally sound.
他身体虽弱,但思想健康。

例 9 The machine can dimensionally be changeable according to consumers' need.
机器的大小(或尺寸)可以根据用户的需要改变。

例 10 They showed a sympathetic understanding of our problem.
他们对我们的问题表示同情和理解。

但需要注意的是,词类转换只是一种翻译技巧,并不是说一遇到这些情况就非得转换词类不可。重要的是,在进行英汉互译时,不要拘泥于词类,误认为英语名词只能译成汉语名词,动词只能译成动词。转类的基本原则是,抓住短语和整句的大意,化整为零,在充分理解的基础上灵活变通,让译文出彩;英译汉时,要摆脱词性的纠缠,一切以译文能否自然流畅地传递意义为准。

五、具体与抽象

1.具体化

英译汉时,经常会遇到原作中有的词汇,短语以致整个句子的含义非常抽象、笼统、空泛或含糊,为了使读者能看懂,达到翻译的社会交际功能,有必要把它们译得比较具体,明确来保证与原文相适应的可读性,这就是翻译的具体化(Specification)。具体化包括抽象词在语义、语言形式和比喻形象等方面的具体化。

(1)词义具体化

原文中有词义比较宽泛、笼统的表抽象概念或一般行为的词语,翻译时可引申为具体的意义或动作。

例 1 As a boy, he was the disappointment of all his teachers.
小时候,他是使全体老师失望的孩子。

例 2 He put unpleasant memories behind him.
他把那些不愉快的往事置之度外。

例 3 Action and foresight will be needed as well as brightness and ambition.
不但需要聪明和有抱负的人,而且需要有远见卓识的实干家。

例 4 The **presence** in China of Coca cola, Mc Donald's and Kentucky Fried Chicken has certainly helped spur the development of the domestic soft drink and fast food industries.
可口可乐、麦当劳以及肯德基在中国**投资经营**,无疑有助于促进国内软饮料及快餐业的发展。

例 5 I marveled at the relentless **determination** of the rain.
雨无情地**下个不停**,我感到惊异。

例 6 I climbed the heights above Yosemite Valley, California in order to see the splendid granite mountain, Half Dome, in its fullest view.

为了饱览壮丽的花岗岩山峰半穹顶的全景,我登上了加州约塞米蒂谷的高地。

(2) 添加范畴词使抽象概念其体化

范畴词(category words)用来表示行为、现象、属性等概念所属的范畴,是汉语常用的特指手段。在翻译英语抽象词汇上,往往可以添加范畴词,以符合汉语表达规范。

例1 We have winked at these irregularities too long.
我们对这些越轨行为宽容得太久了。

例2 He discussed greatness and excellence.
他探讨了伟大和杰出的含义。

例3 Both we and the Chinese approached that first opening toward each other with cautions uncertainty, even trepidation. (R. Nixon: The Real War)
我们和中国人双方都是怀着谨慎、不安甚至是惶恐的心情,来相互探过这初次的接触的。

例4 He spoke with firmness but his face was very sad and his eyes at times were dim.
他讲话时,态度坚定,但面带愁容,时而眼神黯淡。

例5 The stars twinkled in transparent clarity.
星星在清澈的夜空中闪烁。

(3) 译为形象性词语使抽象意义具体化(figuration)

汉语虽较缺乏抽象词语,但形象性词语(如比喻、成语、谚语、歇后语等)却相当丰富。汉语常常借助这类生动具体的词语来表达英语抽象笼统的含义。如:

例1 He was open now to charges of willful blindness.
这时人们指责他装聋作哑。

例2 He waited for her arrival with a frenzied agitation.
他等着她来,急得像热锅上的蚂蚁。

例3 I talked to him with brutal frankness.
我对他讲的话,虽然逆耳,却是忠言。

例4 When young he quitted his home and travelled to the metropolis, which he reached in a state of almost utter destitution.
年轻时代,他背井离乡,徒步来到首都,几乎身无分文。

例5 Oh, but all the rules of self-preservation were broken when we saw that little face, filled with the terror of death, being sucked downstream. (N. Rigg)
是啊!不过一看见那张小脸带着害怕淹死的恐怖神情被激流越冲越远,我们就把明哲保身的金科玉律统统打破了。

例6 Many men have recognized the similarity of plants to the behavior of animals, and have dreamed wistfully but forlornly upon some method or source of rejuvenation such as Ponce de Leon sought in the Fountain of Youth several centuries ago. (Compton's Encyclopedia)
许多人认为,植物的习性与动物相似,于是梦寐以求地去探求什么"返老还童"的"灵丹妙药",就像数百年前彭斯·德·利昂在青春泉祈求仙水一样,结果只能是竹篮打水。

2. 抽象化

如果原文出现了较为具体化的表达方式,在译文中采用较为抽象或笼统的虚化表达方式来翻译,这就是抽象化方法(Generalization),也称宽泛化。

例1 He has a few marbles missing because he is a wrestler.
他是个角斗士,他有点缺心眼。

例2 Arabs rub shoulders with Jews, and have been doing so from the earliest settlement of the territories.
阿拉伯人和犹太人居住在一起,自从他们在这片土地上定居以来就是如此。

例3 For generations coal and oil have been regarded as the chief energy sources used to transport men from place to place.
好几十年以来,煤和石油一直被认为是交通运输的主要能源。

例4 Today there may be no more than 1,000 giant pandas left in the wild, restricted to a few mountain strongholds in the Chinese provinces of Sichuan, Shaanxi and Gansu.
今天,仍处于野生状态的大熊猫可能只有一千只,仅限于中国的四川、陕西和甘肃省内的一些山区。

例5 Inflation in capitalist countries erodes the purchasing power of middle class.
资本主义国家的通货膨胀削弱了中产阶级的购买力。

例6 This auto is a bargain indeed, but I didn't see it was a gas guzzler.
买这辆车钱倒没花多少,但没想到那么耗油。

翻译实践

Columbine at 20: How School Shootings Became 'Part of the American Psyche'
Amanda Holpuch
17 Apr 2019
from www.theguardian.com

It was an attack that could have been exception. Instead, its brutality has been made routine. When the US's glaring failure to respond to gun violence was spotlighted-again-after 50 people were killed and dozens wounded in mass shootings at two mosques in New Zealand, Tom Mauser looked on in pain.

Not only was the Christchurch attack a brutal reminder of the assault at Columbine high school that left his 15-year-old son, Daniel, dead, in 1999, but New Zealand's decisive action to ban assault rifles threw into stark relief decades of US inaction.

"In America, we often see ourselves as this great model for the rest of the world in so many arenas, but this is not one of those arenas," said Mauser. "…We do nothing, we just shake our heads and say our thoughts and prayers and wait for the next one to happen."

Mauser spoke with the Guardian from Colorado, ahead of the 20th anniversary of the shooting at Columbine high school. The attack on 20 April 1999 saw two boys murder 12 students and one teacher before killing themselves.

It was an attack that could have been exceptional. Instead, its brutality has been made routine. The series of mass killings that followed Columbine have failed to result in a dramatic change to US gun culture, unlike similar events in comparable countries.

"It's not so much the sheer numbers of voters who support the very extreme view of gun rights and are pro-gun, it is more that that group is incredibly mobilized politically," said Philip Cook, the co-author of The Gun Debate.

"If you ask any of the pro-gun people: 'have you written to your congressional representative, have you made a contribution, have you gone to a public meeting' ... the answer is more likely to be yes for somebody who is pro-gun."

Columbine was not the first school shooting in the US, but it was the most deadly since 1966. The media sprinted into the tempest of confusion and shock, firing out inaccurate reports about a "trenchcoat mafia" and how Marilyn Manson's music influenced the shooters.

Eventually, the public learned other people bought the shooters' guns and that their actual goal was to kill hundreds more people with poorly made bombs police found in the cafeteria and parking lot.

In its wake, mass shooter drills became a normal part of the education system. And the federal government froze.

From 1994 until February of this year, not a single gun restriction bill advanced in Congress. The drought ended with a bill to expand federal background checks to all gun buyers and most gun transfers, closing a loophole that allows unlicensed gun sellers to not run background checks. That bill is unlikely to be taken up by the Republican-held Senate, and the president has said he would veto it.

"The USA is failing to protect individuals and communities most at risk of gun violence, in violation of international human rights law," Amnesty International warned. "The right to live free from violence, discrimination and fear has been superseded by a sense of entitlement to own a practically unlimited array of deadly weapons."

Public spaces: from sacred to killing grounds

School shootings are not the leading cause of gun deaths in the US. In 2017, there were 39,773 gun deaths in the US, according to the Centers for Disease Control and Prevention – about 60% of those deaths were suicide.

But the idea that public spaces such as schools, churches and music festivals can be-turned so quickly into killing grounds is one of the many outliers in the US attitude towards guns.

Last month, a student at Columbine during the attack, Craig Scott, said at an anniversary event that he worried school shootings have become "a part of the American psyche".

When 10 students and teachers were killed in a shooting at Santa Fe high school in Texas in May 2018, a reporter asked a 17-year-old student, Paige Curry: "Was there a part of you that thought this isn't real, this wouldn't happen in my school?"

Curry answered, with chilling calm: "No, there wasn't. It's been happening everywhere. I've always kind of felt like eventually it was going to happen here, too."

Today's teenagers were born after Columbine. They were children during Virginia Tech and Sandy Hook. They saw conservative politicians resist change after each attack, tightening the gun lobby's grip on government, refusing to back even moderate gun reform.

And in 2018, they asked why an atrocity depicted in their textbooks continued to take place.

The February 2018 shooting at Marjory Stoneman Douglas high school, ended the lives of 17 students and staff in Parkland, Florida.

Teenagers at the school broadcast their disgust on social media and to television cameras, spurring the most prominent movement against gun violence in decades.

The students delivered impassioned speeches and challenged critics, while also building up what would be one of the largest student demonstrations in US history-the March for Our Lives. Hundreds of thousands of people gathered at marches and walked out of class, including at Columbine high school, in March 2018 in support of stronger gun control measures.

'There is hope'

The groundswell of public support wasn't just in the streets, but also represented in March for Our Lives' demands, which included universal background checks for all gun sales and a ban on the sale of high-capacity magazines in the US, both of which are supported by a majority of Americans. In the 2018 midterm elections, Democratic candidates were more outspoken about guns, and won.

"There is hope on the part of folks that support reasonable regulation on guns and gun safety," Cook said. "There has been some shift, maybe partly as the result of Parkland, and the remarkable effectiveness of those students in garnering attention and support."

Mauser said the Parkland kids have had a "tremendous" impact, particularly in strengthening gun control in Florida. But Mauser has seen so many glimmers of promise before, that each one inspires a breath of caution.

"I really have to add, I've seen other things come up in the past. You think you are going to make some progress and it doesn't sustain itself," Mauser said. "I think these young people have the capability to keep it sustainable, but they have to keep working at it."

Mauser knows better than most what it is like to tread through the muck of the gun control fight in the US.

Ten days after Daniel was killed, Mauser joined thousands of others to protest outside the National Rifle Association (NRA)'s annual convention in Denver, 15 miles from Columbine.

The NRA has for decades steered elections towards pro-gun candidates, despite being less financially powerful than other lobbies. It relies on a minority of impassioned individuals to block laws and regulations favored by most Americans.

Mauser for 20 years has come up against that dedicated minority while pushing for stronger gun control in Colorado. At the moment, he is supporting a "red flag" law that allows law enforcement or family to ask a judge to block someone considered to be in danger of harming themselves or someone else from purchasing a gun.

At key moments in these campaigns, Mauser wears the same shoes his son was wearing when he died in April 1999.

But the climate has changed since then, he said, with people who oppose gun restrictions more deeply entrenched than they were in the wake of Columbine, when he was able to speak with Republicans about possible gun restrictions.

"In the case of the red flag law, not a single Republican voted for the bill," Mauser said. "The level of resistance and the intensity of the opposition has gone up significantly."

No matter how badly Mauser wishes this all to change, the Columbine anniversary is simply another day without his son.

He and his family will steer clear of public events, instead privately remembering Daniel, a quiet, thoughtful boy who liked BBQ chicken and his dad's homemade waffles.

"He was extremely shy and yet he chose to join the debate team at Columbine, where he had to get up and talk in front of people," Mauser said. "That's been the inspiration for me-if Daniel can do it, as tough as it is to do what I do and to talk about it, he took it on so I can take it on too."

(1408 words)

第五章

翻译技巧(2)

Beyond Life

I want my life, the only life of which I am assured, to have symmetry or, in default of that, at least to acquire some clarity. Surely it is not asking very much to wish that my personal conduct be intelligible to me! Yet it is forbidden to know for what purpose this universe was intended, to what end it was set a-going, or why I am here, or even what I had preferably do while here. It vaguely seems to me that I am expected to perform an allotted task, but as to what it is I have no notion. And indeed, what have I done hitherto, in the years behind me? There are some books to show as increment, as something which was not anywhere before I made it, and which even in bulk will replace my buried body, so that my life will be to mankind no loss materially. But the course of my life, when I look back, is as orderless as a trickle of water that is diverted and guided by every pebble and crevice and grass-root it encounters. I seem to have done nothing with premeditation, but rather, to have had things done to me. And for all the rest of my life, as I know now, I shall have to shave every morning in order to be ready for no more than this!

(230 words)

On Growing Old Gracefully

英语文本	汉语文本
On Growing Old Gracefully From The Importance of Living Lin Yutang	乐享余年 《生活的艺术》 林语堂

续上表

英语文本	汉语文本
This desire to grow old and in any case to appear old is understandable when one understands the premium generally placed upon old age in China. In the first place, it is a privilege of the old people to talk, while the young must listen and hold their tongue. "A young man is supposed to have ears and no mouth," as a Chinese saying goes "Men of twenty are supposed to listen when people of thirty are talking, and these in turn are supposed to listen when men of forty are talking. As the desire to talk and to be listened to is almost universal, it is evident that the further along one gets in years, the better chance he has to talk and to be listened to when he goes about in society. It is a game of life in which no one is favored, for everyone has a chance of becoming old in his time. Thus a father lecturing his son is obliged to stand suddenly and change his demeanor the moment the grandmother opens her mouth. Of course he wishes to be in the grandmother's place. And it is quite fair, for what right have the young to open their mouth when the old men can say, "I have crossed more bridges than you have crossed streets!" What right have the young got to talk?	我们如了解中国人之如何珍视老年，便能明了为什么中国人都喜欢倚老卖老，自认为老。第一，照中国的礼貌，只有长者有发言的权利，年轻的人只许静听。所以中国有"少年用耳不用口"那句老话。凡有年龄较高的人在座时，年轻的人只许洗耳恭听。世人大都欢喜发言而受人听，因此，在中国必须到相当的年龄才有发言权利这件事，便使人期望早些达到老年，以便无论到什么地方都可以多说几句话。这种生活程序之中，人人须循序而进，每个人都有同等达到老年的机会，而没有一个人能躐等超前。因此，当一个父亲教训他的儿子时，如若祖母走来插口，那做父亲的便须停口，谨敬恭听。这时他当然很羡慕那祖母的地位。年老的人能说："我所走过的桥比你所走过的街还要多几条。"因此，以经验而言，年轻的人在长者之前，没有发言的权利，自只能洗耳恭听，这是很公允的。
In spite of my acquaintance with Western life and the Western attitude toward age, I am still continually shocked by certain egressions for which I am totally unprepared. Fresh illustrations of this attitude come up on every side. I have heard an old lady remarking that she has had several grandchildren, but, "It was the first one that hurt." With the full knowledge that American people hate to be thought of as old, one still doesn't quite expect to have it put that way. I have made allowance for people in middle age this side of fifty, who, I can understand, wish to leave the impression that they are still active and vigorous, but I am not quite prepared to meet an old lady with gray hair facetiously switching the topic of conversation to the weather, when the conversation without it when allowing an old man to enter an elevator or a car first; the habitual expression "after age" comesup to my lips, then I restrain myself and am at a loss for what to say in its place. One day, being forgetful, I blurted out the usual phrase in deference to an extremely dignified and charming old man, and the old man seated in the car turned to his wife and remarked jokingly to her, "This young man has the cheek to think that he is younger than myself!"	我虽然已很熟悉西方的生活，并很明白西方人对于老年的态度，但有时所听见的话仍使我非常诧异，很出我的意料。这种使我奇异的态度，常有所遇。我曾听见过一位年老的妇人说，她已有几个孙儿女，其中以长孙儿使她受到的感触最大。她的意思是长孙儿已如此长大，将反映她自己的年龄之高。我很明白美国人最恨别人说他已老，但我意料不到他们的畏惧心竟会到这个地步。五十岁以下的人大都希望旁人视他为依然年富力强，这很在意料中。但是一个头发已经花白的老妇人，在旁人提到她的年龄时尚要顾左右而言他，实在使我觉得出于意外。当我在让一位老者先走进电梯或公共汽车时，我心中自不免有认为他已老的意思，但我总不敢形之于口。有一天遇到这样一件事时，我无意之间说了出来。不料那位很尊严的老者于坐下去时，竟会向坐在他下手的太太用着讥笑的口气说我："这年轻的人，竟以为他比我年纪轻得多啊！"

认知升级

一、替换与加注

1.替换法

替换法(substitution)是一种常常用于典故、成语等文化负载词(culture-loaded words, culture-specific items)的翻译方法,即使用目标语言中意义相近的典故或成语等直接替换原语的典故或成语,使得双方的语用功能、意义和读者反应大致相当。替换法的好处在于读者能够比较轻松地理解译文,译文可读性、表现力得到增强;缺点在于失去了原文的异域风情,不能非常精确地表达原文的意义,不利于传达源语文化特质。

例1 It was packed like sardines.
简直像芝麻糊煮饺子。

例2 No smoke without fire.
无风不起浪。

例3 Great men are not always wise.
人有失手日,马有失蹄时。

例4 He who keeps company with the wolf will learn to howl.
近朱者赤,近墨者黑。

例5 Her beauty, her pink cheeks, and golden curls, seemed to give delight to all who looked at her, and to purchase indemnity for every fault. (Jane Eyre)
她的美貌,红润的面颊,金色的卷发,使得她人见人爱,一俊便可遮百丑。

例6 This state of things should have been to me a paradise of peace, accustomed as I was to a life of ceaseless reprimand and thankless fagging.
对我来说,过惯了那种成天挨骂、吃力不讨好的日子后,这光景就好比是平静的乐园。

例7 I alleged: "that I have awakened out of glorious dreams, and found them all void and vain, is a horror I could bear and master."
黄译:我断言:"我从一场美梦中醒来,发现全是竹篮打水一场空,这种恐惧我既能忍受,也能克服。"

例8 "Meantime, you forget essential points in pursuing trifles; you do not inquire why Mr. Briggs sought after you—what he wanted with you."
"同时,你捡了芝麻忘了西瓜,没有问问布里格斯先生为什么在找到你——他找你干什么。"

2.加注法

由于英汉文化存在许多差异,因此英语中某些术语、文化词语或者表达方式在汉语中根本就没有对等词,形成了词义上的空缺。在这种情况下,英译汉时常常要采用加注法(Annotation)来弥补空缺。加注通常可以用来补充诸如背景材料、词语起源等相关信息,便于读者理解。

加注法可分为:脚注(footnote)、尾注(end-note)和文内加注(in-text note)。脚注一般位于页面的底部;尾注一般位于文档的末尾;文内加注有时直接写入正文,有时加括号与正文分开,放在所注词语后面。

例1　Like a son of Bachus, he can drink up two bottles of whisky at a breath.

译文:他简直像巴赫斯*的儿子,能一口气喝光两瓶威士忌。

注释:*巴赫斯是古希腊神话中的酒神。

例2　He saw himself, in a smart suit, bowed into the opulent suites of Ritzes*.

译文:他发现自己身着漂亮的礼服,被恭恭敬敬地引进了像里兹饭店一般豪华的旅馆客房里下榻。

注释:里兹饭店:原为瑞士人里兹(1850—1919)开设,以豪华著称。

例3　But I am short-tempered, frazzled from all responsibilities. I am the "sandwich generation"*, caught between kids and parents.

译文:但我的脾气不好,都是这些事给烦的。我是个夹在孩子和父母之间的"三明治人"。

注释:*三明治人:指既要照顾孩子又要照顾父母的人。

例4　At all events the war has done one good thing for us. It's smashed up the power of the aristocracy. The Boer War started it, and 1914 put the lid on.

译文:不管怎样,战争还是为我们做了一件好事,就是把贵族势力一扫而光。布尔战争*开始对它有所触动,而1914年的世界大战终于使它荡然无存。

注释:*布尔战争:1899—1902年英国人与布尔人之间的战争。

例5　Hygeia herself would have fallen sick under such a regimen; and how much more this poor old nervous victim?

按照这样的养生之道,别说这可怜的老太太了,就连哈奇亚(希腊神话中的健康女神)也会害病。

例6　People considered that what he had played on that occasion was no more than a Judas kiss.

人们认为他在那种场合所表演的不过是犹大之吻,居心险恶。

二、分译与合译

1.分译法

英译汉时,如果某个英语句子不能用一个汉语单句清楚地表达出来,可以把原句拆开,用两个或两个以上汉语单句来表达,这就是分译(Division)。

(1)单词的分译

将原文中的一个单词分离出来单独译为汉语的一个句子,使原文的一个句子分译成两个以上的汉语单句。

例1　He is having an identifiable trouble with his teeth.

他正患牙病,这是大家都看得出来的。

例2　The day dawned misty and overcast.

那天天亮时雾气很重,天上布满乌云。

例3　As a shy young visitor to Einstein's home, I was made to feel at ease when Einstein said," I have something to show you."

小时候有一次去爱因斯坦家做客,由于我很腼腆,他就对我说:"我有样东西给你看。"于是我便感到不拘束了。

例4 Not surprisingly, those who were praised improved dramatically.
那些受到表扬的人进步显著,这是不足为怪的。

例5 We recognize and share China's resolve to resist the attempts of any nation which seeks to establish global or regional hegemony.
我们认识到中国决心抵抗任何国家寻求建立全球霸权和地区霸权的企图,我们也有这样的决心。

例6 She left home a child and came back a mother of three children.
离家时她还是个孩子,回来时已是三个孩子的妈妈了。

(2)短语分译

将原文中的一个短语译为一个句子,使原文的一个句子分译成两个或两个以上的汉语句子。

例1 He handed me my draft of the plan completely modified.
他把我的计划草案交还了我,内容全改动了。

例2 With all his faults, I like him.
尽管他有种种缺点,我还是喜欢他。

例3 Alice, normally a timid girl, argued heatedly with them about it.
阿丽丝平时是个腼腆的姑娘,现在也和他们热烈地辩论起来。

例4 So I swam and, presumably because of the long absence of foreigners from Sichuan, before an undeservedly large and enthusiastic audience.
于是我就下水游泳了;大概在四川省人们很久没见过外国人了,所以我游泳时,旁边有一大群热心的观众;而单凭我的游泳技术是不配引来这样一大群观众的。

(3)长句分译

长句分译这里主要是指将含有一个或多个定语从句的英语长句分译为两个或多个汉语句子。

例1 But underneath the sympathetic talk, they actually feel a little wistful envy of the men who brave the winds, rain, snow, cold, and storms upon the restless water.
然而,在这种富于同情的闲聊下面,他们实际上都有着一种强烈的羡慕之情;他们羡慕那些在惊涛骇浪中搏风斗雨、傲雪顶寒的人们。

例2 We have nothing to do with David Swan until we find him at the age of twenty on the main road from his home to the City of Boston where his uncle, a businessman, is going to give him work in the store which he owns.
我们与戴维·斯旺本来毫无关系。直到有一天,我们见到20岁的他离家上了大路,去波士顿他舅舅家。他舅舅是做生意的,开了个店,安排他去那里做事。

2.合译法

所谓合译法(combination),是指为了符合汉语表达习惯,为了更清楚地表达原文意思,把英语原文中两个或两个以上的简单句、并列句合译为一个句子,或将一个主句和从句在译文中用一个单句来表达。合译法多用于英语简单句的翻译,特别是两个或两个以上的英文句子共用相同的主语的时候,汉语往往将合译为一句。

(1)将两个或两个以上的英语简单句合译为一个汉语单句

例 1 It was 2 a.m. on a hot August night. In a San Francisco suburb, a man staggered out of a bar.
一个炎热的 8 月夜晚凌晨两点钟,在旧金山郊区,有个人摇摇晃晃地走出酒吧间。

例 2 When someone asks me what business I am in, I become embarrassed. I stutter and stammer. My face feels hot.
当有人问我从事什么职业时,我感到很尴尬,脸发烫,结结巴巴地难以启齿。

例 3 People are the same everywhere. They are born. They are babies. They are children. They are adults. They grow old. They die.
各地的人都是一样的。人们生下来都要经历从婴儿、儿童、成年人直至衰老死亡的各个人生阶段。

例 4 Her dress was grey and plain, but it fitted her body nicely.
她一身素装,简单而合身。

例 5 The river is very wide. One cannot see the opposite bank.
河宽得看不到对岸。

例 6 He came back to his hometown. He has left it for quite many years.
他回到了阔别已久的故乡。

例 7 He was very stupid. He even didn't know how to do the simple counting.
他笨得连简单的算数都不会。

(2)并列复合句的合译
英译汉中有时候可以将一个并列句合并成一个单独的句子。

例 1 It was in mid-August, and the repair section operated under the blazing sun.
八月中旬,维修人员在烈日下工作。

例 2 Mark wasn't able to escape from the fire. Neither were the children.
马克和孩子都没能从火里逃生。

例 3 The Post Office was helpful, and Marconi applied in June, 1896, for the world's first radio patent.
在邮局的帮助下,马可尼于 1896 年 6 月获得了世界上第一项无线电专利。

(3)复杂句及主从复合句的合译
在英译汉中,有时可以把原文中的主从复合句合译成一个简单句。例如定语从句的翻译中,即将定语从句翻译成一个短语,放在被修饰名词之前。

例 1 He is not the one who will give up easily.
他不是一个轻易服输的人。

例 2 Our two countries are neighbors whose friendship is of long standing.
我们两国是友谊长存的友好邻邦。

例 3 When I negotiate, I get nervous. When I get nervous, I eat.
我在谈判时总是有些紧张,而我紧张时,就想吃东西。

例 4 It was my liver that was out of order.
我的肝脏出了毛病。

例 5 When we praise the Chinese leadership and the people, we are not merely being polite.
我们对中国领导人和中国人民的赞扬不仅仅是出于礼貌。

三、正译与反译

1. 正说反译

英语里有些从肯定表达的词或句子，译文可使用否定词汇来表达，即正说反译法（Negation, Antonymic translation）。该方法的主要目的是让译文晓畅明白，增强修辞效果或者符合译文的表达习惯。

常常采用正说反译法翻译的动词有：fail(to do)（未能、没做到），lack（缺乏，没有），deny（不承认，不给），defy（不服从，不遵从，不让），differ（不同，不同意，不合），miss（未打中，未见到，未达到），forbid（不许），stop（不准），ignore（不理，不肯考虑）等。

例1 You are quite a stranger here.
这儿的人都不认识你。

例2 Only five customers remained in the bar.
酒吧间只有五个顾客还没走。

例3 I failed to understand your meaning.
我弄不懂你的意思。

例4 All international disputes must be settled through negotiations and the avoidance of any armed conflicts.
一切国际争端应通过谈判而不是武装冲突来解决。

例5 Her child was in a terrible state of neglect.
她的孩子简直没人管。

例6 There was a complete absence of information on the oil deposit in that area.
关于该地区的石油储藏情况，人们毫无所知。

常常采用正说反译法翻译的形容词及其短语有：absent（不在，不到），awkward（不熟练，不灵活，使用起来不方便），bad（令人不愉快的，不受欢迎的，不舒服的），blind（看不到、不注意），dead（无生命的、无感觉的），difficult（不容易的），foreign to（不适合于，与……无关），short of（不够），poor（不好的，不幸的），ignorant of（不知道）等。

例1 He would be the last man to say such things.
他决不会说这种话。

例2 These elements are shielded so that they are free from the influence of magnetic field.
这些组件已加屏蔽，因此不受磁场的影响。

例3 She was deaf to all advice.
她不听一切劝告。

例4 Your work is far from satisfactory.
你的工作一点儿也不令人满意。

常常采用反译法的介词有：below（与……不相称，不足，不值得），beneath（不值得，与……不相称），beyond（为……所不及），under（未满足，不足），without（无，不，没有，毫不），except（不包括），within（不超出，不出），instead of（而不是）等。

例1 What you said is beside the question.
你所说的与本题无关。

例2 But that's very extraordinary. It seems against nature.
不过那件事很不平常,似乎不符合自然规律。

例3 The Theory of Relativity put forward by Einstein is now above many people's understanding.
爱因斯坦提出的"相对论",现在还有不少人不理解。

2.反说正译

英语里有些否定表达的词或句子,译文可采用肯定表达,即反说正译法(Affirmation)。英文中的双重否定句也可以译为肯定句。

例1 The dishonesty of the city officials was exposed by the newspaper.
市政府官员们的欺诈行为被报纸披露。

例2 By a sudden attack we uncovered the enemy's right flank.
我们以突袭使敌人右翼暴露。

例3 The cannons were dismounted for shipping.
这些炮弹被拆卸了以便运输。

例4 He gave me an indefinite answer.
他给我一个含糊的答复。

例5 It was inconsiderate of him to mention the matter in her hearing.
他实在轻率,竟在她在场时谈论此事。

例6 "I Don't know if I ought to have come," she said breathlessly, grasping Sandy's arm.
"我不知道我该不该来,"她气喘吁吁地说,一把抓住桑迪的胳膊。

例7 This country is now unprecedentedly expanding its industry.
这个国家目前正在以空前的规模发展其工业。

例8 Don't lose time in cleaning this machine.
赶快把这部机器擦好。

四、转态与重组

1.语态转换

在英译汉时,英语被动句的大部分要转换成汉语的主动句,就是语态转换法(Changing of Voice),简称转态。根据统计❶,Edgar Snow 的书 *Red Star over China* 中,有明显标志的被动句1381句,被翻译成《西行漫记》之后,有13%译成有明显标志的被动句,16%译成了无标志的被动句,62%译成了各种形式的主动句。这一数据可以为英汉翻译提供借鉴。

(1)英语被动句转换成汉语的主动句,增补泛指性的词语(人们、大家等)作主语。

例1 <u>It could be argued</u> that the radio performs this service as well, but on television everything is much more living, much more real.
可能有人会指出,无线电广播同样也能做到这一点,但还是电视屏幕上的节目要生动、真实得多。

例2 <u>It is generally accepted</u> that the experiences of the child in his first years largely determine his character and later personality.

---

❶周志培.汉英对比与翻译中的转换.上海:华东理工大学出版社,2003:449.

人们普遍认为,孩子们的早年经历在很大程度上决定了他们的性格及其未来的人品。

例3 Television, it is often said, keeps one informed about current events, allows one to follow the latest developments in science and politics, and offers an endless series of programmes which are both instructive and entertaining.

人们常说,电视使人了解时事,熟悉政治域的最新发展变化,并能源源不断地为观众提供各种既有教育意义又有趣的节目。

(2)转换成汉语的主动句,将英语原文中的主语翻译为宾语。

例1 By the end of the war, 800 people had been saved by the organization, but at a cost of 200 Belgian and French lives.

大战结束时,这个组织拯救了八百人,但是其代价是两百多比利时人和法国人的生命。

例2 And it is imagined by many that the operations of the common mind can be by no means compared with these processes, and that they have to be acquired by a sort of special training.

许多人认为,普通人的思维活动根本无法与科学家的思维过程相比,而且认为这些思维过程必须经过某种专门的训练才能掌握。

(3)翻译成汉语的无主句。

例1 By this procedure, different honeys have been found to vary widely in the sensitivity of their inhibit to heat.

通过这种方法分析发现不同种类的蜂蜜的抗菌活动对热的敏感程度也极为不同。

例2 Many strange new means of transport have been developed in our century, the strangest of them being perhaps the hovercraft.

在我们这个世纪内研制了许多新奇的交通工具,其中最奇特的也许就是气垫船了。

(4)当然,有时候英语被动句也会翻译成具有显著标记的汉语的被动句,常用"被""给""遭""挨""为……所""使""由……""受到"等表示。

例1 Over the years, tools and technology themselves as a source of fundamental innovation have largely been ignored by historians and philosophers of science.

工具和技术本身作为根本性创新的源泉多年来在很大程度上被科学史学家和科学思想家们忽视了。

例2 Early fires on the earth were certainly caused by nature, not by Man.

地球上早期的火肯定是由大自然而不是人类引燃的。

(5)英语被动句也可以翻译成隐含的,没有标记的汉语被动句。

例1 The shipping charges are included in the price.

运费包括在价格里。

例2 Certain questions have yet to be clarified.

有些问题还需要澄清。

例3 Nuclear power's danger to health, safety, and even life itself can <u>be summed up</u> in one word: radiation.
核能对健康、安全,甚至对生命本身构成的危险可以用一个词"辐射"来<u>概括</u>。

例4 The decision to attack <u>was not taken lightly</u>.
进攻的决定不是<u>轻易做出</u>的。

2.重组

翻译时要根据汉语习惯,进行语序的调整、句子的组合,以适合汉语表达习惯。这一方法就是重组(Restructuring)。重组的原因是英汉句子在语序上存在巨大差异。在翻译的时候,我们必须考虑到英汉语句子在繁简、长短方面的差异;如果过分拘泥于原文顺序就会导致译文死板,不符合目标语规范,降低译文的可读性。重组包括对定语位置、状语位置的调整,对信息重点,对众多小句句序的调整等。

(1)对定语位置进行重组 由于英语和汉语在定语位置方面表现出十分明显的差异,所以,我们在英汉互译时,需要根据上下文语境等因素对定语的位置进行调整。

例1 He has just bought a small round red wooden table.
他刚买了一张红木小圆桌。

原文中,table的定语依次有:①a+②small+③round+④red wooden,译为汉语,需要将汉语定语顺序的习惯调整为:①一张+④红木+②小+③圆桌。

例2 It is <u>the only wild straw</u> berry <u>edible here in this area</u>.
这是<u>该地区唯一能食用的野草莓</u>。

原文中,berry的前置定语有①the +②only+③wild +④straw,后置定语有⑤<u>edible</u> + ⑥<u>here in this area</u>,根据汉语定语习惯前置的特点,可以转化成:⑥该地区+②唯一+⑤能食用的+③野+④草。

例3 Everybody <u>present at the dinner party</u> stood up and applaud.
<u>出席晚宴的人</u>都站起来鼓掌。

原文中,everybody的后置定语是present at the dinner party,译文中将定语前置。

例4 The people <u>who worked for him</u> lived in mortal of him.
在他手下工作的人对他怕得要死。

原文中,people的定语从句who worked for him后置,译文则做了调整、前置。

(2)对状语位置进行调整 由于英汉在状语位置上的差异,我们在翻译时要进行必要的调整,以适应目标语的习惯。

例1 The news briefing was held in Room 301 at about nine o'clock yesterday morning.
新闻发布会于昨天上午大约九点在301会议室召开。

例2 Suddenly the President, looking out over the vast landscape, said, with an underlying excitement in his voice, the words I gave earlier…
总统眺望着辽阔的景色,突然用很兴奋的语调说了我在前文已经提到过的话。

例3 We, the developing countries, should not only support one another politically but also help each other economically.
我们发展中国家不仅在政治上应该互相支持,在经济上也应该互相帮助。

例4 An interesting experiment was done in July, 1971, at the space flight crescent near Houston, Texas, the USA.

1971年7月,在美国得克萨斯州休斯敦附近的太空飞行中心,举行了一场有趣的试验。

(3) 信息重心的调整　汉语在语序上往往一个动作之后接着下一个动作,先发生的事情先说,后发生的事情后说,先因后果,先事实后结论,先次要信息、后重要信息。而英语在行文过程中,由于使用较多的形合手段,往往用关系副词或连词表示逻辑关系,其语序与汉语并不一样。比如,英文经常重心在前,即把要强调的重要信息放在句首。也可能先果后因,后发生的事情先叙述。根据解英汉句子在信息重心上的差异,我们在翻译时,需要进行语序的必要调整。

例1　We work ourselves into ecstasy over the two superpowers' treaty limiting the number of anti-ballistic missile systems that they may retain and their agreement on limitations on strategic offensive weapons.

两个超级大国签订了限制它们可保留的弹道导弹系统的数目的条约和达成了限制进攻型战略武器的协议,因此,我们感到欣喜若狂。

例2　The solution to the problem of Southern Africa cannot remain forever hostage to the political maneuvers and tactical delays by South Africa nor to its transparent proposals aimed at procrastination and the postponement of the solution.

不管是南非政府耍政治花招和策略上的拖延手段,还是提出显然旨在拖延问题解决的建议,都不能永远阻挡南部非洲问题的解决。

(4) 对疑难长句的调整　根据前面第三章所讲,英语中从句居多,长句居多,汉语散句流水句、小句居多。因此,在翻译时,也有必要对句子的长短、繁简程度等作出调整。

在具体操作时,可以采用以下程序:①分析句子主干结构,找出等基本句型,识别主谓语,区分时态、语态、语气;②区分主语与从句、修饰语与被修饰语,分析各成分之间的逻辑关系;③逐层划分意群,按照意群分译;④重组润色,将解构出来的意群,分译出来的小句,根据时间顺序或逻辑顺序,按汉语的行文习惯进行重组。此时,不必拘泥于原文的语言形式,可发挥汉语以意统形、句子短小精悍的优势,甚至可以采用流水句式,并在此基础上加以润色。

例1　The problem is that in the last generation or so we've come to assume that women should be able, and should want, to do everything that by tradition men could have done at the same time as pretty well everything that by tradition women have done.

分析:首先,本句主语是 the problem,谓语是 is,表语是 that 从句。基本句型为 SVC。其次,that 表语从句中,we 是主语,have come to assume 是动词短语,that women should be able, and should want, to do everything 是宾语从句。everything 又被 that by tradition men could have done 这个定语从句修饰。再次,意群分译如下:①问题是;②在过去的20年时间里,我们已经认为;③妇女应该能够,而且应该想做男性传统意义上所做的一切;④而且同时,也能够做得跟妇女传统意义上所做的一切同样好。最后,该英文的语序和汉语的语序特点一致,因此可以顺其自然地翻译,即采用顺序法。

在简单的润色之后,译文如下:①问题在于;②在过去的20年间,我们已经认为;③妇女应该能够,而且应该希望从事传统意义上属于男性角色的一切事业;④而且同时能够一样做好在传统意义上属于妇女角色的一切事情。

例2　The news that a small planet was going to collide with the Earth spread over a frightened world.

分析：首先，本句主干结构是 the news spread over a frightened world，从句 that a small planet was going to collide with the Earth 是 news 的同位语。其次，需要分析逻辑关系，先有 news spread，后有 the world is frightened。spread 是原因，frightened 是结果。再次，将意群分解整理如下：①The news is that a small planet was going to collide with the Earth，②The news spread，③a world is frightened。最后，调整语序翻译如下：一颗行星将要撞击地球的消息传了开来，举世为之震惊。

例3　I take heart from the fact that the enemy, which boasts that it can occupy the strategic point in a couple of hours, has not yet been able to take even the outlying regions, because of the stiff resistance that gets in the way.

分析：首先，本句主干句型 SVO 为 I take heart from the fact，而 that the enemy has not yet been able to take even the outlying regions 是 fact 的同位语从句。其次，which boasts that it can occupy the strategic point in a couple of hours 是一个非限制性定语从句，修饰 the enemy。介宾短语 because of the stiff resistance 做状语，说明 has not been able to take the outlying regions 的原因。再次，意群分割如下：①I take heart from the fact that，②the fact is that the enemy has not yet been able to take even the outlying regions，③the enemy boasts that it can occupy the strategic point in a couple of hours，④because of the stiff resistance that gets in the way。之后，分析意群之间的关系，一是时间上，敌人吹嘘在前，不能攻克其次，我有了信心在后；二是在逻辑关系上，遭遇抵抗是因，不能攻克为果。由于汉语流水句通常按照时间先后以及前因后果的顺序排列，因而，可以将意群调整为③-④-②-①。最后，在调整润色之后，译文如下：敌人吹嘘能在几小时内占领战略要地，由于遭到了顽强的抵抗，甚至连外围地带也没有占领，这让我增强了信心。

例4　It seems to me that the time is ripe for the Department of Employment and the Department of Education to get together with the universities and produce a revised educational system which will make a more economic use of the wealth of talent, application and industry currently being wasted on certificates, diplomas and degrees that no one wants to know about.

译文：我认为时机已成熟。就业部门和教育部门应同大学携起手来，修正我们的教育制度，使之能比较合理地使用学生的才能、勤奋和刻苦。而现在他们这些才能和努力都浪费在无人感兴趣的证书、文凭和学位上。

例5　But we are much less conscious of the extent to which work provides the more intangible, but more crucial, psychological well being that can make the difference between a full and an empty life.

译文：工作对心理健康所起的作用虽然难以捉摸，却更加至关重要，它是人生过得是否充实的决定性因素。但是这种作用的程度之深，我们很少认识到。

五、摘译与编译

1.摘译

所谓摘要翻译（Abstract translation, summary translation），有时也称要旨翻译（Gist Translation),就是选取一些传达重要信息的段落或内容进行摘译,保留原文的中心思想、主要观点和主要信息,而将一些次要信息剔除,以便译文读者在较短的时间内获取文中的主要信息。摘译是指译文展现的是原文内容的浓缩版,或者说译文提供的是原文的梗概。摘译的方法特别适用于篇幅较长的报告、讲话、社论、评论以及科技新闻。

摘要长度一般不超过原文的三分之一。必须要把关键词和核心内容译出,如论文摘要则包括试验研究的目的、范围、方法、手段、步骤、结论等可能涉及的方面。译法上可摘取原文照译,也可适当改变其句子结构或段落安排,增加连接性词语等。

例1 Fifteen wild turkeys strutted into a suburban hamlet of N. Y. on Thanksgiving Day and then left just in time to avoid dinner.

The turkeys showed up Thursday morning, drawing crowds of spectators, but left—marching in single file—at about 1 p. m.

Suffolk County police were called because the turkeys created a traffic hazard while crossing a road. But the officers didn't have to intervene because the birds kept walking— and hadn't been seen or heard from since, residents said Friday.

Resident Joyce Logan said there was no practical joke involved and the turkeys may have wandered into the Long Island neighborhood about 40 miles east of Manhattan from a nearby wooded area, where she had been hearing gobbles since summer.

Logan said the birds walked away In a straight line between her house and her neighbors, and she went back inside to prepare a store-bought turkey dinner for her family. Unlike some neighbors, Logan said, she never had thoughts of catching one of the turkeys in her yard and turning it into dinner.

"I can't eat something that I've met," she said.

分析:全文共七段,此类事件报道主要是"时间、地点、事件"这些主要信息,所以只需要摘译重要段落,如第一段和第二段就可以了。其他段落是对主题进一步的补充和说明,可以不译。所以,可以摘译如下:

感恩节当天,15只野火鸡"大摇大摆地"闯进美国纽约市郊的一个村庄,之后又"及时地"在晚饭前撤离了该地。

这群火鸡于上周四早上出现在当地,吸引了众多居民围观,但到了下午一点钟左右,它们又排着队离开了此地。

摘译具有快捷、有的放矢的特点。所以上文进行摘译处理后,删除了不必要的段落和文字,节约了读者时间,突出了重点内容,增强了目的性,符合新闻报刊的特点。

比较:虽然编译和摘译都是对原文有所取舍,可是二者是有不同的。编译必须保持原文的整体框架,在内容上可以进行取舍整合,而摘译是根据所需从原文中零星地抽取,一旦确定抽取的内容后,必须完整地将其翻译出来。

例2 A distinction must be made between a fault and an overload. An overload implies only that loads greater than the designed values have been imposed on system. Under such a circumstance the voltage at the overload point may be low, but not zero. This undervoltage condition may extend for some distance beyond the overload point into the remainder of the system. The current in the overload equipment are high and may exceed the thermal design limits. Nevertheless, such currents are substantially lower than in the case of a fault. Service frequently may be maintained, but at below-standard voltage.10,000.

Overloads are rather common occurrences in homes. For example, a housewife might plug five waffle irons into the kitchen circuit during a neighborhood part. Such an overload, if permitted to continue, would cause heating of the wires from the power center and might eventually start a fire. To prevent such trouble, residential circuits are protected by fuses or circuit breakers which open quickly when currents above specified values persist. Distribution transformers are sometimes overloads as customers install more and more appliances. The continuous monitoring of distribution circuits is necessary to be certain that transformers sizes are increased as load grows.

摘译:超负荷仅指施加于系统的负荷大于设计值。发生这种情况时,超负荷处的电压可能很低,但并不等于零。超负荷设备的电流变大而超过预定的热极限。

超负荷的情况常常发生在家里,倘若不能迅速处理的话,就会造成电力线发热甚至酿成火灾。为了避免这种情况的发生,须采用保险丝或断路器来保护住宅区电路免受损坏。

2.编译

编译是指在翻译过程中,根据客户要求,译者风格和读者的口味,对源文本进行较大幅度的改编,以提高文本在目标语境中的交际影响力。编译的典型特征是运用大量释义、口语表达形式、额外的明喻及隐喻、旁白和现代化措辞等。值得注意的是,改译者虽然对作品的表现形式做了很大改动,但文本的主要内容和思想与原文基本相同。

例1 It is an object of this invention to provide potato chips by a process which eliminates deep frying.

It is another object of this invention to provide potato chips having a fat content significantly lower than that obtained heretofore by commercial processes.

It is still another object of this invention to provide potato chips by a process which utilizes microwave heating as the sole means of reducing the water content of the potato piece to the required level and providing the color, crispness and flavor of deep fried potato chips.

编译为:本发明的目的是提供一种生产低脂油炸马铃薯片的工艺。该工艺无须浸炸,只靠微波加热即可使生薯片的水分降到所要求的含量,并保持浸炸薯片的色、脆、味,而含脂量却比用现有工艺生产的油炸薯片低得多。

例2 Four charged with plotting terror attacks in LA.

Wed Aug 31, 2005 10:18 PM ET Wed Aug 31, 2005 7:56 PM ET

LOS ANGELES (Reuters)—The imprisoned founder of a radical Islamic group and his three followers were indicted on Wednesday for plotting attacks on Los Angeles' area military facilities and synagogues, the Israeli consulate and £|A| airlines, authorities said.

The four men had purchased firearms with silencers, investigated making bombs and were ready to carry out attacks when two of them were caught robbing a gas station to fund the operation, U.S. Attorney Debra Yang told a news conference in Los Angeles. The evidence in this case indicates that the conspirators were on the verge of launching their attack," she said, adding that the arrest had exposed a chilling plot based on one man's interpretation of Islam."

She declined to elaborate on the timing or nature of the attack but said it could have included "shooting up military facilities" or bombing a synagogue and may have been planned to coincide with the Jewish holidays in October.

**Had these four defendants succeeded in their alleged plots, their attacks would have taken an untold number of Americans, M U.S. Attorney General Alberto Gonzales told a separate news briefing in Washington.

Prosecutors say Kevin James, a 29-year-old gang member from Los Angeles who was serving time for attempted robbery and possessing a weapon in prison, had formed the radical organization Jamiyyat Ul-Islam Is-Saheeh at a California correctionalfacility in the late 1990s and preached violence against the United States and Israel.

James distributed to other prisoners a document setting forth his teachings on Islam, including the justification for killing nonbelievers, and recruited fellow inmate Levar Washington in November of 2004, the indictment said.

When Washington, 25, was released from a California prison a short time later, the indictment charges, he recruited his roommate Gregory Patterson and a friend, Hammad Samana, both 21, to the cause. The four men allegedly researched possible targets—including military facilities, synagogues, the Israeli consulate and El A1 airlines.

The men robbed 11 gas stations across Southern California beginning in May to fund their operation, prosecutors say. When they were caught after the final robbery, authorities say, police conducted a search and discovered the list of potential targets and evidence of the larger plot.

The four men each face life in prison if convicted.

编译：

策划在洛杉矶制造恐怖袭击的四人被正式起诉

[据路透社洛杉矶8月31日电] 涉嫌策划袭击美国洛杉矶国民卫队和以色列领事馆等设施的一个在押的一个穆斯林激进组织创立者和他的3名同伙8月31日被正式起诉。

四人分别是莱瓦尔·华盛顿（25岁）、格雷戈里·帕特森（21岁）、哈马德·萨马纳（21岁）和凯文·詹姆斯（29岁）。起诉书称，因抢劫未遂和非法拥有枪支，凯文·詹姆斯目前是美国加利福尼亚州一座监狱的在押因犯，是激进组织"真实伊斯兰会议"（Jamiyyat Ul-Islam Is-Saheeh）的创始人。莱瓦尔·华盛顿在该监狱服刑期间被这个组织吸收为成员，假释出狱后又吸收了他的室友格雷戈里·帕特森和一个朋友哈马德·萨马纳。

据称，他们已经购置了枪支，并对洛杉矶地区的国民卫队军事设施、以色列领事馆和数座犹太教堂进行调查，并准备发动袭击。

为了获取行动经费，三人抢劫了南加利福尼亚的11个加油站。他们在实施最后一次抢劫后被捕，袭击计划也随之被警方发现。

如果罪名成立，他们四人将面临终身监禁。

Moment in Peking (Excerpt)
Chapter 1 The Daughters of a Taoist
Lin Yutang

(1) Mulan greatly admired her father. He had refused to flee from Peking until the evening of the eighteenth; and, now that they had decided to seek safety in their home at Hangchow, he had made extremely cool and unperturbed1 preparations for the departure. For Mr. Yao was a true Taoist^ and refused to be excited.

(2) "Excitement is not good for the soul," Mulan heard her father say. Another argument of his was: "When you yourself are right, nothing that happens to you can ever be wrong". In later life Mulan had many occasions to think about this saying of her father's, and it became a sort of philosophy for her, from which she derived much of her good cheer and courage. A world in which nothing that happens to you can ever be wrong is a good, cheerful world, and one has courage to live and to endure.

(3) War clouds had been in the air since May. The allied foreign troops had taken the fort at the seacoast, but the railway to Peking had been destroyed by the Boxers, who had grown in power and popularity and swarmed over the countryside.

(4) The Empress Dowager had hesitated between avoiding a war with the foreign powers and using the Boxers, a strange, unknown, frightening force whose one object was to destroy the foreigners in China and who claimed magical powers and magic protection against foreign bullets. The Court issued orders one day for the arrest of the Boxer leaders, and the next day appointed the pro-Boxer Prince Tuan as minister for foreign affairs. Court intrigue played an important part in this reversal of the decision to suppress the Boxers. The Empress Dowager had already deprived her nephew the Emperor of his actual power, and was planning to depose him. She favored Prince Tuan's son, a worthless rascal 'as successor to the throne. Thinking that a foreign war would increase his personal power and obtain the throne for his son, Prince Tuan encouraged the Empress Dowager to believe that the Boxers' magic actually made them proof against foreign bullets. Besides, the Boxers had threatened to capture "One Dragon and two Tigers" to sacrifice to heaven for betrayal of their nation, the "Dragon" being the reformist Emperor whose "hundred days of reform" two years earlier had shocked the conservative mandarinate, and the Tigers' being the elderly Prince Ching and Li Hungchang, who had been in charge of the foreign policy.

(5) The Boxers were actually within the capital. A lieutenant colonel who had been sent out to fight them had been ambushed and killed, and his soldiers had joined the Boxers. Highly popular and triumphant, the Boxers had captured Peking, killing foreigners and Christian Chinese and burning their churches. The diplomatic corps protested but Kang Yi, sent to "investigate" the Boxers, reported that they were sent from Heaven to drive out the Oceanic People and wipe out China's shame, and secretly let tens of thousands of them into the capital.

(6) Once inside, the Boxers, under the covert protection of the Empress Dowager and Prince Tuan, terrorized the city. They roamed in the streets, hunting and killing "First Hairies" and "Second and Third Hairies." The "First Hairies" were the foreigners; the "Second and Third Hairies" were the Christians, clerks in foreign firms, and any other English-speaking Chinese. They went about burning churches and foreign houses, destroying foreign mirrors, foreign umbrellas, foreign clocks, and foreign paintings....

(7) Mr. Yao, being a well-read man and in sympathy with the reformist Emperor, thought the whole thing silly and dangerous child's play, but kept his convictions to himself. He had his own good reasons to be "anti-foreign" in a sense, and hated the church as a foreign religion protected by a superior foreign power; but he was too intelligent to approve of the Boxers, and was grateful that Lota and his brother Lotung had kept away from the rabble.

(656 words)

第六章

专有名词的翻译

The First Black Hole image: What Can We Really See?
Brenna Cooper
The Guardian 14 April 2019

It's not actually a photo of a black hole.

This week, scientists produced the first real image of a black hole, in a galaxy called Messier 87. The image is not a photograph but an image created by the Event Horizon Telescope (EHT) project. Using a network of eight ground-based telescopes across the world, the EHT collected data to produce the image. The black hole itself is unseeable, as it's impossible for light to escape from it; what we can see is its event horizon. The EHT was also observing a black hole located at the centre of the Milky Way, but was unable to produce an image. While Messier 87 is further away, it was easier to observe, due to its larger size.

Event horizon

The golden ring is the event horizon, the moment an object approaching a black hole reaches a point of no return, unable to escape its gravitational pull. Objects that pass into the event horizon are thought to go through spaghettification, a process, first described by Stephen Hawking, in which they will be stretched out like a piece of pasta by gravitational forces.

The hole in the centre

Heino Falcke, professor of radio astronomy and astroparticle physics at Radboud University in Nijmegen, and chair of the EHT science council, says the image shows a silhouette of the hole against the surrounding glow of the event horizon, all of the matter being pulled into the hole. At the centre of the black hole is a gravitational singularity, where all matter is crushed into an infinitely small space.

How big is the black hole?

The black hole lies 55m light years away from us. It is around 100bn km wide, larger than the entire solar system and 6.5bn times the mass of our sun.

What does this mean for physics?

Through creating an image of a black hole, something previously thought to be impossible, the EHT project has made a breakthrough in the understanding of black holes, whose existence has long been difficult to prove. The image will help physicists to better understand how black holes work and images of the event horizon are particularly important for testing the theory of general relativity.

(336 words)

佳译赏析

请阅读以下英文原文和中文译文段落,找出其中的专有名词,对它们分类,并研究它们的翻译方法。

Brain-computer Interfaces

英 语 文 本	汉 语 文 本
Brain-computer Interfaces (excerpt) From Economist (Jan 4th 2018)	脑机接口(节选) 摘自经济学人(2018年1月4日)
Brain-computer interfaces may change what it means to be human	脑机接口可能会改变对人的定义
Technologies are often billed as transformative. For William Kochevar, the term is justified. Mr Kochevar is paralysed below the shoulders after a cycling accident, yet has managed to feed himself by his own hand. This remarkable feat is partly thanks to electrodes, implanted in his right arm, which stimulate muscles. But the real magic lies higher up. Mr Kochevar can control his arm using the power of thought. His intention to move is reflected in neural activity in his motor cortex; these signals are detected by implants in his brain and processed into commands to activate the electrodes in his arms.	人们常用"具变革性"来宣传某种技术。对威廉·科切瓦尔(William Kochevar)来说,这个词并无夸张。一次自行车事故后,科切瓦尔自肩部以下瘫痪,但还是能自己用手吃饭。这个非凡的成就部分要归功于植入他右臂用来刺激肌肉的电极,但真正施展魔力的还在更高的部位:科切瓦尔可以用意念控制手臂。他移动手臂的意图反映在他大脑运动皮层的神经活动中,而他大脑中的植入物会探测到这些信号并将之转化成指令,激活他手臂里的电极。
An ability to decode thought in this way may sound like science fiction. But brain-computer interfaces (BCIs) like the BrainGate system used by Mr Kochevar provide evidence that mind-control can work. Researchers are able to tell what words and images people have heard and seen from neural activity alone. Information can also be encoded and used to stimulate the brain. Over 300,000 people have cochlear implants, which help them to hear by converting sound into electrical signals and sending them into the brain. Scientists have "injected" data into monkeys' heads, instructing them to perform actions via electrical pulses.	用这种方式解码思想听起来可能像科幻小说。但是像科切瓦尔使用的"脑门"(BrainGate)系统之类的脑机接口证明思维控制的确可以实现。研究人员仅凭人们的神经活动就能知道他们听到了哪些词语、看到了哪些图像。信息还可以经编码用于刺激大脑。超过30万人已经植入了人工耳蜗,这种装置把声音转换成电信号,再将信号传入大脑,帮助人们听到声音。科学家还曾将数据"注射"到猴子的大脑里,通过电脉冲命令它们做出动作。

英语文本	汉语文本
The pace of research into BCIs and the scale of its ambition are increasing. Both America's armed forces and Silicon Valley are starting to focus on the brain. Facebook dreams of thought-to-text typing. Kernel, a startup, has $100m to spend on neurotechnology. Elon Musk has formed a firm called Neuralink; he thinks that, if humanity is to survive the advent of artificial intelligence, it needs an upgrade. Entrepreneurs envisage a world in which people can communicate telepathically, with each other and with machines, or acquire superhuman abilities, such as hearing at very high frequencies.	脑机接口的研究进程正在加快,并且越来越雄心勃勃。美国军方和硅谷都开始关注大脑。Facebook 希望能实现"思想转文字",让大脑直接输出文字。创业公司 Kernel 获得了一亿美元的融资,用于研发神经技术。伊隆·马斯克成立了一家名为 Neuralink 的公司,他认为人工智能出现后,人类如果还想生存下去,就需要升级。在企业家们设想的世界中,人们可以通过心灵感应与他人或机器交流,或是获得超人般的能力,比如能听到非常高频的声音。
These powers, if they ever materialise, are decades away. But well before then, BCIs could open the door to remarkable new applications. Imagine stimulating the visual cortex to help the blind, forging new neural connections in stroke victims or monitoring the brain for signs of depression. By turning the firing of neurons into a resource to be harnessed, BCIs may change the idea of what it means to be human.	这些能力即便真能实现,也要到几十年后。但在那之前,脑机接口或许会打开通往非凡新应用的大门。想象一下,人类或许可以通过刺激视觉皮层来帮助盲人视物,为中风患者建立新的神经连接,或是监控大脑是否有抑郁症的迹象。脑机接口将神经元放电转化为一种可利用的资源,在此过程中或许会改变对人的定义。
That thinking feeling	思维的感觉
Sceptics scoff. Taking medical BCIs out of the lab into clinical practice has proved very difficult. The BrainGate system used by Mr Kochevar was developed more than ten years ago, but only a handful of people have tried it out. Turning implants into consumer products is even harder to imagine. The path to the mainstream is blocked by three formidable barriers- technological, scientific and commercial.	持怀疑态度的人对此嗤之以鼻。事实证明,把医用脑机接口从实验室带到临床实践中就非常困难。科切瓦尔使用的"脑门"系统是十几年前开发的,但试用过的人屈指可数。将植入物变为消费品更加难以想象。脑机接口要成为主流面临三大难以逾越的障碍:技术、科学和商业。
Start with technology. Non-invasive techniques like an electroencephalogram (EEG) struggle to pick up high-resolution brain signals through intervening layers of skin, bone and membrane. Some advances are being made—on EEG caps that can be used to play virtual-reality games or control industrial robots using thought alone. But for the time being at least, the most ambitious applications require implants that can interact directly with neurons. And existing devices have lots of drawbacks. They involve wires that pass through the skull; they provoke immune responses; they communicate with only a few hundred of the 85bn neurons in the human brain. But that could soon change. Helped by advances in miniaturisation and increased computing power, efforts are under way to make safe, wireless implants that can communicate with hundreds of thousands of neurons. Some of these interpret the brain's electrical signals; others experiment with light, magnetism and ultrasound.	先说技术。像脑电图(EEG)这样的非侵入性技术很难透过层层皮肤、骨骼和脑膜来提取高分辨率的大脑信号。这项技术有所改进,体现在用来玩虚拟现实游戏和仅靠思想控制工业机器人的脑电图帽上。但至少在目前,那些最具雄心的应用仍需要能与大脑神经元直接交互的植入物。现有的设备也有很多缺点,例如都有穿过头骨的电线,还会引起免疫反应,且只能与人类大脑 850 亿个神经元中的几百个交流。但这种情况可能很快会改变。随着微型化技术的进步以及计算能力的提高,研究人员正在努力制造安全、无线且能与几十万个神经元交流的植入物。它们当中有些解读大脑的电信号,另一些则尝试利用光、磁和超声波信号。

续上表

英语文本	汉语文本
Clear the technological barrier, and another one looms. The brain is still a foreign country. Scientists know little about how exactly it works, especially when it comes to complex functions like memory formation. Research is more advanced in animals, but experiments on humans are hard. Yet, even today, some parts of the brain, like the motor cortex, are better understood. Nor is complete knowledge always needed. Machine learning can recognise patterns of neural activity; the brain itself gets the hang of controlling BCIS with extraordinary ease. And neurotechnology will reveal more of the brain's secrets.	攻破了技术壁垒,还要面对另一个障碍。大脑仍然是个非常陌生的领域。科学家们对于它的确切工作原理知之甚少,如果涉及记忆形成这样的复杂功能就更是如此。在动物身上的研究进展更快,但在人体上试验却很困难。不过即便是目前,我们还是加深了对大脑某些部分的了解,如运动皮质。而且这方面的知识并不总要面面俱到。机器学习可以识别神经活动的模式;大脑自己也能游刃有余地控制脑机接口。神经技术还将揭示更多大脑的秘密。
Like a hole in the head The third obstacle comprises the practical barriers to commercialisation. It takes time, money and expertise to get medical devices approved. And consumer applications will take off only if they perform a function people find useful. Some of the applications for brain-computer interfaces are unnecessary—a good voice-assistant is a simpler way to type without fingers than a brain implant, for example. The idea of consumers clamouring for craniotomies also seems far-fetched. Yet brain implants are already an established treatment for some conditions. Around 150,000 people receive deep-brain stimulation via electrodes to help them control Parkinson's disease. Elective surgery can become routine, as laser-eye procedures show.	就像开"脑"洞 第三个障碍是难以实现商业化。医疗设备获批需要时间、资金和专业知识。而消费应用只有具备对人们有用的功能时才能大行其道。有些脑机接口的应用并无必要,比如,要想不动手指就能打字,使用好的语音助手比使用大脑植入物更便捷。认为消费者会哭着喊着要做开颅手术的想法似乎也很离谱。但是在某些情况下,大脑植入物已经是一种成熟的治疗手段。大约有15万人通过电极接受深脑刺激,帮助自己控制帕金森氏症。激光眼科手术也已证明选择性手术可以成为常规手术。
All of which suggests that a route to the future imagined by the neurotech pioneers is arduous but achievable. When human ingenuity is applied to a problem, however hard, it is unwise to bet against it. Within a few years, improved technologies may be opening up new channels of communications with the brain. Many of the first applications hold out unambiguous promise—of movement and senses restored. But as uses move to the augmentation of abilities, whether for military purposes or among consumers, a host of concerns will arise. Privacy is an obvious one: the refuge of an inner voice may disappear. Security is another: if a brain can be reached on the internet, it can also be hacked. Inequality is a third: access to superhuman cognitive abilities could be beyond all except a self-perpetuating elite. Ethicists are already starting to grapple with questions of identity and agency that arise when a machine is in the neural loop.	所有这些都表明,要抵达神经技术先锋们设想的未来,道路虽艰辛,但仍可实现。无论一个问题有多难,一旦人类发挥创造力,赌它无法被攻克就是不明智的。随着技术进步,也许在几年内人们就会开启与大脑沟通的新渠道。很多最先投入应用的脑机接口都是为了实现非常明确的效果:恢复运动和感知能力。但随着应用转向增强人体能力——无论是用于军事目的还是消费活动,就会产生种种担忧。隐私是一个突出的问题:内心声音的庇护所可能会消失。另一个问题是安全:如果能够通过互联网连接上大脑,那么它也可能被黑客攻击。还有第三个问题:不平等。除了自我永续的精英,也许再无人能承担得起获得超人般的认知能力。伦理学家已经开始为机器被引入神经回路所引发的身份认同和主体性问题挠头。
These questions are not urgent. But the bigger story is that neither are they the realm of pure fantasy. Technology changes the way people live. Beneath the skull lies the next frontier.	这些问题并不紧迫。但更重要的一点是,它们都不属于纯粹幻想。科技改变人类的生存方式。头骨之下是下一个前沿。

认知升级

一、人名的翻译

1.人名翻译,问题多多

人名翻译是一个需要高度重视的问题。著名翻译家思果曾说过:"翻译有多难,由译人名地名等固有名词可以看出。没有一处可以掉以轻心,没有一处不需要学问。"

作为专有名词的一种,人名不仅是人的称呼,还具有悠久的历史和浓厚的文化色彩,语源广,典故多。了解英姓名的文化内涵有助于我们准确翻译人名。

屈文生❶在《谈人名翻译的统一与规范化问题》中指出了当今众多译著中出现的各有关外国人名翻译的问题。先将部分内容摘录如下,以供参考。

第一,胡译乱译。比如把日本姓田端(Tabata)误为"塔巴塔";把日本近世儒学家获生徂徕(Ogyu Sorai)翻译为"大给空井";把著名法学家罗纳德·德沃金(Ronald Dworkin)译成"罗纳德·德沃科";把大名鼎鼎的哈耶克(Friedrich Hayek)译成"弗瑞锥奇·海克"等。即便是中国人名回译的,也有人曾错将 Mencius 翻译为"门修斯"(应为孟子),将 Chiang Kai-shek 翻译为"常凯申"(应为蒋介石)。

第二,另起炉灶。例如,将寻找金羊毛的伊阿宋(Jason)翻译为"贾森";Leigton Stuart 约定俗成译为"司徒雷登",有人将之翻译为"斯图尔特";John K. Fairbank 应翻译为费正清(曾任哈佛大学终身教授,美国最负盛名的中国问题观察家),有人误译为"费尔班克";有人把美国总统马丁·范布伦(Martin Van Buren)译成"马丁·范·伯瑞";把美国著名法学家、案例教学法创始人兰德尔(Langdell)翻译为"郎德尔"。凡此种种,不再列举。

第三,将普通实词误当为人名翻译。以普罗菲特·穆罕默德为例,实际上这是"先知穆罕默德"的意思,英文 prophet 是指"先知",这并非名字。

第四,姓名混用,将名用作姓。在姓名的排列顺序上,中国人、朝鲜人、越南人及泰国人的姓名排列顺序是姓在先,名在后;而西方人的姓名则大多名在先,姓在后。此外,尽人皆知,当在尊称某人先生、女士或主席时,是要使用对方的"姓"而不是"名"的。

第五,把俄语、德语、法语、西班牙语中的姓名按照英语发音来翻译。比如有人将 Bolsheviks 翻译为"博利舍维克斯",若非译者把原文附上,谁能猜到这就是"布尔什维克"?还有"库斯科夫"是谁?若无原文 Khrushchev,大概无论如何也想不到这是"赫鲁晓夫"。

……

还有,不少人把"van"和"von"混淆。前者一般翻译为"范",后者常是德语人名中的介词,翻译为"冯"。17世纪以前,von 只是用来连接某人的名字和他的出生地,表示"某地的某某",以区别于其他同名人。到17世纪,它演变成了贵族出身的标志。现在,它已失去了其贵族含义,成了姓名的一个组成部分。称呼时,必须把 von 和其后的姓连在一起使用。

第六,前后不一致。音译人名应当采取同名同译、同姓同译的原则。但翻译实践中,有不少人在同一著作或同一论文中将同一人名译成不同的汉语人名。

第七,写错别字。有的译者甚至还写错别字,例如把卢梭写为"卢俊";把里森亲王写成"黑森亲王"等。

---

❶屈文生.谈人名翻译的统一与规范化问题.中国科技术语.2009,(5):39-45.

英语原文	大陆译名	香港译名	台湾译名
Thatcher	☑撒切尔	戴卓尔	柴/佘契尔
Reagan	里根	列根	雷根
Peres	佩雷斯	佩雷斯	☑裴瑞斯
Bush	☑布什	布殊	布希
Kennedy	☑肯尼迪	甘乃地	甘乃迪
Kissinger	☑基辛格	☑基辛格	季辛吉
Putin	普京	普京	☑蒲亭/普丁
Nixon	尼克松	尼克逊	☑尼克森
Merkel	墨克尔	墨克尔	☑梅克尔
Che Cuevara	☑切·格瓦拉	哲·古华拉	☑切·格瓦拉
Theresa Mary May	☑特雷莎·梅	文翠珊	德蕾莎·梅伊
Sydney	☑悉尼	☑悉尼	雪梨

了解在翻译人名时,首先需要区分是历史和现实生活中的真实人名,还是文学作品中的虚构人名;区分姓名的国籍或者语言来源,然后按照名从主人、约定俗成、音译为主、规范统一等原则进行翻译。

2. 英美人姓名来源

英美人姓氏,若从词源的角度来看,主要来源于自然界、地名、动植物、体貌特征、职业、家族长幼关系、神话宗教等。

一些姓氏来源于自然界。如 Snow(斯诺)、Frost(弗罗斯特)、Hill(希尔)、Brook(布鲁克)等。

另一些来源于地名。如 Everest(埃弗里斯特)、Bradley(布拉德利)、London(伦敦)、Ford(福特)、Thames(泰晤士)、Scott(司科特)等。

有的来源于动植物。如 Fox(福克斯)、Finch(芬奇)、Bull(布尔)、Wood(伍德)、Bush(布什)、Rice(莱斯)等。

还有的与人的体貌特征相联系。如 Small(斯莫尔)、Longfellow(朗费罗)、Bunch(邦奇)、Armstrong(阿姆斯特朗)等。

有的来源于职业。如 Hunter(亨特,猎人)、Miller(米勒,磨坊主)、Blacksmith(铁匠,布莱克史密斯)、Goldsmith(戈德史密斯,金匠)、Carter(马车夫,卡特)等。

还有的根据家族中长幼关系来命名。如 Henderson 亨德森(亨特的儿子),Johnson 约翰逊(约翰的儿子)、Richardson 理查森(理查德的儿子)、等。绝大多数情况下,以男子个人名作为词干的家姓,但亦有少数以女子个人名作为词干的,如 Ibson(伊布森)= Ib(Isabel 伊莎贝拉)+son,Magson = Mag(Margaret 玛格丽特)+son 等。也可以用-es 表所属关系,如 Hughes(休斯)等。

还有一些与神话宗教有关。如月亮女神 Diana(黛安娜)、智慧女神 Athena(阿西娜)、Adam(亚当)、David(大卫)等。

在英语家姓中,除了借助后缀构成的家姓外,也有不少是通过加前缀构成,有以下四种不同情况:

第一类是加盖尔语前缀 mac-的。如:MacKay(麦凯)、Mackey(麦基)、MacNab(麦克纳布）、MacAlister（麦卡利斯特）、MacDonald（麦当劳）等。

第二类是加爱尔兰语前缀 o'的。如 O'Clery（奥克利里），O'Flynn（奥弗林），O'Neil（奥尼尔）等。

第三类是加尔士语前缀 ab-或 afep)-、b-或 p-的。如：Absimon（阿布西蒙），Abbell（阿贝尔），Appleman（阿普尔曼），Badam（巴达姆），Penny（彭里）等。

第四类是加古英语或诺曼法语的前缀 fitz。如 Fitzalan（菲查伦），Fitzgerade（菲茨杰拉德），Fitzwalter（菲茨沃特）等。

若从语种来源的角度来看，现代英语家姓则主要来源于古英语、古斯堪的纳维亚语和诺曼法语。

例如，有的姓氏来源于古英语。如 Pink（平克），Fatt（法特），Marry（梅里），Baxter（巴克斯特）等。

有的来源于古斯堪的纳维亚语。如 Asikettle（阿仕凯特尔），Askwith（阿斯克威司），Kettle（凯特尔），Thorold（索罗尔德）等。

还有的来源于诺曼法语：如 Baskerville（巴斯克威尔），Bayard（贝亚德），Cheever（奇弗）等。

3. 外国人名的翻译原则与方法

英文中出现外国人名的情况非常复杂，需要根据具体情况，按照一定的原则和步骤进行翻译。通常，应在第一个译文后面附注原文名字备查，还可以加注生卒年份，以避免混淆。

（1）先名后姓

西方人强调个性，因此，英美人姓名的排列顺序是表示个性的名在前，表示共性的姓在后。常见形式为：Given name（名）+Middle Name（中间名或教名）+Family name（家姓）。如：Percy Bysshe Shelly（柏西·比希·雪莱）等。在汉译这类人名时，一般是先名后姓，中间用符号"·"隔开。如 David Copperfield（大卫·科波菲尔），Thomas Hardy（托马斯·哈代）等。

①含有缩写的姓名

若原文姓名中有缩写的英文字母，可照录英文缩写，直接出现在译文中。如：C. S. Butler（C.S.布特勒）、J. Edger. Hoover（J.埃德加·胡佛）、H. G. Alexander（H. G.亚历山大），F.H.Fonk 的汉译就应是 F.H.冯克等。G .Paget Thomson 译为 G.佩吉特·汤姆森，而 George P .Thomson,译为乔治·P.汤姆森。

②含有地名的人名

含有出生地的人名是一种常见的英美人名，指的是家姓产生前的历史人物。人名中的出生地名，是区分个人名相同的不同人的手段之一。英语的书写形式为：人名+介词+出生地。如：Paul of Venice（威尼斯的保罗），William of Occam（奥康的威廉）。还有一种是既包括出生地，又包括封建领地的人名。如英格兰军事家 John of Gaunt Duke of Lancaster，汉译就译为"冈特约翰，兰开斯特公爵"，或者"冈特的约翰，兰开斯特领地的公爵"。

③含有序数词、绰号或附加名的人名

含序数词的人名通常由个人名与序数词构成，序数词常常写为罗马数字。序数词通常汉译作"几世"或"第几"。凡是皇室，国君或拥有爵号的贵族，其人名中的序数词通常都汉译作"几世"。如：Henry IV 应译作"亨利四世"。Napoleon III 译作"拿破仑三世"（法兰西第二帝国皇帝）。但如果人名中的序数词不表示承袭关系，就译作"第几"。如 C. E. Ragan III 则应译作"拉根第三"（美国科学家）。

④含有绰号或附加号的人名

英美人名,有时会加上绰号或附加名,表示该人据有某些外部或者内部特征。例如:William Short 中的 Short(矮子),Geoffrey Hunch 中的 Hunch(驼背者),Henry Brag 中的 Brag(爱说大话者)。由于这些人名中的绰号或附加名,并没有失去其固有的词汇意思,所以在汉译时应按照名从主人的原则而将其予以意译。

英美人姓名的另一个特点是父子使用同名的很多。为了与父名有所区别,在其姓名之后加上 Jr.(Junior 的缩写)一词,意思是"小……"。例如:Charles Brown, Jr.;Howard Gammage Jr.等。

女子婚前概用父姓,婚后随夫姓,保留自己的名字,例如:未婚女子 Ann Lally 嫁给一个叫 David Nelson 的男子后,在正常情况下,她的姓名应为 Ann Nelson(本人名字加夫姓)或 Ann Lally Nelson,本人姓氏列在夫姓之前,起实际上的名字作用〉。在社交中,人们也直接称呼她 David Nelson(用其丈夫全名再加上"夫人"一词)。当然,有时也会出现妇女婚后仍保留父姓而并未随夫姓的例子。

(2)音译为主

一般人名指的是没有添加其他的"言外之意",又没有像文学作品中的有些人名那样包含了作者特殊意图的人名,只是起到一种指称代码的作用。这种情况通常采用音译法。如英文的 Smith 译成"史密斯",Hunter 译成"亨特"。虽然这些名字本身具有内涵意义,即"铁匠"和"猎人",但是叫这个名字的人本身可能不是铁匠或猎人,如果采用意译则会导致误解。

翻译外国人名主要是译音。译音用字应采用常见易懂的字,不用冷僻的字。如常见的人名及其翻译有:Laura(劳拉)、Jones(琼斯)、Taylor(泰勒)、James(詹姆斯)Brown(布朗)、Smith(史密斯)、Mike(迈克)、Sharp(夏泼)等。

①分清男女

英美姓名有男女之分,汉译时凡是在用字上能予以区分的,习惯上都应予以区分。如英语中常见的女名 Catherine, Maria, Lilly, Louisa 通常分别译作凯瑟琳,玛利亚,玛丽,莉莉,露伊莎。翻译女性姓名时,可以选用的汉字有:娅,玛,妮,娜,琳,丽,丝,莎,黛等。如果男女共用一个名,翻译时,也可以在用字上调整,以示区分。如 Sidney,男名译为"西德里",女名则译为"西德妮",Hillary,男名为"西拉里",女名则为"希拉里",Jocelin 男名译为"乔瑟林",女名译为"乔瑟琳"。

②避免歧义

还有,音译时尽量不使用那些容易引起联想的字词,以免闹笑话。如把 Bumble(本伯)译作"笨伯",Kuless(孔雷飒)译成"裤里塞"。

(3)名从主人

人名翻译中的一个重要原则就是尊重主人。如外国人本身已有中国名字,则不用按发音翻译,直接采用中文姓名。如:参加翻译《几何原理》的 Matto Ricci,应译为"利玛窦";美北长老会派至中国的传教士 William Alexander Parsons Martin(1827—1916)应译为"丁韪良",美国汉学家、历史学家,哈佛大学教授 John K Fairbank(1907—1991)应译为"费正清"。其他如 Leighton Stuart 应译为"司徒雷登",Joseph Needham 译为"李约瑟",诺贝尔文学奖得主、著名美国女作家 Pearl Buck 中文名字"赛珍珠"。

翻译人名时,还要坚持名从主籍的原则,即要遵循其所在国语言的发音,尽可能从姓名使用者的母语译出。例如,东罗马帝国的皇帝 Justinian 译为"优士丁尼"而不译为"查士丁尼";法国法学家 Doneau 应按照法语发音译为"多诺",而不译为"德尼奥"或"德纽";法国比较法学家 René David 按照法语音译为"勒内·达维德",而不译为"勒内·大卫"或者"勒内·戴卫";Rasputin 应译作"拉斯·普京"而非"拉斯·普丁"。

英语中有些人名,虽然拼写方式相同,但是来自不同的语言,也要注意区分,应根据所在国家的官方或通用语言的标准语音为准音译。例如"Weiss",如果是德国人就根据其德语读音译成"怀斯",如果是美国人则应译成"韦斯"。英国王储"Charles"译作"查尔斯王子",法国人"Charles de Gaulle"应按照法语译为"夏尔·戴高乐",其中"Charles"既不能译为"查理",也不能译为"查尔斯",应该按照法语"Charles"的发音译为"夏尔"。

有些西方语言中,会出现双名和复姓的情况。法语姓名中有使用双名或复姓的,则在两词之间用连字符分开,汉译时作相应处理。如:Jean-Pierre 让—皮埃尔(双名),Jacques-Yves 雅克—伊夫(双名),Bourges-Maunoury 布尔热—莫努里(复姓)。复姓的组成情况不一,可以是父姓+母姓,承袭其父的复姓,或者女子婚后用夫姓+父姓。翻译时,可以加连词符号,用以明示。

如果英文中出现了韩国人的姓名,应该找到韩语的中文表达方式,而不用根据韩语发音进行翻译。例如,Roh Moo Hyun 译为"卢武铉",Cho Hunhyun 译为"曹熏铉"。Kim Taek Su "金泽株",韩国人气偶像 Cha Tae-hyun 为"车太铉",Jeon Ji-hyun 为"全智贤"等。据悉,韩国最常见的姓氏有金(Kim)、朴(Park)、崔(Choi)、李(Lee)、卢(Roh)等十个,占韩国全部姓氏的90%以上。

如果英文中出现日本人的姓名,则有三种处理办法。首先,应查找有无该名的汉字对应形式,如有,在翻译时,直接采用日文汉字即可。例如 Itō Hirobumi 日文平假名为いとう ひろぶみ,汉字为"伊藤博文",Abe Shinzō 日文平假名为あべしんぞう,汉字为"安倍晋三";Ken Takakura 日文平假名けんたかくら,汉字为高仓健,Namie Amuro 日文平假名なみえあむろ,汉字"安室奈美惠"。这类姓名在翻译时,照搬日文汉字即可。其次,假如该名字中的汉字为日本自造,在中文缺少对应的汉字,则应沿用日文汉字。例如,英文中如果出现日本侵华祸首之一的 Fumimaro Konoe,其日语平假名书写形式ふみまろこのえ,对应的日文汉字形式"近卫文麿",其中的"麿"字为日本自造。Nagi Noda 的日文平假名为なぎのだ,日文汉字为"野田凪"其中的"凪"也是自造汉字。在翻译此类姓名时,也可以沿用日文汉字。最后,如果实在不能查到其确切的中文写法,可参照日文发音写出其可能性较大的汉字,同时用小括号注明采用音译处理。

(4)约定俗成

在早期的译著中,一些外国人名的翻译往往个性化十足,延续至今,形成五花八门的历史遗留译名。尽管这些译名不符合今天的标准,但它们已经耳熟能详、广为接受,如果再改,反而读者不易接受,容易产生歧义且引发混乱。因此,我们仍需尊重历史,保留旧译。

例如,虽然按今天的标准"Smith"音译应为"史密斯",但英国政治经济学家"Adam Smith"的中国译名"亚当·斯密"已经深入人心,无须改为"史密斯"。又如,Bernard Shaw 译作"肖伯纳","Bethune"音译为"贝修恩",敬爱的加拿大医生"Norman Bethune"的历史译名为"诺尔曼·白求恩";西班牙传奇故事中的"Don Juan"被翻译成"唐璜"而不是"唐·故安",NBA 著名篮球运动员 Kobe Bryant 翻译为"科比·布莱恩特",而不是"科贝",著名侦探小说中的人物 Holmes 译成"福尔摩斯",意大利航海家 Christopher Columbus 译作"哥伦布"。

这些翻译是约定俗成的,已为大多数的中国人所接受,译者和出版社可以继续沿用。

又如,意大利伟大画家达·芬奇的名字 Leonardo da Vinci 是由个人名+介词+出生地名构成意为"生于芬奇村的莱奥纳多",达·芬奇的名字显然是误译,但因广泛流传,大家都接受了这个译名,也就没必要改译了。这样的例子还有 Charles de Gaulle(夏尔·戴高乐),Johan Wolfgang Von Goethe(约翰·沃尔夫岗·封·歌德)等。

(5)符合标准

外国人名翻译,应该符合都必须统一实行我国新华通讯社译名室编写的《世界人名翻译大辞典》等行业标准。首先优先参照新华通讯社译名室编辑、中国对外翻译出版公司 1993 年出版的《世界人名翻译大辞典》及其附录"世界各国及地区语言、民族、宗教和人名翻译主要依据",以及《中国大百科全书》各卷所附的"外国人名译名对照表"。其次可参照新华社编辑、商务印书馆出版的针对各个语种的姓名译名手册,如《英语姓名译名手册》《法语姓名译名手册》《德语姓名译名手册》《西班牙语姓名译名手册》《葡萄牙语姓名译名手册》《罗马尼亚语姓名译名手册》《意大利语姓名译名手册》等。

以上均未收录的人名,可根据新华社编辑,商务印书馆出版的《译音表》中相应语言的译音表进行音译拼组。

(6)同名同译

对同一个外国人,应该同名同译。但因政治、历史、社会、文化等多种复杂原因,同名不同译的情况屡见不鲜,如本文开头所提到的功能学派代表人物的译名。如著名德国哲学家 A. G. Baumgarter 的家姓见于出版物的译法至少有六种:鲍姆伽登、鲍姆加顿、鲍姆加滕、鲍姆嘉通、鲍谟加登和鲍姆加登;经典世界文学名著《红与黑》的作者 Stendhal 的译法目前有:斯当达、司汤达、斯汤达、斯丹大尔、斯唐达尔、斯汤达尔、司丹达尔、斯丹达尔、斯当达尔九种。

作为译者,我们应该尽量选择符合标准、采用已经通用的译名,避免闭门造车,另创译名,使得译名的不统一的情况雪上加霜。

4.华人华裔人名的回译

在英文或其他外语文献中,也会经常出现华人、华裔的人名。在这种情况下,译者需要认真查证,小心处理,以免张冠李戴。

有些中国人、包括港澳台胞或者外籍华侨华裔,本身既有汉语名,又有英文名,两者之间存在较大差异。在翻译时,直接恢复其已有的汉语姓名即可,不用另行翻译。例如,Samuel Chao Chung Ting 译为"丁肇中",Jewel Lee 指澳门小姐李菲,Andy Lau"刘德华",Edmund Ho Hau-Wah 澳门特别行政区行政长官"何厚铧",Vincent Siew"萧万长",Run Run Show 为"邵逸夫",Bruce lee 为李小龙,Jackie Chan 为"成龙",Eason Chan 陈奕迅,Mavis Hee 新加坡女歌手许美静,Yue Sai Kan 是著名的羽西化妆品公司的总裁靳羽西女士英文名字,Jack Ma 是阿里巴巴集团创始人马云的英文名字,Yong Hock-kin 为马来西亚体育明星杨景福。这些名字在英汉翻译时都应谨慎处理。

例1 In addition to Ting, Wang, Pei, other Chinese-Americans today include: Nobel laureates in physics Yang Chen-Ning (1922-) and Tsung-Dao Lee (1926-), and composer Wen-Chung Chou (1923-).

除了丁(肇中)、王(安)、贝(聿铭)之外,当前有名的其他华裔美国人还包括诺贝尔物理学奖获得者杨振宁(1922 年出生)、李政道(1926 年出生)以及作曲家周文中(1923 年出生)。

例 2 That includes the CEO of the local company giving eBay fits there, Jack Ma of the Alibaba-Taobao.

这样的人物包括阿里巴巴淘宝网的首席执行官马云,这家公司曾让 eBay 如坐针毡。

此外,外国文献中,如果出现了中国历史上的人名,也要根据约定俗成的原则进行回译。例如,英文中的 Confucius 指"孔子",Mencius 指"孟子",Sun Tzu 指"孙子",Chiang Kai-shek 为"蒋介石"。

5.文学作品中人名的翻译

翻译既涉及真实人物的姓名,也涉及文学作品中的姓名。作家在塑造人物时,为更深刻地刻画人物性格,预示人物的命运和结局,常常精心而慎重地为人物选择名字。文学作品中的许多人物的姓名往往会被作者赋予某种含义。

例如,萨克雷给《名利场》(Vanity Fair)中两个性格迥异的女性起名:一个起名 Rebecca Sharp,意为尖刻,其人狡诈自私;另一个起名 Amelia Sedley,意为勤劳,其人堪称善良勤劳的典范。前者音意融合译成"利蓓加·夏泼",不用"普"而用"泼"字,把人物泼辣、势利、机灵而不择手段的性格译得听音而知义了;后者译为"爱米丽亚·赛特笠",对人物的褒贬自现。

在翻译文学作品时,译者应在把握人物性格特征的基础上,结合上下文语境以及了解姓名的文化内涵、民族心理、语言特征等,在可能的范围内用适当的翻译方法,尽量传达原作者赋予的内涵。否则,就会造成文化信息的缺失,引起读者理解的偏差,无法使译文读者得到阅读原文同等的效果。译者根据具体情况需要,可以采用音译和意译结合的方法,也可以在音译后附加注释,或舍弃原文中具体人名直接译出这类人的性格特征及所代表的行为。

英国 17 世纪小说家 John Bunyan 小说《天路历程》里大部分人名,直接用普通名词构成,寓意明显,如 Evangelist, Mr. Worldly Wiseman, Faithful, Giant Despair, Mercy, Greatheart, Christiana 等。在几种汉译本中,不同译者均采用意译的方法来处理人名:Christian 基督徒,Evangelist 传教士,Mr. Worldly Wiseman 世故先生,Faithful 诚实人/诚信者,Giant Despair 巨人失望,Mercy 慈悲者,Greatheart 大勇,Christiana 基督徒之妻等。此类人名的翻译采取意译的方式既可以展示人物性格,引导读者的思维,同时有助于体现原作者的起名意图。

有些作者会从历史、神话、圣经以及其他文学作品中借用人名,或者自己创造新的名字。作者能决定是选择意义隐晦的名字还是选择意义外露的名字,也就是说意义外露的名字会使读者在读小说时一看到这些带有象征意义的名字时便会对这些名字所预示的人物性格和命运有大概的了解。

例如,英国小说家 George Orwell 的小说(《动物农庄》)中,有头公猪叫 Napoleon,这便是借用法国的历史人物 Napoleon 的名字来暗示人物的性格和命运。小说中的 Napoleon 是法国大革命时的独裁统治者 Napoleon 的一个变体。按照历史人物拿破仑的名字进行翻译,符合作者的原始意图。这样的人名可以按照历史人物或者所借用的人名的原名翻译,否则译成其他的名字,原作者的意图就无法准确地传达出来。

例 1 Even before they were acquainted, he had admired Osborn in secret. Now he was his valet, his dog, his man Friday. ["星期五(Friday)"是《鲁滨孙漂流记》中鲁滨孙的忠实奴仆。]

没有认识奥斯本之前已经暗地佩服他。如今他成了他的听差,他的狗,他的忠仆星期五。

例 2 They have, by this very act, opened a Pandora's Box. (Pandora's Box 意为"灾祸之

根源",此习语取自希腊神话。)

他们这种做法犹如打开了潘多拉的盒子,造成了极大的混乱和不幸。

例3 Several of the country's most respected doctors have stated that smoking cigarettes harms one's health, but there are still many doubting Thomases who are not yet persuaded. (此处原文有"Doubting Thomas"一词,译为"怀疑的托马斯",此习语源自《圣经》,意指那些不肯相信别人的人。)

虽然这个国家几位最有名望的医生都说吸烟有害健康,但还是没有说服几个顽固的怀疑者。

例4 I am no Hamlet. (注释:Hamlet 即哈姆雷特,是莎士比亚戏剧中的人物,性格犹豫。)

我绝不犹豫。

在此具体语境中,可以直接译出代表这类人物的性格特征并加以注释说明。

人名翻译参考书目

[1] 新华通讯社译名室.世界人名翻译大辞典[M].北京:中国对外翻译出版公司,1993.
[2] 新华通讯社译名室.英语姓名译名手册[M].4版.北京:商务印书馆,2004.
[3] 李忠华.英语人名词典[M].上海:上海外语教育出版社,2005.
[4] 刘复华.最新英文人名词典6600[M].台北:文鹤出版有限公司,2004.
[5] 宋兰臣,李淑舫.常用英美人名词典[M].石家庄:河北教育出版社,2001.
[6] 白云晓.圣经人名词典 汉英对照[M].北京:中央编译出版社,2015.
[7] 新华通讯社名室.西班牙语姓名译名手册[M].北京:商务印书馆,2015.
[8] 新华通讯社译名室.意大利语姓名译名手册[M].北京:商务印书馆,2012.
[9] 新华通讯社译名室.德语姓名译名手册(修订本)[M].北京:商务印书馆,1999.
[10] 辛华.罗马尼亚姓名译名手册[M].北京:商务印书馆,1997.
[11] 新华通讯社译名室.法语姓名译名手册[M].北京:商务印书馆,1996.
[12] 新华通讯社译名室.葡萄牙语姓名译名手册[M].北京:商务印书馆,1995.
[13] 杭州大学哲学系古希腊哲学研究室.古希腊罗马姓名译名手册[M].杭州:杭州大学,1984.
[14] 陈玉书.日本造船界姓名译名手册[M].无锡:中国船舶科学研究中心,1982.
[15] 赵福堂.日英汉对译日本人名地名词典[M].北京:世界知识出版社,1998.
[16] 中国社会科学院近代史所翻译室.近代来华外国人名辞典[M].北京:中国社会科学出版社,1981.
[17] 唐敬杲.现代外国人名词典[M].北京:商务印书馆,1939.
[18] 于鹏彬.外国人名词典[M].上海:上海辞书出版社,1988.
[19] 陈观胜,安才旦.常见藏语人名地名词典 汉英藏对照[M].北京:外文出版社,2004.
[20] 胡芳毅,熊欣.中英人名地名的特点与翻译[M].南京:东南大学出版社,2012.

二、地名的翻译

地名(place name, geographic name)是人们在生活实践中创造性的产物,它具有民族性、地理性、社会性以及准确性和相对稳定性。同时,地名又是国家领土主权的象征,是社会交往的媒介。在当今社会,地名作为特殊的信息载体,在国际政治、经济、科技、文化交流以及人类社会生活方面起着非常重要的作用。地名的翻译需要加以重视。

外国地名的翻译需要遵循音译为主、意译为辅、名从主人、约定俗成、坚持标准等原则。这些原则的运用可以促进地名翻译的规范性。

(1)音译为主

外国地名一般都采取专名音译,通名意译的方法。大多数外国地名一般不含太多的内涵意义,可以音译为主。外国地名的音译要严格遵守源语和译语的标准发音规则。比如说英语发音要根据通用的国际音标。如美国的 Florida(福罗里达州)、Wisconsin(威斯康星州)等。

①外国居民点名称原则上都应采取音译,不宜采取意译。如美国居民点 Snow Hill 音译为"斯诺希尔",不意译为"雪丘",古巴居民点 Rio Grand 音译为"里奥格兰德",不意译为"大河城"。

②在由复合词组成的居民点名称中,如果专名和通名连写,通名也一律采取音译,例如德语的 Darmstadt 译为"达姆施塔特"(Stadt 在德语中是"城市"之意)。

③对地名通名部分起修饰作用的形容词采用音译。譬如 Great Island 译为"格雷特岛",不宜译为"大岛";Little River 译为"利特尔河",不宜译为"小河";Front Range 译为"弗兰特山脉"等。

④有两种以上官方语言的国家,其地名译音要以该地名所属地区语言的读音为依据。如:瑞士有德语、法语、意大利语 3 个语区,则应按 3 个语区的语言译写地名。瑞士地名 Buchs(德语区),La Chaux de Fonds(法语区),Mendrisio(意大利 语区),分别按德语、法语和意大利语译为"布克斯""拉绍德封""门德里西奥"。

(2)意译为辅

如果一些外国地名都具有一定的含义,可以采用意译,以便更好地表达地名的特点,达到一目了然的效果。《关于改用汉语拼音方案拼写中国人名地名作为罗马字母拼写法的实施说明》第三条规定:"在各外语中地名的专名部分原则上音译,用汉语拼音字母拼写,通名部分(如省、自治区、市、江、河、湖、海等)采用意译。但在专名是单音节时,其通名部分应视作专名的一部分,先音译,后重复意译。文学作品、旅游图等出版物中的人名、地名,含有特殊意义,需要意译的,可按现行办法译写。"

"New Zealand"是太平洋西南部的一个岛国,荷兰探险家塔斯曼(Abel Tasman)于1642年发现该岛屿。因其海岸地貌特征与荷兰的"Zealand"岛相似,塔斯曼将其命名为"New Zealand",意为"新的西兰岛",也就是说,"New"是一个实义词,而并非只是一个地理符号。鉴于此,"New Zealand"应译为"新西兰",而非"纽西兰"。

具有以下特点的地名应该意译:

①地物名称中的通名一般意译。英国 Culdrose Airbase 卡德罗斯空军基地,印度尼西亚语 Laut Djawa 爪哇海,南非共和国 Grootrivier 赫鲁特河(rivier 在阿非利堪语是"河"),芬兰语 Maltiotunturi 马尔蒂奥山(Tunturi 在芬兰语中是"山")。

②具有明显地理特征、特点(地形、地貌、物产、颜色)的地名应该意译。例如,中东的死海(Dead Sea),因湖中及湖岸均富含盐分,鱼虾等水生物都难以生存,水中只有细菌和绿藻,岸边及周围地区也没有花草生长,故称"死海"。南极洲的鲸鱼湾(Bay of Whales)、美国的云峰(Cloud Peak)等,都是以意译为主。还有中东地区的红海(Red Sea)、黑海(Black Sea)等。

③对地名专名起修饰作用的形容词(如表示方位、大小、新旧等)、方位词区别词(如东、南、西、北、上、下、前、后)等,一般意译。方位如马来西亚的北婆罗洲(North Borneo)、西澳大利亚(Western Australia)、加拿大的西北地区(West Territories)、苏格兰的东劳欣(East Lothian)、美国的中途岛(Midway Island);大小如美国的小密苏里河(Little Missouri)、大提顿山(Grand Teton)、澳洲的大分水岭(Great Dividing Range)、加拿大的大奴湖(Great Slave Lake)、印度的大尼科巴岛(Great Nicobar Island)、新旧如澳大利亚的新南威尔士(New South Wale)、新西兰(New Zealand)等。其他如非洲的"好望角"(Cape of Good Hope)。

④带有数词或日期的地名一般要意译。譬如,美国的八十八村 Eight-eight Village)、印度洋的一度半海峡(One-and-Half Degree Channel)、八度海峡 Eight Degree Channel)、十度海峡(Ten Degree Channel)、加拿大的魁北克省的三河城(法语 Trois-Riviere)、美国的万烟谷 Valley of Ten Thousand Smokes 等。

⑤凡有职务、称呼、绰号等与姓氏分写的人名和凡有衔称的人名命名的地名,这些成分等一律意译,如阿根廷的"General San Martin"译成"圣马丁将军城",加拿大的"Queen Elizabeth Is."译成"伊丽莎白女王群岛"等。

⑥凡具有政治、历史或其他意义的地名,音译又过长者,则可意译,如阿根廷和智利的 Isla Grande de Fuego 译成"火地岛",俄罗斯的 Ostrov Oktyabriskiy Revolyutsiy 译成"十月革命岛",南极洲的 South Magnetic Pole 译成"南磁极"等。

⑦在印欧语系各种语言中,凡是以圣贤命名的地名,尽管拼写不尽相同,可以统一意译为"圣"。如英语 St. Austell Bay 圣奥斯特尔湾,法语 St. Brieuc 圣布里厄,德语 Sankt Jürgen 圣于尔根,西班牙语 San Lorenzo, Sa. de 圣洛伦索山,葡萄牙语 Santa Maria 圣玛丽亚岛,意大利语 San Marino 圣马力诺等。

⑧但在文学作品、旅游景点中的地名,由于含有特殊意义需要意译。如王汉川博士在汉译英国文艺复兴后期著名作家 John Bunyan(约翰·班扬)的名著 The Pilgrim's Progress(《天路历程》)中的地名时将 Land Beulah 译为"良缘国"等。又如旅游图中"Eiffel Tower"译成"艾菲尔铁塔","Wellington Museum at Waterloo"译成"滑铁卢惠灵顿博物馆"等。

(3)名从主人

"名从主人"是各国翻译和转写外国地名所必须遵循的一条基本原则。根据联合国经社理事会所属联合国地名标准化会议的要求,国际地名标准化要以各国地名标准化为基础。因此,外国地名的译写要依据要以各国主权范围内所定地名的标准名称及其罗马字母书写为准,不能用其他语种或其他国家的转手资料作依据。这就要求对人名、地名和所有专名中包含的人名、地名以及地名性专名(如建筑物、公园、广场、街道、名胜古迹等),都应以各自所在国家的官方或通用语言的标准语音为准音译,以便能最忠实于主权所有者,最忠实于原文。

例如,翻译波兰地名 Gdansk,不能采用德语名称 Danzig,译为"但泽",而应该译为"格但斯克"。华盛顿(Washington)、伦敦(London)都是根据其英语标准发音来翻译。譬如,意大利首都罗马 Roma 是根据意大利语发音来翻译的,而不能按照英语 Rome 翻译,法国首都 Paris 按照法语的发音译成"巴黎"。如果按照英语发音则应译为"巴黎斯";法国东南部城市里昂 Lyons,如果按照英语发音应为"莱恩斯";德国首都 Berlin 也是按照德语发音译成"柏林",只是发音与英语相似。

应用名从主人原则,还需注意以下具体情况:

①如果一国有两种或两种以上的官方语言,如比利时、瑞士、加拿大等,以每种语言的分布地区为转移来汉译。以比利时为例,有三种官方语言:北部地区的人用荷兰语,其地名以荷兰语发音汉译,如地名 Hoegaarden 译成"胡哈尔登";南部地区的人用法语,其地名按法语发音汉译,如 Hondelange 译成"翁德朗日";东南部与德国接壤部分的人用德语,其地名须按德语发音,如 Lommersweiler 译为"洛默尔斯韦勒"。又如南非,有 11 种官方语言,则应视其人名地名源于何种语言而翻译,如英语地名 Worcester 译为"伍斯特",南非语地名 Bloemfontein 译为"布隆方丹"。

②如果一国除官方语言外,还有在法律上享有自治权的少数民族语言,则应按少数民族语实际发音翻译。例如在西班牙,除西班牙语外,还有几种少数民族语。如东北部加泰罗尼亚自治区的地名应按加泰罗尼亚语音译,如 Puigcerda 译为"普奇塞达",Serchs 译成"塞尔克斯"。还有少数带有强烈外来语特征的人名地名,可按相应的外来语读音翻译,如以西班牙语为官方语言的智利,其英语地名 Cochrane 译为"科克伦",Isla Byron 译成"拜伦岛"。

③第三世界的不少国家,独立后的地名,不能按原宗主国的语言文字转译,只能按各国政府颁布的罗马字母转写方案或国际上较为通用的方案,以该国的官方语言或通用语言的标准语音为准音译。如非洲的"Botswana"应汉译成"博茨瓦纳",而不是原"Bechuanaland 贝专纳兰",其首都"Gaborone"应汉译成"哈博罗内",而不是原"Gaberones 加贝罗内斯"。

④有不少英语人名地名,即使拼写相同而读音在英国、美国、澳大利亚、加拿大却不一致,相应的译名也不一样。如 Greenwich 英国标音为[ˈgrinidʒ],译为"格林尼治";美国标音为[ˈgrinwitʃ],译为"格林威治"。Launceston 英国标音为[lɔːnstən],译为"朗斯顿",澳大利亚标音为[lɔːnsetən],译为"朗塞斯顿"等。对这些专名,需要括注其所属的国家或地区,以便区别。

⑤跨国度的河流、山脉、岛屿等,也按各国所用名称分别翻译。如欧洲一河名在法国拼写为 Escault,译为"埃斯科河";在比利时和荷兰却拼写为 Schelde,则译为"斯海尔德河"。如果原文名称的拼写及其发音各国之间差别不大,可采用统一的译名。有时还可以括号加注副名表示。如我国与尼泊尔之间的界峰,这样表示:珠穆朗玛峰(萨加玛塔峰)[中·尼] Qomolangma Feng(Sāgarmāthā Peak),Sāgarmāthā Peak(Qomolangma Feng)萨加玛塔峰(珠穆朗玛峰)[尼·中]。又如大洋洲的一岛屿,国际上通名是 New Guinea,属巴布亚新几内亚和印度尼西亚两国共有,而印度尼西亚却叫 Irian Pulau,所以汉译为"新几内亚岛(伊里安岛)"[巴布·印尼]。

⑥凡属国际共有的公海、海峡有两个不同名称的,以正副名括号加注表示。如英法之间的海峡 English Channel(La Manche)英吉利海峡(拉芒什海峡)[英·法],La Manche(English Channel)拉芒什海峡(英吉利海峡)[法·英]。

⑦凡属有领土争议的地区,双方都有各自的拼写名称,如南美洲东南有一群岛,为阿根廷与英国争议地,汉译时,也客观公正地表示为:Malvinas, Islas(Falkland Islands)马尔维纳斯群岛(福克兰群岛)[阿·英],Falkland Islands(Malvinas, Islas)福克兰群岛(马尔维纳斯群岛)[英·阿]。

(4)符合标准

首先是坚持国际标准。对世界各国的所有英语专名汉译时,都可根据尊重主人、尊重主权的国际原则,依据其主人、主权国的官方规定的或国际通用的罗马字母拼写或转写的标准形式,进行翻译。

英语专名汉译时,还必须依据中华人民共和国国家标准(GB/T 16159—1996)《汉语拼音正词法基本规则》(Basic Rules for HanyuPinyin Orthography)和《汉语拼音方案》,必须使用普通话的标准语音和规范的汉字译写英语人名地名和所有英语专名中的英语地名人名,必须始终实行国家的有关法规,坚持国家标准的原则。

地名翻译时,还必须依照翻译行业的标准。为了逐步克服外国地名译名的混乱现象,实现外国地名译写的统一和规范,我国于1977年成立了中国地名委员会。后来又成立了由新华通讯会等单位组成的外国地名译写小组,该小组制订出在全国试行的《外国地名汉字译写通则》和英、法、西、德、俄、阿拉伯语地名汉字译音表以及波、捷、罗、意、印地、波斯、阿姆哈拉语55种外语汉字译音表,先后编制了《外国地名译名手册》《美国地名译名手册》《德国地名译名手册》《苏联地名译名手册》,并组织人力审定了《世界地名录》等工具书。上述努力,初步结束了以往外国地名译写混乱局面,为译名规范化打下了良好基础。

地名的翻译可能涉及国家主权、政治立场。例如,不能把钓鱼岛称为"尖阁群岛",把肯尼亚称为"怯尼亚",把莫桑比克称为"莫三鼻给"等。地名翻译事关重大,应尽可能找到出处,请查工具书。

(5)约定俗成

"约定俗成"是指把人们经过长期实践而确定或形成的某种事物的名称、形式或某种社会习俗。而专名的翻译必然要受到译者所处的历史背景、文化氛围等因素的影响,反映出时代、文化特色。地名与语言里的其他词语一样,一经约定俗成,就代代相传。具有相对的稳定性。

有些地名的翻译经过前面几代人的传承,已经深入人心,广为接受,在翻译的时候,则可延续旧有翻译,以免另起炉灶,带来混乱。比如俄罗斯首都"莫斯科"(Moscow)是按英文音译的,如按俄文应为"莫斯克娃"(MOCKBA),但前者已约定俗成。Cambridge,一为美国马萨诸塞州内的一个地名,译为"坎布里奇"市,而另一为英国的地名,译为"剑桥"。又如San Francisco,一为河流名,译为"圣弗朗西斯科",另一为美国城市"旧金山"。

(6)同名同译

名从主人,理所当然应是同名同译。但因政治、历史、社会、文化等多种复杂原因,同名不同译的情况,屡见不鲜。同名不同译,哪怕只有两个,因客观存在只有一个,也会引起混乱。例如,德国东南部一州,一般地图按德语Bayern译为"拜恩州",《世界地图集》仍用这个译名,而报刊上却常按英语Bavaria译为"巴伐利亚州",现在的《世界地图集》也只好把同一州同时写上两个译名,英文及其译名作为副名括注于后。

欧洲的另一大河流经9个国家,德国和奥地利将其写为Donau,斯洛伐克写为Dunaj,匈牙利写为Duna,克罗地亚、南斯拉夫和保加利亚写为Dunav,罗马尼亚写为Dunărea,乌克兰语写为Dunai,常见的英语惯用名写为Danube。尽管写法不尽相同,但差别甚少,因此统一译为"多瑙河"。

有时不同地点(书写可能不同,读音相近或相同)译成同一汉名,这时需要注明各自的详情和特征,以便区分。如巴西的Sao Luis,阿根廷的San Luis和美国的Saint Louis汉名均为"圣路易斯"。而名为"圣地亚哥"的城市有四个:智利首都Santiago,美国城市San Diego(又名"圣迭戈"),古巴东南岸港市Santiago以及多米尼加的圣地亚哥省省会Santiago。对于异地同名者,翻译可注明国别,或译出该城市的全称(因命名来源不同,全称往往有别)。

(7)灵活处理

以下有些情况需要灵活处理。

①有些专名翻译时可以音意兼译。如 Cambridge 译成"剑桥",Casterbridge 译成"卡斯特桥"等。

②含有冠词的外国地名的翻译需要根据语种不同而定。西班牙语、法语、意大利语的人名地名中的冠词,汉译时采用音译。如西班牙语地名 La Paz 译为"拉巴斯",而自然地理实体名称中的冠词一般则省译,如西班牙语 Isla la Tortuga 译为"托尔图加岛",德语 Der Ruden 译为"鲁登岛"。阿拉伯语地名中的冠词,汉译时按传统习惯省译。如利比亚地名 Bir ash Shuwayrif 译为"比尔舒韦里夫"。

③有些地名含有连词成分,如 and(英语),i(塞尔维亚语),et(法语),y(西班牙语),e(葡萄牙语)。凡属国名和行政区划名称汉译时,中间一律加"和"字;一般居民点一律以连词符"-"表示。如 Trinidad and Tobago 译为"特立尼达和多巴哥",Kosovo i Metohija 译为"科索沃和梅托希亚",Vaux-et-Borset 译为"沃-博尔塞",archipelago de San Andrésy Providencia 译为"圣安德烈斯-普罗维登西亚群岛",São Tomée Príncipe 译为"圣多美和普林西比"。

④含有介词的地名汉译时,可以有如下处理方法。例如,Boulogne-sur-Mer 译为"滨海布洛涅",Castrillo de Duero 译成"杜罗河畔卡斯特里略",Kingston-upon-Hull 译为"赫尔河畔金斯顿"等。

值得注意的是,地名翻译涉及众多历史文化因素。例如韩国首都(Seoul)的中文译名由汉城改为首尔。首尔古时因位于汉江之北,得名"汉阳"。14 世纪末,朝鲜王朝定都汉阳后改名为"汉城"。1945 年朝鲜半岛光复后,更名为韩国语固有词,罗马字母标记为"Seoul",语意为"首都",汉语名为"首尔"。此后,世界上绝大多数国家都将"Seoul"按照与英文标记相似的发音来称呼。后来,时任汉城市长李明博提出将韩国首都中文译名变更为"首尔"。2005 年 10 月,我国民政部和外交部发出通报作出相应变更,中国各政府机关、商业部门以及中央电视台等许多新闻媒体和各类出版物,相继采用"首尔"这个名称,原名"汉城"译名不再使用。

地名翻译参考书目

[1]汉语拼音方案(1958 年 2 月 11 日第一届全国人民代表大会第五次会议通过).

[2]汉语拼音正词法基本规则　中华人民共和国国家标准(GB/T 16159—1996).

[3]关于改用汉语拼音方案拼写中国人名地名作为罗马字母拼写法的实施说明(1978.9.26.国务院转批).

[4]地名管理条例(1986 年 1 月 23 日国务院发布).

[5]新华通讯社译名室.世界人名翻译大辞典[D].北京:中国对外翻译出版公司,1993.

[6]世界地名翻译大辞典[M].北京:中国对外翻译出版公司,2014.

[7]中国地名委员会.外国地名译名手册[M].北京:商务印书馆,1983.

[8]中国地名委员会.外国地名译名手册　中型本[M].北京:商务印书馆,1993.

[9]中国地名研究所.外语地名汉字译名互查手册[M].北京:旅游教育出版社,2014.

[10]中国地名委员会.美国地名译名手册[M].北京:商务印书馆,1985.

[11]米来提·达依尔巴也夫.东亚、东南亚、南亚各国地名译名手册[M].乌鲁木齐:新疆人民出版社,2004.

[12]彭曦.日本常用姓名地名译名辞典[M].南京:南京大学出版社,2007.

[13]丛国胜.越南行政地名译名手册[M].北京:军事谊文出版社,2004.
[14]周俊英.新编俄罗斯地名译名手册[M].北京:商务印书馆,2003.
[15]中国地名委员会.苏联地名译名手册 上[M].北京:商务印书馆,1991.
[16]中国地名委员会.苏联地名译名手册 下[M].北京:商务印书馆,1991.
[17]李夜,周俊英合.俄汉地名形容词译名手册[M].北京:商务印书馆,2005.
[18]外国地名编译组.东南亚地名译名手册[M].北京:星球地图出版社,1996.
[19]中国地名委员会.联邦德国地名译名手册[M].北京:商务印书馆,1988.

三、术语的翻译

术语是准确地标志科学技术和社科领域的一定概念的词语,是反映科学技术和社科领域进步的特殊标记,用来记录和表述各种现象、过程、特征、关系、状态等不同名称。术语对自然现象或人类活动的描记。长期以来,我国科技术语大多参考或引自外来语,因此正确翻译术语具有十分重要的意义。

1.术语的特点

"术语是凝结一个学科知识系统的关键词"(郑述谱),它们准确地表达该学科领域的重要概念。每门学科都必须有自己的术语系统,如数学、化学、物理学、生物学、哲学、语言学等。在某种程度上,我们可以说每个学科都具有并且依赖一定数目的术语才成其为科学。术语和概念构成一个学科的骨架或架构。"没有术语就没有科学。"(侯国金,2009)由术语构成的知识框架是科学论著的必然构件,因此术语翻译就成为国际间学科交流的重要组成部分,对学科的发展具有重要的影响。

术语具有准确性、单义性、系统性、正确性、简明性、稳定性和能产性等特点。

(1)准确性

术语要确切地反映概念的本质特征。科学性就是从科学的概念出发,准确地反映所指事物的特征,根据概念的全部特征来掌握事物的内涵,即"名副其实"。

(2)单义性

至少在一个学科领域内,一个术语只表达一个概念;同一个概念只用同一个术语来表达(钱三强,1989),即理论上讲的"一词一义"。

(3)系统性

在一个特定领域中的各个术语,必须处于一个明确的层次结构之中,共同构成一个系统。如 close circuit television, large screen television, stereoscopic television,三词处于同一领域,构词的方式相同,均为"限定词+television",有一个明确的层次结构,形成词汇链。比如包含关系,而"数码电视机""液晶电视机"以及"背投电视机"形成并列的关系。"电视机"与上述三种形成上义词与下义词的关系。

(4)正确性

术语结构要符合该语言的构词法和组词规则。例如"柴油机",英语为 diesel engine,德语为 Diesel motor,两者中 diesel 均置前;而法语为 moteur Diesel,Diesel 置后,符合法语规则。

(5)简明性

术语要简明扼要,易读易记。中文特性是指术语翻译要体现汉语表意文字的特点,要"望文生义""顾名思义",中外文字不同,不能拘泥于外文。交流。比如"刻度"一词的意思是 gradual scale,但是在具体命名时只要使用 scale(刻度)就可以了。英语中把 Severe Acute

Respiratory Syndrome 通过使用首字母简化法简化为 SARS 就是一个很好的例证。这种利用首字母简化法化简的科学术语在西方语言中非常普遍。这既便于科技交流,也符合语言的经济规律。

(6)稳定性

术语一经定名,不轻易改动。例如 atom(原子),原指物质最小的不能分割的单元,后来证明 atom 是可以分割的,但术语依旧。有的词随着科学技术发展,词义自然变化。如 mineral 一词,源自拉丁文 mirn era(或 mineri),其意为矿山、矿山掘出物之总称。后来,词义范围缩小。

(7)能产性

术语还具有构词的能力。例如"电",可以组成"电话""电脑""电炉""电灯"等词语。英语也一样,比如 telephone 的词头 tele-可以用来组成 telegram,telescope,telecommunication 等词语。这就是科技术语的能产性原则。(冯志伟,1997:3)

2.术语与普通词汇

术语的来源有三种。一是通过新造而创建,例如 Clone 克隆、nanometer 纳米、autopilot 自动驾驶等。对于这部分新词,译者容易辨别。二是从非科技术语转化而来,即普通词汇的专业化。如:shield 原指古代战争中使用的"盾",现在多指一种开凿隧道的工具"盾构",但是在磁化工艺中通常译为"屏蔽";swan neck 转化为专业词汇应译为"鹅颈管"或者"弯管";carrier 其基本含义是"搬运工",其专业含义非常丰富:航空母舰(军事)、媒体(计算机)、刀架(机床)、搬运车(运输)、载波(航天)、带菌体(医学)、运载火箭(无线电)、载体(集成电路)、载流子(半导体)、运输机(航空)。三是利用固有的词或者语素,通过不同的构词方法(派生法、合成法、混成法、转化法等)构成新的科技术语。例如 wavelength(波长)、telesat(telecommunicationsatellite 通信卫星)、Internet(互联网、因特网)、soft landing(软着陆)等。

由日常生活中的各类普通名词,诸如人体器官名称、动植物名称、日常用具、食品以及人的称谓等,因为某方面的语义特征不断得到强化、广泛使用或者经过规定,往往能转变为专业术语,翻译时,需要准确区分这些普通词和术语。

语义特征	例 词	普通词义—专业词义	词的搭配举例	汉译
形状	ball banana butterfly crane	球—滚珠 香蕉—香蕉状物 蝴蝶—蝶形物 鹤—起重机	ball bearing banana pin butterfly nut arm crane	滚珠轴承 香蕉形插头 蝶形螺母 悬臂吊车
功能	carrier cushion distributor storage	搬运工—运载工具 垫子—缓冲器 分配器—配电盘 储藏—存储器	carrier rocket pneumatic cushion cable distributor file storage	运载火箭 气压式缓冲器 电缆配线架 外存储器
动作	grass-hopper monkey pecker worm	蚱蜢—跳动物 猴—打桩锤 啄木鸟—穿孔器 蚯蚓—螺旋,蜗杆	grass-hopper conveyor monkey driver automatic pecker auger worm	跳动式运输器 锤式打桩机 自动穿孔器 螺旋钻

续上表

语义特征	例 词	普通词义—专业词义	词的搭配举例	汉 译
性质	baby master mother sister	婴儿—小型物 主人—主导装置 母亲—母体 姐妹—同类型物	baby car master oscillator mother machine sister metal	小型汽车 主控振荡器 工作母机 同类型金诚
结构	sandwich tree wall bed	三明治—夹层结构 树—树枝物,分支结构 墙壁—器壁 床—底座	sandwich concrete tree system cylinder wall test bed	夹层混凝土 分支配电系统 汽缸壁 试验台

需要特别注意的是,一个术语,如果用在不同的学科和专业领域,其含义往往大相径庭,容易使人混淆,译者在处理时要加倍小心。

例如,shield 原来指用来防御敌人的刀枪等利器刺伤自己使用的叫作"盾"的兵器。可是在科学术语中它的含义不同,可以是一种用来开掘隧道的工具;在磁化工艺中又是一种"屏蔽";在采矿工艺中翻译成"铠装"或"掩护支架"等。所以,不能把它一概而论地翻译成"盾"。

再如英语的 shield 本来意思是"屏蔽"。可是在句子 It is the measure of most of its ceramic heat-shield tiles. 和 Almost any calamity ultimately would involve the breach of the heat shield and the breakup of the spacecraft. 中,shield 的译文就变化了。它们的译文分别是:这是航天飞机大多数陶瓷防热瓦的尺寸;几乎任何灾难最终都会涉及防热罩的破裂而使航天飞机崩裂。

Dog 本来是个普通名词,译为"狗",用在技术术语中,它有多种含义。在建筑学上的意思是"铆件";在机械工程领域又翻译成"齿轮栓";是机床上的"挡块"或"止动器";而在船上又是"(水密门的)夹扣"。另外,还有许多带有 dog 的科学术语,翻译时也应当特别留心,不要译错。例如:dogberry 山茱萸的果实;dog-box 铁路上运狗的车厢;dog-cart(单匹马拉的)马车;dog-fall(摔跤比赛的)平局;dog-paddle(狗爬式)游泳;dog-shore(船)(下水滑道的)抵键,(下水前用的)斜支柱;dog-spike(铁路上的)钩头道钉;dog's tooth(男子衣料的)格子花纹;dog-vane(桅杆上的)风向指示器等。

比如英语的 packing 通常是"包装"的意思。可是若这个词出现在句子 The function of the packing in this case is to provide a large interfacial area. 中,我们就不能把 packing 翻译成"包装",因为这里不是"包装"的意思。根据科学术语概念转换的方法可以判断出 packing 在这里有"填充"的意思,所以这里 packing 是"填料"的意思。所以全句应译为:在这种情况下填料的作用是提供一个较大的接触面积。

再举一例,英语的 bit 在不同专业中有不同的意思。在石油钻探中是"钻头",在机械加工业中是"车刀",在数学中是"二进位数",现在电脑中又有了"字节""存储单元"的意思。所以 bit 的概念内涵越来越多。可是在具体的上下文当中,bit 当然只能有一个准确的意思。

再如,英语的 container 是"容器"的意思。可是在不同专业中 container 也有不同的意思。虽然这些不同意思的术语都是由"容器"的基本含义引申来的,可是它已经发生了概念的变化,比如它可以是"水杯""油罐""锅炉"等。

vehicle 的意思是"运载工具",可是在不同领域也有"车辆""机动车""飞行器"等意思。

这就是科学术语翻译中根据逻辑判断进行的概念转换。

我们还有注意区分通俗词和术语在使用语境上的区别。专业文献采用严谨的文体,必须采用术语表述。正式程度较高的论文学术专著中,必须使用正规的术语。可是,术语对于普通大众读者来说,往往成了阅读的障碍。于是大众媒体常用解释性词语替代专业术语,以使读者一目了然。

意 义	术 语	通 俗 词
安乐死	euthanasia	physician assisted suicide/mercy killing
隆胸	augmentation mammoplasty	breast enlargemen timplants
隆鼻	augmentation rhinoplasty	nose reshaping
疯牛病	bovine spongiform encephalopathy(BSE)	mad cow disease

3. 术语翻译的基本方法

术语的翻译方法主要有直译、意译、音译、音意兼译、形译、创译等方法。

①直译。直译是指根据原词的实际含义译成对位的汉语术语。这种译法具有概念明确、简明易记的优点,被广泛用于术语的翻译中。例如,airline rework(航线网),celestial guidance(天体制导),earth orbit(地球轨道),orbiting station(轨道站),operating system(操作系统),multimedia(多媒体),NC(Numerical Control,数控),semiconductor(半导体),radio active isotopes(放射性同位素),guided missile(导弹),holograph(全息摄影),damping resistance(阻尼,阻力)等。

翻译时,分析词语的构成方式有助于确切定义。

codec=coder+decoder(编码译码器),cermet=ceramics+metal(金属陶瓷),insullac=insulation+lacquer(绝缘漆),astronics=astronomical+electronics(天文电子学),voder=voice operation demonstrator(语言合成专业术语)

如果译名太长,在不影响词义的情况下还可进一步简化。如 modem=调制解调器——解调器,transfer modling=传递模塑法——递模法。

掌握前缀、后缀的意义,对术语翻译也会有很大帮助,如 coaxial(同轴的,共轴),counteraction(反作用),superconductor(超导体),preheating(预热),telecommunication(电信),waterproof(防水的),noiseless(无噪声的),dust-free(无尘的)。

②意译。某些科技术语很难找到相对应的汉语词汇来表达,或者字面的翻译不足以表达其专业意义时,可以采用意译的方式,能够被广大读者和科技工作者接受的方式。例如:光学术语"narcissus effect"若按字面意义译为"水仙花效应",会让读者摸不着头脑,应该按意义改为"冷光效应";经贸术语"more or less clauses",如果直译为"或多或少条款",显得不够正式,应该改为"溢短装条款";"contact lens"译为隐形眼镜;"ejection seat"译为"喷射""喷出",若将其直译为"喷射座位",很可能会让人啼笑皆非,所以意译为"弹射座椅";"obstacle free zone"直译为"障碍自由区",恰恰与该术语的本意相悖,应意译为"无障碍区"。又如"error recovery"如果直译为"差错恢复",虽然字面上对应得工整,但在汉语中意思不明,其实原文的含义应对应于"恢复常态""差错排除"或"错后恢复"。译者在翻译时,要从定义中细心体会术语中各同语字面意义之外的隐含意义,并力求从大型辞书中得到印证。

③音译。即根据术语的发音,选择与发音相似的汉字作为该英语术语的汉语译名,以代表术语所表达的技术概念的一种翻译方法。这种用于音译的汉字不再有本身的原义,只保

留其语言和拼写形式。这种翻译方法多用于计量单位与新材料、新发现和新发明等术语,在汉语中还没有确切的对应词时,按照意译又比较冗长和麻烦时,就可以用音译法。如:quark 夸克,volt 伏特,gauss 高斯(磁场强度单位),joule 焦耳(功或能的单位),hertz 赫兹(频率单位),freon 氟利昂,skydrol 斯开德劳尔(耐火液压油)等。需要说明的是,有些采用音译的专业术语虽然已经为人们所熟悉和接受,却有许多后来被意译词代替,如:motor 马达—电动机、engine 引擎—发动机等。

④音意兼译。即在音译之后加一个表示类别的词,或者一部分音译,一部分意译。此类术语多为人名加原料或某种理论组成的术语。如:Holman orbit 霍曼轨道,Posson's constant 泊松系数,这类术语的翻译很好地实现了源语和目的语的对等,同时也反映了源语中的发明者、创造者的名字,也是对发明专利和发现的一种保护和尊重。还有的例子是:domino effect 多米诺效应,decibel 分贝,millibar 毫巴,kilovolt 千伏等。还有的"音义神结合"最为理想。例如 WWW(World Wide Web)译为"万维网",Hacker 译为黑客,gene 译为基因等术语翻译。其中,"维"是几何学及空间理论的基本概念,构成空间的每一个因素(如长、宽、高),"万维网"意为连接无数个小网的大网。三个"W"分别是"万""维""网"三字汉语拼音的开头字母。所以把 WWW 译为"万维网",可说是神音(形)兼备。又如,hacker 是指用非法手段进入他人的电子系统窃取秘密信息的人,译为"黑客",与源语发音相近,且令人联想起黑夜蒙面的盗贼,也是神音(形)兼备。

⑤形译。一些术语的前半部分用大写字母表示事物的形状,翻译时,应将这一部分译成能表示具体形象的汉字,或保留原来的字母,这种译法叫作形译。这样的翻译既生动形象,又明白准确,容易被广大读者和科技工作者理解和接受。如:X-axis X 轴,S-band S 波段,T-square 丁字尺,S-turning S 形弯道,C-network,I-beam 工字梁,cross-bar 横梁十字头,butterfly nut 蝶形螺母等。

⑥创译。根据原文中包含的某个音或所代表的某个概念来创造新词,但需要得到科学家或专家的认可。对于化学元素、医药和化学品等,可通过创造新词来进行翻译。如:ether 醚,titanium 钛。

⑦增译。有些英语术语,虽无"防"或"耐"等词语或者词素出现,但表示"防""耐"等意思,翻译时需要适当增加,以符合汉语的表达习惯。dusk mask 不能译为灰尘面罩,只能翻译成"防尘面罩"。fire engine 不能译为"火灾车",只能添加词语,译成"救火车"或"消防车"。wet strength 译为"耐湿强度",firebrick 译为"耐火砖",tear strength 译为"抗扯强度"等。

⑧转译。有些术语带有否定词缀的形容词,可以用汉语的肯定表达方式反译,另一些肯定表达的术语,却往往需要汉语的否定表达翻译;其主要目的是符合汉语表达规范。例如 undesired signal 不能翻译成"不希望的信号",而应译成"干扰信号",unenclosed construction 译为"敞开式结构",就是将否定表达转换为肯定表达。quiet circuit 译成"安静电路"不合汉语习惯,不如译为"无噪声电路"好;quiet hydraulic valve 译成"安静液压泵",读来感觉奇怪,不如译为"低噪声液压泵"符合实际。

译者在掌握上述翻译方法的基础上,还要注意术语翻译应该遵循的基本原则。一是尊重规范。只要所译术语在汉语中已有规范,译者就必须立足于现有的规范,不能另起炉灶。"尊重规范"不仅是因为规范所具有的权威性,而且还因为规范中术语的普适性。二是译名统一的原则。科学术语翻译的"统一性"(unification)是指在翻译科学术语时,为了避免出现不同人翻译同一术语可能出现译名不同的现象,科学术语翻译者要遵循统一规定的规范(或标准)。这样有利于科学研究事业的发展和教学的顺利进行,有利于科技文献的写作、编辑、出版、情报检索和术语数据库的建立。

请将下列篇章译为汉语,特别注意专有名词的翻译方法(小组翻译)。

Demography and Automation

Because of ageing, the world needs a robotics revolution. The machines don't seem ready for one.

When Gill Pratt sat down to discuss the job of running the Toyota Research Institute, the carmaker's new research division, his Japanese interviewers wrote one word on a piece of paper and asked him to talk about it. The word was dementia. That might seem a strange topic to put to one of the most respected figures in the world of robotics, a man who had previously run a competition to find artificially intelligent, semi-autonomous robots for the Pentagon. But, Mr Pratt says, the company's interest in ageing was a big reason for him to take the job. "The question for all of us", he says, "is, how can we use technology to make the quality of life better as people get older?"

Ageing and robots are more closely related than you might think. Young countries with many children have few robots. Ageing nations have lots. The countries with the largest number of robots per industrial worker include South Korea, Singapore, Germany and Japan, which have some of the oldest workforces in the world.

The connection does not merely reflect the fact that young countries tend to be poor and cannot afford fancy machines, which they do not need anyway. It holds good within rich countries, too. Those with relatively few robots compared with the size of their workforce include Britain and France, both of which (by rich-country standards) are ageing slowly.

Two recent studies quantify the connection. Daron Acemoglu of the Massachusetts Institute of Technology (MIT) and Pascual Restrepo of Boston University show that, between 1993 and 2014, the countries that invested the most in robotics were those that were ageing the fastest—measured as a rise in the ratio of people over 56 compared with those aged 26-55. The authors posit a rule of thumb: a ten-point rise in their ageing ratio is associated with 0.9 extra robots per thousand workers.

A study from Germany used different measures but reached the same conclusion. Ana Abeliansky of the University of Göttingen and Klaus Prettner of the University of Hohenheim found that the growth in the number of robots per thousand workers rises twice as fast as the fall in the growth rate of the population (ie, if population growth falls by 1%, the growth in robot density rises by 2%). Population growth is closely related to age structure.

These findings should not be surprising. Robots typically substitute for labour. That is why many people fear that they will destroy jobs. Countries with plenty of young workers do not need labour substitutes. Wages there also tend to be low, making automation unprofitable. But ageing creates demand for automation in two ways. First, to prevent output falling as more people retire, machines are necessary to substitute for those who have left the workforce or to enable ageing workers to continue to do physical labour. Second, once people have retired they create markets for new kinds of automation, including robots that help with the medical and other requirements of caring for people who can no longer look after themselves.

Automation is destiny

As a result, the connection between robots and ageing is a powerful one. Mr Acemoglu reckons that ageing is the biggest single influence upon how many robots a country has. He estimates it explains close to 40% of the variation in the numbers of robots countries introduce.

The influence will grow. This year, there will be more people over 65 than under five for the first time in human history. By 2060, the number of Americans over 65 will double, to 98m, while in Japan, 40% of the population will be 65 or older. There will not be enough younger people to look after so many, unless robots help (and probably an influx of migrants is permitted, too).

Shrinking and ageing workforces matter as much. China is now the world's largest robot maker, producing 137,900 industrial robots (typically, machines used in assembly lines) in 2017. Between 2015 and 2040, according to the UN, China's working-age population (aged 20 to 64) will fall by a staggering 124m, or over 13%. Applying Mr Acemoglu's rule of thumb to this decline, China would by the end of the period need to install roughly 2m more robots. That is more than four years' worth of all the industrial robots produced in the world in 2018 and six times as many as the increase in worldwide production over the past nine years.

Such problems loom even in countries ageing more slowly than China—such as Britain. Between 2016 and 2025, according to Mercer, a consultancy, the proportion of British workers who are under 30 will fall by four percentage points and that of over 50s will rise by ten points. That sounds manageable. But it masks big regional swings. In that period, London (which is relatively youthful) will see the share of its labour force under 30 fall by a quarter and the share over 50 rise even more.

That will put enormous pressure on some industries. A third of teachers and building workers in Britain are over 50, as are more than a third of health-care workers, farmers and lorry drivers. They are quitting in droves. A poll in 2015 found that a third of doctors planned to retire by 2020. And this is in a country whose ageing is relatively gentle. Automation is not the only way to deal with skills shortages (immigration and later retirement also help) but it is one of the most important.

Over the next few years, demography will change the kinds of robots people need, as well as increase the number in use. At the moment, the robotics market is dominated by industrial machines, the sort used to assemble cars or electrical equipment. Sales of industrial-robotics systems were $48bn in 2017, seven times as much as "service robots", a category that includes logistics robots for running warehouses, medical robots, robotic milking machines, exoskeletons that help people lift heavy objects and household robots that vacuum the floor.

As demographic change speeds up, service robots will become more important. One day, their makers hope, they will enable old people to live alone and stay mobile for longer. Robots will help assuage loneliness and mitigate the effects of dementia. They will make it easier to look after people in nursing homes and enable older workers who want to stay employed to keep up with the physical demands of labour. These robots will also be fundamentally different from industrial ones, which usually replace human activity—fitting a car windscreen, for example. By contrast, service robots extend it. For example, if an exoskeleton helps someone lift something heavy, the person still has to be there.

You can see the stirrings of this robot revolution most clearly in Japan. AIBO, a robotic puppy with artificial intelligence (AI) made by Sony, and Paro, a furry seal made by Japan's National Institute of Advanced Industrial Science and Technology, are therapeutic robots for children and patients with dementia. Pepper, made by SoftBank, is a humanoid robot which can carry out conversations on a limited range of topics, so long as its human interlocutor does not stray too far from the script. MySpoon is a robot for those who cannot feed themselves. HAL, by Cyberdyne and Muscle Suit, by Innophys, are exoskeletons, helping nurses pick up and carry patients (HAL stands for hybrid-assistive limb). Panasonics' Resyone is a robotic bed that transforms itself into a wheelchair. And so on.

Demand for these gizmos is growing fast, if from a low base. Sony said it had sold 11,111 AIBOs in the three months after the new model went on sale in January 2018. Japan's government reckons that 8% of nursing homes now have lifting robots, and its national robot strategy (every country should have one) calls for four-fifths of the elderly receiving care to have some care provided by a robot by 2020.

For the time being, though, the technology remains a long way from transformative. According to the International Federation of Robotics, an estimated 20,000 robots were sold in 2018 that could realistically be described as helpful for ageing (medical robots, handicap assistance, exoskeletons and the like). That is less than 5% of industrial robots.

The number will doubtless grow. The question is how quickly. Mr Pratt is optimistic. Over the past five years, he argues, there have been huge advances in artificial intelligence, enabling machines to surpass humans in certain kinds of information-processing, notably pattern recognition which (within limits) robots can perform more quickly and reliably than humans. New firms are pouring into the business. A third of robot companies are less than six years old and make service robots. The costs of research and development are coming down and investment is rising. Within a decade, Mr Pratt reckons, domestic robots will help people cook at home and car-guidance systems will keep them mobile for longer.

Machine learning

But for that to happen, robots will have to perform a dauntingly long list of things they cannot yet do. They cannot navigate reliably around an ordinary home, move their hands with human dexterity, or conduct open-ended conversations. Although they can provide some physical assistance to the elderly, one robot can do only one thing, so multiple tasks would require your home to be stuffed with machines.

Their pattern recognition is not 100% reliable. One image classifier could not tell the difference between a snow plough and an overturned school bus. Robots struggle to operate on the basis of incomplete information, or to adapt to novelty as quickly as humans do. Driverless cars are proving harder to develop than most people expected. Rodney Brooks, a professor at MIT, reckons that driverless services comparable to those offered by conventional taxis are unlikely before 2032. Google's Duplex, an AI-enabled personal assistant launched in 2018, can so far make appointments only for hair salons and restaurants. All this suggests that, as solutions to the problems of ageing, robots have some way to go.

  Their limitations have significant implications. Robots that make the end of life more bearable are likely to remain expensive for many years, so only rich people will buy them. That may limit their wider social acceptance. Companies may not be able to automate their way out of future skills shortages. Other responses, such as raising wages, attracting more women into paid work and allowing more migration, will be just as important. Last, there may be room for the expansion of global supply chains, as work shifts from ageing China and other middle-income countries, to Africa and poorer places with more labour. Ageing demands a robotics revolution but it may be slow to arrive.

(1794 words)

第七章

修辞、文化与翻译

Notre Dame: The Human Spark

"What is civilisation?" asked Kenneth Clark 50 years ago in the seminal BBC series on the subject. "I Don't know, and I can't define it in abstract terms, yet. But I think I can recognise it when I see it, and I'm looking at it now." And he turned to gesture behind him, at the soaring Gothic towers and flying buttresses of Notre Dame.

It seems inhuman to care more about a building than about people. That the sight of Notre Dame going up in flames has attracted so much more attention than floods in southern Africa which killed over 1,000 arouses understandable feelings of guilt. Yet the widespread, intense grief at the sight of the cathedral's collapsing steeple is in fact profoundly human—and in a particularly 21st-century way.

It is not just the economy that is global today, it is culture too. People wander the world in search not just of jobs and security but also of beauty and history. Familiarity breeds affection. A building on whose sunny steps you have rested, in front of which you have taken a selfie with your loved one, becomes a warm part of your memories and thus of yourself.

This visual age has endowed beauty with new power, and social media have turned great works of art into superstars. Only a few, though, have achieved this status. Just as there is only ever a handful of world-famous actors, so the pantheon of globally recognizable cultural symbols is tiny: the Mona Lisa, Michelangelo's David, the Taj Mahal, the Great Pyramid—and Notre Dame. Disaster, too, is visual. In the 24 hours after the fire started videos on social media of the burning cathedral were viewed nearly a quarter of a billion times.

(291 words)

佳译赏析

Beauty(Excerpt)

英 语 文 本	汉 语 文 本
Beauty (excerpt) Scott Russel Sanders	论美(节选) 司各特·罗素·桑德斯 集体讨论,贾文波执笔
Judging from the scientists I know, including Eva and Ruth, and those whom I've read about, you can't pursue the laws of nature very long without bumping into beauty. "I Don't know if it's the same beauty you see in the sunset," a friend tells me, "but it feels the same." This friend is a physicist, who has spent a long career deciphering what must be happening in the interior of stars. He recalls for me this thrill on grasping for the first time Dirac's equations describing quantum mechanics, or those of Einstein describing relativity. "They're so beautiful," he says, "you can see immediately they have to be true. Or at least on the way toward truth." I ask him what makes a theory beautiful, and he replies, "Simplicity, symmetry, elegance, and power."	我认识的(包括伊娃和鲁思认识的)和书中读到的科学家们都认为,只要去探寻自然法则,不用多久,必有与美邂逅的一天。"那种美,"用我一位朋友的话来说,"不知能否与夕阳晚照媲美,但感受绝对是一样的。"我的这位物理学家朋友,为破解星体内部之谜耗去了大半辈子的光阴。回想初次顿悟量子力学狄拉克方程式或爱因斯坦相对论所带给他的那份狂喜,他会说:"真是太美了!一看就知道那必是真理,或至少接近真理。"当问及何谓理论之美,答曰:"简洁、对称、典雅、力量。"
Why nature should conform to theories we find beautiful is far from obvious. The most incomprehensible thing about the universe, as Einstein said, is that it's comprehensible. How unlikely, that a short-lived biped on a two-bit planet should be able to gauge the speed of light, lay bare the structure of an atom, or calculate the gravitational tug of a black hole. We're a long way from understanding everything, but we do understand a great deal about how nature behaves. Generation after generation, we puzzle out formulas, test them, and find, to an astonishing degree, that nature agrees. An architect draws designs on flimsy paper, and her buildings stand up through earthquakes.	大自然为何与我们所见之"美的理论"这般吻合?个中道理尚不得而知。然而,如爱因斯坦所言,宇宙之妙就在于其最不可知者其实可知。试想,在一颗丁点儿大的星球上,一群生命不长的两足动物竟能测定光速、解构原子、计算黑洞引力,是何等的不可思议!诚然,知晓世间万物尚远非人力所及,但自然界的活动规律,的确被人类弄清了许多。一代又一代,人类推导出的各种公式定理,几经验证,竟发现与自然界惊人的一致;建筑师在薄纸上绘制出的建筑蓝图,建成后竟能经地震而屹立不倒。
We launch a satellite into orbit and use it to bounce messages from continent to continent. The machine on which I write these words embodies hundreds of insights into the workings of the material world, insights that are confirmed by every burst of letters on the screen, and I stare at that screen through lenses that obey the laws of optics first worked out in detail by Isaac Newton.	人类将卫星送入空间轨道,便可在地球各大洲传递信息;我用来打字的这台电脑,同样是人类千百次探索与认知物质世界的结晶,眼前跳现于荧屏上的一个个字母就是最好的例证;而我的双眼透过镜片凝视荧屏,这镜片又是遵循艾萨克·牛顿当年阐释的光学原理研制而成。
By discerning patterns in the universe, Newton believed, he was tracing the hand of God. Scientists in our day have largely abandoned the notion of a Creator as an unnecessary hypothesis, or at least an untestable one. While they share Newton's faith that the universe is ruled everywhere by a coherent set of rules, they cannot say, as scientists, how these particular rules came to govern things. You can do science without believing in a divine Legislator, but not without believing in laws.	牛顿认为,认知宇宙结构模式,乃探索上帝造物之谜。而当今之科学家们,早已将造物主一说抛至脑后,视其为虚妄假说,或至少认为它无从验证。他们虽认同牛顿的观点,认为宇宙万物无处不由一套连贯严整的法则来主宰,但作为科学家,却又讲不出这些特定法则是如何统领天地万物的。从事科学研究可不信上帝立法之说,但绝不可不信其法则的存在。

英 语 文 本	汉 语 文 本
I spent my teenage years scrambling up the mountain of mathematics. Midway up the slope, however, I staggered to a halt, gasping in the rarefied air, well before I reached the heights where the equations of Einstein and Dirac would have made sense. Nowadays I add, subtract, multiply, and do long division when no calculator is handy, and I can do algebra and geometry and even trigonometry in a pinch, but that is about all that I've kept from the language of numbers. Still, I remember glimpsing patterns in mathematics that seemed as bold and beautiful as a skyful of stars.	青少年时,我曾攀登过数学之峰。然而,行至半山,距爱因斯坦和狄拉克理论之巅尚遥不可及之地,便已步履蹒跚,胸闷气短,气喘吁吁而颓然止步了。如今,手头虽无计算器,我也能加、减、乘、除(甚至做多位数长除法),必要时还会做代数、几何和三角一类的运算。但就数字符号而言,就已穷尽我毕生所学了。至今我仍记得,一瞥之下,那些数学图式恰如漫天繁星闪烁,曾是那般美丽而耀眼。
I'm never more aware of the limitations of language than when I try to describe beauty. Language can create its own loveliness, of course, but it cannot deliver to us the radiance we apprehend in the world, any more than a photograph can capture the stunning swiftness of a hawk or the withering power of a supernova. Eva's wedding album holds only a faint glimmer of the wedding itself. All that pictures or words can do is gesture beyond themselves toward the fleeting glory that stirs our hearts. So I keep gesturing.	直到用语言描绘美,我才深感语言的贫乏与无奈。语言固然能创自身之美,却无法言传人们在世间感悟的那番美的意境,这恰如照片不能捕捉飞鹰掠天的惊人迅疾与超新星爆耀的慢人威力一样,伊娃的新婚相册,也不过是整个婚礼淡淡的一瞥。照片也好,文字也罢,要表达那种动人心魄、稍纵即逝的辉煌之美,充其量不过是"比划"一下而已!因而,我只好在这儿跟着"比画"下去了。
"All nature is meant to make us think of paradise," Thomas Merton observed. Because the Creation puts on a nonstop show, beauty is free and inexhaustible, but we need training in order to perceive more than the most obvious kinds. Even 15 billion years or so after the Big Bang, echoes of that event still linger in the form of background radiation, only a few degrees above absolute zero. Just so, I believe, the experience of beauty is an echo of the order and power that permeate the universe. To measure background radiation, we need subtle instruments; to measure beauty, we need alert intelligence and our five keen senses.	托马斯·默顿曾感言:"天地万物欲使我们想到天堂。"上天造物,生生不息,犹如连番上演的舞台剧,美亦展示得无拘无束、无穷无尽。若要从最显见的物类中获得更多美的感悟,则须经专门训练。即使在宇宙大爆炸的一百五十亿年后,其反射仍以背景辐射的形式,略略徘徊于绝对零度之上。正因为此,人们对美的体验,实则是对宇宙间无处不在的秩序与力量的回应。测量背景辐射,要有精巧的仪器;体验美,则需机敏的智能与敏锐的五官了。
Anyone with eyes can take delight in a face or a flower. You need training, however, to perceive the beauty in mathematics or physics or chess, in the architecture of a tree, the design of a bird's wing, or the shiver of breath through a flute. For most of human history, the training has come from elders who taught the young how to pay attention. By paying attention, we learn to savor all sorts of patterns, from quantum mechanics to patchwork quilts. This predilection brings with it a clear evolutionary advantage, for the ability to recognize patterns helped our ancestors to select mates, find food, avoid predators. But the same advantage would apply to all species, and yet we alone compose symphonies and crossword puzzles, carve stone into statues, map time and space.	凡眼见于俏脸、鲜花,无人不觉赏心悦目。然而,要参透数学、物理或棋弈之美,欣赏树之有形、鸟之翼趣,乃至对长笛奏出的悠悠颤音心领神会,则必经专门训练方可体味。在人类大部分历史上,这种训练就是学会如何观察,历来由长者教之于幼者。通过观察,人类学会鉴赏天地万化之模式,从量子力学到百纳被无所不包。此痴情所至,亦使人类在进化过程中占尽先机,能辨万化之象,有助于先人们择偶、觅食、逃避猛兽。按理,同一进化优势本应造福世间一切物种,然唯独人类能谱出交响曲、制作填字游戏、创造石雕艺术、标示时空天体。
Have we merely carried our animal need for shrewd perceptions to an absurd extreme? Or have we stumbled onto a deep congruence between the structure of our minds and the structure of the universe?	那么,是人类为获敏锐的感知而一味将其动物的本能需求推向了乖戾之极致,还是人脑构造与宇宙天体碰巧契合呢?

英语文本	汉语文本
I am persuaded the latter is true. I am convinced there's more to beauty than biology, more than cultural convention. It flows around and through us in such abundance, and in such myriad forms, as to exceed by a wide margin any mere evolutionary need. Which is not to say that beauty has nothing to do with survival: I think it has everything to do with survival. Beauty feeds us from the same source that created us. It reminds us of the shaping power that reaches through the flower stem and through our own hands. It restores our faith in the generosity of nature. By giving us a taste of the kinship between our own small minds and the great Mind of the Cosmos, beauty reassures us that we are exactly and wonderfully made for life on this glorious planet, in this magnificent universe. I find in that affinity a profound source of meaning and hope. A universe so prodigal of beauty may actually need us to notice and respond, may need our sharp eyes and brimming hearts and teeming minds, in order to close the circuit of Creation.	后一说法令我信服。我相信，美之契合甚于生物进化，更甚于文化习俗，它流经我们身边、贯通我们心灵，其内涵之丰富、形态之多样，大大超越了人类起码的进化需求。当然，这并非说美与生存无关，恰恰相反，它们之间可谓息息相通。美用人类生命之源滋养人类，使我们想起了经由花茎与人的双手产生的创造力。美恢复了人类对大自然慷慨富有的信念，唤起了渺小人类与浩瀚宇宙心灵间的亲缘感应。美使我们深信，如此妙绝天成的人类，原本就是为这煌煌星球、泱泱宇宙应运而生的。从这一天缘巧合中，我悟出那种深长的蕴意与博大的希望。一个流芳溢美的大千世界，兴许真要我们对它处处留意并做出回应，需要我们用敏锐的双眼、充沛的情感、博大的胸怀，去沟通人类与大自然的交流和循环，使之周而复始、生生不息。

认知升级

一、修辞与翻译

修辞格（Figure of speech, Rhetorical device）是人们在长期的语言交际过程中，在本民族语言特点的基础上，为提高语言表达效果而形成的格式化的方法、手段。修辞格是提高语言表达效果的语言艺术，它能使语言生动形象、具体活泼，给人以美的享受。

修辞格可以分为三类：音韵修辞格（phonological），如拟声等；词义修辞格（semantic）如比喻、拟人等；句法修辞格（syntactical），如排比、对偶等。

中文的辞格大致有20多种[1]：比喻、比拟、借代、拈连、夸张、双关、仿词、反语、婉曲、设疑、对偶、排比、层递、顶真、回环、对比、映衬、反复、设问、反问、引用、拟声等。

英文修辞格也有20多种[2]：Simile, Metaphor, Analogy, Personification, Hyperbole, Understatement, Euphemism, Metonymy, Synecdoche, Antonomasia, Pun, Syllepsis, Zeugma, Irony, Innuendo, Sarcasm, Paradox, Oxymoron, Antithesis, Epigram, Climax, Anti-climax, Apostrophe, Transferred Epithet, Alliteration, Onomatopoeia等。

可以看出，英汉两种语言中既有相类似的常用修辞格，如Personification 拟人，Zeugma 拈连，Punning 双关，Parallelism 排比，Euphemism 婉曲，Rhetorical Question 反问，Onomatopoeia 拟声，Irony 反语等。

英汉两种语言中的修辞格又有各自的特点。例如，英语中常用而汉语中罕用或不用的修辞格有 Oxymoron、Paradox、Alliteration、Transferred Epithet（移就）等。汉语中常用而英语中

---

[1] 黄伯荣，廖序文.现代汉语（增订五版）.北京：高等教育出版社，2011.
[2] 冯翠华.英语修辞格.北京：商务印书馆，1983.

少用的修辞格,如顶真、回环、歇后语、镶字、析字、析词、联边等。此外,汉语中的修辞格夸张,在英语中为 hyperbole 和 understatement 两种形式,前者是夸大,后者是缩小。汉语中的比喻在英文中则分为 Simile, Metaphor, Metonymy 三种。

涉及修辞格的翻译方法有四种:直译法、意译法、替换法以及增译法。

1.直译法 A→A

对近似的辞格,尽可能直译,保留原有辞格,以使语言生动活泼,保留语言的风格特色。一般来说,句法修辞如对偶、排比等均能直译。

例1 The pen is to a writer what the gun is to a fighter.
作家的笔犹如战士的枪。

例2 Jane's uncle is an old fox, up to all kinds of evils.
简的叔叔是个老狐狸,什么坏事都干得出来。

例3 How soon hath Time, the subtle thief of youth, stolen on his wing my three and twentieth year! (John Milton)
时间,这个盗窃青春的狡猾的小偷,盗窃了我二十又三年飞走了。

例4 Paper and ink cut the throats of men, and the sound of a breath many shake the world. (= written words; speech)
纸墨能割断人的喉管,嗓音能震动整个世界。(纸墨=写几个字;嗓音=说几句话)

例5 His brother is a disturber of the piano keys.
他哥哥是一个跟钢琴键找麻烦的人。

例6 In the examination, the boy threw a nervous glance at the teacher, who was obviously suspicious of his cheating.
在考场上,那个男孩用紧张的眼光瞥了老师一眼,老师显然怀疑到他在作弊。

2.意译法或省译法 A→0

对一些不可译或者翻译难度极大的辞格,可以摒弃修辞格的形式,阐释其大意即可。此种译法有损原文之美。

例1 No X in Nixon.
尼克松心中没有谜。(这是有人对美国前总统尼克松的赞语。)

例2 Able was I ere I saw Elba.
在我看到厄尔巴岛之前,我曾所向无敌。(这是拿破仑被流放到厄尔巴岛时的豪言,原文使用了回环的修辞方法。翻译起来极度困难,采用意译,阐释其意思,而放弃其形式。)

3.替换法 A→B

如果某一修辞格难度较大,可以换用其他辞格,以达到类似的修辞效果,此法具有异曲同工之妙。

例1 He is all fire and fight.
他怒气冲冲,来势汹汹。(原文使用修辞 Alliteration,译文换用对偶的四字格译出,且押韵,保留了修辞效果。)

例2 The sixth sick sheik's sixth sheep's sick.
四只狮子私吃四十只涩柿子。(赵彦春译)

例3 Peter Piper picked a pack of pickled peppers.
吃葡萄不吐葡萄皮,不吃葡萄偏吐葡萄皮。

例4 —The professor rapped on his desk and shouted:"Gentlemen,order!"
—The entire class yelled:"Beer!"
译文1:—教授敲了敲讲桌,大声问道:"同学们,我们上什么?"
—全班同学大叫:"上啤酒。"
译文2:—教授敲了敲讲桌,大声问道:"先生们,吆喝什么(要喝什么)?"
—全班同学大叫:"要喝啤酒。"

例5 Better late that the late.
译文1.晚了总比完了好。(译文中用谐音替换原文的双关)
译文2.宁迟一时,不迟一世。(用对偶换双关。)

例6 A:It's an order from President Bush.
B:I Don't care if it is from bush,tree or grass.
译文1.这是布什总统的命令。
管他什么布什、布头、布片呢,与我无关。
译文2.这是布什总统的命令。
我才不管他什么布十、布七、还是布一呢。

4.增益法 0→A

原文本无修辞格,可以根据翻译目的和译文读者需要,无中生有,添加修辞格,以加强修辞效果,美化译文。

例1 I repair to the enchanted house, where there are lights, chattering, music, flower, officers, and the eldest Miss Larkins, a blaze of beauty.
我现在朝着那家仙宫神宇走去,那儿灯光辉煌、人声嘈杂、乐音悠扬、花草缤纷、军官纷来(这是我看着极为心痛的),还有拉钦大小姐,简直是仪态万方、丰姿千状。(张谷若译)

例2 The mayor of Toledo said in 1932:"I have seen thousands of these defeated, discouraged, hopeless men and women, cringing and fawning as they come to ask for public aid. It is a spectacle of national degradation." (W. Manchester: The Glory and the Dream)
译文1.托莱多市长在1932年说过:"我见到数千万遭受了挫折的、失去了信心和希望的男人和女人又奉承又乞怜地前来请求救济。这么一个情景给国家丢了脸。"
译文2.托莱多市长在1932年说过:"我见到成千上万的山穷水尽、灰心绝望的男男女女前来请求救济。他们低声下气,苦苦哀求。此情此景,真是丢尽了美国的脸。"

例3 Dairyman Crick's household of maids and men lived on comfortably, placidly, even merrily.
克里克老板牛奶厂里的男男女女,都过得舒舒服服、平平静静,甚至于还嬉嬉笑笑、闹闹嚷嚷。

修辞翻译的原则不妨总结如下:功力深厚,尽量直译;灵活变通,采用替换;无计可施,选择意译;美化译文,不妨增益。

例1 He is as tight as a drum.

译文1.他像鼓一样紧。

译文2.他非常吝啬,不肯花钱。

译文3.他像只铁公鸡,一毛不拔。

例2 "Mine is a long and a sad tale!"said the Mouse,turning to Alice and sighing. "It is a long tail,certainly,"said Alice,looking down with wonder at the Mouse's tail; "but why do you call it sad?"(L.Carroll:Alice's Adventures in Wonderland)

译文1."我的故事说来真是又长又伤心!"耗子转向爱丽丝叹口气说。"你的尾确实很长,"爱丽思惊奇地朝下看着耗子尾巴说,"可是干吗说它伤心呢?"

译文2.那老鼠对着爱丽丝叹了口气道,"唉!我的身世说来可真是又长又苦又委屈呀!"

爱丽丝听了,瞧着那光滑的尾巴说,"你这尾是曲呀!可是你为什么又叫它苦呢?"(赵元任)

例3 On Sunday,they pray for you and on Monday they prey on you.

译文1.周日他们祈祷你,周一他们吃掉你。(曹顺发)

译文2.星期天他们祈祷你的幸福,星期一他们欺盗你的财产。(廖七一)

译文3.今天他们祈福你,明天他们欺负你。(杨全红)

例4 If we Don't hang together,we shall most assuredly hang separately.(Benjamin Franklin)(美国富兰克林可称一代语言大师。在其诸多妙语中,本句富兰克林在《独立宣言》上签名时说的那句话,采用双关的修辞格,妙用两个hang。本句在翻译界有诸多讨论)。

译文1.我们要是不抱在一起,保准会吊到一起。

译文2.我们必须共同上战场,要不就得分别上刑场。

译文3.我们必须共赴沙场,否则就会分赴杀场。

例5 It was a splendid population,for all the slow,sleepy,sluggish-brained sloths stayed at home.

译文1.那是一批卓越的人——那些慢慢吞吞、昏昏沉沉、反应迟钝、形如树懒的人都留在了家乡。

译文2.那是一批卓越能干的人——因为所有那些行动迟缓、头脑愚钝、睡眼惺忪、呆如树懒的人都待在家乡了。

译文3.这帮人个个出类拔萃——因为凡是呆板、呆滞、呆头呆脑的呆子都待在了家里。(马红军)

译文4.这帮人个个出类拔萃——因为凡是懒散、懒惰、懒洋洋的树懒(懒汉,懒虫)都赖在了家里。(罗天)

例6 Able was I ere I saw Elba.

我在看到厄尔巴岛以前是强有力的。(钱歌川)

不见棺材不掉泪,不到厄岛我不倒。(许渊冲)

落败孤岛孤败落,若非孤岛孤非弱。(马红军)

例7 I love my love with an E, because she's enticing; I hate herewith an E, because she's engaged; I took her to the sign of the exquisite, and treated her with an elopement; her name's Emily, and she lives in the east. (Charles Dickens: David Copperfield)

本短话出自狄更斯小说《大卫·科波菲尔》第二十二章，这是一段令译者颇感棘手的文字游戏。这段话翻译的难度较高，看似无解。但是，它吸引了众多译家一试身手，历经演化的译文最终不仅较好地传达了原文的意义，而且在修辞效果上有过之而无不及。

译文1.我爱我的爱人为了一个E，因为她是Enticing（迷人的）；我恨我的爱人为了一个E，因为她是Engaged（订了婚了）。我用我的爱人象征Exquisite（美妙），我劝我的爱人从事Elopement（私奔），她的名字是Emily（爱弥丽），她的住处在East.（东方）。（董秋斯）

译文2.我爱我的爱，因为她长得实在招人爱。我恨我的爱，因为她不回报我的爱。我带着她到挂着浮荡子招牌的一家，和她谈情说爱。我请她看一出潜逃私奔，为的是我能和她长久你亲我爱。她的名字叫爱弥丽，她的家住在爱仁里。（张谷若）

译文3.吾爱吾爱，因伊可爱；吾恨吾爱，因伊另有所爱。吾视吾爱，神圣之爱，吾携吾爱，私逃为爱；吾爱名爱米丽，吾东方之爱。（中国翻译杂志）

译文4.我爱我的那个"丽"，可爱迷人有魅力；我恨我的那个"丽"，要和他人结伉俪；她文雅大方又美丽，和我私逃去游历；她芳名就叫爱米丽，家住东方人俏丽。（马红军）

译文5.爱她也为一个"人"，魅力无边迷死人；恨她也为一个"人"，错订终身许他人。满眼看她是完人，带她私奔瞒众人。她叫爱弥丽好可人，家住东边想煞人。（马红军）

译文6.我爱我的那个"丽"，落落大方真美丽；我恨我的那个"丽"，要和他人结伉俪；我的心里她最靓丽，带她私奔路迤逦；她名字就叫爱弥丽，家在东方好瑰丽。（马红军）

二、文化与翻译

翻译不仅是一项双语活动，也是一种跨文化活动。文化在翻译中的作用不可低估。王佐良说过："翻译者必须是一个真正意义的文化人"[1]。

"文化"这个概念，使用率颇高，然而要下一个简单而明确的定义，却非易事。文化是人类社会特有的产物，是有关人类社会知识体系、思想品德、思维模式等一系列活动的综合体，是人类创造的共同财富。文化具体可以划分为物质、制度及观念这三个层面，物质文化与人类的现实生活有着密不可分的关系，比如建筑、雕塑等就是物质文化的重要代表；制度文化与各种规范息息相关，比如礼仪、法律制度等是制度文化的典型代表；观念文化与思维息息相关，比如审美意识、宗教信仰等都是有代表性的观念文化。

Tylor(1871:1)对文化的定义是："Culture, or civilization, taken in its broad, ethnographic sense, is that complex whole which includes knowledge, belief, art, morals, law, custom, and any

---

[1] 王佐良.翻译中的文化比较.中国翻译,1984(1):2.

other capabilities and habits acquired by man as a member of society". 根据 Harris & Moran (1996) that culture is "a set of knowledge, beliefs, values, religion, customs, acquired by a group of people and passed on from generation to generation."

语言与文化的关系密不可分。一方面,语言是文化的一部分,属于制度文化,受到文化长期的沁润和影响;另一方面,文化需要语言来表达,文化因语言的表达而变得生动、丰富、具体可见。

中西文化之间存在着差异,可以体现在地理环境、社会习俗、宗教信仰、历史典故等多方面。这些差异可以在各自的语言上反映出来,并且对英汉翻译过程中的语义理解和传达产生一定的干扰和影响。因此在英汉翻译活动中,必须要考虑到中西文化差异的问题,从各自文化的角度充分理解原文的含义,并采取适当的语义表达方式,精确地译出原文。

例如,地理环境的不同会引起文化上的个性和差异,形成一些独特的文化概念并会体现在语言中。例如,中国东临大海,西部为高山,所以在中国,"东风"是"春天的风","西风"却是凛冽的。而英国的地理环境与中国不同,英国西临大西洋,报告春天消息的却是西风。西风在英国人心中是温暖宜人的。英国著名诗人雪莱的《西风颂》就是对温暖西风的讴歌:"It's a warm wind, the west wind, full of bird's cries."在英汉翻译时,要充分理解这些差异,才能更好地理解原文。再如,英国的天气变化无常,所以人们见面喜欢谈论天气。而中国人见面打招呼则会说:"去哪儿啊?""吃饭了吗?"

中西文化的历史背景也会反映在语言中。在英语中,与 Dutch 有关的词语往往带有贬义。例如以下短语和句子:Dutch act(自杀);Dutch courage(酒后之勇);I got mad and I talk like a Dutch uncle(我勃然大怒,于是就严厉地训人);If it is the fact, I'm a Dutchman(如果这是事实,我就不是人)等。这是因为在 17 世纪初,英国和荷兰曾经激烈交战二十多年,使英国大伤元气,所以英国普通民众对荷兰人不含好感。这些历史原因导致英语中有关 Dutch 有关的词语具有贬义。

在社会风俗习惯方面。欧美人和中国人也存在很多差异。同一件事物,来自不同的文化背景,人们的看法大相径庭。比如,龙是古代汉族人崇拜的图腾,象征着吉祥、尊贵、权势和奋发向上。我们自称是龙的传人,意思是一个伟大而杰出的民族。龙象征皇帝,凤象征皇后。在汉语中,有关龙、凤的词语大都是褒义的,如藏龙卧虎、龙飞凤舞、生龙活虎、龙凤呈祥等。但是在英语中,dragon 却是具有破坏性的喷火的怪兽,通常含有贬义。根据《圣经》记载,与上帝作对的恶魔撒旦被称为 the Great Dragon,dragon 在西方被看作是邪恶的象征,在现代英语中,dragon 用以指"凶暴的人"或"严厉透顶的人"。例如说 She is a bit of dragon around this place. (她是一个专横跋扈的人)。凤在中国被视为是百鸟之王,还被比作出类拔萃的人,如"山窝里飞出了金凤凰"。而在西方传说中,phoenix 是一种鸟,在沙漠生活了五六百年后将自己烧成灰烬,又从中诞生出一只新的 phoenix,所以在英语中 phoenix 有再生、复活、浴火重生的意思。

中西文化的历史渊源不同,宗教信仰不同,典故的来源不同,也会对英汉翻译造成一定的影响。对中国影响深远的是佛教、道教和儒家伦理文化。英美人大多信仰基督教,《圣经》文化,希腊、罗马神话对英美文化和社会的影响比较深刻久远。如中国人说"菩萨保佑",西方人则说 God bless you(上帝保佑你);中国人说"天知道",西方人则说 God knows(上帝才知道)。还有不少典故、谚语,如中国的成语典故中有"叶公好龙""空城计""东施效颦"等,多来自中国古代的文学名著。而西方人会讲 He's a Shylock. (他是个守财奴),a Pandora's box

(潘多拉之盒), That's all Greek to me.(我对此一窍不通)。这些西方谚语、典故,都源于莎士比亚作品和希腊罗马神话。在翻译这类词语时,要在了解中西宗教文化背景的前提下,知道其出处,充分理解其深层文化内涵,再用恰当文字精确翻译出来。

再比如中西方对颜色有着不同的文化差异,红色是我国文化里的崇尚色,它象征吉祥、喜庆、繁华、热闹、漂亮等,如女子美艳的容颜为"红颜"。西方文化中红色主要指鲜血的颜色,多指血腥、暴力、恐怖、危险等,如"red ruin"指火灾;红色也常用于情感上,当某人生气时,常用"see red"或"red with anger"形容;另外,其还有"亏本"等消极意义。

英汉文化上的差异体现在两种语言中无处不在的文化专有项(culture-specific items)上。文化专有项有时也称为文化负载词(culture-loaded words)或者文化专属词(culture-bound words)。翻译理论家哈维·佛朗哥·艾克西拉(Javier Franco Aixela)于1996年在其著作《翻译中的文化专有项》中率先提出了文化专有项的概念。文化专有项是"在文本中出现的某些项目,由于在译语读者的文化系统中不存在对应项目或者与该项目有不同的文本地位,因此其在源语文本中的功能和含义转移到译文时发生了翻译困难"。

文化专有项可以是表示衣物、建筑、人名、称谓、地名、度量衡、历史及神话人物、宗教的词组或短语,也可以是较长的俗语、谚语、成语,甚至可以延伸到段落和篇章层面。

艾克西拉还提出四类影响翻译策略选择的因素:(1)超文本因素,例如译语社会语言规范性的程度、潜在读者的性质和期望、翻译发起人的性质和目的、译者的工作条件、培训和社会地位。(2)文本因素,例如与文本配合的影像、已有的译本、源文的经典化程度。(3)文化专有项的性质,例如透明度、意识形态地位、对其他文化的指涉以及有没有定译。(4)文本内因素,例如项目在文本中的重要性和出现次数,以及译文的连贯性等(Aixeld,1996:65-70)。

1995年,美国翻译理论家劳伦斯·韦努蒂(L.Venuti)在《译者的隐身》(The Translator's Invisibility)中指出,翻译的策略可以分为两种:异化和归化。

1.异化策略

异化(foreignization)是指偏离本土主流价值观,保留原文的语言和文化差异(Venuti,2001:240),或指在一定程度上保留原文的异域性,故意打破目标语言常规的翻译。它主张在译文中保留源语文化,丰富目的语文化和目的语的语言表达方式。异化法则要求译者向作者靠拢,采取相应于作者使用的原语表达方式,来传达原文的内容。

一些文化词汇和典故影响很广,几乎众所周知,翻译时可以采用异化策略。在异化策略下,可以采用的翻译方法有直译、音译等。

一些文化专有项经过长期的异化翻译,已经在汉语中固化下来,读者往往难以觉察到它们是舶来品。例如crocodile tears 鳄鱼的眼泪, an olive branch 橄榄枝, sour grapes 酸葡萄, the Cold War 冷战, Iron Curtain 铁幕, grasp a straw 捞救命稻草, a stick-and-carrot policy 大棒加胡萝卜政策, armed to teeth 武装到牙齿, black horse 黑马, crocodile tears 鳄鱼的眼泪, ivory tower 象牙塔等。

以下是一些句子对文化专有项进行异化翻译的例子:

例1 The wealth he had boasted for years turned out to be the emperor's new clothes.
他吹嘘了多年的所谓财富实际上只是"皇帝的新装"。

例2 He doesn't have an idea of his own. He just parrots what others say.
他没有自己的观点,只是鹦鹉学舌罢了。

例3 A lion at home, a mouse abroad.

在家如狮,在外如鼠。

例4 High-speed communications in oncoming years can either produce the most informed generation in history or reduce the globe to a **Tower of Babel**.

不久的将来,高速的交往既可以产生在历史上最信息化的时代,也可能使世界变得喧哗嘈杂、语言混乱如**通天塔**重现。

"Tower of Babel"出自《圣经·旧约》。洪水退后,诺亚子孙想在巴比伦修建一座通天塔,作为自豪的象征,以此反抗上帝。上帝则扰乱了他们原来统一的语言,使他们彼此语言不同,建塔的工程也半途而废。后用"通天塔"比喻混乱的局面。

例5 A week after a Chinese envoy compared Japan to **Lord Voldemort**, Japan's ambassador to Britain has also invoked Harry Potter's arch-enemy to accuse Beijing of raising tensions amid disputes over territory and wartime history. ("Japan hits back at China over Voldemort comparisons", *The Guardian*, 6 January 2014)

在中国大使将日本比作"**伏地魔阁下**"的一周之后,日本驻英大使也借用这位哈利·波特的主要敌人,谴责北京利用领土与战争历史的争议制造紧张局势。

"伏地魔"(Voldemort)是小说、电影《哈利·波特》中最邪恶的巫师,也是主人公哈利·波特最强大的敌人,将自己的灵魂分藏在七个"魂器"中。因为预言说他或将被哈利杀死,伏地魔曾追杀哈利,却最后还是死在哈利手中。鉴于小说和电影的风靡程度,一般读者都理解"伏地魔"一词背后的含义与典故,因此直译即可。

例6 IPhone: Apple's **Trojan horse** into the business world(BGR News by Chris Smith, Jan 10, 2014)

Iphone:苹果公司打入商业世界的**特洛伊木马**。

"特洛伊木马"(Trojan horse)语出希腊神话传说。古希腊人在攻打特洛伊城之时,诱使特洛伊人将藏有精兵的巨型木马搬入城中,里应外合,赢得这场战争。后广泛用来比喻先期打入内部的颠覆者和决定因素。这一典故中国读者业已熟知,故直译即可。

2.归化(domestication)策略

归化是指在翻译中采用透明、流畅的风格,最大限度地淡化原文陌生感的翻译策略。它尽可能地使源语文本所反映的世界接近目的语文化读者的世界,从而达到源语文化与目的语文化之间的"文化对等"。归化法要求译者向译语读者靠拢,采取译语读者习惯的译语表达方式,来传达原文的内容。

翻译时,遇到英汉语言、文、思维等方面差异较为巨大的文化专有项,这些词语如果坚持异化译法,势必导致译文的晦涩难懂。在这种情况下,译者可以采取归化的策略。具体的翻译方法有意译、文化替换、省译等。

有些习语可以采用文化替换法进行翻译。如 as stupid as a goose 蠢得像头猪,like a duck to water 如鱼得水,cherish a snake in one's bosom 养虎遗患等。请看以下句子翻译的例子:

例1 Your honor, I confess the corn. I was royally drunk.

法官先生,我承认错误,我当时酩酊大醉了。

例2 Don't play your ace in the hole until the critical moment.
不到关键时刻不要亮出你的绝招。

例3 George Washington adopted a Fabian policy during the war of Independence.
乔治·华盛顿在独立战争期间采取过拖延战术。

例4 You can not make a crab walk straight.
狗改不了吃屎。

例5 Once the wife of a parson, always the wife of a parson.
嫁鸡随鸡,嫁狗随狗。

例6 One boy is a boy, two boys half a boy, three boys no boy.
一个和尚挑水吃,两个和尚抬水吃,三个和尚没水吃。

例7 I was limp as a dish rag. My back felt as though it had been beaten with wires.
我软得像一团棉花,脊背疼痛得好像被钢丝抽打过一样。(limp as a dish rag,如直译为"像洗碟布一样柔软",既不地道,又让人产生一种较恶心的感觉,不如用汉语中常说的"软得像一团棉花"加以归化。)

例8 "No, if they try anything it will be salami tactics." [Salami tactics was the description customarily given to a "slice by slice" manoeuvres, i.e., not a full scale invasion of the West, but the annexation of one small piece at a time.-Ed.] (66)
"不会的。他们一定会用蚕食战术。"
[编者按:就是说,每次只吞吃一小片土地。[……]](71)

原文是在谈论苏联可能用什么方法吞并西欧。所谓"salami tactics"(意大利香肠战术),看来并非英语的惯用语,所以原文作者要加上按语。译文代之以汉语成语"蚕食战术",就能把按语简化了。

例9 With the help of then-CEO Russell T. Lewis, he reinvented the "**Gray Lady**"…("The Future Of The New York Times", *Business week*, 2005)
在当时任该报首席执行官的拉塞尔·刘易斯的帮助下,他使**报纸**获得了新生……

Gray Lady 指纽约时报,因其传统版面风格高贵严肃,但拘谨保守,版面上一片黑灰色,故有"灰贵妇"之称。此处没有强调纽约时报风格的需要,采取了意译,弱化了原文的文化特色,译成"报纸"。

3. 异化与归化相结合的策略

采用异化归化相结合的策略下,可以既保留源语文化,丰富译入语文化和语言表达方式,又保证译文的可读性。这时,可采用多种翻译方法的组合,例如直译+注释;音译+意译等方式。

例1 Curiosity enough, he prophesied with oracular accuracy to the amazement of all.
译文:说也奇怪,他料事真准,像神启一样应验,让所有的人都惊讶不止。
注释:"oracular"的名词形式是"oracle",在希腊神话中指"神示、神启"。

例2 Would any of the stock of **Barrabbas** Had been her husband rather than a Christian!
(*The Merchant of Venice*)

译文:哪怕她跟**巴拉巴**的子孙做夫妻,也强似嫁给了基督徒!

注释:巴拉巴:古时强盗名,见《新约·马太福音》XX-VII,15-20。(方平译)

由于这一典故出自《圣经》,大多数中国读者并不熟悉,因此译者采用了直译加注的翻译策略,既体现了原文的意思,又保留了原文典故的文化内涵,有助于读者了解西方文化。

例3 The relationship between Google and the newspaper industry has always been somewhat tumultuous, so this revenue-sharing model can be seen as Google extending an **olive branch** to content producers. ("Is Fast Flip Really the Best Google Can Do to Save the News?")

谷歌和报业之间的关系一直有些纷乱,因此这一收入共享模式可以被视为谷歌向生产商伸出**求和的橄榄枝**。

"橄榄枝"寓意和平,源于《圣经·创世纪》,洪水后,诺亚为了解地面状况在船上连续放了三次鸽子,等第三次鸽子衔回橄榄枝后,说明洪水已经退去。这里将"olive branch"译作"求和的橄榄枝",加上"求和"的释义,更清晰地表达了原文的文化寓意。

例4 "We have not yet **met our Waterloo**, Watson, but this is our **Marengo**." (Arthur Conan Doyle, *Return of Sherlock Holmes*, 1905)

译文:华生,我们还没有遭遇滑铁卢呢,但这是我们的马伦哥之役。

注释:马伦哥是拿破仑在意大利战场上几近失败,后转败为胜的一场战役。

Meet one's Waterloo 遭遇滑铁卢,意即一败涂地,这个典故众人皆知,直译即可。而马伦哥战役(1800)虽是拿破仑引以为傲的一场战役,然而中国读者对这段历史并不熟悉,因此采用直译加注的方式更有助于读者的理解。

例5 The US government expresses the fear that retaliatory operation abroad could open a **Pandora's box** of terrorism in America.

译文:美国政府表示担心,在国外采取报复行动可能会在美国本土打开恐怖主义的**潘多拉盒子**。

注释:"潘多拉盒子"来自希腊神话传说,意即一切灾难、麻烦、祸害的根源。

本句若单纯直译,对于不了解希腊神话的读者来说可能会造成误解,加上注释可以使读者理解原文所要传达的文化信息。

例6 The news struck me like **a bolt from the blue**, and I could not believe it.

译文:当时听到这一消息,犹如**晴天霹雳**,我无论如何不敢相信这是真的。

例7 All you can do is to **burn your boats** and fight them in the hope that one day you'll come out on top.

译文:只有**破釜沉舟**地跟他们拼,还许有翻身的一天。

英语 burn one's boat 与汉语"破釜沉舟"无论从字面意思还是文化内涵都极为相似。欧洲古罗马的恺撒(Julius Caesar,公元前 100—44 年)将军曾率领大军乘船横渡卢比庚河(the Rubicon),登岸之后,即刻下令把自己部队所乘的船只全部焚毁,自断退路,以示只进不退、非决一死战不可的决心。现在人们借此表达在做一件事时不惜牺牲、孤注一掷的决心。

A Hero Reborn: "China's Tolkien" Aims to Conquer Western Readers
The world's most popular kung fu fantasy series is finally set to become a UK bestseller.
By Vanessa Thorpe

Guo Jing, a young soldier among the massed ranks of Genghis Khan's army and son of a murdered warrior, may soon become as familiar a questing literary figure as Frodo Baggins from Tolkien's Lord of the Rings, or Jon Snow from Game of Thrones. In fact, this Chinese fighting hero is already part of phenomenon that can match both of those epics in size. For the books of Guo Jing's creator, the author known as Jin Yong, have already sold more than 300m copies.

The world's biggest kung fu fantasy writer, Jin Yong enjoys huge popularity in the Chinese-speaking world. In the west, however, his name is barely the world he has created and the puzzle that has posed for translators.

Now, for the first time, the beginning of his extraordinarily popular series, Legends of the Condor Heroes, has been translated into English for a mainstream readership. It is a task that has already defeated several translators, yet Anna Holmwood, 32, from Edinburgh has managed it-or at least the first volume. Her British publisher, MacLehose Press, plans a 12-volume series, with Holmwood's first volume, A Hero Born, due out in February.

Agent Peter Buckman, who sold the rights to the series to the publisher, came across the works almost by chance as he searched the internet for "bestselling authors". "Jin Yong was in the top 10, though I'd never heard of him; nor did I read Chinese," he said this weekend.

Comparisons with Tolkien or George RR Martin might sound overblown, but in and around China, Jin Yong's works are classics, loved like fairytales or national legends.

"These books are read by so many Chinese people when they are teenagers, and the work really stays in their heads," Hollywood told the Observer. "So, of course, I felt a great weight of responsibility in translating them-and even more as publication draws near."

Set in China in 1200, A Hero Born tells of an empire close to collapse. Under attack from the Jurchen Jin dynasty, the future of the entire Chinese population rests in the hands of a few lone martial arts exponents. A novel in the wuxia, or fighting hero, tradition, it was written under the pen name Jin Yong by Chinese journalist, Louis Cha Leungyung. A founding editor of the Hong Kong daily newspaper Ming Pao, in the 1950s he put together a set of stories charting the progress of a young martial arts fighter during the Song dynasty and serialised them. The plots were fictional but the historical background was real.

They became the biggest Chinese publishing hit of the last century. Cha, who is now 93 and lives in seclusion, created a vast imaginary world over 15 novels, which spawned [2] films, games, comics and television shows.

Buckman bought the rights and sold them on to a British publisher after meeting Holmwood and discovering how little of the series was available in English. "Anna did a sample chapter of the first of the Condor Heroes books and I sent it out to various publishers. My old friend Christopher

MacLehose, who specialises in translated masterpieces, had discovered from a Chinese friend how Jin Yong's work was like Simenon's is to the French or Tolstoy's to the Russians-a part of the common culture, with one generation of readers passing on their enthusiasm to the next," he said.

Although there have been academic translations published over a decade ago, including an edition of The Deer and the Cauldrontranslated by John Minford, attempts to tackle the wider work have been abandoned. Holmwood, who studied Chinese at Oxford University, first discovered the book in Taipei and later moved to Hangzhou, in east China, while she worked on her translation.

Fellow translators are now being drafted in to help with the task, but the challenge facing all of them is to faithfully represent the kung fu moves along with the Chinese philosophies and religions that are all woven through the plot. Even the fighting skill of the warrior in A Hero Born, for instance, which literally translate as "the 18 palm attacks to defeat dragons", is in fact derived from a Taoist classic ascribed to Lao Tzu, dating from 2,500 years ago, and has a strong philosophical element in addition to movement.

"I am of the belief that a lot of readers like a bit of a challenge as they go along," said Holmwood, who now lives in Malmö, Sweden, with her Taiwanese husband and son. "That is why fans of Lord of the Rings try to learn Elvish. So I Don't explain everything, although I have written a very short prologue to introduce some of the elements of the story."

(800 words)

第八章

语篇分析与翻译

Cuban Missile Crisis Address to the Nation(Excerpt)
John F. Kennedy
delivered 22 October 1962

Good evening, my fellow citizens:

This Government, as promised, has maintained the closest surveillance of the Soviet military buildup on the island of Cuba. Within the past week, unmistakable evidence has established the fact that a series of offensive missile sites is now in preparation on that imprisoned island. The purpose of these bases can be none other than to provide a nuclear strike capability against the Western Hemisphere.

Upon receiving the first preliminary hard information of this nature last Tuesday morning at 9 a.m., I directed that our surveillance be stepped up. And having now confirmed and completed our evaluation of the evidence and our decision on a course of action, this Government feels obliged to report this new crisis to you in fullest detail.

The characteristics of these new missile sites indicate two distinct types of installations. Several of them include medium range ballistic missiles, capable of carrying a nuclear warhead for a distance of more than 1,000 nautical miles. Each of these missiles, in short, is capable of striking Washington, D.C., the Panama Canal, Cape Canaveral, Mexico City, or any other city in the southeastern part of the United States, in Central America, or in the Caribbean area.

Additional sites not yet completed appear to be designed for intermediate range ballistic missiles—capable of traveling more than twice as far—and thus capable of striking most of the major cities in the Western Hemisphere, ranging as far north as Hudson Bay, Canada, and as far south as Lima, Peru. In addition, jet bombers, capable of carrying nuclear weapons, are now being uncrated and assembled in Cuba, while the necessary air bases are being prepared.

This urgent transformation of Cuba into an important strategic base—by the presence of these large, long-range, and clearly offensive weapons of sudden mass destruction—constitutes an explicit threat to the peace and security of all the Americas, in flagrant and deliberate defiance of the Rio Pact of 1947, the traditions of this nation and hemisphere, the joint resolution of the 87th Congress, the Charter of the United Nations, and my own public warnings to the Soviets on September 4 and 13. This action also contradicts the repeated assurances of Soviet spokesmen, both publicly and privately delivered, that the arms buildup in Cuba would retain its original defensive character, and that the Soviet Union had no need or desire to station strategic missiles on the territory of any other nation.

(408 words)

佳译赏析

The Declaration of Independence

英 语 文 本	汉 语 文 本
The Declaration of Independence In Congress, July 4, 1776 Thomas Jefferson	独立宣言 大陆会议（一七七六年七月四日） 赵一凡译❶
The Unanimous Declaration of The Thirteen United States of America	美利坚合众国十三个州一致通过的独立宣言
When in the Course of human events, it becomes necessary for one people to dissolve the political bonds which have connected them with another, and to assume among the Powers of the earth, the separate and equal station to which the Laws of Nature and of Nature's God entitle them, a decent respect to the opinions of mankind requires that they should declare the causes which impel them to the separation.	在有关人类事务的发展过程中，当一个民族必须解除其和另一个民族之间的政治联系，并在世界各国之间依照自然法则和上帝的意旨，接受独立和平等的地位时，出于对人类舆论的尊重，必须把他们不得不独立的原因予以宣布。
We hold these truths to be self-evident, that all men are created equal, that they are endowed by their Creator with certain unalienable Rights, that among these are Life, Liberty, and the pursuit of Happiness.	我们认为下面这些真理是不言而喻的：人人生而平等，造物者赋予他们若干不可剥夺的权利，其中包括生命权、自由权和追求幸福的权利。
That whenever any form of Government becomes destructive of these ends, it is the Right of the People to alter or to abolish it, and to institute new Government, laying its foundation on such principles and organizing its powers in such form, as to them shall seem most likely to effect their Safety and Happiness. Prudence, indeed, will dictate that Governments long established should not be changed for light and transient causes; and accordingly all experience has shown, that mankind are more disposed to suffer, while evils are sufferable, than to right themselves by abolishing the forms to which they are accustomed. But when a long train of abuses and usurpations, pursuing invariably the same Object, evinces a design to reduce them under absolute Despotism, it is their right, it is their duty, to throw off such Government, and to provide new Guards for their future security.	为了保障这些权利，人类才在他们之间建立政府，而政府之正当权力，是经被治理者的同意而产生的。当任何形式的政府对这些目标具破坏作用时，人民便有权力改变或废除它，以建立一个新的政府；其赖以奠基的原则，其组织权力的方式，务使人民认为唯有这样才最可能获得他们的安全和幸福。为了慎重起见，成立多年的政府，是不应当由于轻微和短暂的原因而予以变更的。过去的一切经验也都说明，任何苦难，只要是尚能忍受，人类都宁愿容忍，而无意为了本身的权益便废除他们久已习惯了的政府。但是，当追逐同一目标的一连串滥用职权和强取豪夺发生，证明政府企图把人民置于专制统治之下时，那么人民就有权利，也有义务推翻这个政府，并为他们未来的安全建立新的保障。

---

❶赵一凡.美国的历史文献.北京：生活·读书·新知三联书店，1989：16-21.

续上表

英语文本	汉语文本
Such has been the patient sufferance of these Colonies; and such is now the necessity which constrains them to alter their former Systems of Government. The history of the present King of Great Britain is a history of repeated injuries and usurpations, all having in direct object the establishment of an absolute Tyranny over these States. To prove this, let Facts be submitted to a candid world.	这就是这些殖民地过去逆来顺受的情况,也是他们现在不得不改变以前政府制度的原因。当今大不列颠国王的历史,是接连不断的伤天害理和强取豪夺的历史,这些暴行的唯一目标,就是想在这些州建立专制的暴政。为了证明所言属实,现把下列事实向公正的世界宣布。
He has refused his Assent to Laws, the most wholesome and necessary for the public good.	他拒绝批准对公众利益最有益、最必要的法律。
He has forbidden his Governors to pass Laws of immediate and pressing importance, unless suspended in their operation till his Assent should be obtained; and when so suspended, he has utterly neglected to attend to them.	他禁止他的总督们批准迫切而极为必要的法律,要不就把这些法律搁置起来暂不生效,等待他的同意;而一旦这些法律被搁置起来,他对它们就完全置之不理。
He has refused to pass other Laws for the accommodation of large districts of people, unless those people would relinquish the right of Representation in the Legislature, a right inestimable to them and formidable to tyrants only.	他拒绝批准便利广大地区人民的其他法律,除非那些人民情愿放弃自己在立法机关中的代表权,但这种权利对他们有无法估量的价值,而且只有暴君才畏惧这种权利。
He has called together legislative bodies at places unusual, uncomfortable, and distant from the depository of their public Records, for the sole purpose of fatiguing them into compliance with his measures.	他把各州立法团体召集到异乎寻常的、极为不便的、远离他们档案库的地方去开会,唯一的目的是使他们疲于奔命,不得不顺从他的意旨。
He has dissolved Representative Houses repeatedly, for opposing with manly firmness his invasions on the rights of the people.	他一再解散各州的议会,因为他们以无畏的坚毅态度反对他侵犯人民的权利。
He has refused for a long time, after such dissolutions, to cause others to be elected; whereby the Legislative powers, incapable of Annihilation, have returned to the People at large for their exercise; the State remaining in the mean time exposed to all the dangers of invasion from without, and convulsions within.	他在解散各州议会之后,又长期拒绝另选新议会;但立法权是无法取消的,因此这项权力仍由一般人民来行使。其时各州仍然处于危险的境地,既有外来侵略之患,又有发生内乱之忧。
He has endeavoured to prevent the population of these States; for that purpose obstructing the Laws of Naturalization of Foreigners; refusing to pass others to encourage their migrations hither, and raising the conditions of new Appropriations of Lands.	他竭力抑制我们各州增加人口;为此目的,他阻挠外国人入籍法的通过,拒绝批准其他鼓励外国人移居各州的法律,并提高分配新土地的新条件。
He has obstructed the Administration of Justice, by refusing his Assent to Laws for establishing Judiciary powers.	他拒绝批准建立司法权力的法律,借以阻挠司法工作的推行。
He has made Judges dependent on his Will alone, for the tenure of their offices, and the amount and payment of their salaries.	他把法官的任期、薪金数额和支付,完全置于他个人意志的支配之下。
He has erected a multitude of New Offices, and sent hither swarms of Officers to harass our People, and eat out their substance.	他滥设新官署,派遣大批官员,骚扰我们的人民,并耗尽人民必要的生活资料。
He has kept among us, in times of peace, Standing Armies without the Consent of our legislatures.	他在和平时期,未经我们的立法机关同意,就在我们中间维持常备军。

续上表

英 语 文 本	汉 语 文 本
He has affected to render the Military independent of and superior to the Civil power.	他力图使军队独立于民政之外,并凌驾于民政之上。
He has combined with others to subject us to a jurisdiction foreign to our constitution, and unacknowledged by our laws; giving his Assent to their Acts of pretended Legislation:	他同某些人勾结起来,把我们置于一种不适合我们的体制且不为我们的法律所承认的管辖之下,他还批准那些人炮制的各种伪法案来达到以下目的:
For quartering large bodies of armed troops among us: For protecting them, by a mock Trial, from Punishment for any Murders which they should commit on the Inhabitants of these States: For cutting off our Trade with all parts of the world: For imposing Taxes on us without our Consent: For depriving us in many cases, of the benefits of Trial by Jury: For transporting us beyond Seas to be tried for pretended offences: For abolishing the free System of English Laws in a neighbouring Province, establishing therein an Arbitrary government, and enlarging its Boundaries so as to render it at once an example and fit instrument for introducing the same absolute rule into these Colonies: For taking away our Charters, abolishing our most valuable Laws, and altering fundamentally the forms of our Governments: For suspending our own Legislatures, and declaring themselves invested with power to legislate for us in all cases whatsoever.	在我们中间驻扎大批武装部队; 用假审讯来包庇他们,使他们杀害我们各州居民而仍然逍遥法外; 切断我们同世界各地的贸易; 未经我们同意便向我们强行征税; 在许多案件中剥夺我们享有陪审制的权益; 罗织罪名押送我们到海外去受审; 在一个邻省废除英国的自由法律,在那里建立专制政府,并扩大该省的疆界,企图把该省变成既是一个样板又是一个得心应手的工具,以便进而向这里的各殖民地推行同样的极权统治; 取消我们的宪章,废除我们最宝贵的法律,并从根本上改变我们各州政府的形式; 中止我们自己的立法机关行使权力,宣称他们自己有权就一切事宜为我们制定法律。
He has abdicated Government here, by declaring us out of his Protection and waging War against us.	他宣布我们已不属他保护之列,并对我们作战,从而放弃了在这里的政务。
He has plundered our seas, ravaged our Coasts, burnt our towns, and destroyed the Lives of our people.	他在我们的海域大肆掠夺,蹂躏我们沿海地区,焚烧我们的城镇,残害我们的人民的生命。
He is at this time transporting large armies of foreign mercenaries tocomplete the works of death, desolation and tyranny, already begun with circumstances of Cruelty & perfidy scarcely paralleled in the most barbarous ages, and totally unworthy the Head of a civilized nation.	他此时正在运送大批外国雇佣兵来完成屠杀,破坏和肆虐的勾当,这种勾当早就开始,其残酷卑劣甚至在最野蛮的时代都难以找到先例。他完全不配作为一个文明国家的元首。
He has constrained our fellow Citizens taken Captive on the high Seas to bear Arms against their Country, to become the executioners of their friends and Brethren, or to fall themselves by their Hands.	在公海上俘虏我们的同胞,强迫他们拿起武器来反对自己的国家,成为残杀自己亲人和朋友的刽子手,或是死于自己的亲人和朋友的手下。
He has excited domestic insurrections amongst us, and has endeavored to bring on the inhabitants of our frontiers, the merciless Indian Savages, whose known rule of warfare, is an undistinguished destruction of all ages, sexes and conditions.	他在我们中间煽动内乱,并且竭力挑唆那些残酷无情、没有开化的印第安人来杀掠我们边疆的居民;而众所周知,印第安人的作战规律是不分男女老幼,一律格杀勿论的。
In every stage of these Oppressions We have Petitioned for Redress in the most humble terms; Our repeated Petitions have been answered only by repeated injury. A Prince, whose character is thus marked by every act which may define a Tyrant, is unfit to be the ruler of a free people.	在这些压迫的每一阶段中,我们都是用最谦卑的言辞请求纠正;但屡次请求所得到的答复是屡次遭受损害。一个君主,当他的品格已打上了暴君行为的烙印时,是不配做自由人民的统治者的。

续上表

英语文本	汉语文本
Nor have We been wanting in attention to our British brethren. We have warned them from time to time of attempts by their legislature to extend an unwarrantable jurisdiction over us. We have reminded them of the circumstances of our emigration and settlement here. We have appealed to their native justice and magnanimity, and we have conjured them by the ties of our common kindred to disavow these usurpation, which would inevitably interrupt our connections and correspondence. They too have been deaf to the voice of justice and of consanguinity. We must, therefore, acquiesce in the necessity, which denounces our Separation, and hold them, as we hold the rest of mankind, Enemies in War, in Peace Friends.	我们不是没有顾念我们英国的弟兄。我们时常提醒他们,他们的立法机关企图把无理的管辖权横加到我们的头上,我们也曾把我们移民来这里和在这里定居的情形告诉他们。我们曾经向他们天生的正义感和雅量呼吁,我们恳求他们念在同种同宗的份上,弃绝这些掠夺行为,以免影响彼此的关系和往来。但是他们对于这种正义和血缘的呼声,也同样充耳不闻。因此,我们实在不得不宣布和他们脱离,并且以对待世界上其他民族一样的态度对待他们,和我们作战,就是敌人;和我们和好,就是朋友。
We, therefore, the Representatives of the United States of America, in General Congress, Assembled, appealing to the Supreme Judge of the world for the rectitude of our intentions, do, in the Name, and by Authority of the good People of these Colonies, solemnly publish and declare, That these United Colonies are, and of Right ought to be Free and Independent States; that they are Absolved from all Allegiance to the British Crown, and that all political connection between them and the State of Great Britain, is and ought to be totally dissolved; and that as Free and Independent States, they have full Power to levy War, conclude Peace, contract Alliances, establish Commerce, and to do all other Acts and Things which Independent States may of right do.	因此,我们不得不在大陆会议上集会的美利坚合众国代表,以各殖民地善良人民的名义,并经他们授权,向全世界最崇高的正义呼吁,说明我们的严正意向,同时郑重宣布:这些联合一致的殖民地从此是自由和独立的国家,并且按其权利也必须是自由和独立的国家,它们取消一切对英国王室效忠的义务,它们和大不列颠国家之间的一切政治关系从此全部断绝,而且必须断绝;作为自由独立的国家,它们完全有权宣战、缔合、结盟、通商和采取独立国家有权采取的一切行动。
And for the support of this Declaration, with a firm reliance on the Protection of Divine Providence, we mutually pledge to each other our Lives, our Fortunes and our sacred Honor.	为了支持这篇宣言,我们坚决信赖上帝的庇佑,以我们的生命、我们的财产和我们神圣的名誉,彼此宣誓。
JOHN HANCOCK, President Attested, CHARLES THOMSON, Secretary	约翰·汉考克,主席 鉴定无误,查尔斯·汤森,秘书

认知升级

一、语篇特征与翻译

语篇是指一段有意义,传达一个完整信息,逻辑连贯,语言衔接,具有一定交际目的和功能的语言单位或交际事件。语篇(Text)是指口头或书面语的一个单位,或短或长。一个语篇可能只有一个词,如书写在机场的 Entrance;也可能是很长的一段话或文字,如一次访谈、一本小说或一场辩论。它依赖于语境,可以被读者接受,篇章的制作和解读都不能脱离语境。

语篇特征指的是作为语篇必须具备的特征的复合体,是某个语言客体(linguistic object)在社会和交际制约中所折射出来的特质。在翻译研究中,语篇特征原则可用来解释如何获得原文和译文在语篇层面上的对等。

比格兰德和德斯拉(Beaugrande & Dressler 1981)及纽伯特和史赖夫(Neubert & Shreve 1992)都认为,典型的语篇应具有以下七个标准:衔接性(cohesion)、连贯性(coherence)、意图性(intentionality)、可接受性(acceptability)、信息性(informativity)、情境性(situationality)和互文性(intertextuality)。下文以衔接、连贯和信息性为例来说明这些语篇特征在翻译过程中的处理方法。

衔接的形式(基于 Halliday and Hasan,1976)

Type of cohesion	Description	Example
Reference	A semantic relation where meaning needs to be interpreted through reference to something else, linked using a pronoun (*I*, *you*, *it* …), demonstrative(*this*/*that*), etc.	*I know Bill followed the match.* ***He*** *saw* ***it*** *on TV* -he refers to *Bill* and *it* to *the match*
Substitution	A grammatical substitution within the text	*Arctic foxes threatened by* ***red ones*** -*red ones* substitutes for *red foxes*
Ellipsis	A kind of zero substitution, where and element needs to be supplied	*For every dollar donated federally,* ***three more*** *are donated by the State* -the element *dollars* needs to be supplied
Conjunction	A semantic relation indicating how what follows is linked to what has gone before	Typical examples are additive (***and***…), adversative (***but***, ***however***…) and temporal (***at first***, ***then***, ***finally***…)
Lexical cohesion	A lexical relation where cohesion is produced by the selection of vocabulary; these can be through reiteration (some form of repetition or linkage) and/or collocation (the typical co-occurrence of lexical items)	Reiteration, through: -repetition of the same word (*lion*…***lion***) -synonym (*lion*…***hunter***) -superordinate (*lion*…***cat***) -general word (*lion*…***creature***) Collocation, through: -pairs of words (***inclement weather***, ***quirk of fate***, ***make a mistake***) -words occurring in the same semantic field (***inclement weather***…***rain***…***wind***…***cold***…).

衔接手段在语篇中的地位十分重要。由于英汉语思维方式和表达习惯的不同,其衔接方式也有许多不同之处,原文中的衔接方式有时必须做些调整,否则便会造成译文表达不准确或不自然。因此,在翻译的过程中,如何恰当地处理好译文中的衔接方式尤为重要。

例1 Business is pretty slack, to begin with, and then I m fixing up a little house for Ned and Ruth, when they re married.
原译:生意清淡,这是其一;此外,当纳德和路德结婚时,还得给他们盖房子。
改译:一来生意清淡,二来我正预备给纳德和路德盖个小房子,他们快结婚了。
(吕叔湘)

Coherence concerns the ways in which the components of the textual world, i.e., the configuration of concepts and relations which underlie the surface text, are mutually accessible and relevant. Cause, enablement, and reason, temporal proximity, Coherence can be illustrated particularly well by a group of relations subsumed under causality. These relations concern the ways in which one situation or event affects the conditions for some other one.

例2 If today it is often true, a hundred and fifty years ago it was invariably so. The hopes of a family rested on the male child. Parents and daughters all sacrificed to promote the son; if there were more than one, the eldest.

原译:如果今天情况经常是这样,150年前就更是如此。一家人的希望寄托在男孩身上。父母、女儿们为他的发展甘愿做出牺牲;假若不止一个儿子,就寄希望于长子。

改译:如果说在今天,一家人往往把希望寄托在男孩子身上,那么150年前,情况无不如此。做父母的也好,做女儿的也好,为了使男孩成才,都甘愿自己作出牺牲。男孩多的则寄希望于长子。

信息性指的是语篇能够"给接受者传达新的或意想不到的东西"(Beaugrande & Dressler,1981:139),它是指文本能够提供给目标语读者关于事件、状态、过程、物体、个人、地方和机构等方面的信息。从翻译的角度来看,信息性也指一个译本对目标语读者所提供的关于原文的信息是否适度(Neubert & Shreve,1992:89)。

根据"合作原则"(Co-operative principle)中"量"(Quantity)的准则,语言交际过程中,说话者所提供的信息的量应该不多不少,恰好满足达到交际目的所需的必要信息(Grice,1975:45)。如果包含的信息太少,语篇就会枯燥无味;如果包含的信息太多,就会给读者/听者带来困难。

比尔格兰和德斯拉(Beaugrande & Dressler 1981)把语篇的信息性分为三级:如果一个语篇只包含已知信息或读者意料之中的信息,其信息性属一级。只含一级信息性的语篇会令人觉得乏味,没有价值。如果语篇具有部分未知的或意料不到的信息,其信息性属二级,属正常程度。如果一个语篇包含的未知信息太多,又没有加以解释,其信息性属三级。

翻译时,要把原文的信息用目标语表达出来,需要对比原文和译文的信息层级。由于不同文化背景的读者的知识结构不同,语篇的信息性层级也就不能一概而论。同一个语篇,对原文读者来说其信息性是二级,但是对目标语读者来说可能是一级,也可能是三级。因此,译者就成了目标语语篇信息性的调节者,他要根据目标语读者的阅读经验和期待视野对语篇中的信息进行适当的调节。

例1 A great-grandmother of mine, who was a friend of Gibbon, lived to the age of ninety-two, and to her last day remained a terror to all her descendants. (Bertrand Russell, How to Grow Old)

译文:我的一位曾祖母,和吉本是朋友,活到了九十二岁,她直到临终都使孙儿望而生畏。(庄绎传,1999:149)

译注:吉本(Edward Gibbon,1737—1794)是英国历史学家,著有《罗马帝国之衰亡》(The Decline and Fall of the Roman Empire)。

对于一般的英国人而言,Gibbon是英国的历史学家,因此译文信息层级可以归为二级,但对大多数中国人而言,吉本是个非常陌生的信息,这样信息层级就会升为三级。因此,译者用加注脚的方法处理,帮助目标语读者了解此信息,又保持了译文的简洁流畅。

例2 My maternal grandfather, it is true, was cut off in the flower of his youth at the age of sixty-seven, but my other three grandparents all lived to be over eighty. (Bertrand Russell, How to Grow Old)

译文:我外祖父固然是在风华正茂之年就弃世了,当时他只有六十七岁,但是我的祖父、祖母和外祖母却都活到了八十岁以上。(庄绎传,1999:149)

在英汉翻译中,亲属称谓的翻译是一大难题,受到的文化制约非常明显,信息层级也不一样。英语中"grandparents"可以兼顾祖父、祖母、外祖父、外祖母,一个cousin既指堂兄弟姐妹,又指表兄弟姐妹,而汉语中却没有这样的词。因此,翻译时要根据上下文,把这类词具体化。

二、文本类型与翻译①

在很多情况下,译者以翻译对等理论作为翻译的指导标准。可是,在翻译实践中,有时译文所要实现的目的或功能不同于原文的目的或功能,因此翻译并不要求对等。例如将一篇散文改写成舞台剧,把莎士比亚的戏剧翻译成外语课堂教材,将一首阿拉伯诗歌逐字翻译出来作为不懂阿拉伯文的英国诗人意译的基础,把《格列佛游记》翻译成儿童读本,或是由于宗教、民族或商业的原因将之编辑成具有不同意识形态的版本等,翻译对等理论不再灵验。

在这些情况下,翻译的功能是译者需要考虑的首要因素。译者不仅要对原文进行特征分析,还要判断译文的文本类型,以此来判断译文具有什么样的功能及译文的最终目的。语言功能的文本类型理论可以帮助译者确定特定翻译目的所需的合适的对等程度。

卡塔琳娜·莱思对文本的两种分类形式作了区分。

一类是文本类型(Texttypen),按照主体交际功能分为三种:信息型(informative)、表情型(expressive)、操作型(operative)。

(1)信息型文本通常是文字简朴,所陈事实包括信息、知识、观点等。传递信息的语言特点是逻辑性强,其内容或"话题"是交际的焦点。

(2)表情型文本指的是"创作性作品",作者或"发送者"地位显著,传递信息的形式特别,语言具有美学特点。

(3)操作型文本的目的是"引诱行为反应",即感染读者或"接受者"并使其采取某种行动。语言的形式通常是对话性的,其焦点是呼吁或感染。

另一种文本分类方式是语篇体裁(Textsorten)(莱思 1976:20),按照语言特征或惯例常规分类(如划分工具书、讲演稿、讽刺作品或广告所依照的标准)。

值得注意的是,每种文本类型都可能包括多种不同的体裁。但一种体裁(如书信)不一定只涉及一种文本类型,因此也不限于一种交际功能:情书可为表情,商务信函可为传意,求助信可为操作。

莱思曾举例说明哪些文本属她所说的三种类型,后来切斯特曼(Chesterman)用图表描绘了她的文本分类。

莱思的文本类型与文本种类(根据 Chesterman 1989:105)

---

①本书重点参考了张美芳《功能途径论翻译:以英汉翻译为例》第三章的内容。

根据上图,参考资料类的书籍(例如百科全书)是最为明显的信息型文本。诗歌是高度表情型的文本,十分注重形式。广告则是最具感染力的文本(试图说服某人去做某事或者买某样商品)。在这三极之间,存在着很多混合型文本。例如传记(如一本关于重要政治人物如奥巴马的传记)可能就位于信息型和表情型文本之间,因为传记一方面提供了相关主题的信息,同时也在一定程度上起着一部文学作品的作用。如果它试图唤起读者采取某种行动的话,它甚至还会包含感染功能。同样,一篇宗教演说可能在传递宗教信息的同时也在试图说服听众采取某种行为,因此这篇宗教演说辞在信息功能之外也同时具备感染功能。如果这篇演说还使用了一些修辞,那它就又多了表情功能。

原文的主要功能决定了翻译的方法。换句话说,译者应该根据文本类型来选择翻译方法"(莱思 1976:20)。如下表所示。尽管很多文本都是混合型的,具有多种功能,但是"评判译文的最重要因素是,它是否传达了原文的主要功能"(莱思 1977/1989:109)。

文本类型及其翻译方法(根据 Munday 2001:74)

文本类型 Text type	信息型 Informative	表情型 Expressive	操作型 Operative
语言功能 Language function	信息的(表达事物与事实) Informative (representing objects and facts)	表情的(表达情感) Expressive (expressing sender's attitude)	感染的(感染接受者) Appellative (making an appeal to text receiver)
语言特点 Language dimension	逻辑性 Logical	审美性 Aesthetic	对话性 Dialogic
文本焦点 Text focus	侧重内容 Content-focused	侧重形式 Form-focused	侧重感染作用 Appellative-focused
译文目的 TT should	表达内容信息 Transmit referential content	表现审美形式 Transmit aesthetic form	激发出所期望的反应 Elicit desired response
翻译方法 Translation method	使用简朴的白话文,采用明晰化的方法 'Plain prose', explicitation as required	从原作者出发,采用"等同"方法 'Identifying' method, adopt perspective of ST author	采用编译方法,达到等效 'Adaptive', equivalent effect

(1)翻译信息型文本应将其中的全部信息都译出来。译文应是简明的白话文,没有冗余,并且在必要的时候使用明示的方法。例如,在翻译百科全书里的"雷克斯·暴龙"这一条目时,应当将全部的信息和术语翻译出来而不必拘泥于与有关风格的细枝末节。

(2)翻译表情型文本时,在确保信息准确的基础上,译文应当反映出原文的艺术形式和审美特点。翻译方法应当是仿效法,忠实于原作。译者应采取和原文作者相同的视角行文。因此,詹姆斯·乔伊斯(James Joyce)作品的译者应当从詹姆斯·乔伊斯的角度行文。翻译文学作品时,原文作者的写作风格应是重点考虑之一。

(3)感染型文本的译文应能在译文读者中产生预期的反应。应采取"编译"的方法以实现等效。因此,广告文本的译文应能对译文读者产生感染力,尽管因此而可能添加新词或者新图像。

莱思(1971/2000:48—88)还列举了一系列语言和非语言方面的标准(Instruktionen),用于评估译文的恰当性。这些标准包括语言要素(如语义对等、词汇对等、语法和文体特征)和非语言要素(情境、主题、时间、地点、国家和文化的特点、译文读者、原文读者、情感暗示等)。

这些因素的重要性因文本类型和体裁不同而不一样。例如，任何侧重内容的文本，如百科全书，其翻译应首先确保语义对等。对于科普读物的翻译，应当注意译文的可读性和原文作者的个人风格。而如果读者是专家的话，译文应当符合相关的学术规范。莱思认为相对于信息型文本里的隐喻，表情型文本里的隐喻在翻译时保留下来显得更为重要，而信息型文本里的隐喻只要将其真实语义翻译出来就足够了。

如果原文和译文的功能一样，上述的标准便可有效衡量译文质量。不过，莱思(1977/1989:114)也指出，有时原文和译文的功能可能不一样。例如，乔纳森·斯威夫特(Jonathan Swift)的《格列佛游记》(*Gulliver's Travel*)最初是一部抨击当时政府的讽刺小说，因而主要是感染型文本；如今被当作一部"普通的娱乐小说"翻译，也就变成了表情型文本。译文的交际功能也可能与原文的交际功能不同：一篇感染型的竞选演讲，在另一个国家的用途可能只是供分析者研究里面的政策以及这些政策信息是如何表述的(也就变成了信息型和表情型文本)。

功能学派的另一位重要学者，克里斯蒂安·诺德对文本类型和功能进行了补充和细化。如下表所示。

诺德的文本类型

Referential function 指称功能	Expressive function 表情功能	Appellative function 感染功能			Phatic function 寒暄功能
		Direct appellative 直接感染	Indirect appellative 间接感染	Poetic appellative 诗型感染	

三、功能目的与翻译❶

1. 翻译目的论

翻译目的论(Skopos Theory)的基本原则是：翻译是一种交际性行为，是为了达到某种特定的目标，而译文目的决定其翻译策略和方法。Skopos 一词源自希腊语，意为"目的""目标"。弗米尔和莱思合著的《通用翻译理论基础》一书是目的论的奠基之作。该书认为，弄清楚翻译原文的目的以及译文的功能对于译者而言至关重要。该书基本论点如下：(1)翻译目的决定翻译行为；(2)译文在目的语及其文化中传递信息，该信息与原文在源语文化中传递的信息相关；(3)译文所提供的信息，不一定可以清晰地译回原文；(4)译文必须内在连贯；(5)译文必须与原文连贯。

这些内容可以概括为三大原则：目的原则、连贯原则与忠实原则。目的原则指目的决定翻译行为，译文是为某目的服务的。也就是说，翻译的目的决定了翻译策略、方法和技巧的采用。

连贯原则要求做到译文与目的语环境相连贯，要考虑译文读者的需要、所处的环境、所具备的知识，译文必须能让读者看得懂；如果译文没能符合译文读者的需要，那它就不"合适"，不能达到预定的目的。

忠实原则要求译文对原文尽量保持忠实。具体而言，指下述各方之间的连贯：译员从原文接收到的信息，译员对信息的解读，为译文读者所传递的信息。目的论三原则有主次之分，目的原则是首要原则，连贯原则与忠实原则从属于目的原则。

---

❶ 本书重点参考了张美芳《功能途径论翻译：以英汉翻译为例》第三章的内容。

目的论的重要优点之一在于允许原文基于译文之目的和译者之任务而以不同的方式翻译。用弗米尔的话说就是:目的论想表达的是译者必须有意识地且始终如一地遵照一些顾及译文的翻译原则。弗米尔举例说,一份用法语写成的存在歧义的遗嘱,如果是翻译给一位处理相关案子的律师看的话,就应该直译,同时加脚注或评语。而这份遗嘱如果是小说里的一个情节,那译者可能就不会以加脚注的方式去翻译。目的论此时就允许译者在这份遗嘱的译文里创造出未加评注的歧义,以达到功能对等。

执行具体的翻译实例,要做到翻译行为恰当,就必须明白翻译"任务"(brief/commission),搞清楚翻译目的。弗米尔认为翻译任务应包括:(1)目的;(2)目的达成的条件(包括交付日期及费用)。这两点都需要译者和翻译委托人之间协商。译者需要告知委托人或客户翻译任务的可行性。译文的本质"首先由其目的或使命决定",在评估翻译行为时,合适比对等更为重要。此处的合适指在翻译过程中,遵守了目的准则后所形成的原文和译文间的关系。换言之,如果译文满足了翻译委托书里所规定之目的,那么在功能上和交际上,译文就是合适的。

诺德在此基础上提出了"功能加忠诚原则"的理论模式。对于诺德来说,忠诚是翻译互动中译者对其合作伙伴的责任。译者应该忠于原语和译语双方。但不能把它与忠信这一概念混为一谈,因为忠信(fidelity/faithfulness)仅指原文与译文的关系,而忠诚(loyalty)是一个人际范畴概念,指的是人与人之间的社会关系。(诺德1997:125)

诺德接着解释说,"译文目的应与原文作者之目的和谐相容"。当然,有时原文目的不一定总是那么清楚。忠诚原则的重要性在于"限制了某一原文的多种译文功能之范围,增加了译者与客户之间对翻译任务的商榷与沟通的必要性"。

2.翻译中的文本分析

在1997年出版的《译有所为——功能翻译理论阐述》(*Translating as a Purposeful Activity*)一书中,克里斯蒂安·诺德提出了一个更加灵活的分析模式,该模式综合了本章描述的许多成分,从句子到句子以上的文本分析所涉及的诸多要素,并突出强调了功能主义翻译理论中对译员培训尤其有用的三个方面:翻译委托书的重要性(translation brief)、原文分析的作用以及翻译问题的功能排序。

(1)翻译委托书的重要性

在进行详细的文本分析前,译者需要比较委托书中对原文和译文的描述,从而找出二者之间可能的差别。翻译委托书应该给出关于原文与译文的如下信息:预期的文本功能,译文读者(发出者和接收者),文本接收的时间和地点,媒介(口头语或者书面语),动机(为什么撰写原文和翻译该文)等。

委托书的信息应有助于译者决定译文中所含信息的轻重缓急。诺德举例说,德国海德堡大学的宣传册的目的是要庆祝海德堡大学成立600周年,因此其最重要的内容便是与周年纪念有关的事件。

(2)原文分析的作用

译者一旦了解有关原文和译文的委托书后,便可开始分析原文从而确定:(a)翻译的可行性;(b)为了实现功能翻译必须考虑到的原文中最相关的内容;(c)为完成翻译任务所必需的翻译策略。诺德的模式列出的文本内部因素如下(2005:87-142):

题材:包括与原语和译语语境在文化上的关联。

内容:文本的"意义",包括隐含意义和衔接。

预设:这与原文和译文读者的相关背景知识以及特定的文化和体裁惯例有关。因此,原文中可能存在冗余的部分(例如注释、重复等),而在译文中可能会被忽略。比方说,原文中对唐宁街10号所做的解释:唐宁街10号是英国首相办公所在地。如果译文读者是英国人,这样的解释在译文中则是多余的。另一方面,原文中隐含意义可能需要对译文读者进行解释。例如,在英语文化中,猫头鹰象征着智慧,在汉语文化中,红色象征着幸福,或者在古埃及、佛教和其他文化中,莲花的重要意义等。

文本构成:包括微观结构(如信息单位、情节阶段、逻辑关系、主位结构等)和宏观结构(如开头、结尾、脚注、引证等)。

非语言因素:插图、斜体字、字体等等。

语言:包括方言、语域和专业术语。

句子结构:包括修辞特点,比如括号和省略号的用法。

超语段特征:包括重读、语调、节奏和文体上的标点。

不过,诺德强调,这只是文本分析的一个模式,还可以采用其他语篇语言学模式分析。重要的是,分析模式应包括对所涉及的交际情境的语用分析,且分析原文和翻译任务应使用同一种模式,这样的分析结果才具有可比性(诺德 1997:62)。

(3)翻译问题的功能排序

诺德(1997:62;2005:189)列出了执行翻译任务时需要遵守的功能排序,该排序从语用角度出发,以预期译文功能为最高级别,自上而下排序如下:

①对原文和译文的预定功能进行比较,有助于决定译文的功能类型(文献型还是工具型)。

②如上述(1)中所提及,通过对翻译委托书的分析,可以确定哪些功能需要复制以及哪些因为要迎合译文读者的情境而需要改编。

③翻译类型决定翻译风格。因此,文献型翻译应以原语文化为导向,而工具型翻译则以译语文化为导向。

④有关文本的问题可以在较低的语言层面上得以解决,如上述(2)中所提及的原文分析。

Afghan's Time of Endless Crisis

By Mujib Mashal

(Zabihullah Ghazi contributed reporting from Jalalabad, Afghanistan.)

New York Times, 19, Oct.2018.

Elections raise little hope in a war-ravaged nation where peril is at every turn.

In the past 17 years of war and crisis in Afghanistan, no one remembers a season quite like this one, with peril and hopelessness at every turn. People here struggle for words to explain how it feels.

A former minister, fit with healthy habits and hardened by years of battle and politics, said he could barely force himself out of bed in the morning. A young professional, after years of dedicated work in civil society and government jobs, teared up as she tried to explain why she was losing hope, her usual clarity choked by emotion. A poet in the country's east said his verse had dried up.

"Every time something bad happened, I would turn to poetry-it would give me calm," said the poet, Sajid Ba-har, 26, who lives in the city of Khost. "It's been seven months that I can't write. It no longer gives me calm. When I sit down to focus on one incident for a poem, 30 others flash through my head. My words do not have the strength for all of them."

If there is a common theme in this up-swell of alarm and worry that seems so widespread, it is a sense that no one sees any clear path through a minefield of crises.

And with a parliamentary election coming on Saturday, in which 2,500 candidates are contesting 250 seats, the possibility of widening political disputes and intractable division poses an immediate concern. After five elections and nearly $1 billion spent on them, there is little consensus on how voting should happen, and elections have become flash points for instability.

Any one of the problems facing Afghanistan right now would be an urgent national issue. Together, they have created an existential moment.

Afghan and international officials consider government security forces' losses to the Taliban to be unsustainable, as the insurgents continue to threaten districts and towns. The daily toll, all sides of the war included, often reaches 100 dead.

Officials acknowledge the only hope is to bring the Taliban to a political reconciliation through peace talks—even though the insurgents have offered no convincing indication they are willing to accept any basic tenet of the democratic program here, including elections or hard-earned rights for women. This best-case scenario for ending the war is chilling for an entire generation of politically active young Afghans who do not want to go back to repression or civil war.

At the same time, an intensified campaign of suicide bombings by Islamic State loyalists in Kabul, the capital, has brought new menace and deepened sectarian divisions. The repeated violence against Afghanistan's Shiite minority has soured people on the government's promises of protection, and it is raising fears that national unity cannot hold in the face of an increasingly complicated war.

Criticism of President Ashraf Ghani's coalition government has grown intense, on both the security and political fronts.

A growing opposition movement of political elites accuses him of trying to rig the electoral system. These politicians have pushed to bypass elections altogether and declare an interim government, and some who can call on armed militias have even threatened to reject the election results by force.

"We waited a long time, hoping that it would get better next year, and then the year after, and then the year after."

But many Afghans still believe in the promise of some kind of democracy, and they want to vote even though they are disillusioned.

Despite the tensions, and the fact that at least a third of polling stations across the country will not open because of the war, the parliamentary vote will go ahead on Saturday.

At least 10 candidates and dozens of their supporters have already been killed, including a parliamentary hopeful, Abdul Jabar Qahraman, who died in Helmand Province on Wednesday when a Taliban bomb blew up under his chair.

Geopolitically, worsening American relations with three crucial neighbors of Afghanistan—Pakistan, Russia and Iran—have raised fears that those countries will intensify their meddling in the war to punish the United States. Afghan and Western officials say Pakistan refuses to stop sheltering the insurgency^ leaders or use its influence to slow the Taliban's momentum. And both Russia and Iran, they say, are increasing their aid to the Taliban.

In this fragile environment, the physical encroachments of violence have given a new shape to life's routine in Afghanistan.

In Kabul, there is no more visible symbol of the change than the network of concrete blast walls protecting the elite, turning the streets into a maze. Behind those walls, political and diplomatic energy is sapped by problem after problem, each solution offering a bit of relief but no breakthrough toward ending the war.

A concerted military and intelligence push over the past month has brought a rare reprieve from suicide bombings. Suspects have been rounded up in large numbers, and insurgent networks disrupted somewhat, officials say.

But the fear of that next big bombing remains, and with it a conviction that ordinary Afghans will again bear the brunt. So residents see in those blast walls a reminder of their own vulnerability, and life continues as a daily resistance.

The teacher on his bicycle navigates armored vehicles and armed guards on his way to school. The cafe is briefly deserted after a blast, and then it returns to its normal chatter. The blown-up wrestling gym starts rebuilding, one brick at a time. The student who survived a massacre in a lecture hall shows up for an exam days later, his head wrapped in gauze.

Some see the crumbling of an untenable structure created by the foreign presence as a necessary trial by fire to get to a new and more sustainable way.

"We had a fake economy, fake money and fake prosperity. Security was provided by foreigners, said Mirwais Arya, who has been trying to grow a small chain of burger cafes called Mazadar.

"Our role, our input, our understanding was limited."

"My sense is that the situation will get worse as that fakeness crumbles, that we will reach the edge of collapse before there is a move for the better," he said.

"But once it crumbles, we will see that underneath, the society has actually transformed."

Others continue with the routine of advocacy and politics, in the face of tremendous uncertainty. At the core of that resistance is the generation of Afghans who have come of age in the past 17 years, enjoying some happier times and possibilities.

President Ghani sees this group as key to escaping the quagmire—what he has described as putting out a fire in one house while simultaneously building a new foundation next door.

He has appointed many young officials to important government jobs, ignoring criticism that he is abandoning experience at a crucial time. But thousands of other youths are fleeing, risking a dangerous trek even when it is clear that Europe has shut its gates.

The vote on Saturday is turning into an important contest between an entrenched elite and young, educated Afghans who have decided to stay and try their chances.

"This election is an arena for two generations: one that is about the glories and the grievances of the past, and a younger generation that wants to build the Afghanistan of the future," said Sami Mahdi, a journalist who is running for a Parliament seat in Kabul.

"In my conversations, people still have a lot of hope in this new generation—that they can stand against the corruption, against the warlords, against the stereotypes," Mr. Mahdi said.

Muqadessa Ahmadzai, 25, is running in Nangarhar Province, where many districts are under threat from the Taliban or the Islamic State, and where the provincial capital, Jalalabad, has been wrecked by repeated suicide attacks.

She says she is running for Parliament to try to correct some of the wrongs of the elites, in any way she can.

We have not received the kind of representation we expected, said Ms. Ah-madzai, who led a nonprofit group that established literary hubs in schools for female writers. "Not only did they not fight for our rights, but they actually abused our rights." She added: "They are the reason for Afghanistan's crisis."

The months ahead will likely prove even more testing to the patience of ordinary Afghans, and to the coherence of the government.

The voting on Saturday is likely to produce the kind of localized disputes that will, once again, put the coalition government and its international partners in firefighting mode.

Mr. Bahar, the poet, said he was trying a variety of things to ease his mind, like talking long walks.

"We waited a long time, hoping that it would get better next year, and then the year after, and then the year after. But it's not happening," Mr. Bahar said. "I will wait another few months, until the presidential elections. If it doesn't improve, I will have to find a smuggling route to another country."

He added: "In a different country, at least I can go up a mountain, sit by the water. At least my mind will be at ease.

(1543 words)

第九章

译文校改

Of Virtue
Francis Bacon(1561-1626)

VIRTUE is like a rich stone, best plain set; and surely virtue is best, in a body that is comely, though not of delicate features; and that hath rather dignity of presence, than beauty of aspect. Neither is it almost seen, that very beautiful persons are otherwise of great virtue; as if nature were rather busy, not to err, than in labor to produce excellency. And therefore they prove accomplished, but not of great spirit; and study rather behavior, than virtue. But this holds not always: for Augustus Caesar, Titus Vespasianus, Philip le Belle of France, Edward the Fourth of England, Alcibiades of Athens, Ismael the Sophy of Persia, were all high and great spirits; and yet the most beautiful men of their times. In beauty, that of favor, is more than that of color; and that of decent and gracious motion, more than that of favor. That is the best part of beauty, which a picture cannot express; no, nor the first sight of the life. There is no excellent beauty, that hath not some strangeness in the proportion. A man cannot tell whether Apelles, or Albert Durer, were the more trifler; whereof the one, would make a personage by geometrical proportions; the other, by taking the best parts out of divers faces, to make one excellent. Such personages, I think, would please nobody, but the painter that made them. Not but I think a painter may make a better face than ever was; but he must do it by a kind of felicity (as a musician that maketh an excellent air in music), and not by rule. A man shall see faces, that if you examine them part by part, you shall find never a good; and yet altogether do well. If it be true that the principal part of beauty is in decent motion, certainly it is no marvel, though persons in years seem many times more amiable; pulchrorum autumnus pulcher; for no youth can be comely but by pardon, and considering the youth, as to make up the comeliness. Beauty is as summer fruits, which are easy to corrupt, and cannot last; and for the most part it makes a dissolute youth, and an age a little out of countenance; but yet certainly again, if it light well, it maketh virtue shine, and vices blush.

佳译赏析

Of Great Place

英语文本	汉语文本
Of Great Place Francis Bacon(1561-1626)	谈高位 王佐良译
MEN in great place are thrice servants: servants of the sovereign or state; servants of fame; and servants of business. So as they have no freedom; neither in their persons, nor in their actions, nor in their times. It is a strange desire, to seek power and to lose liberty: or to seek power over others, and to lose power over a man's self. The rising unto place is laborious; and by pains, men come to greater pains; and it is sometimes base; and by indignities, men come to dignities. The standing is slippery, and the regress is either a downfall, or at least an eclipse, which is a melancholy thing. Cum non sis qui fueris, non esse cur velis vivere. Nay, retire men cannot when they would, neither will they, when it were reason; but are impatient of privateness, even in age and sickness, which require the shadow; like old townsmen, that will be still sitting at their street door, though thereby they offer age to scorn. Certainly great persons had need to borrow other men's opinions, to think themselves happy; for if they judge by their own feeling, they cannot find it; but if they think with themselves, what other men think of them, and that other men would fain be, as they are, then they are happy, as it were, by report; when perhaps they find the contrary within. For they are the first, that find their own griefs, though they be the last, that find their own faults. Certainly men in great fortunes are strangers to themselves, and while they are in the puzzle of business, they have no time to tend their health, either of body or mind. Illi mors gravis incubat, qui notus nimis omnibus, ignotus moritur sibi.	居高位者乃三重之仆役,帝王或国家之臣,荣名之奴,事业之婢也。因此不论其人身、行动、时间,皆无自由可言。追逐权力,而失自由,有治人之权,而无律己之力,此种欲望诚可怪也。历尽艰难始登高位,含辛茹苦,唯得更大辛苦,有时事且卑劣,因此须做尽不光荣之事,方能达光荣之位。既登高位,立足难稳,稍一倾侧,即有倒地之虞,至少亦晦暗无光,言之可悲。古人云:"既已非当年之盛,又何必贪生。"殊不知人居高位,欲退不能,能退之际亦不愿退,甚至年老多病,理应隐居,亦不甘寂寞,犹如老迈商人仍长倚店门独坐,徒令人笑其老不死而已。显达之士率需借助他人观感,方信自己幸福,而无切身之感,从人之所见,世之所羡,乃人云亦云,认为幸福,其实心中往往不以为然。盖权贵虽最不勇于认过,却最多愁善感也。凡人一经显贵,待己亦成陌路,因事务纠缠,对本人身心健康,亦无暇顾及矣,诚如古人所言:"悲哉斯人之死也,举世皆知其为人,而独无自知之明!"
In place, there is license to do good, and evil; whereof the latter is a curse: for in evil, the best condition is not to win; the second, not to can. But power to do good, is the true and lawful end of aspiring. For good thoughts (though God accept them) yet, towards men, are little better than good dreams, except they be put in act; and that cannot be, without power and place, as the vantage, and commanding ground.	居高位,可以行善,亦便于作恶。作恶可咒,救之之道首在去作恶之心,次在除作恶之力;而行善之权,则为求高位者所应得,盖仅有善心,虽为上帝嘉许,而凡人视之,不过一场好梦耳,唯见之于行始有助于世,而行则非有权力高位不可,犹如作战必据险要也。
Merit and good works, is the end of man's motion; and conscience of the same is the accomplishment of man's rest. For if a man can be partaker of God's theatre, he shall likewise be partaker of God's rest. Et conversus Deus, ut aspiceret opera quae fecerunt manus suae, vidit quod omnia essent bona nimis; and then the sabbath.	行动之目的在建功立业,休息之慰籍在自知功业有成。盖人既分享上帝所造之胜最,自亦应分享上帝所订之休息。圣经不云乎:"上帝回顾其手创万物,无不美好。"于是而有安息日。

续上表

英 语 文 本	汉 语 文 本
In the discharge of thy place, set before thee the best examples; for imitation is a globe of precepts. And after a time, set before thee thine own example; and examine thyself strictly, whether thou didst not best at first. Neglect not also the examples, of those that have carried themselves ill, in the same place; not to set off thyself, by taxing their memory, but to direct thyself, what to avoid. Reform therefore, without bravery, or scandal of former times and persons; but yet set it down to thyself, as well to create good precedents, as to follow them. Reduce things to the first institution, and observe wherein, and how, they have degenerate; but yet ask counsel of both times; of the ancient time, what is best; and of the latter time, what is fittest.	执行职权之初，宜将最好先例置诸座右，有无数箴言，可资借镜。稍后应以己为例，严加审查，是否已不如初。前任失败之例，亦不可忽，非为揭人之短，显己之能，以其可作前车之鉴也。因此凡有兴革，不宜大事夸耀，亦不耻笑古人，但须反求诸己，不独循陈规，而且创先例也。凡事须追本溯源，以见由盛及衰之道。然施政定策，则古今皆须征询：古者何事最好，今者何事最宜。
Seek to make thy course regular, that men may know beforehand, what they may expect; but be not too positive and peremptory; and express thyself well, when thou digressest from thy rule. Preserve the right of thy place; but stir not questions of jurisdiction; and rather assume thy right, in silence and de facto, than voice it with claims, and challenges. Preserve likewise the rights of inferior places; and think it more honor, to direct in chief, than to be busy in all. Embrace and invite helps, and advices, touching the execution of thy place; and do not drive away such, as bring thee information, as meddlers; but accept of them in good part.	施政须力求正规，俾众知所遵循，然不可过严过死；本人如有越轨，必须善为解释。本位之职权不可让，管辖之界限则不必问，应在不动声色中操实权，忌在大庭广众间争名分。下级之权，亦应维护，与其事事干预，不如遥控总领，更见尊荣。凡有就分内之事进言献策者，应予欢迎，并加鼓励；报告实况之人，不得视为好事，加以驱逐，而应善为接待。
The vices of authority are chiefly four: delays, corruption, roughness, and facility. For delays: give easy access; keep times appointed; go through with that which is in hand, and interlace not business, but of necessity. For corruption: do not only bind thine own hands, or thy servants' hands, from taking, but bind the hands of suitors also, from offering. For integrity used doth the one; but integrity professed, and with a manifest detestation of bribery, doth the other. And avoid not only the fault, but the suspicion. Whosoever is found variable, and changeth manifestly without manifest cause, giveth suspicion of corruption. Therefore always, when thou changest thine opinion or course, profess it plainly, and declare it, together with the reasons that move thee to change; and do not think to steal it. A servant or a favorite, if he be inward, and no other apparent cause of esteem, is commonly thought, but a by-way to close corruption. For roughness: it is a needless cause of discontent: severity breedeth fear, but roughness breedeth hate. Even reproofs from authority, ought to be grave, and not taunting. As for facility: it is worse than bribery. For bribes come but now and then; but if importunity, or idle respects, lead a man, he shall never be without. As Solomon saith, To respect persons is not good; for such a man will transgress for a piece of bread.	掌权之弊有四，曰：拖、贪、暴、圆。拖者拖延也，为免此弊，应开门纳客，接见及时，办案快速，非不得已不可数事混杂。贪者贪污也，为除此弊，既要束住本人及仆从之手不接，亦须束住来客之手不送，为此不仅应廉洁自持，且须以廉洁示人，尤须明白弃绝贿行。罪行固须免，嫌疑更应防。性情不定之人有明显之改变，而无明显之原因，最易涉贪污之嫌。因此意见与行动苟有更改，必须清楚说明，当众宣告，同时解释所以变化之理由，决不可暗中为之。如有仆从稔友为主人亲信，其受器重也别无正当理由，则世人往往疑为秘密贪污之捷径。粗暴引起不满，其实完全可免。严厉仅产生畏惧，粗暴则造成仇恨。即使上官申斥，亦宜出之以严肃，而不应恶语伤人。至于圆通，其害过于纳贿，因贿赂仅偶尔发生，如有求必应，看人行事，则积习难返矣。索罗门曾云："对权贵另眼看待实非善事，盖此等人能为一两米而作恶也。"

续上表

英 语 文 本	汉 语 文 本
It is most true, that was anciently spoken, A place showeth the man. And it showeth some to the better, and some to the worse. Omnium consensu capax imperii, nisi imperasset, saith Tacitus of Galba; but of Vespasian he saith, Solus imperantium, Vespasianus mutatus in melius; though the one was meant of sufficiency, the other of manners, and affection. It is an assured sign of a worthy and generous spirit, whom honor amends. For honor is, or should be, the place of virtue; and as in nature, things move violently to their place, and calmly in their place, so virtue in ambition is violent, in authority settled and calm. All rising to great place is by a winding star; and if there be factions, it is good to side a man's self, whilst he is in the rising, and to balance himself when he is placed. Use the memory of thy predecessor, fairly and tenderly; for if thou dost not, it is a debt will sure be paid when thou art gone. If thou have colleagues, respect them, and rather call them, when they look not for it, than exclude them, when they have reason to look to be called. Be not too sensible, or too remembering, of thy place in conversation, and private answers to suitors; but let it rather be said, When he sits in place, he is another man.	旨哉古人之言，"一登高位，面目毕露。"或更见有德，或更显无行。罗马史家戴西特斯论罗马大帝盖巴曰："如未登基，则人皆以为明主也。"其论维斯帕西安则曰："成王霸之业而篾有德，皇帝中无第二人矣。"以上一则指治国之才，一则指道德情操。尊荣而不易其操，反增其德，斯为忠诚仁厚之确征。夫尊荣者，道德之高位也：自然界中，万物不得其所，皆狂奔突撞，既达其位，则沉静自安，道德亦然，有志未晒则狂，当权问政则静。一切腾达，无不须循小梯盘旋而上。如朝有朋党，则在上升之际，不妨与一派结交。既登之后，则须稳立其中，不偏不倚。对于前任政绩，宜持论平允，多加体谅，否则，本人卸职后亦须清还欠债，无所逃也。如有同僚，度恭敬相处，宁可移樽就教，出人意外，不可人有所待，反而拒之。与人闲谈，或有客私访，不可过于矜持，或时刻不忘尊贵，宁可听人如是说："当其坐堂议政时，判若两人矣。"

认知升级

好的翻译作品大多是多次修改出来的，并非一蹴而就。在译文的校改与润色阶段，译者需要着重掌握以下几方面的问题。

一、词义的推敲

在翻译校对阶段，我们首先需要处理的最基本的翻译单位就是词语。译者需要进一步辨别词类，分清词形变化，根据语境确定词义，对比中英语义关系，并将初步译文放在具体语境中，检验翻译结果。

1.词语的概念和分类

词语是语言组织中能独立运用的，具有一定的读音、意义和句法功能的基本单位。

英语中的词语可以根据不同的标准分为不同的类别。例如，可以根据词语的来源分为本族词语(native words)和外来词语(loan words)。根据词语的使用情况可以分为基本词(basic words)和普通词(non-basic words)，后者包括 literary, colloquial, slang, technical words。

根据词语在句中的用法和功能，可以分为功能词(function words)和实义词(content words)。前者指没有完整词汇意义但有语法意义或语法功能的词语，例如代词(pronoun)、介词(preposition)、连词(conjunction)、助动词(auxiliary)；后者主要有名词(noun)、动词(verb)、形容词(adjective)、副词(adverb)等。

2.词义的分类

词义由各种相互联系与相互依存的不同成分组成,这些成分就是词义的种类。词义可以分为语法意义和词汇意义,后者又可分为概念意义和联想意义。

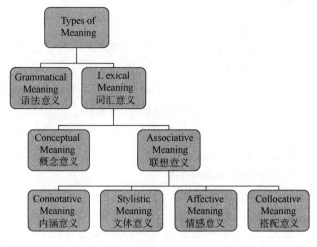

词语的意义

(1)语法意义(Grammatical meaning)

语法意义指词义中表示语法概念或关系的那部分意义。例如词类、名词的单复数、动词的时态意义及它们的屈折形式。

词类不同,意义不同。要理解词义,首先应在句中根据该词的搭配确定其词类。现以 light 一词为例,分析它在具体语境下所充当的不同词类。

例1 Suddenly there was a flash of white **light** in the sky.
突然,天空中白光一闪。(此处,light 为名词)

例2 Dry wood **lights** easily.
干木柴容易**点燃**。(不及物动词)

例3 His face was **lighted by happiness.**
他脸上**喜气洋洋**。(及物动词)

例4 The bag was very **light**, as though there were nothing in it.
那只包很**轻**,似乎里面是空的。(形容词)

再如 back 一词,也有名词、动词、形容词等不同词性,其代表的意义也不相同。

例1 He rides on a horse's **back.**
他骑在马**背**上。(名词)

例2 The car **backed** through the gate.
汽车**倒车**开出大门。(不及物动词)

例3 Don't worry. I will **back** you up.
不要发愁,我**支持**你。(及物动词)

例4 I know a **back** way from our place to the graveyard.
我知道一条由此通往墓地的**偏僻**小路。(形容词)

例5 Please go **back** three steps.

请后退三步。(副词)

(2) 词汇意义 (Lexical meaning)

词汇意义是词典中一个独立词的意义。在该词的所有形式中,其词汇意义相同。词汇意义又分为概念意义和联想意义。

(3) 概念意义 (Conceptual meaning)

概念意义是词汇意义的核心,也是指词典中列出的第一义,是最基本、最本质的意义,一般用来界定和描述一个事物、一种特性、一个过程或一种状态。

一个词的概念意义可能随着上下文的不同而不同。由于所处的语境不同,一个词可能有几个不同的概念意义。例如,foot 一词的不同概念意义如下。

例1 He hurt his feet this morning.
他今天上午脚受伤了。

例2 The man is five feet two inches tall.
此人身高5英尺2英寸。

(4) 联想意义 (Associative meaning)

联想意义是概念意义的补充意义,是次要意义。它受语言外界因素如文化、经历、宗教、地域、出身、教育等的影响而变化,所以是开放性的,是不定的。联想意义有内含意义、文体意义、感情意义和搭配意义。

① 内涵意义 (Connotative Meaning)

内涵意义是由概念意义产生的言外之意或联想。词的内涵意义可以因人而异,因不同年龄而异,例如 home 这个单词对一些人来说,意味着"家庭成员""亲情",East or west, home is best. 千好万好,自家最好。对另一些人来说,可能是"冷冰冰的""令人烦恼的""如坟墓似的"。

某些词语的内涵意义带有民族特征。例如,dog 在西方常常意味着"忠心""人类的朋友",而"狗"在一些中国人看来,可能意味着"趋炎附势""帮凶"。再如"肥肉"一词,中国人听到"肥肉"就会联想到"美差""好东西",到嘴的"肥肉"要是吃不上可就遗憾得要命,而美国人听到 fat meat,会觉得那是"毫无价值、该扔掉的东西"。

② 语体意义 (Stylistic Meaning)

语体意义是个人或某一特定领域所使用的语言的特点或倾向。从广义上讲,语体一般分为正式 (formal) 和非正式 (informal);口语语体 (spoken) 和书面语体 (written) 两大类。按正式程度分,语体还可分庄严 (solemn) 的、正式的 (formal)、商议性的 (consultative)、随意的 (casual) 以及亲密的 (intimate)。每一种语体的特点都可以通过各自使用的语音、词汇、句法和篇章特点体现出来。例如:

非正式	正式
leave	depart
job	position, occupation
tired	fatigued
can't	cannot
ad	advertisement
fridge	refrigerator

例如:thereunder, hereinafter 为正式语,一般只在法律条文中出现;cardiovascular, semiconductor, glucose 为特定行业内的科技词汇;而 sunbeam, comely 则富有文学色彩。一些词汇可以

出现在不同语体中,但在不同语体中的语体色彩又各不相同,这尤其需要我们加以注意。

例如:kidney 出现在科技文体中时,是一个带有科技语体色彩的词语,汉语称作"肾脏",而在日常口语中,尤其指称动物体内可供食用的内脏时,又成为一个带有口语色彩的普通名词,汉语常称作"腰子"。再如 probability,在统计学或某些特定科技文体中,常译为"概率、或然性",而在其他文体中,常译作"可能性"这一普通表达。

很多因素可以帮助我们识别词语在具体语境中的语体色彩。从非语言层面来看,包括作者的思想情感、说话人的身份特征、会话情景、对象等;从语言层面来看,包括文本内容、用词和句式特点、修辞等。翻译时应对这些因素加以综合考虑,使译文用词的语体色彩与原文相符。

在翻译中,要再现词汇的语体色彩,首先应把握不同词语所具有的不同语体意义。

例1 Anyone who **accomplishes** a lot must be equipped with an excellent quality——an open mind.(accomplish 为较正式的书面语。)
任何取得巨大**成就**的人都具备一项优秀的品质——心胸宽广。
Work harder, chaps, if you really want to **get ahead**.(get ahead 口语色彩浓厚,且多用于非正式场合,这是短语动词的一个普遍特征。)
伙计们,想要**搞出点名堂**来,得再加一把劲儿啊。

例2 A receiver around the patient's **abdomen** records the images.(abdomen 为带有科技语体色彩的书面语。)
患者**腹部**周围的接收器会记录下这些影像。
Two frogs in the **belly** of a snake were considering their altered circumstances.(belly 常用于口语和非正式场合。)
蛇**肚子**里的两只青蛙正琢磨着自己的处境怎么就被改变了呢。

例3 The Chinese Government has always opposed and **condemned** all form of terrorism.
中国政府一贯反对和**谴责**一切形式的恐怖主义。("condemn"为正式的政论语体。)
I wish you wouldn't **call** me **down** in public.("call down"语气不及"condemn"正式,用于一般场合。)
请不要当着众人的面**责骂**我行吗?

其次,应把握具体语境所赋予同一词语的不同语体意义。试比较下面几组例子:

例1 Both groups afford students regular opportunities to meet, eat, and **talk** philosophy with each other and with graduate students and faculty in the department.
每个小组都会定期组织同学与系里的其他同学、研究生以及教师会面、就餐,并在一起**探讨**哲学。(大学哲学系介绍,较正式。结合 philosophy 一词,将 talk 译为"探讨"。)
I'm kinda hoping so, just so it takes a little more time and we can **talk** some.(交通事故中小伙子和一位不相识的姑娘搭讪。结合场景,talk 此处显得极为随意。)
我倒有点希望。这样一来,我们也可以多点儿时间好好**聊聊**啊。

例2 I said hello to her, but she **ignored** me completely!(口语或一般语境中,用法较随意。)
我向她打招呼,可她根本**不理**我。
A grand jury **ignores** an indictment.(正式法律语体。)
大陪审团**驳回**刑事起诉。

③情感意义(Affective meaning)

词语的感情色彩是词语所反映出来的人们对客观事物的情感态度,一般分为褒义(commendatory,appreciative,positive)、贬义(derogative,pejorative,or negative)和中性(neutral)。这种意义可以通过表情词直截了当地表现出来。褒义词主要表达欣赏或肯定的意思。贬义词表达否定、轻蔑或批评的意思。翻译时,需要译者去理解和认同作者的思想与情感,灵活地发挥译入语的特点,使原文的感情色彩在译文中得到再现。情感意义反映作者或说话人对所谈论的人或物、事态等表示的个人情感或态度。

在感情色彩传译的过程中,一般有以下几种情况:一种情况是词语本身就含有褒义或贬义,其感情色彩是固有的,例如:

褒义	贬义
famous 出名的,有名的	notorious 臭名昭著的
publicity 宣传	propaganda 宣扬,鼓吹
achievement 成果	consequence 后果
statesman 政治家	politician 政客
encourage 鼓励	instigate 鼓动、唆使
praise 赞扬	brag 吹嘘
cooperate 合作	collude 勾结
charm 使……着迷	seduce 诱使
active 积极的	radical 激进的
plump 丰满的	obese 肥胖的
slim/slender 苗条	skinny 骨瘦如柴
firm 坚定的	stubborn 固执的
confidence 信心	complacency 自负

把握词语固有的感情色彩,能够让译文生动传神,保持原有的意蕴。例如:

例1 When he smiled, his grave, even rather gloomy, look was instantaneously replaced by another—a **childlike**, kindly, even rather silly look, which seemed to ask forgiveness.

当他笑起来的时候,脸上那种严肃,甚至有些阴沉的表情顷刻间被另一种表情所取代——**天真**,和善,还有些傻傻的,就好像在乞求宽恕似的。(褒义)

例2 The truth is the truth; and neither **childish** absurdities, nor unscrupulous contradictions, can make it otherwise.

事实就是事实,无论用**幼稚的**谬论,还是用无耻的反驳,都是无法改变的。(贬义)

例3 Our excellent technical talents and **strict** management are the guarantee of high-quality products.(褒义)

优秀的技术人才和**严格的**管理是产品质量的保证。

例4 **Harsh** regulations were made to punish and exploit the workers.(贬义)

制定**苛刻的**规章制度对工人进行惩罚和压榨。

第二种情况是词语的感情色彩,既可为褒义,也可为贬义,我们应结合句子的上下文判断作者的态度,以恰当的译入语展现原文的感情色彩。例如:

例1 Jack, enthusiastic and **aggressive**, was often unjustly accused of being a politician.

杰克热情而**有进取心**,却老有人不公正地指责他是在玩弄政治权术。(褒义)

例2 U.S.business today is challenged by **aggressive** overseas competitors.

美国今天的商业受到**咄咄逼人的**海外竞争者的挑战。(贬义)

第三种情况是,有时为了实现反讽、幽默等特殊的修辞效果,作者会将褒义词用于表示否定的场合,或将贬义词用于肯定的场合,这就是所谓的"褒义贬用"或"贬义褒用"。例如:

例1 You make your mother like a servant;you are a **filial** son.Indeed!

你把你妈当作佣人使唤,你可真**孝顺**啊!(将褒义词用作贬义)

例2 How **clever** you are! You broke the glass and laid the blame on others.(将褒义词用作贬义)

你可真**聪明**啊,砸了玻璃还赖在别人身上。

④搭配意义(Collocative Meaning)

搭配意义即与之一起使用的词语所赋予的那部分意义。搭配意义是由一个词从与它相结合的词的意义中所获得的各种联想构成的。它是由其前后的相关词所决定的。有些同义词虽然"概念意义"相同,但搭配能力不同,因而具体意义也有所不同。

比如,pretty 和 handsome 虽然都有"面目好看"的含义,但是它们可以搭配的词语却有着很大的不同。Pretty 常常和 boy,woman,girl,colour,village,garden flower 等词(组)搭配;handsome 常常与 boy,man,car,vessel,overcoat,airliner,typewriter 等搭配。

例如,strong 的意义为"强壮的,强大的",根据搭配的不同,其意义和表达就相当丰富了。如:strong pressure 巨大的压力,a strong majority 绝大多数,a strong will 坚定的意志,a strong argument 有力的论据,strong tea 浓茶,strong perfume 浓郁的香水,strong beat 强烈的节拍,a strong economy 实力雄厚的经济,a strong microscope 高倍显微镜等。

单词 hard 能搭配的词语有:a hard nut 硬坚果,a hard task 艰巨的任务,a hard life 艰难的生活,hard study 刻苦的学习,hard rain 大雨,a hard winter 严冬,hard evidence 铁证,a hard policy 强硬政策,give sb.a hard look 狠盯某人一眼等。

搭配对于翻译中词义的选择是至关重要的。语境为词语提供了赖以生存的框架结构。这一点,在很多所谓"万能词"身上体现得尤为突出,如:take,do,get,go,make,put,set 等。这类词的意义很不明确,必须放在具体语境下,或者与其他词构成固定搭配才能将其意义明确下来。以 take 为例:

例1 Go and **take** a larger spoon.

去**拿**一个大点的勺子来。

例2 The scarf **took** her eye.

她**看中**了那条围巾。

例3 We usually **take** a nap after lunch.

午饭后我们通常会**打**个盹。

例4 She **took** the position of chair of the committee.

她**当上**了委员会主席。

例5 The picture was **taken** on Monica Drane's wedding day in 1989.

这张照片是 1989 年莫尼卡·德雷恩结婚当天**拍摄**的。

例6 Butter often **takes** the flavour of the substances near it.

黄油和什么东西搁在一块儿,就常常会**带上**那种东西的味道。

有时，就是同一个动词短语，其意义仍然需要我们结合上下文，才能确定。例如短语 take in：

例1 Tankers were **taking in** cargoes of finished oil products.
油船正在**装**石油成品。

例2 He **took** some refugees **in** during the Second War.
第二次世界大战期间他**收留**了不少难民。

例3 I'm not sure how much of her teacher's explanation she **took in**.
我不知道老师的解释她**听懂**了多少。

例4 Don't be **taken in** by their promises.
不要被他们的许诺给**欺骗**了。

例5 My skirt is a little loose round the waist. Could you **take** it **in** for me?
我的裙子腰身稍稍大了点，你能帮我**改小**吗？

在具体语境中，我们不仅要学会选择恰当的词语，还要学会对词语进行适度的引申。在翻译中的引申，是指根据上下文的内在联系，通过句中词语或词组，乃至整句的字面意义，由表及里，运用符合译入语习惯的表达方式，将原文的深层意义表达出来。例如：

例1 You can **stretch** your dollars by leaving the city.
原译：离开城市，钱就可以**伸展**开了。（未加引申）
改译：离开城市，钱就耐花。

stretch 一词原意为"伸展、延长"，但由于译文照搬原义而未将意义加以引申，译文显得令人费解。就算勉强能够接受，也极不符合汉语表达习惯。因此，可以将 stretch 引申为"发挥最大效用"，该句便可做以上改译。

例2 If you're **hooked on** Britain, France or Italy, skip the $200-and-up hotels and forgo those gourmet meals.
如果你**非去**英国、法国或意大利**不可**，不要住200美元以上的饭店，也别去吃那些美食。

hook 原指"钩子"，用作动词表示"钩住"，因此，be hooked on 常引申为"沉溺于，对……入了迷"。译文正是根据其引申义，结合搭配的宾语，将其灵活地处理为"非去……不可"。

例3 She was effectually prevented, but she **wasn't on speaking terms** with her family for several weeks.
原译：她家里人想尽办法才没有让她走成，从而使她**反目成仇**，一连几个星期不跟家里的任何人说话。
改译：她家里人想尽办法才没有让她走成，不过事后好几个星期，她都不跟家里的任何人说话。

在英语中，on speaking terms 为固定表达，意为"与……关系好"，常与 not 连用表否定。根据原文提示，she 同 her family 之间存在矛盾，而且还持续了好几周，但我们无论如何是看不出有"反目成仇"这层意思的。

3.英汉语词义关系

"辩义乃翻译之本"。作为最基本的语言单位，词语意义的确定与表达在翻译过程中十分重要，同时也是翻译中的难题之所在。要在翻译中确定词义，寻求恰当的表达，我们必须首先考查英汉两种语言中词语的相互关系。

无论英语还是汉语,每个词的词义都涵盖了一定的范围,这个范围决定了该词能否与译入语中的词语建立对应关系。在英汉互译中,词与词之间对应关系可大致分为:①词义相符;②词义部分相符;③词义空缺。

(1)词义相符

词义相符,是指原语和译入语中对应词语的概念意义和内涵意义相符。概念意义是词的确切意义和字面意义(strict and literal meaning),是人们进行语言交际时所表达的最基本的意义;内涵意义是词汇隐含的意义(implied and suggested meaning),内含了丰富的情感和联想,能体现该民族特有的思维方式和社会文化。

由于我们人类都生活在地球上,所处生态环境大致相似,而人类大脑的结构也基本相同。这使得人类无论处于何种社会和文化背景下,对于客观世界的认识都有着许多共同之处。此外,在中西方文化交流的过程中,各自语言中的一些词汇和表达,也逐渐被对方所接受。因此,不同语言间的词义相符关系也是必然存在的。

我们身边的很多词语,在一般语境下只具备概念义,因此翻译中用词义相符的词译出即可,如:water 水,fire 火,forest 森林,sky 天空,sun 太阳,planet 行星,desert 沙漠,wind 风,rain 雨,liver 肝脏,plastics 塑料,computer 电脑,telephone 电话,book 书,paper 纸,market 市场,museum 博物馆,green-house effect 温室效应,avian influenza/bird flu 禽流感,等等。

还有一些词语或表达既有概念义,又有内涵义,而且在英、汉两种语言中概念义和内涵义基本相同。例如:fox 狐狸(生性狡猾),parrot 鹦鹉(模仿他人说话,人云亦云),trap 陷阱(圈套,困境),face 脸(颜面,尊严),with tail between legs 夹尾巴(垂头丧气,灰溜溜的),add fuel to the fire 火上浇油(使事态严重)等。例如:

例1 Juventus have been slayed there three times, Manchester United and PSV Eindhoven twice each, while Galatasaray, Arsenal, Bayern Munich and Milan have all left Galicia with **tail between legs.**

尤文图斯曾三次在这里遭到绞杀,曼联和埃因霍温各有两次受挫。加拉塔萨雷、阿森纳、拜仁慕尼黑以及米兰也都曾**夹着尾巴**离开加利西亚。

例2 但是,如果你晚上睡眠不好,白天总想着来补补瞌睡,那是万万不可行的,那样做无异于**火上浇油**。

However, if you are having trouble sleeping then, the last thing you need to do is to **add fuel to the fire** by sleeping some during the day.

不难看出,对于词义相符的对应关系,我们可以直接使用相应的概念义来表达原文的意思,让读者去体会其中的含义。如果舍弃概念义,而只将其内涵义译出,如将例1中 tail between legs 译作"失败地离开";将例2中"火上浇油"译作 make it worse,原文的意味就无法得到生动的再现。

但是,对于接下来要讲到的第二类对应关系,在很多情况下则不得不舍弃概念义。

(2)词义部分相符

词义部分相符的第一种情况是两个词语的部分概念义相同,但由于两种语言所存在的社会文化差异和发展差异,人们对所指事物存在认知上的不同,导致两个词的外延不同。例如,在英语中,pen 指代书写工具时,包括钢笔(fountain pen)、圆珠笔(ballpoint pen)、蘸水笔(dip pen)羽毛笔(quill)等,大致与汉语中的"笔"相对应,但是汉语中的"笔"还包括铅笔(pencil)和毛笔(ink brush),这是英语 pen 的外延所不具备的。因此,在翻译的过程中,我们必须根据上下文判断原文所指的究竟是哪一种"笔"。再如,当我们在翻译"羊"这一汉语词汇时,在用 goat 还是 sheep 的问题上常常无法抉择,这是因为"羊"本身就包含了 goat 和 sheep,同时还包括了 ram(公羊)、ewe(母羊)以及 lamb(羊羔),这几个词都是"羊"的下义词(hyponym),词义就蕴涵在"羊"里面,而在"羊"这一语义层面就难以找到对应的英文表达了。

第二种情况是两个词语的概念义基本相同,但内涵义不同或空缺。例如,熊(bear)在汉语和英语中都指哺乳动物中的一类,但在两种语言中的内涵义却大相径庭。在英语中,bear 有"粗鲁,脾气坏"的含义。在汉语中,很多由"熊"构成的词都有此含义,如"装熊""熊包""熊样儿"等。这需要我们在翻译中特别加以注意。例如:

例1 Mrs. Smith is very kind, but her husband is a **bear**.
史密斯太太为人很不错,但她丈夫的**脾气大得很**。

如果将此句译为"史密斯太太为人很不错,但她丈夫却是一只熊",不仅不能传达原文的意思,还会让汉语读者产生误解,因为在汉语中,"熊"有"无能,怯懦"的含义,例如:

例2 到了节骨眼上,你怎么**熊**了?
It's a **coward** thing that you back out at this critical moment.

(3)词义空缺

词义的空缺是文化现象空缺的结果。任何语言都根植于自身特有的文化土壤,而表现特有文化的词语在另一种语言中可能无法找到对应表达,从而出现译入语文化中语义的空缺。翻译时可以灵活运用音译、直译、意译等方法来表达意义。

比如,以下例子采用的是音译法,主要针对词义完全空缺的词汇:engine 引擎,cartoon 卡通,AIDS 艾滋,carnival 嘉年华,sauna 桑拿,ballet 芭蕾。

对于一些外来音译,我们也可以加上表示其类别的语素,以明确词语的意义。如上述 sauna 也可译为"桑拿浴",ballet 也可译为"芭蕾舞"。

但是,直译法的局限在于,译文读者了解的仅仅是词语的字面意义,很难深入理解这些词汇的文化内涵和背景。在必要的时候,译者可为直译加上注释,更好地传达词语的内涵义。

为了文化交流的便利,以下例子采用了意译法:narcissism 自恋,Oedipus complex 恋母情结,Achilles' heel 致命的弱点,peeping Tom 好窥视的人,lazy Susan 餐桌上的转盘,Dear John letter 绝交信等。

值得一提的是,以上的翻译方法都并不是孤立使用的,有时为了交流的需要,我们往往将多种译法结合在一起使用。

二、逻辑的判断

1. 查找逻辑漏洞

翻译不仅是个语言问题(词汇、语法、修辞等),它牵涉到许多非语言方面的因素。逻辑便是其中最活跃、最重要的因素。钱歌川说:逻辑是翻译者的最后一张王牌,是他必须具有的基本要素。凡是翻译出来的一字一句、一事一物,都必须合乎逻辑,合乎情理,否则必然有误。以下例证充分说明逻辑在译文校改中非常重要。

例1 Jefferson refused to accept other people's opinions without careful thought.
原译:杰斐逊没有认真考虑,就拒绝了别人的意见。

改译1：只有经过认真思考，杰斐逊才接受别人的意见。

改译2：未经认真考虑，杰斐逊绝不接受别人的意见。

分析：原文此处谈论的是杰斐逊的优点。可以原译所表达的是一个缺点。这样与逻辑相悖。认真分析原文，就会发现实际上是双重否定结构，相当于 Only with careful thought, jefferson would accept other people's opinions.

例2 Shortly before the uninhabited space station reached orbit in May 1973, aerodynamic pressure ripped off a meteoroid and heat shield.

原译：在1973年5月无人空间站到达轨道前不久，空气动力压力扯破了一个流星体和挡热板。

改译：在1973年5月无人空间站到达轨道前不久，空气动力压力扯破了一个防流星体和防热护罩。

分析：首先，从逻辑上看，"空气动力压力扯破了一个流星体"是不合事理的。其次，按照译文，应该扯破了两个物体，可是译文中，为何 meteoroid 前面有不定冠词 a，而 heat shield 前没有？进一步分析发现，名词 meteoroid 和名词 heat 原来都是名词 shield 的定语，对其修饰说明。A meteoroid and heat shield 的意思是：一个防流星体和防热护罩。

例3 This country has many challenges. We will not deny, we will not ignore, we'll not pass along our problems to other Congress, to other presidents, and other generations. We will confront them with focus and clarity and courage.

原译：我国面临着许多挑战。对此，我们并不否认，也不会置之不理。我们不会把眼前的难题留给其他的国会、其他的总统和其他的后代。我们将集中精力，立场鲜明，勇敢应对。

改译：我国面临着许多挑战。对此，我们并不否认，也不会置之不理。我们不会把眼前的难题留给以后的国会、以后的总统和子孙后代。我们将集中精力，立场鲜明，勇敢应对。

分析：原译三个 other 按其字面意义翻译成"其他的"，产生了"逻辑"混乱，好像美国同时并存着几个国会和总统。其实，根据全段的整体意义可以看出，这里的 other 指的是"以后的"或"下几届"，因而在翻译时要用有相应含义的词语替换之，才合乎汉语的逻辑。

例4 The 20th century will not be remembered as the era when space was conquered, or the power of the atom, harnessed, but that in which were made the first machines having intelligence.

原译：将来人们回忆起20世纪时候，不会把它看成是征服了太空和利用了原子动力世纪，而是看成制造了首批具有智能机器的世纪。

改译：如果在20世纪没有制造出具备智能的首批机器，我们就不会称20世纪为征服宇宙的世纪或者原子能利用的世纪。

分析：原译中的问题在于，究竟是把20世纪看作是什么样的世纪合适，是制造了首批智能机器的世纪，还是征服宇宙的世纪或原子能利用的世纪，原译意味着二选一。常识告诉我们：20世纪既是征服宇宙的世纪，也是利用原子能的世纪。在发现译文不符合逻辑后，要注意研究原文语言。从技术逻辑上看，当今世界，如果没有智能计算机一类的机器，火箭就不能上天，原子能生产就无法控制。因此，译文需要做逻辑上的调整。

例5 After all, all living creatures live by feeding on something else, whether it be plant or animal, dead or alive.

原译:因为,毕竟所有活着的生物,不论是植物还是动物,死的还是活的,都靠吃某种别的东西生存。

改译:所有活着的动物毕竟都是靠吃别的东西生存,无论这些东西是植物还是动物,是死还是活。

例6 The absence of intelligence is an indication of satisfactory developments.

原译1:信息的缺失表明发展很顺利。

原译2:信息的缺乏是发展充分的表现。

改译:没有消息即表明有令人满意的进展。

语篇中,逻辑是服务于主题思想的重要因素,其主要作用是连贯、衔接、照应和过渡,使通篇的语义有机地形成一体;篇章的主题思想和整体含义则是逻辑借以发挥其关联作用的条件(上下文)。

逻辑的存在方式可以是有形的,如具体的词语(连接词、代词、上坐标词等),也可能是无形的,即通过语序和结构反映出来。一般来说,汉语重"意合",所以其逻辑关系往往可以通过后一种方式体现出来;英语重"形合",因此英语中表示连接手段的词语使用频率很高。但是,在英汉翻译过程中,原文中的部分逻辑关系有时也需要细心体会,并且设法把"隐含"的逻辑意义"显现"出来。从广义上说,逻辑是连接篇章与交际环境的纽带之一,而篇章所处的文化背景也是充分理解该篇章逻辑的重要依据。

例1 Some other factors which may influence reasoning are (a) faulty analogizing, (b) the inhibiting effect on further research of concepts which have been widely accepted as satisfactory…

原译:其他会影响推理的一些因素是:(a)错误类比,(b)对一些概念进一步研究抑制性影响,而这些概念被广泛认为满意……

改译:影响推理的其他一些因素有:(a)错误类比;(b)某些概念广为接受,阻碍人们对其进一步研究……

分析:什么叫"抑制性影响",它怎么会成为影响推理因素?原译语意不明确,判断不严密。一查原文,发现原译果然有误。原译者把介词短语of concepts 看成是research这个动作名词逻辑上的宾语了。实际上,句中关键结构是 the effect A(up)on B,意思是:A 对 B 的作用(或影响)。由此可见,the inhibiting effect on further research of concepts…并不是"对一些概念进一步研究抑制住影响",而是"某些被公认的正确概念对进一步研究的阻碍作用"。

例2 Corrosion is an elctro-chemical process by which a metal such as mild steel, returns to its natural state, state, such as iron oxide or rust.

原译:腐蚀是一种电化过程,像低碳钢一类金属,因腐蚀而恢复到自然状态,如氧化铁,即铁锈。

改译:腐蚀是金属(如低碳钢)返回其天然状态(如氧化铁即铁锈)的电化学过程。

分析:原文是一个关于"腐蚀"的定义。但译文由于不恰当地采用了分译法,把一个完整定义弄得支离破碎、面目全非了。大家知道,定义是揭示概念内涵即揭示事物本质属性的逻辑方法。下定义的第一个任务就是把被下定义对象同其他一切对象区分开来。原文很好地完成了这个任务,原译则条块分割,犯了过宽的错误,没有完成下定义这个任务(未把"腐蚀"同其他电化过程如电解、电镀等区分开来)。

2.防范"假朋友"

Mona Baker 这样定义"假朋友"(false friends):False friends are words or expressions which have the same form in two or more languages but convey different meanings。"假朋友"形式上看似相符,实则意义上有天壤之别,在翻译时要特别小心。

下表中列有更多英汉翻译时的假朋友,它们结构相同但意义迥异。

英汉翻译中的假朋友

英　文	"假朋友"	"真朋友"
Vice-chancellor	副总理	大学校长
Sweet water	甜水	淡水、饮用水
dry goods	干货	纺织品
white night	白夜	不眠之夜
Indian summer	印度夏天	秋季的晴暖天气;小阳春
capital idea	资本主义思想	好主意
morning glory	晨光	牵牛花
Spanish athlete	西班牙运动员	吹牛的人
liberal arts	自由艺术	文科
English disease	英国病	软骨病
pull one's leg	拖后腿	开玩笑
You don't say!	你别说!	是吗!
guinea pig	几内亚猪	豚鼠,天竺鼠;试验品,实验对象
pigtail	猪尾巴	辫子
marriages go off the rails	婚姻出轨	家庭出现小矛盾
eat one's words	食言	收回说过的话,承认前言有失,说错了

翻译中的"假朋友"常常使译者误入歧途,有些"假朋友"常常被当作"真朋友"。例如,Out of sight,out of mind 常被译为"眼不见,心不烦",而其真正意义是"久别情疏"。lady killer 常被认为是"少奶杀手",但其主要意义是"爱情骗子"。

例1 Tom said Nancy would never succeed in her business, but after seeing her business grow, he had to eat his words.

原译:汤姆曾经说南希不可能把生意做好,但是看着她的事业风生水起,他不得不食言。

改译:汤姆曾经说南希不可能把生意做好,但是看着她的事业风生水起,他不得不承认自己说错了。

例2 Microsoft's decision to offer new employee perks, initially only at its headquarters campus near Seattle but eventually also in other sites around the world, marks a reversal of an earlier, unpopular cost-cutting policy. A decision to scrap the free towel service two years ago became a lightening rod for employee dissatisfaction. (Microsoft plans perks to retain staff, May 20, 2006)

原译:美国微软公司决定向新员工提供福利,起初仅限于邻近西雅图总部的员工,后来扩展到全球的所有员工,这标志着该公司对此前不受欢迎的节约成本政策的彻底否定。两年前微软曾取消免费提供毛巾,此举成了员工不满的避雷针。

改译:美国微软公司决定向新员工提供福利,起初仅限于邻近西雅图总部的员工,后来扩展到全球的有员工,这标志所着该公司彻底否定了此前不受欢迎的节约成本的政策。两年前,微软曾停止提供免费毛巾,此举成为了引发员工不满的导火索。

分析:汉语中"避雷针效应"的寓意是:"善疏则通,能导必安。"而英语中 lightening rod 则有"招惹麻烦、众矢之的"等意义。

例3 Emina Zaimovic: During the time of war… we also did not have social and medical coverage and, you know, pension funds and stuff, but we were in a way taken care of. For example, there was a girl who had a broken arm, and she was taken to Zagreb hospital, at the expense of the UN. It wasn't arranged as part of the contract, but they made sure to take care of people if something should happen to them.

原译:埃米娜·扎莫维奇:在战争时期……我们也没有社会和医疗保险,也没有养老基金之类的东西,但是我们在某种程度上被照顾了。例如,有一个女孩手臂骨折,她被送往萨格勒布医院,代价是联合国。这不是合同的一部分,但如果有什么事情发生在他们身上,一定要照顾他们。

改译:埃米娜·扎莫维奇:在战争时期……我们也没有社会和医疗保险,也没有养老基金之类的东西,但是我们在某种程度上被照顾了。例如,有一个女孩手臂骨折,她被送往萨格勒布医院,由联合国出钱。这不是合同的一部分,但如果译员出了什么事,他们肯定要照顾。

例4 When their expectations were not met, they typically turned to the locally employed interpreters who tended to assume the technical language roles of formal interpreting and translating as well as the routine work of accompanying patrols. This was particularly apparent once the level of violence had reduced and civilian linguists were able to work safely. As with colloquial linguists, a clearer title would be an advantage.

原译:当他们的期望得不到满足时,他们通常求助于当地雇用的口译员,这些口译员往往承担着正式口译和笔译的技术语言作用以及陪同巡逻的日常工作。一旦暴力程度降低,民间语言学家能够安全工作,这一点就变得尤为明显。如同口语语言学家一样,更清楚的标题将是一个优势。

改译:当他们的期望得不到满足时,他们通常求助于当地雇用的口译员,这些口译员往往承担着正式口笔译的技术语言工作以及陪同巡逻的日常工作。一旦暴力程度降低,民间语言学家能够安全工作,这一点就变得尤为明显。对口语语言工作者而言一样,定义更加清楚的头衔将是一个优势。

例5 Interlocutors also had to attempt to determine the backgrounds of their counterparts in order to decide whether, or how far, to trust. Great weight was placed in these calculations on discerning the nationality and ethnicity of language intermediaries.

原译:对话者还必须设法确定对方的背景,以便决定是否信任,或信任到何种程度。在对语言中介机构的国籍和民族的识别方面,这些计算有很大的分量。

改译:对话者还必须设法确定对方的背景,以便决定是否信任,或信任到何种程度。要花很大精力来考虑如何识别语言调停者的国籍和民族身份。

三、风格的统一

1.语域与文体风格

风格是指作家、艺术家在创作中所表现出来的艺术特色和创作个性的作家由于生活经历、立场观点、艺术素养、个性特征的不同,在处理题材、驾驭体裁、描绘形象、表现手法和运用语言等方面都各有特色,这就形成了作品的风格。风格体现在文艺作品内容和形式的各要素中。

风格可以归纳为以下三个方面:第一,文学作品的题材和体裁及作家对它们的处理手法。第二,作家文章的风采和作品的基调。所谓风采,指作家的文笔,是清新、华丽、细腻或者粗犷等;所谓基调,指作家"表达手法的一致性",是严肃、欢乐、沉闷或者悲哀等。第三,作家驾驭语言的本领,遣词造句的特色,作家对语言的习惯用法、句型结构的特点以及贯穿作品始终的作家本身的语言"个性"等。

风格的决定因素在于语域。所谓语域(register)就是指语言随着使用场合环境不同而区分的语言变体,是指在特定的语言环境中使用的、有一定的语言特征的语言变体。语域(Register)是语言使用的场合或领域的总称。语言使用的领域种类很多,例如:新闻广播、演说语言、广告语言、课堂用语、办公用语、家常谈话、与幼童谈话、与外国人谈话、口头自述等。

决定语域的三个社会变量是:语场(field)、语旨(tenor)及语式(mode)。语场指的是实际发生的事,或者说是指语言发生的环境,包括谈话的话题;语旨是指参与者之间的关系,包括参与者的社会地位以及他们之间的角色关系;语式是指语言交际的渠道或媒介,比方说是口头的还是书面的,是即兴的还是有准备的。

随着一个人在不同的社会环境中角色的转变,他所使用的语言也应作相应不同的改变:作为一个孝顺儿子对年迈的母亲、作为一个体贴的丈夫对心爱的妻子和作为一个严厉的父亲对逃学的孩子所使用的语言是不同的。

在不同的领域使用的语言会有不同的语体。根据语域变化的范围,德国语言学家Martin Joos归纳出英语的五种语体:

①庄重文体(frozen style):最正式语体,一般都有固定的格式,用词讲究,结构严谨、句子冗长,用于典礼等正规场合。

②正式文体(formal style):正式语体,句法规范,句子具有一定的长度,用于官方报道、演说等重要的场合。

③商议文体(consultative style):半正式语体,用于日常工作、购物和旅行等场合。

④随意文体(casual style):非正式语体,特点是简略,常常省略主语和助动词,多用于朋友之间。

⑤亲密文体(intimate style):最不正式语体,高度省略,夹杂俚语和行话,语气十分随意,有时甚至粗俗,多用于家人和十分亲近的朋友之间。

庄重文体在法律条文和部门的规章制度、重大仪式上的演说中,有着独特的功用。

例1 We hereby declare that all the candidates here have passed their thesis defense and therefore degrees will be conferred on them.

兹宣布:所有参加答辩的考生都已通过论文答辩,因此授予他们学位。

例2 Discourse with the chauffeur is strictly prohibited while this vehicle is in motion.

本车行驶期间严禁与司机交谈。

与这种文体形成鲜明对照的是随意文体。随意文体可以是口语,也可以是书面语,结构较为松散、简单,有时甚至杂乱。它的另一个特点是大量使用俚语和省略的表达方式。有人认为正式文体是最佳文体,但这种说法是带有偏见的。有时候,一些不堪登大雅之堂的俚语可以由作者信手拈来的,变成神来之笔。

例1 Dear Ann Landers:

Is our daughter normal? Am I crazy or what? Linda is 16, does not lift a finger around the house, yells bloody murder if I misplace something that she should have put away. She has a tantrum if I Don't have her blouses pressed in time. If I ask her to run an errand for me, she says I'm exploiting her. I'm exhausted and disgusted. What goes?

——Beat Mom.

译文:

亲爱的安·兰德丝:

我们的女儿正常吗?是我疯了还是咋的?琳达已经16岁,但她对家务事却从不伸手。如果我把本应该由她收拾的东西放错了地方,她就会大惊大闹;如果我没有及时把她的衬衫熨好,她就会歇斯底里;如果我差她帮我跑个腿,她就说我在剥削她。我被她弄得筋疲力尽,腻烦透了。这到底是个啥事情?

——垮了的母亲

原文是一封信,其中的俚语 yell, bloody murder, what goes 和 beat (as in Beat Generation) 在译文中得到了较好的传达,再现了女儿被宠不孝和母亲无可奈何的神情,译文与原文风格相近。

王佐良先生曾经指出:要准确地再现原文的风格和精神,"译者必须首先对译出译入两种语言的不同文体、语气、细微差别和语域具备鉴赏的能力"。

语域研究不只适用于口语翻译,也适用于书面语翻译。根据题材(subject matter)或根据语场(field of discourse),我们还可以把语域细分为政治、科技、法律、宗教、新闻、广告等。这些语域都有各自的不同特征。如政治题材的文章语言庄重规范,结构严谨,长句多,句子的扩展大,逻辑性强,语言冗赘现象少,采用正规或极正规的文体;科技英语准确凝练、客观冷静、逻辑严密、术语丰富、从句叠套、有名词化倾向、广泛使用被动语态和一般现在时;新闻英语力求内容准确、文字简洁和文章结构条理上的清新感,也就是要遵循所谓的新闻英语 ABC 三原则:Accuracy, Brevity 和 Clarity。

除了这些大家都很熟悉的语域,英语的语域还有地域和时间变体之分。所谓地域变体就是我们常说的 regional dialect;所谓时间变体,也就是我们常说的 historical dialect。这两种语言变体能使作品具有异国情调、地方色彩或古色古香。有时候,作者为了取得特定的文章效果而故意偏离现代英语的常规,仿效古人的"之乎者也",以取得类似金庸武侠小说的巨大魅力。马克·吐温就是这样的文体大师,请看下例。

例1 So these two knights came together with great random that Sir Uwaine smote Sir Marhaus that his spear brast in pieces on his shield, and Sir Marhaus smote him so sore that horse and man he bare to the earth, and hurt Sir Uwaine on the left side.

于是,两个骑士不期而遇,厄韦恩爵士重击马豪斯爵士,结果将长矛在他的盾上打得粉碎。马豪斯爵士痛打厄韦恩爵士,将他连人带马掀翻在地,伤其左肋。

评论家 Ian Ousby 认为,著名的《亚瑟王之死》的作者 Thomas Malory 的风格在此处被马克·吐温模仿得惟妙惟肖。

2.风格翻译的 5 个层次

美国翻译理论家 Eugene A.Nida 认为翻译就是要在目标语言中重构源语言信息的自然对等,这种自然对等首先是在意义方面,其次是在风格方面。

翻译时,特别是文学翻译时,为保持风格统一,译文所采用的语言必须与原作语言特色相一致。原作的语言清新淡雅,译作的语言也就应该清新淡雅;原作的语言诙谐幽默,译作的语言也应该诙谐幽默;原作的语言隐晦、生涩,译作的语言也应该隐晦、生涩。把粗俗的文字译得文雅,或者把文雅的文字译得粗俗,都会严重损害原作风格。

但是,要在译语中重构原作的风格,我们必须首先识别原作的风格。翻译家刘宓庆(1990:264)认为"就语际转换而言,对原语的风格分析工作至关重要,它是理解阶段的基本任务之一。忽视对原语风格的分析,就谈不上对原作全部意义的把握"。

一部作品,特别是一部宏大的作品,其风格往往不易掌握。这时,我们就要从大处着眼、小处着手,从微观到宏观,分 5 个层面对原作进行风格分析。这 5 个层面分别是:语音、词汇、句法、修辞和篇章。

(1)语音层面

在语音层面,作者可以借助单音、双音以及多音节的巧妙安排,通过对拟声、叠韵、谐音等语音修辞法的调配,以及节奏和停顿的配合,营造出独特的风格。

例1 It was a splendid population, for all the slow, sleepy, sluggish-brained sloths stayed at home.

译文1.那是一批卓越的人——那些慢慢吞吞、昏昏沉沉、反应迟钝、形如树懒的人都留在了家乡。

译文2.这帮人个个出类拔萃——因为凡是呆板、呆滞、呆头呆脑的呆子都待在了家里。(马红军)

译文3.这帮人个个出类拔萃——因为凡是懒散、懒惰、懒洋洋的树懒(懒汉,懒虫)都赖在了家里。(罗天)

例2 After a few preliminary tries, the whole farm burst into "Beasts of England" in tremendous unison.The cows lowed it, the dogs whined it, the sheep bleated it, the horses whinnied it, the ducks quacked it.They were so delighted with the song that they say it right through five times.

……牛儿哞,狗儿嗷,羊儿咩,马儿嘶鸣,鸭儿嘎嘎,个个眉飞色舞,一连唱了五遍方才尽兴。

(2)词汇层面

词汇的正式程度是文体风格的重要特征之一。正式语体使用正式词汇;非正式语体则常常使用非正式用语。英语的词汇有两个主要来源:一是英国本族词汇(native words),即古英语盎格鲁撒克逊(Anglo-Saxon)词,如 house, fire, red, green, make, talk 等;盎格鲁撒克逊词语最为短小、朴实,是构成日常非正式交谈与一般写作的主要成分。二是外来词,如 residence, domicile, conflagration, scarlet, verdant, manufacture, conversation 等。英语的外来词主要来自法语,即 11 世纪诺曼底人征服英国时所使用的法语词汇;法语词文雅、华丽,大都用于较为正式的语体语言。然后是拉丁词和希腊词,即文艺复兴时期英国学者、作家为了表达新的思想而大量借用的拉丁词和希腊词。拉丁词和希腊词抽象、冷僻,常被称作"学究词"(inkhorn),主要用于学术、政论等极为正式的语体。

翻译的时候,我们要根据原文中正式词汇和非正式词汇的使用频率,来综合判断词汇方面的风格。

例1 "Why can't you be like the Happy Prince?"asked a sensible mother of her little boy who was crying for the moon," The Happy Prince never dreams of crying for anything."

"你为什么不能像快乐王子那样呢?"一位聪明的母亲对她那个哭着要月亮的孩子说,"快乐王子连做梦也没想到会哭着要东西。"

王尔德的《快乐王子》是篇优美的散文似的童话,吸引着一代又一代的大人和孩子,可是如果没有巴金先生那传神的译文,恐怕我们就没有这么幸运了。

例2 One night there flew over the city a little Swallow.His friends had gone away to Egypt six weeks before, but he had stayed behind, for he was in love with the most beautiful Reed.

某一个夜晚一只小燕子飞过城市的上空。他的朋友们六个星期以前就到埃及去了,但是 他还留在后面,因为他恋着那根最美丽的芦苇。

原文使用的是口语化的语言,流畅质朴,译文同样清新动人,读起来朗朗上口,如母亲对孩子使用的语言。例如,"连做梦也没想到""不停地飞来飞去""用他的翅子点水"等等,一如原文那么清新、明丽,真正将原文的风格充分保留。

例3 "Makes you look younger" might be a reasonable claim for a cosmetic.But pledging to "take years off your life" would be an overclaim akin to a promise of eternal youth.A garden center's claim that its seedings would produce "a riot of color in just a few days" might be quite contrary to the reality.Such flowery words would deserve to be pulled out by the roots.

"使您看上去更加年轻"也许是化妆品厂家的合理许诺。但保证"去年20,今年18",那恐怕只是一句过头话,它无异于在允诺使您青春永驻。如果一个园艺中心声称他的幼苗只需数日就能争芳斗妍,那恐怕是相当有悖实情的。这种华丽的辞藻应当杜绝。

这个段落是对广告的批判。既然是华丽的辞藻,就不能说笔者译过了头,这样译既是对作者的忠实,也是对译文读者的忠实。词汇能引起读者的联想,有褒贬之分,能够在读者的脑海产生不同的意象(image)。准确的翻译能够反映作者待人接物的态度。例如,印度作家拉什迪(Salman Rushdie)在描写印度儿童贫困受人轻视时采用尖酸刻薄冷嘲热讽的笔调:

例4 I, Saleem Sinai, later variously called Snotnose, Stainface, Baldy, Sniffer, Buddha and even Piece-of-the-Moon, had become heavily embroiled in Fate.

我叫塞利姆·斯赖,后又先后被人蔑称为烂鼻子、脏脸、秃顶、抽鼻涕者、木头人,甚至月碴儿,已深深地被卷入命运的漩涡。

显然,译者把 sniffer, Buddha 和 piece-of-the-Moon 译成"嗅探者、佛爷和月牙儿",人物便在读者脑海里形成截然不同的意象,在风格上便与原作不符。

(3)句法层面

有的作家擅长使用简单的字词和短句,写就优美的文字。例如美国作家海明威总共只用100多个单词就写出12个句子,且这100多个单词又都是英语中的常用词,但却把旅馆附近的海边景色描写得淋漓尽致。

例1 It is a truth universally acknowledged, that a single man in possession of a good fortune must be in want of a wife.

译文 1.有钱的单身汉总要娶位太太,这是一条举世公认的真理。

译文 2.有这样一条举世公认的真理,这就是,有钱的单身汉总要娶位太太。

例2 There were only two Americans stopping at the hotel. They did not know any of the people they passed on the stairs on their way to and from their room. Their room was on the second floor facing the sea. It also faced the public garden and the war monument.

只有两个美国人在该旅馆歇息。对于他们在进出房间时在楼梯上遇到的任何人,他们一个也不认识。他们的房间在二楼,朝着大海,也朝着公园和战争纪念碑。

海明威一生都以文学风格的简洁而出名,他精选短小精悍的句子、朴实无华的词汇以及习用口头语。译文也较为简洁。

当然,也有作者展现出繁复的文风。例如,亨利·詹姆斯是著名的美国现实主义小说家,擅长描写人物心理。他寻求叙述的绝对准确,养成了使用错综复杂的长句、密集难懂的句法和堆砌修饰从句的习惯。下面是他的小说《专使》(The Ambassadors)中的一个典型的句子:

例3 Why Miss Barrace, mature, meagre, erect and eminently gay, highly adorned, perfectly familiar, freely contradictious, and reminding him of some last century portrait of a clever head without powder — why Miss Barrace should have been in particular the note of a trap Strether couldn't on the spot have explained; he blinked in the light of a conviction that he should know later on, and know well — as it came over him, for that matter, with force, that he should need to.

为什么巴拉士小姐,亭亭玉立,欢快卓绝,佩戴华丽,悉如知己,辩驳自如并使他想到一幅上世纪的不施粉著的俏丽头像——为什么巴拉士小姐会特别是一个"圈套"的标志?斯特雷塞不能当场作出解释;他由于确信自己以后会知道会弄清楚而眯缝着眼睛——由于他在这个问题上强烈地感到他需要弄清楚。

这句话繁复难懂,但是有其特定目的。运用大量的形容词,独具特色的细腻描写,捕捉人物在某个特别瞬间的心境。这样的句子,有别于海明威简洁明快的风格。译者也使用了较多书面词语,基本保留了原文的长句。

有时候,作者为了最恰当地表现自己的思想和感情,故意在使用语言时有所选择和变化,甚至使用偏离语言常规的句式,这就是风格的变异。乔伊斯在写作《尤利西斯》(Ulysses)时,故意打破标点符号常规,让句子连成一体,旨在表现人物的意识流动。这是乔伊斯独特的意识流的语言风格。如果译者一味用自己喜爱的句式来翻译不同的作者风格,那么中国读者就可能以为英语文学中只有赵树理或汪国真的风格。所以,我们在翻译时,应该在句法这一层面尽量再现原作的风貌。

(4)修辞层面

修辞格是人们在长期的语言交际过程中,在本民族语言特点的基础上,为提高语言表达效果而形成的格式化的方法、手段。修辞往往背离正常的词句顺序或者词语的字面含义。正确使用修辞可以贴切、生动地表现思想内容,加深文章留给读者的印象,提高对读者的说服力,给读者以美的享受。

英语修辞主要分为三类:音韵修辞、词义修辞及结构修辞。

音韵修辞主要包括头韵法(alliteration)、尾韵法(end-rhyming)及拟声词(onomatopoeia)。

音韵美是语言美的一个重要因素。好的作品抑扬顿挫,节奏鲜明,读起来朗朗上口。许多作家都是运用音韵取得修辞效果的文学大师。

词义修辞主要包括夸张(hyperbole)、委婉(euphemism)、矛盾修饰法(oxymoron)和一语双关(pun)。最常用的手法当数比喻,包括明喻(simile)、暗喻(metaphor)、换喻(metonymy)和提喻(synecdoche)。比喻能使语言生动、逼真和富有感染力,还能使深奥的哲理浅显易懂。

结构修辞主要包括重复(repetition)、对照(antithesis)、平行结构(parallelism)和反诘问句(rhetorical question)等。重复经常用来加强语气,保持句子平衡对称,使得行文生动,看起来醒目,听起来悦耳,读起来节奏感强,给人印象深刻,容易记住。用得好还可造成一种跌宕起伏的气势,增加文体的力量。

修辞手法是作家展现自己风格的法宝。因此,在如果读者能够理解接受,译文应该尽量保留原文修辞方法;如果原文的修辞格不合译文的表达规范,读者难以理解接受,那么可以采用变通的方法,使用另一种修辞法,尽量达到原文修辞同样或近似的效果。

例1 East and west, home is the best.
金窝银窝,不如自家的穷窝。

例2 An apple a day keeps the doctor away.
一天一苹果,医生别管我。

例3 In certain industrial areas, it can still excite resentment, despite the fact that it no longer necessarily goes hand in glove with power or privilege.
在某些工业地区,尽管它事实上不再与权力或特权狼狈为奸,但它仍然会激起人们的不满情绪。

在这句话中,英文把东部方言和特权比作手和手套,而汉语则把它们比作狼和狈,手法不同,但是异曲同工。

例4 You paid homage to your favorite star; you dutifully communed with the fan magazines. You wore the clothes they wore in the movies; you bought the furniture you saw on the screen.You shared your adulation with Shanghai, Sydney and Santiago.
人们向自己最爱的明星致敬;虔诚地和影迷杂志通信;人们追随影片中衣服;买他们在银幕上看到的家具;人们和上海、悉尼以及圣地亚哥的观众崇拜着共同的偶像。

本例描写无声电影风靡一时的景象。采用排比的修辞方法,把影迷们追星的狂热描写得淋漓尽致,译文也较好地保留了原文的排比修辞法。

(5)篇章层面

奈达在论述最佳翻译程序时曾说:"译者首先应借助尽可能大的单位进行翻译。如果可能的话,翻译必须以段落为单位进行;如果行不通,译者应至少努力考虑两三句话,而不是以单个的词、词组或句子为单位来考虑翻译。考虑的单位愈大,译文就愈显自然。"

以段落为单位进行翻译,其优点是多方面的:①能在语义层面揭示原作的逻辑关系和作者的思维模式,即句与句之间的语义连贯 coherence);②能在句法层面揭示原作的过渡衔接与连贯的手段,即语篇的形式连接(cohesion);③能在特定的语境发挥解构(deconstruction)的优势,"前后引衬,以显其义",即语篇的场合性(contextuality)。通过研究篇章的格调、体例和布局的合理性,译者可以在比字词句更高的层面把握原作特有的行文风格。

语篇分析最重要的手段是研究衔接。衔接包括词汇衔接(lexical cohesion),如前面所说的重复法。其他重要的篇章衔接手段还有：照应(reference)、替代(substitution)、省略(ellipsis)和连接(conjunction)等，其中以连接最为典型。

我们在语篇分析中所说的连接，不是语法分析中所说的从属连词或并列连词，而是语篇中表示逻辑思维关系的过渡性连接词语(transitional connective words or phrases)。这些连接词语(sentence connectors)可用来表示时间与空间、列举与例证、原因与结果、强调与重述、推理与转折、推论与总结等。

一般来说，英语文章大量使用连接手段。在翻译时，尤其是在翻译科技论文或其他功能性文体时，往往不用那么多的连接词语，而以"意合"代替"形合"，甚至采用编译，使得译文的语体风格契合原文。

但是，也有作家风格独特，少用连接手段。例如，英国作家 James Joyce 所著 Ulysses 中的一段描述：

and the sea the sea crimson sometimes like fire and the glorious sunsets and the fightrees in the Alameda gardens yes and all the queer little streets and pink and blue and yellow houses and the rosegardens and the jessamine and geraniums and cactuses…

金译：还有海洋深红的海洋有时候真像火一样的红嘿夕阳西下太壮观了还有阿拉梅达那些花园里的无花果树真的那些别致的小街还有一幢幢桃红的蓝的黄的房子还有一座座玫瑰花园还有茉莉花天竺葵仙人掌……(金隄译)

萧译：大海 有时候大海是深红色的 就像火似的 还有那壮丽的落日 再就是阿拉梅达园 里的无花果树 对啦 还有那一条条奇妙的小街 一座座桃红天蓝淡黄的房子 还有玫瑰园啦茉莉花啦 天竺葵啦仙人掌啦……(《尤利西斯》萧乾、文洁若译，1994:244)

《尤利西斯》中的这段文字，和其他段落一样，通篇无标点符号；没有大小写之分，句子难辨主从，没有一定的思维模式，逻辑飘忽不定，一个个思维片段像溢出的流水，顺着地势自上而下如泉涌一阵一阵地流淌。然而，这正是乔伊斯的独特的文体风格，我们在翻译时再现他的这种意识流风格尤为重要。

两种译本都在尽力传达原文风格的基础上，充分体现了译者个人的风格和观点。作为具有记者、作家和文艺刊物编辑等身份的萧乾、文洁若夫妇从读者出发，一心让译文易懂、可读，冒着改变原文风格的风险创造出"丰腴灵透"的译文；而金隄先生则从一个理论研究者的角度努力印证"等效'翻译的可能性，带给读者一个"方正端严"的译本。

四、译文的美化

1. 去掉翻译腔

"翻译腔"(translationese)其实就是指翻译出来的译文有洋化现象或不符合汉语的习惯表达方式。表现为译文不自然、不流畅、生硬、难懂、费解等特点。翻译腔也称译文体。

2000年某期的《参考消息》曾连载了香港中文大学教授金圣华先生的一篇文章，指出"译文体"的弊端。他写道：

何谓"译文体"？"译文体"是一种不中不西、非驴非马、似通非通、佶屈聱牙的表达方式。翻译时如果只会对照原文字字死扣，就会译出累赘不堪的文字。译文体，总括来说，是一种"英文没有学好，中文却学坏了"的文体。

很多人以为把欧化语法及词汇照搬过来,可以丰富中文的内涵,使之充满活力,增添生机,于是不顾目的语的语言规范、习惯用法、词语搭配、语境、文化形态、民族心理、接受者心理等,生搬硬套原语的句式、词义和用语习惯、修辞手法,不求甚解地引进外域文化,承袭原语风格,一味死译、硬译,结果往往适得其反,使得译文生涩硬化,面目可憎,无人愿读,失去翻译的根本目的。

翻译腔的具体表现形式很多,比如滥用介词,滥用被动句,滥用抽象动词,滥用"的""性""们""作为""关于"等词缀或字眼。下面举例说明。

(1)滥用"的"字

余光中曾经撰写《论的的不休》一文,对"的""地""得"等的滥用进行曝光与批评。他认为:

> 许多人写文章,每逢需要形容词,几乎都不假思索,交给"的"去解决。更有人懒得区分"的"与"地","的"与"得"之间的差异,一律用"的"代替。……一律的的到底,说成"他一路心不在焉的走着",不然就是"他唱的累了"。这么一来,当然更是的的不休[3]。(余光中)

余光中甚至认为:少用"的"字,是一位作家得救的起点。"他举例说,"An old, mad, blind, despised, and dying king"这个诗行,最懒的译法就是"一位衰老的、疯狂的、瞎眼的、被人蔑视的、垂死的君王"了,但21字也实在太长了。为求简洁,"的"必须少用,不定冠词 an 也可免去,"君王"可以缩成单字"王"。以便搭配较为可接的某形容词。因此,该句可以改译为:"又狂又盲,众所鄙视的垂死老王"。

同样,金圣华对滥用"的"字也深感延误。她在审定《牛津高阶英汉双解词典》第6版翻译例句时,发现原译"的"的泛滥成灾,并列举了两个例子说明。

例1 She was forced to face up to a few unwelcome truths about her family.
　　原译:她不得不正视有关她的家族的几个尴尬的事实。
　　改译:她不得不正视有关她家(庭)的几桩尴尬事。

译文共用3个"的"字,如此译法,是否必要?事实上,"的"字用作"possessive case"(所有格)及"adjective"(形容词)时,在中文里可以酌量省略。

例2 There are plenty of restaurants for those who tire of shopping.
　　原译:有很多的餐馆可以成为厌烦购物的人的去处。
　　改译:厌烦购物的人有很多餐馆可去。

这些例子使用了一连串"的"字!需要指出的是,译文中,有时"的"字用得越多,反而可能使人越看越糊涂。

潘文国也发现,2004年7月1日《参考消息》第9版,有一则题为"直击权力移交后的伊拉克"的新闻译文,其中一句为:"每个伊拉克人都拥有生活在一个建立在友谊、兄弟般情谊和公正的基础上的尊严的社会的权利。"这个句子后半部分,几个"的"字连用,就体现了十足的翻译腔。

(2)照搬原文表达方式

翻译时,如果不会调整,译文就有半通不通的符合"语法"的新鲜表达。"睡着了"要说成"进入了睡眠状态";"她又哭了"要修饰为"她又再度哭了一次";"为人父母"要说成"作为子女的父母"等。"作为"一词的滥用已到了可笑的地步,电视画面上,我们经常看到各行各业的被采访者在那里侃侃而谈:"我作为我……"令人忍俊不禁。(潘文国)

"作为"是一个教人非常忧心的词语。罪魁祸首是英文里的"as"。"To abolish as soon as possible Hong Kong's status as a port of first asylum",立法局议员和秘书处的中译都说是"尽快取消香港作为第一收容港的地位"。其实,"作为"可以不要,也应该不要。像样的说法是:"尽快取消香港的第一收容港地位"……我们不会对一位漂亮的小姐说:"你作为一位大美人,实在不必花太多钱买化妆品了!"我们说:"你是个大美人,不用花太多钱买化妆品了!"用简介的语言表达清楚的思路最重要。(董桥)

余光中发现,粗心的译者总是用"当……的时候"这个僵化的公式,来应付一切的 when 子句,公式化的翻译体,既然见 when 就"当",五步一当,十步一当,当当之声,遂不绝于耳了。如果你留心听电视和广播,或者阅览报纸的外国消息版,就会发现这种莫须有的当当之灾,正严重地威胁美好中文的节奏。例如:

①当他自己的妻子都劝不动他的时候,你怎么能劝得动呢?
②弥尔顿正在意大利游历,当国内传来内战的消息。
③当他洗完了头发的时候,叫他来找我。

上面几句,译者如能稍加思考,就应该知道如何用别的字眼来表达。

①连自己的妻子都劝他不动,你怎么劝得动他?
②弥尔顿正在意大利游历,国内忽然传来内战的消息。
③他洗完头之后,叫他来找我。

(3)照搬原文语序

较长的英语句子中存在着比较复杂的关系,如果照搬,会导致翻译腔。应该分析句子内在的逻辑关系,按照汉语的表达习惯进行翻译。例如:

例1 The chances are that the dwellers of the new caves would see more greenery, under ecologically healthier conditions, than dwellers of surface cities do today.

原译:新洞穴里的居民能见到青枝绿叶,如果生态环境比较健康,同今天地面城市里的居民相比。

改译:同今天地面城市里的居民相比,新洞穴里的居民如果在比较健康的生态环境中生活,会有更多的机会见到青枝绿叶。

例2 But a broader and more generous, certainly more philosophical, view is held by those scientists who claim that the evidence of a war instinct in men is incomplete and misleading, and that man does have within him the power of abolishing war.

原译:但是一个更开阔,更富有普遍性和哲理性的由大多数科学家所持有的观点认为:人类战争本能的证据尚不完全,而且容易引起误解,事实上,人类自身具有消除战争的能力;以及人类事实上自身具有消除战争的能力。

改译:有些科学家的观点更开阔,更富有普遍性和哲理性。他们指出,有关人类战争本能的证据尚不完全,而且容易引起误解,事实上,人类自身具有消除战争的能力。

例3 It was that population that gave to California a name for getting up astonishing enterprises and rushing them through with a magnificent dash and daring and a recklessness of cost or consequences, which she bears unto this day.

原译:这是一群富于大无畏的开创精神,建立庞大的企业,敢冒风险,势如破竹,一干到底,不顾及成本,为加利福尼亚赢得了声誉的人。

改译:那里的人们富于大无畏的开创精神,建立庞大的企业,敢冒风险,势如破竹,一干到底,不顾及成本,因此为加利福尼亚赢得了声誉。

这个句子虽长,但结构不复杂,如果进行直译,其译文将十分逊色,如果进行综合处理,译文将有声有色地传达原文的神韵。

(4)硬译修辞

有一些英语修辞格很难用直译方式表达清楚,即便是同一修辞格,由于处于不同场合,有的能直译,有的则不能直译。下列几种情况有时不宜直译:

例1 He went west by stage coach and succumbed to the epidemic of gold and silver fever in Nevada's Washoe Region.

原译:他乘公共马车到了西部,患了瓦肖地区的金银发烧流行病。

改译:他乘公共马车到了西部,卷入了淘金热和淘银热。

例2 The rather arresting spectacle of little old Japan adrift amid beige concrete skyscrapers is the very symbol of the incessant struggle between the kimono and the miniskirt.

原译:古老的小日本漂游在灰棕色的钢筋混凝土摩天大楼之间的引入景象是和服与超短裙之间的不断斗争的象征。

改译:式样古老小巧的日本房屋像小船一般,漂游在灰棕色的钢筋混凝土摩天大楼之间,这引人注目的景象象征着旧传统和新发展之间的不断斗争。

例3 At the door to the restaurant, a stunning, porcelain-faced woman in traditional costume asked me to remove my shoes.

原译:在通往餐厅的门口有一位妇女,一位迷人的陶瓷般脸蛋的妇女,身着和服、十分迷人,叫我脱下鞋子。

改译:在通往餐厅的门口有一位妇女,涂脂抹粉、细皮嫩肉、身着和服、十分迷人,她叫我脱下鞋子。

原译把 stunning, porcelain-faced woman 译作"一位迷人的陶瓷般脸蛋的妇女"就显得粗俗滑稽,但是不是作者的本意。这时意译就比较好。

余光中指出:公式化的翻译体,毛病当然不只这些。一口气长达四五十字,中间不加标点的句子;消化不良的句子;头重脚轻的修饰语;画蛇添足的所有格代名词;生涩含混的文理;毫无节奏感的语气。这些都是翻译体中信手拈来的毛病。所以造成这种种现象,译者的外文程度不济,固然是一大原因,但是中文周转不灵,词汇贫乏,句型单调,首尾不能兼顾的苦衷,恐怕要负另一半责任。至于文学修养的较高境界,对于公式化的翻译,一时尚属奢望。我必须再说一遍:翻译,也是一种创作,一种"有限的创作"。译者不必兼为作家,但是心中不能不了然于创作的某些原理,手中也不能没有一枝作家的笔。

2.精心校改,美化译文

著名翻译家傅雷先生说:"以效果而论,翻译应当像临画一样,所求的不在形似而在神似。"当然,这个"临画"不是"照猫画虎","照猫画虎"的结果难免会"画虎不成反类犬",重点是最后几个字——"不在形似而在神似"。字字对译,看起来似乎忠于原文,但往往字到意不到,顾及了死的字面却遗落了活的神采。要透过字面,顾其义而传其神,这样译文才能生动逼真,赏心悦目。

翻开名家佳译,颇有出彩之处,看似"随手拈来"或"神来之笔"。但这些佳译,得来不易,依靠的不仅是译者正确传达信息,还要精益求精,不断修改,让语句传神。这样的译者往往"吟安一个字,捻断数茎须"(卢延让),或者"两句三年得,一吟双泪流"(贾岛),甚至"为人性僻耽佳句,语不惊人死不休"(杜甫)。

我们先看林语堂自译 The Importance of Living《生活的艺术》中的两个句子。

例1 For a nation to have a few philosophers is not so unusual, but for a nation to take things philosophically is terrific.

一个民族产生过几个大哲学家没什么稀罕,但一个民族能以哲理的眼光去观察事物,那是难能可贵的。

英语原文中的"terrific""unusual"是寻常用词,译文里"难得可贵""稀罕"更出彩。在林语堂笔下,工整紧凑的成语和白话文松散的词法句式相得益彰。

例2 A Chinese poet has already warned us that the fountain of youth is a hoax, that no man can yet "tie a string to the sun" and hold back its course.

中国某诗人早已提醒我们说,青春之泉是无稽之谈,无人能系住光阴不让它前进。

译文将比喻"tie a string to the sun"轻松化解为"系住光阴",将"hoax"化解为"无稽之谈",都精简而传神。

下面是香港中文大学教授金圣华教授修改译文的一些例子,此种校改很见双语功力。

例1 Now that he is buried almost up to the bow tie in government documents, he still finds time to read, for pleasure, fascinating, well-written non-fiction.

原译:现在,虽然无数政府文件堆到了蝴蝶领结之下,他依然忙里偷闲,阅读写得引人入胜的文章。

改译:现在,虽然政府文件堆积如山,他依然忙里偷闲,阅读文采斐然、引人入胜的文章。

英文原文使用了夸张的修辞方法(buried almost up to the bow tie in government documents),语言幽默,用中文习惯用语"堆积如山"翻译,相当传神简练。

例2 How does he keep fit amidst all the demand of business, family, and philanthropy? He swims, he exercises, and plays a bit of golf.

原译:方博士既须处理公司业务,又要照顾家庭和慈善工作,费力劳心,有什么办法保持健康?他的办法是游泳,做体操,偶然还打打高尔夫球。

改译:方博士既须处理公司业务,又要照顾家庭和慈善工作,劳心劳力之余,如何保持健康?游泳,体操,偶然打高尔夫球,即为强身健魄之道。

例3 He also taught English to a very original young woman, the individualistic Ningtsu, later to become his warm and courageous wife.

原译:他又认识了一位很有个性的年轻女郎宁祖,并教她英语,这位热情、勇敢的女郎后来做了他太太。

改译:当时,他又结识一位极有个性的年轻女郎宁祖,并教她英语。嗣后,终与这位热情勇敢的女郎盟订终身。

英文往往可以简单、直接的表达方式运用在正式的场合,而不失之呆板平凡。相反,译成中文时,不得不做出适度的调节。这样,译文方能合乎中文的行文惯例以及读者或听众的审美期待。

下面的更多例子均可为校对过程中的语言美化提供范例,值得认真品读。首先,译文的美化依赖于精妙的选词。

例1 And in these meditations he fell asleep.

他这么思前想后,就睡着了。

赏析:"思前想后"译得妙。这句译文再次提醒我们,妙译有赖才学和两种语文上醇厚的修养,光指着上翻译课学翻译,就抱着几本词典做翻译,是难出好译文的。

例2 Their family had more money, more horses, more slaves than anyone else in the Country, but the boys had less grammar than most of their poor Cracker neighbors.

他们家里的钱比人家多,马比人家多,奴隶比人家多,都要算全区第一,所缺少的只是他哥儿俩肚里的墨水,少得也是首屈一指。

赏析:原文选自 Gone With the Wind。译文忠实且流畅,算得上好译文,特别值得一提的是译者对 grammar 的处理,如果照搬字典自然难于翻译,但译者吃透了原句精神,译为"肚里的墨水",真是再妥帖不过了。

例3 The only concession he made to the climate was to wear a white dinner jacket.

原译:他对气候的唯一让步就是穿了一件白色的短餐衣。

改译:气候变化,他仅稍稍作了一点变通,赴宴时穿了件白色的短礼服。

例4 He was silent for a few moments, then recovered himself, and answered.

他沉默了一会儿,定了定神,作了回答。

赏析:汉语讲究语序,动作在前的语序在前,动作在后的语序在后,因此译者没有将这句的 then 译为"然后……"。字典中 recover oneself 常译为"使自己恢复正常状态",译者如果照搬也未尝不可,但必定是蹩脚的译文,译为"定了定神"不仅符合原意且汉语地道。

例5 An awareness of her graceful nubility gave every movement the value of nature perfectly controlled by art.

她姿影绰约,正当待嫁年华。姑娘心里明白;于是举止之间,无不优雅怡人,把天生丽质发挥得淋漓尽致。

赏析:原文通顺地道,译文贴切优美。句中的难点是 nubility,《英汉大词典》对这个词的解释是"(女子的)适婚性,达结婚年龄"。译者将其译为"待嫁年华"堪称佳译。

例6 Human affairs are all subject to changes and disasters.

人世间,事不由己,变迁灾祸,难以逆料。

例7 It was a day as fresh as grass growing up and clouds going over and butterflies coming down can make it. It was a day compounded from silences of bee and flower and ocean and land, which were not silences at all, but motions, stirs, flutters, risings, fallings, each in its own time and matchless rhythm.

绿草萋萋,白云冉冉,彩蝶翩翩,这日子是如此清新;蜜蜂无言,春花不语,海波声歇,大地音寂,这日子是如此安静。然而并非安静,因为万物各以其独特的节奏,或动,或摇,或震,或起,或伏。

其次,译文的美化可以依靠汉语的四字成语。汉语四字词组特点是精练紧凑,表意丰富,形式整齐。在翻译时,如遇繁杂棘手的语句,可以穿插使用四字结构,有助于使译文凝练达意,雅俗交融,形成对仗,富有节奏。

正如著名翻译理论家许渊冲先生所言:翻译是两种文化竞赛,是一种艺术;而在竞赛中取胜的方法是发挥译文优势,或者说再创造。译文中,如果四字结构运用恰当,会令人感觉译笔老练,丝丝入扣,气势非凡,同时又可体现译者厚实的汉语功底。当然,具体翻译时也要谨防滥用四字,不可脱离原文语境勉强生造;否则,会使译文显得油滑,还会造成译文违背原意。

例1 The presidential candidate and his wife have had two decades, investing each other since their marriage.

总统候选人和夫人婚后20年来,一直恩爱体贴,鱼水难分。

赏析:原文"invest in each other"属于一种比喻的说法,意义是"love and care never stop flowing from one to another between the couple"。显然,译者不能把这个比喻生硬地直接译为"投资";也不能简单处理为"一向对方奉献关爱",以致失去了英文文采。译者选择"恩爱体贴,鱼水难分",与原文貌离神合,是一种扬长避短的译法,译文扬了四字句之"长",避免了行文拖沓之"短"。

例2 From this deficiency of nourishment resulted an abuse which pressed hardly on the younger pupils: whenever the famished great girls had an opportunity they would coax or menace the little ones out of their portion.

食物严重缺乏造成了一种恶劣风气,使年龄小一些的学生大受其害。那些饿坏了的大姑娘一有机会,就会连哄带吓分占她们的那一份。

赏析:coax or menace 译为"连哄带吓"简练而传神,如译为"或哄骗或威胁",则淡而无味矣。

例3 The BBC reporters overwhelmed the police as much with courtesy as with force, and rushed to the scene in time.

英国广播公司记者软磨硬闯,冲破了警察阻拦,及时赶到事发现场。

赏析:英语"as much with courtesy as with force",如果老老实实地译成"不仅显示出礼貌,而且还使出了力气",表达不够流畅,晦涩难度,比原文逊色不少。译为"软磨硬闯",简洁生动,既传达意义,又留下想象余地。

例4 Some personnel executives complained that many college graduates they had interviewed here had two-star abilities with five-star ambitions.

译文1:一些人事经理抱怨,在他们面试过的大学毕业生中,不少人本事只有"二星级",心气儿倒有"五星级"。

译文2:一些人事经理抱怨,在他们面试过的大学毕业生中不少人都眼高手低(或好高骛远)。

赏析:在英语里,"two-star"和"five-star"中的"star"用来泛指等级。译文1采用直译,保留了表达内在含义的外部形象,保留其中的幽默感;同时句式上形成对比,便于读者理解。译文2"眼高手低"或"好高骛远",放弃星级的概念,采用汉语成语来替换,可说是效果对等,值得称道。

例5 The then young senator was struck by the powerful profile of his secretary of Asian descent, her rich black hair falling freely onto her shoulders, the intensity of her dark eyes.

译文1.当时,这位年轻的参议员为他亚裔秘书的出众长相所倾倒:她乌发披肩,亮泽飘逸;一双黑眸,顾盼生辉。

译文 2.当时,参议员还很年轻,他被自己那位亚裔女秘书的出众长相迷住了:垂肩秀发,无拘无束;一双黑眸,波光撩人。

赏析:以上两句都将有关原文表达译成了四字结构,都可以算是成功的译文。例如,"the intensity of her dark eyes"译为"一双黑眸,顾盼生辉""一双黑眸,波光撩人"突破原文局限,生动传神。至于"falling freely on her shoulders",译文1为"乌发披肩,亮泽飘逸",显示"风吹仙袂飘飘举"那样飘然欲飞的状态,比较贴切;译文2为"无拘无束",是一个比较老实的翻译,紧贴原文的内在含义,但是缺少了飘逸头发的那种神韵。

第三,译文的美化,需要译者摆脱原文形式的桎梏,"得意忘形"。

例1 The famous little Becky Puppet has been pronounced to be uncommonly flexible in the joints, and lively on the wire.

那个叫蓓基的木偶人儿非常有名,大家一致称赞她的骨节特别的灵活,线一牵就活泼泼地手舞足蹈。

赏析:译者不拘泥于原句的结构,先是将原句的主语 the famous little Becky Puppet 译为句子"那个叫蓓基的木偶人儿非常有名",再把原句的被动语态转化为汉语的主动语态,"大家一致称赞她……",最后将 lively on the wire 译为分句"线一牵就活泼泼地手舞足蹈"。整句译文丝毫看不出翻译痕迹,一气呵成,地道顺畅,是上佳的译文。如果拘泥于原句形式,译为"那个有名的木偶人儿蓓基被人们称为……",译文必然佶屈聱牙。

例2 Those privileged to be present at a family festival of the Forsytes have seen that charming and instructive sight—an upper middle-class family in full plumage.

碰到福尔赛家的喜庆事,那些有资格参加的人都曾看见过那派中上层人家的兴盛气象,不但看了开心,也增长见识。

译者将破折号后补充说明部分译为名词 sight 的定语,而将 sight 前的形容词 charming 和 instructive 放到后面去处理,译为句子"不但看了开心,也增长见识"。整句译文地道而通顺,这种高明老练的译法值得我们认真体会和学习。

例3 The very laborer, with his thatched cottage and narrow slip of ground, attends to the embellishment.

译文:就这下苦力的农家人,不过几间茅屋栖身,一块窄地养家,也尽心打扮着自己的居所。

很显然,译文由四个短句构成,不论在气韵还是在结构上,符合汉语审美的要求。

例4 Vehicles steering in the conventional manner lacked the rapid response, short turning radius, and ease of handling.

传统的转向机构反应迟钝,转弯半径大,操作不便。

为求得一种好的译文,译者往往反复推敲,不乏采用一定的翻译技巧,本例译文采用正反倒说的技巧。

例5 Eight years ago, the black woman and the white man were married. They have survived their families' shock and disapproval and the stares and unwelcome comments of strangers.

这对夫妇是八年前结的婚,丈夫是白人,太太是黑人。双方家庭对此都感到震惊并加以反对;旁人也对他俩侧目而视且非议纷纷。面对所有这一切,他俩顶住压力,挺了过来。

赏析:原文"black"与"white",在译文中处理成两个小句,强调了两人的种族身份,符合句子的意义。第二句"survive"后面跟上"shock"等四个名词,含义丰富,是英语中的地道表达,可是如果直译,势必生硬难懂,具有严重的翻译腔。因此,译者将这些名词译为小句,符合汉语多小句散句的特点,将意义流畅地表达出来。

例6 Established in 1960s when federal money flowed, the clinics are now a shadow of their former selves. Patients wait hours while the undermanned and sometimes short-tempered staff struggle to meet the demand.

联邦政府在20世纪60年代拨出巨款建起的这些诊所,现在只是徒有其表。病人就诊要久久等候;由于诊所人手不足,医护人员常常是手忙脚乱,难免要发点脾气。

原文中,"a shadow of their former selves"为一个比喻,如果照直翻译,可读性不强。"undermanned and sometimes short-tempered"这一短语,如果照搬语序翻译,则显得过长,让读者喘不过气来。幸好,译文既化解了比喻,又将短语单独成句,读来流畅自然。

例7 The residence of people of fortune and refinement in the country has diffused a degree of taste and elegance in rural economy that descends to the lowest class.

原译:乡间有钱人和有雅趣的人的住宅把一些趣味和风雅浸染到乡间的生计中,它们向平民百姓传递。

改译:豪门雅宅,将风雅和情趣浸染于乡间的生计,连平民百姓也乐于此道。

例8 The air seemed almost sticky from the scent of bursting buds.

原译:由于开放的花蕾的香气,空气似乎稠粘。

改译:花蕾初绽,芳香四溢,空气中似乎弥漫着稠稠的香味。

例9 1 should wish to die while still at work, knowing that others will carry on what I can no longer do and content in the thought that what was possible has been done.

原译:我希望在工作中死去。知道有人会继续做下去自己不再能做的事,并且怀着满意的心情想到,自己能做的事都已做到了。

改译:我倒希望在工作中死去。知道事业后继有人,想到自己不枉此一生,也就心满意足了。

例10 In practice, the selected interval thickness is usually a compromise between the need for a thin interval to maximise the resolution and a thick interval to minimise the error.

原译1.层的厚度的选择是相当困难的,因为这实际上存在着难于调和的矛盾:从提高分辨率的角度来考虑,总希望把层选得尽可能薄;但从减小误差的角度来考虑,又总希望把层选得尽可能厚。那么,究竟要选取多大的厚度才算合适呢?这就往往需要在反复权衡其利弊得失之后,才能得出一个最佳的折中方案。

译文2.实际上,层的厚度的选择,往往需要在下列两者之间得出一个折中方案,即从提高分辨率的要求来考虑,总想把层尽量选得薄一些;但从减少误差的要求来考虑,又总想把层尽量选得厚一些。

译文3.实际上,所选择的层的厚度通常是可最大限度提高分辨率所需的薄层和可使误差降至最小的厚层之间的平均值。

译文4.为保证最大分辨率必须选用薄层,为使误差最小却须选用厚层,实际上通常选择介于两者之间的最佳厚度。

以上四种译文都表达了原文的内容,但就得体而言,是可作一番比较的。

译文 1 添加信息过多,如加上"相当困难""难于调和的矛盾""反复权衡其利弊得失"等主观色彩较浓的文字,使译文表层结构膨胀。这种增加信息容量、不顾原文形式的做法,是不得体的。

译文 2 虽较译文 1 有所改进,但与原文的精练相比仍有差距。原文 a compromise 之后有一个很长的介词短语作修饰,为本句信息中心,但将 compromise 译成"折中方案"(有小题大做之嫌),置于句中,未予突出。

译文 3 虽然简短,但拘泥于原文形式,一个长句,字数太多,读来不畅。

译文 4 畅晓自然,简练通顺,表层结构安排得体,附着信息与中心信息相得益彰,把中心信息译为"最佳厚度"并将其置于句末,形成末尾焦点(end-focus),符合汉语的表达习惯。译者采用词序颠倒、词义引申、词类转换等技巧。

The Sounds of Manhattan
Terry Bragg

New York is a city of sounds; muted sounds and shrill sounds; shattering sounds and soothing sounds; urgent sounds and aimless sounds. The cliff dwellers of Manhattan, who would be racked by the silence of the lonely woods, do not hear these sounds because they are constant and eternally urban.

The visitor to the city can hear them, though, just as some animals can hear a high-pitched whistle inaudible to humans. To the casual caller to Manhattan, lying restive and sleepless in a hotel twenty or thirty floors above the street, they tell a story as fascinating as life itself. And lack of the sounds broods the silence.

Night in midtown is the noise of tinseled honky-tonk and violence. Thin strains of music, usually the firm beat of rock 'n' roll or the frenzied outbursts of the discotheque, rise from ground level. This is the cacophony, the discordance of youth, and it comes on strongest when nights are hot and young blood restless.

Somewhere in the canyons below there is shrill laughter or raucous shouting. A bottle shatters against concrete. The whine of a police siren slices through the night, moving ever closer, until an eerie Doppler effect brings it to a guttural halt.

There are few sounds so exciting in Manhattan as those of fire apparatus dashing through the night. At the outset there is the tentative hint of the first-due company bullying his way through midtown traffic. Now a fire whistle from the opposite direction affirms that trouble is, indeed, afoot. In seconds, other sirens converging from other streets help the sky-top listener focus on the scene of excitement.

But he can only hear and not see, and imagination takes flight. Are the flames and smoke gushing from windows not far away? Are victims trapped there, crying out for help? Is it a conflagration, or only a trash-basket fire? Or, perhaps, it is merely a false alarm.

The questions go unanswered and the urgency of the moment dissolves. Now the mind and the ear detect the snarling, arrogant bickering of automobile horns. People in a hurry. Taxicabs blaring, insisting on their checkered priority.

Even the taxi horns dwindle down to a precocious few in the gray and pink moments of dawn. Suddenly there is another sound. The growl of a predatory monster? No, just garbage trucks that have begun a day of scavenging.

The sounds of the new day are businesslike. The growl of buses, so scattered and distant at night, becomes a part of the traffic bedlam. An occasional jet or helicopter injects an exclamation point from an unexpected quarter. When the wind is right, the vibrant bellow of a ship can be heard.

The whistles of traffic policemen and hotel doormen chirp from all sides, like birds calling for their mates across a frenzied aviary. And all of these sounds are adult sounds, for childish laughter has no place in these canyons.

Night falls again, the cycle is complete, but there is no stop from sounds. For the beautiful dreamers, perhaps, the "sounds of the rude world heard in the day, lulled by the moonlight have all passed away," but this is not so in the city.

Too many New Yorkers accept the sounds about them as bland parts of everyday existence. They seldom stop to listen to the sounds, to think about them, to be appalled or enchanted by them. In the big city, sounds are life.

(577 words)

第十章
文学语篇的翻译（1）

The Adventures of Huckleberry Finn（Excerpt）

YOU Don't know about me without you have read a book by the name of The Adventures of Tom Sawyer; but that ain't no matter. That book was made by Mr. Mark Twain, and he told the truth, mainly. There was things which he stretched, but mainly he told the truth. That is nothing. I never seen anybody but lied one time or another, without it was Aunt Polly, or the widow, or maybe Mary. Aunt Polly—Tom's Aunt Polly, she is—and Mary, and the Widow Douglas is all told about in that book, which is mostly a true book, with some stretchers, as I said before.

Now the way that the book winds up is this: Tom and me found the money that the robbers hid in the cave, and it made us rich. We got six thousand dollars apiece—all gold. It was an awful sight of money when it was piled up. Well, Judge Thatcher he took it and put it out at interest, and it fetched us a dollar a day apiece all the year round—more than a body could tell what to do with. The Widow Douglas she took me for her son, and allowed she would civilize me; but it was rough living in the house all the time, considering how dismal regular and decent the widow was in all her ways; and so when I couldn't stand it no longer I lit out. I got into my old rags and my sugar-hogshead again, and was free and satisfied. But Tom Sawyer he hunted me up and said he was going to start a band of robbers, and I might join if I would go back to the widow and be respectable. So I went back.

The widow she cried over me, and called me a poor lost lamb, and she called me a lot of other names, too, but she never meant no harm by it. She put me in them new clothes again, and I couldn't do nothing but sweat and sweat, and feel all cramped up. Well, then, the old thing commenced again. The widow rung a bell for supper, and you had to come to time. When you got to the table you couldn't go right to eating, but you had to wait for the widow to tuck down her head and grumble a little over the victuals, though there warn't really anything the matter with them,—that is, nothing only everything was cooked by itself. In a barrel of odds and ends it is different; things get mixed up, and the juice kind of swaps around, and the things go better.

Seeing the Wind

英 语 文 本	汉 语 文 本
Seeing the Wind RogerAschem	观风 杨自伍译
To see the wind, with a man his eyes, it is impossible, the nature of it is so fine, and subtle, yet this experience of the wind had 1 once myself, and that was in the great snow that fell four years ago: I rode in the highway between Topcliffe-upon-Swale, and Borowe Bridge, the way being somewhat trodden afore, by wayfaring men. The fields on both sides were plain and lay almost yard deep with snow, the night afore had been a little frost, so that the snow was hard and crusted above. That morning the sun shone bright and clear, the wind was whistling aloft, and sharp according to the time of the year. The snow' in the highway lay loose and trodden with horse feet: so as the wind blew, it took the loose snow with it, and made it so slide upon the snow in the field which was hard and crusted by reason of the frost overnight, that thereby I might see very well, the whole nature of the wind as it blew that day. And 1 had a great delight and pleasure to mark it, which maketh me now far better to remember it. Sometime the wind would be not past two yards broad, and so it would carry the snow as far as I could see. Another time the snow would blow over half the field at once. Sometime the snow would tumble softly, by and by it would fly wonderful fast. And this I perceived also that the wind goeth by streams and not whole together.	观风，凭一个人的眼睛，那是不可能的，因为风性如此虚无而又飘缈；不过有一回，我却获得了这种亲身体验，那是四年前大雪飘落的时分。我骑马经过洼地上段通向市镇桥的大路，这条路是昔日徒步行客渐渐走出来的。两旁的田野一望无际，积雪盈尺；前一天夜间，凝结起薄薄的霜冻，所以地面的积雪变硬结冰了。早晨阳光普照，灿烂明媚，朔风在空中呼啸，一年到了这个季候，已是凛冽侵骨了。马蹄阵阵踏过，大路上的积雪便松散开来，于是风吹雪飘，席卷而起，一片片滑落在田野里。彻夜霜寒地冻，田野也变得坚硬结冰了，因此那一天风雪飞舞，我才有可能把风的属性看得清清楚楚。而且我怀着十分喜悦的心情注目凝视，所以如今我更是记忆犹新。时而风吹过去，不到咫尺之遥，放眼望去，可以看见风吹雪花所到之处。时而雪花一次就飘过半边田野。有时雪花柔缓泻落；不一会儿又会激扬飘舞，令人目不暇接。而此时的情景我也有所感知，风过如缕，而非弥漫天地。
For I should sec one stream within a score on me, then the space of two score no snow would stir, but after so much quantity of ground, another stream of snow at the same very time should be carried likewise, but not equally. For the one would stand still when the other flew apace, and so continue sometime swiftlier, sometime slowlier, sometime broader, sometime narrower, as far as I could see. Nor it flew not straight, but sometime it crooked this way, sometime that way, and sometime it ran round about in a compass. And sometime the snow would be lift clean from the ground up into the air, and by and by it would be all clapped to the ground as though there had been no wind at all, straightway it would rise and fly again.	原来我竟看到相距二十来步之远的一股寒风迎面袭来；然后相距四十来步的雪花没有动静；但是，地面积雪越来越多之后，又有一缕雪花，就在同一时刻，同样地席卷而起，不过疏密相间。一缕雪花静止不动，另一缕则疾飞而过，时而越来越快，时而越来越慢，时而渐渐变大，时而渐渐变小，纵目望去，尽入眼帘。飞雪不是劈面而来，而是忽而曲曲弯弯，忽而散漫交错，忽而团团旋转。有时积雪吹向空中，地面一无所遗，不过片刻又会笼盖大地，仿佛根本没有起风一般，旋即雪花又会飘扬飞舞。
And that which was the most marvel of all, at one time two drifts of snow flew, the one out of the West into the East, the other out of the North into the East: And I saw	

英 语 文 本	汉 语 文 本
two winds by reason of the snow the one cross over the other, as it had been two highways. And again I should hear the wind blow in the air, when nothing was stirred at the ground. And when all was still where I rode, not very far from me the snow should be lifted wonderfully. This experience made me more marvel at the nature of the wind, than it made me cunning in the knowledge of the wind; but yet thereby I learned perfectly that it is no marvel at all though men in a wind lose their length in shooting, seeing so many ways the wind is so variable in blowing.	令人叹为观止的是，两股飘然而来的雪花一起飞扬，一股由西向东，一股北来东去。借着飘雪，我看见两股风流，交叉重叠，就像是在两条大路上似的。还有一回，我竟听见空气中风声吹过，地面一切毫无动静。当我骑到万籁俱静之处，离我相隔不远的地方，积雪竟是无比奇妙地向风披靡。这番体验使我更为赞叹风的属性，而不只是使我对风的知识有所了解；不过我也由此懂得，风中的行人打猎时，失去距离感不足为奇，因为风向变幻不定，视线便转向四面八方。

Vanity Fair (Excerpt)

英 语 文 本	汉 语 文 本
Vanity Fair (Excerpt) By William Thackeray	名利场(节选) 杨必译
Although schoolmistresses, letters are to be trusted no more nor less than churchyard epitaphs; yet, as it sometimes happens that a person departs this life, who is really deserving of all the praises the stone cutter carves over his bones; who is a good Christian, a good parent, child, wife or husband; who actually does leave a disconsolate family to mourn his loss; so in academies of the male and female sex it occurs every now and then, that the pupil is fully worthy of the praises bestowed by the disinterested instructor. Now, Miss Amelia Sedley was young lady of this singular species, and deserved not only all that Miss Pinkerton said in her praise, but had many charming qualities which that pompous old Minerva of a woman could not see, from the differences of rank and age between her pupil and herself.	一般说来，校长的信和墓志铭一样靠不住。不过偶然也有几个死人当得起石匠刻在他们朽骨上的好话，真的是虔诚的教徒，慈爱的父母，孝顺的儿女，尽职的丈夫，贤良的妻子，他们家里的人也真的哀思绵绵地追悼他们。同样的，不论在男学校女学校，偶然也会有一两个学生当得起老师毫无私心的称赞。爱米丽亚·赛特笠小姐就是这种难能可贵的好人。平克顿小姐夸奖她的话，句句是真的。不但如此，她还有许多可爱的品质，不过这个自以为了不起的、像智慧女神一样的老婆子因为地位不同，年龄悬殊，看不出来罢了。
For she could not only sing like a lark, or a Mrs. Billington, and dance like Hillisberg or Parisot; and embroider beautifully; and spell as well as the Dixonary itself; but she had such a kindly, smiling, tender, gentle, generous heart of her own, as won the love of everybody who came near her, from Minerva herself down to the poor girl in the scullery, and the one-eyed tartwoman's daughter, who was permitted to vend her wares once a week to the young ladies in the Mall. She had twelve intimate and bosom friends out of the twenty-four young ladies. Even envious Miss Briggs never spoke ill of her; high and mighty Miss Saltire (Lord Dexter's granddaughter) allowed that her figure was genteel.	她的歌喉比得上百灵鸟，或者可说比得上别灵顿太太，她的舞艺不亚于赫立斯白格或是巴利索脱。她花儿绣得好，拼法准确得和字典不相上下。除了这些不算，她心地厚道，性格温柔可疼，器量又大，为人又乐观，所以上智慧女神，下至可怜的洗碗小丫头，没一个人不爱她。那独眼的卖苹果女人有个女儿，每星期到学校里来卖一次苹果，也爱她，二十四个同学里面，倒有十二个是她的心腹朋友；连妒忌心最重的白力格小姐都不说她的坏话；连自以为了不起的赛尔泰小姐(她是台克斯脱勋爵的孙女儿)也承认她的身段不错。

英语文本	汉语文本
And as for Miss Swartz, the rich woolly-haired mulatto from St. Kitts, on the day Amelia went away, she was in such a passion of tears, that they were obliged to send for Dr. Floss, and half tipsify her with sal volatile. Miss Pinkerton's attachment was, as may be supposed, from the high position and eminent virtues of that lady, calm and dignified; but Miss Jemima had already whimpered several times at the idea of Amelia's departure; and, but for fear of her sister, would have gone off in downright hysterics, like the heiress (who paid double) of St. Kitts. Such luxury of grief, however, is only allowed to parlour-boarders. Honest Jemima had all the bills, and the washing, and the mending, and the puddings, and the plate and crockery, and the servants to superintend. But why speak about her? It is probable that we shall not hear of her again from this moment to the end of time, and that when the great filigree iron gates are once closed on her, she and her awful sister will never issue therefrom into this little world of history.	还有位有钱的施瓦滋小姐，是从圣·葛脱回来的半黑种，她那一头头发卷得就像羊毛；爱米丽职离校那天她哭得死去活来，校里的人只好请了弗洛丝医生来，用嗅盐把她熏得半醉。平克顿小姐的感情是沉着而有节制的，我们从她崇高的地位和她过人的德行上可以推想出来，可是吉米玛小姐就不同，她想到要跟爱米丽亚分别，已经哼哼唧唧哭了好几回，若不是怕她姐姐生气，准会像圣·葛脱的女财主一样（她付双倍的学杂费），老实不客气地发起歇斯底里病来。可惜只有寄宿在校长家里的阔学生才有权利任性发泄哀痛，老实的吉米玛工作多着呢，她得销账，做布丁，指挥佣人，留心碗盏瓷器，还得负责上上下下换洗缝补的事情。我们不必多提她了。从现在到世界末日，我们也不见得再听到她的消息。那镂花的大铁门一关上，她和她那可怕的姐姐永远不会再到我们这小天地里来了。
But as we are to see a great deal of Amelia, there is no harm in saying, at the outset of our acquaintance, that she was a dear little creature; and a great mercy it is, both in life and in novel, which (and the latter especially) abound in villains of the most sombre sort, that we are to have for a constant companion, so guileless and good-natured a person. As she is not a heroine, there is no need to describe her person; indeed I am afraid that her nose was rather short than otherwise, and her cheeks a great deal too round and red for a heroine; but her face blushed with rosy health, and her lips with the freshest of smiles, and she had a pair of eyes, which sparkled with the brightest and honestest good-humour, except indeed when they filled with tears, and that was a great deal too often; for the silly thing would cry over a dead canary bird; or over a mouse, that the cat haply had seized upon; or over the end of a novel, were it ever so stupid; and as for saying an unkind word to her, were any persons hard-hearted enough to do so - why, so much the worse for them. Even Miss Pinkerton, that austere and god-like woman, ceased scolding her after the first time, and though she no more comprehended sensibility than she did algebra, gave all masters and teachers particular orders to treat Miss Sedley with the utmost gentleness, as harsh treatment was injurious to her.	我们以后还有好些机会和爱米丽亚见面，所以应该先介绍一下，让大家知道她是个招人疼的小女孩儿。我们能够老是跟这么天真和气的人作伴，真是好运气，因为不管在现实生活里面，还是在小说里面——尤其在小说里面——可恶的坏蛋实在太多。她反正不是主角，所以我不必多形容她的外貌。不瞒你说，我觉得她的鼻子不够长，脸蛋儿太红太圆，不大配做女主角。她脸色红润，显得很健康，嘴角卷着甜蜜蜜的笑容，明亮的眼睛里闪闪发光，流露出最真诚的快活，可惜她的眼里也常常装满了眼泪。因为她最爱哭。金丝雀死了，老鼠给猫逮住了，或是小说里最无聊的结局，都能叫这小傻瓜伤心。假如有硬心肠的人责骂了她，那就活该他们倒霉。连女神一般严厉的平克顿小姐，骂过她一回之后，也没再骂第二回。在她看来，这种容易受感触的性子，正和代数一样难捉摸，不过她居然叮嘱所有的教师，叫他们对赛特笠小姐特别温和，因为粗暴的手段对她只有害处。

续上表

英 语 文 本	汉 语 文 本
So that when the day of departure came, between her two customs of laughing and crying, Miss Sedley was greatly puzzled how to act. She was glad to go home, and yet most wofully sad at leaving school. For three days before, little Laura Martin, the orphan, followed her about, like a little dog. She had to make and receive at least fourteen presents,—to make fourteen solemn promises of writing every week: 'Send my letters under cover to my grandpapa, the Earl of Dexter' said Miss Saltire (who, by the way, was rather shabby): 'Never mind the postage, but write every day, you dear darling,' said the impetuous and woolly-headed, but generous and affectionate Miss Swartz; and the orphan, little Laura Martin (who was just in round-hand), took her friend's hand, and said, looking up in her face wistfully, 'Amelia, when I write to you I shall call you mamma.' All which details, I have no doubt, Jones, who reads this book at his Club, will pronounce to be excessively foolish, trivial, twaddling, and ultra-sentimental. Yes: I can see Jones at this minute (rather flushed with his joint of mutton and half-pint of wine), taking out his pencil and scoring under the words 'foolish, twaddling', etc,. and adding to them his own remark of 'quite true'. Well, he is a lofty man of genius, and admires the great and heroic in life and novels; and so had better take warning and go elsewhere.	赛特笠小姐既爱哭又爱笑,所以到了动身的一天不知怎么才好。她喜欢回家,又舍不得离校。没爹娘的罗拉·马丁连着三天像小狗似的跟在她后面。她至少收了十四份礼物,当然也得照样回十四份,还得郑重其事地答应十四个朋友每星期写信给她们。赛尔泰小姐(顺便告诉你一声,她穿得很寒酸)说道:"你写给我的信,叫我祖父台克斯脱勋爵转给我得了。"施瓦滋小姐说:"别计较邮费,天天写信给我吧,宝贝儿。"这位头发活像羊毛的小姐感情容易冲动,可是器量大,待人也亲热。小孤儿罗拉·马丁(她刚会写圆滚滚的大字)拉着朋友的手,呆呵呵地瞧着她说:"爱米丽亚,我写信给你的时候,就叫你妈妈。"琼斯在他的俱乐部里看这本书看到这些细节,一定会骂他们琐碎、无聊,全是废话,而且异乎寻常的肉麻。我想像得出琼斯的样子,他刚吃过养肉,喝了半品脱的酒,脸上红彤彤的,拿起笔来在"无聊""废话"等字样底下画了道儿,另外加上几句,说他的批评"很准确"。他本来是个高人一等的天才,不论在小说里在生活中,只赏识大刀阔斧、英雄好汉的事迹,所以我这里先警告他,请他走开。

认知升级

一、散文的翻译

散文是文学中常见的体裁,它一般篇幅较短,但选材广泛,结构灵活,表现手法多样,如叙事、抒情、议论等,主要特点是体物写志,形散神聚。"形散"是指散文运笔如风,不拘形式,清淡自然;"神聚"指意旨鲜明,紧凑集中,既散得开,又收得拢。优美的散文艺术性在于新颖的构思,充沛的感情,丰富的想象,简洁精粹的语言和耐人寻味的意境。

英语散文的结构层次简练,篇幅短小,语言简洁精练,具有文笔流畅、意境清新、前后呼应、浑然一体的特点。英文散文家都十分讲究风格,或是华丽繁丰的风格,或是平实简洁的风格,或是反讥幽默的风格。英国著名散文家 Lord Chesterfield 曾说:Style is the dress of thoughts, and well-dressed thought, like a well-dressed man, appears to good advantage",这足以说明风格的重要。

散文翻译不仅力求完美地保持原文的信息、原文的功能;语言自然流畅、准确细致、雅俗得当;还需要语篇神韵的再创造;译出原文的风格或味道来。在翻译之前,要准确分析,确认该散文是朴实无华,典雅华丽浪漫抒情,还是修辞多样、形式工整,然后采取各种手段,传达原文风格。原文严谨周密,译文也当周密细致;原文朴素自然、语言清新,译文也要清新自然。

在具体处理的时候,可以从词汇、句式、节奏、修辞方法四个方面忠实地重现原文风格。具体来说,译者需要得体选词,运用增减词等翻译技巧,调整句法结构,考虑散文节奏韵律的再现,琢磨如何保留修辞方法的表现力,充分表达原文的感情、韵味、意境,译出原文的风格和神韵。

1.选词

例1 Father's attitude toward anybody who wasn't his kind used to puzzle me. It was so dictatorial. There was no live and let live about it. And to make it worse he had no compunctions about any wounds he inflicted; on the contrary, he felt that people should be grateful to him for teaching them better.

从前我总不懂父亲为什么对那些脾气跟他不一样的人采取那么个态度。那么专制!一点"你好我好"也没有。尤其糟糕的是他伤害了人家还毫无抱歉的意思!正相反,他觉得别人应该感谢他,因为他教他们学好。(吕叔湘译)

这段散文是作者的独白,它靠的是平易、优美、用词得当来感染读者。译文先将第一句调整词序,主语后置与那么专制相呼应,符合汉语前轻后重的表达习惯。将原文中通俗易懂的词 puzzle 译为"不懂",这一词就把全句带活了。随后将 no live and let live 译为"一点你好我好也没有",译文没有对号入座的痕迹。句中定语从句的处理也毫不拖泥带水。译者在这段译文中娴熟地运用了"尤其""正相反""因为"等关联词,使译文和原文一样流转自如,明白晓畅。

例2 This rambling propensity strengthened with years. Books of voyages and travels became my passion, and in devouring their contents I neglected the regular exercises of the schools. How wistfully would I wander about the pier heads in fine weather, and watch the parting ships bound to distant climes — with what longing eyes would I gaze after their lessening sails, and waft myself in imagination to the ends of the earth! (Washington Irving)

译文1.这种浪游的习性在我竟随着年龄而俱增。描写海陆的游记成了我的酷嗜,浸润其中,致废课业。我往往怀着多么渴慕的心情,在天气晴和的日子里漫步在码头周围,凝视着一艘艘离去的船只,驶赴迢迢的远方。我曾以何等希羡的眼神目送着那渐渐消逝的桅帆,并在想象之中自己也随风飘越至地角天涯。(《英语世界》88.4)

译文2.岁月增添,游兴更浓。游记和旅行日记这类书籍成了我的爱好,如饥似渴地阅读使我忽略了学校的正常功课。晴朗的日子里,我常到码头去闲逛,看到船舶离岸远去的情景,不觉心旷神怡。我凝视着点点风帆,看他们逐渐消失,而我的幻觉也跟着它们,驶向天边。(《英语世界》85.2)

在该例中,译文1词语生硬,文白夹杂,句子冗长累赘,文字风格不统一,读起来有佶屈聱牙之感,译文2词语简洁平易,句式结构匀称,首尾平衡,平淡之中充满着舒畅的活力,读起来有轻松自如之感。将两种译文进行比较,可以明显地看出,后者词义选择确切得体,句子之间层次分明。不管是从上下文判断,还是从字面理解,译得较为具体化、形象化,再现了原文的内在美。比译文1略胜一筹。

2. 句式

例1 The year's season in the sun has run its course. Nature begins to prepare for winter. After the color in the woodlands, the leaves will blanket the soil. The litter of autumn will become mulch, then humus for root tender seed. The agency of growth is ended for another year, but life itself is hoard in root and bulb and seed and egg.

阳光下，九月健步走完它的旅程，大自然开始进入冬季。丛林褪色，树叶凋零，大地铺满了厚毯。秋日的馈赠覆盖在大地上，沃土滋养着根茎和幼嫩的种子。生长的冲动中止了，静待来年，但是生命本身却藏身于根茎、籽卵之中，永无止息。

这是译自《读者文摘》上的一段抒情散文，文字结构简易，句子短小精干，笔调清新动人。译文注意了前后连贯、流畅这一环节。顺序安排符合汉语习惯，显然，只有"走完"才能"进入"。大自然的变迁受日月支配，所以"太阳下"这一定语按汉语状语译出，位于句首。不仅如此，译文在结构上把 After the color in the woodlands 这一状语与主句 the leaves will blanket the soil 合为一体，用三个句子译出，紧凑有力。同时"永无止息"是译者根据全段的含意而添加的。添词是为了再现原文的弦外之音，起到统领全段之效果。

英汉两种语言在句法结构与语序上差别很大，翻译时绝对不能生搬硬套，需要重新组合，译文才能通顺流畅。当然，结构可以改变绝对不等于意思可以改变。如果译文与原文含意不符，那么"连贯"与"流畅"就失去了意义。我们所说的"顺"必须是在"信"的前提下。

3. 节奏

语言节奏，是很好体现散文风格的技巧之一，因为每一篇散文精品都是一件艺术品，如同音乐、舞蹈等艺术活动一样，离不开节奏。而节奏是体现文章气势、神韵等的第一要事，因此，保持译文与原文在节奏方面的对应，也使译文与原文在风格方面相吻合，使"译文神似"的有效途径之一。译者应该捕捉散文的节奏美，使译文生动传神，是我们散文译者孜孜以求的最高境界。

散文的节奏可分为意义节奏（Thought rhythm）和声音节奏（Sound rhythm）。本文主要想谈谈散文的意义节奏。意义节奏是指"由短语、从句和句子等句法手段产生的节奏"。散文作家为了体现散文独特的语言风格，常常采用一些修辞手段、变换句子结构等，使思想情感和语体风格浑然一体。诸如排比、并列、重复等修辞手段的使用，变换句式和句子的长短，以调节情感的轻重缓急，从而产生不同效果的节奏。

例1 The car ploughed uphill through the long squalid straggle of Tevershali, the blackened brick dwellings, black slate roots glistening their sharp edge, the mud black with coaldust, the pavements wet and black. It was as if dismalness had soaked through and through everything. The utter negation of natural beauty, the utter negation of the gladness of life, the utter absence of the instinct for shapely beauty which every bird and beast had, the utter death of the human intuitive faculty was appalling. The stacks of soap in the grocers' shops, the rhubarb and lemoms in the green-grocers, the awful hats in the milliners, all went by ugly, ugly, ugly, followed by the plaster and gill horror of the cinema with its wet picture announcements. A Woman's Love and the new big Primitive chapel, primitive enough in its stark brick and big panes of greenish and raspberry glass in the windows. (D. H. Lawrence)

汽车吃力地爬上山坡,穿过特维肖尔镇那漫长肮脏、杂乱无序的矿区。这里的砖屋已变成了黑色;黑色的石板瓦显出轮廓清晰的棱角;泥土混杂着黑色的煤灰;道路污黑潮湿。抑郁阴沉似乎彻彻底底笼罩了这里的一切。一切完全没有了自然的美色;完全缺少了生活的喜悦;完全失去了鸟兽原有的美丽;完全毁灭了人类的直觉,使人充满了惧怕。杂货店里成堆的肥皂;蔬菜水果店里的大黄和柠檬;女帽店里的那些令人嫌恶的帽子,所有这些已变得非常非常丑陋。电影院墙上的灰泥惨不忍睹,上面贴有电影《一个女人的爱》的潮湿的图片公告;那座新建的古式大教堂,因其毫无装饰的砖块显得过分粗糙,窗户上的巨大玻璃已变成了浅绿色和蔗莓色……

  D.H.Lawrence 的这篇散文,淋漓尽致地抒发了自己的情感,深刻表达了对 TEVERSHALL 矿区的嫌恶之情,作者大量运用排比、重复句结构,文章读起来富有节奏感。排比用于叙事,可使语言畅达,层次清楚;用于抒情,能收到节奏和谐、感情奔放的效果。原文第 2 句 through 的重复和第 4 句中 ugly 的三次使用,强调了作者的直观感觉并且加强了语气,可以译为"彻彻底底"和"非常非常丑陋"。第 3 句中,由四个短语 the utter negation of, the utter negation of, the utter absence of, the utter death of 组成的排比结构,读起来铿锵悦耳,层次清楚,节奏感强,淋漓尽致地表达了作者的厌恶心情。在此排比结构中,作者又四次重复使用了 utter 这个词,使得这种节奏前后呼应,语言显得紧凑、连贯,富有很强的感染力。为了保留这种效果,英文 utter 译为"没有了""缺少了""失去了"和"毁灭了",形成汉语的重复和排比结构,体现了原文的节奏,保持了原文的文体风格。第 4 句中,作者再次运用了排比结构"名词+in+名词",其结构相同,语气一致,多项并列,加强了语气,增强了节奏,读起来朗朗上口。为此,我们把这种排比用同样的手法转换成汉语,以达到相同的效果。

  节奏是文学作品,特别是英文散文的美学特征之一。翻译散文时,就应该审视原作中客观存在的节奏美、结构美,识别原作的音美手段。领悟原作的美学特征,把握原作的艺术魅力,不仅对于把握原作的表层和深层意义,而且对于捕捉语境意义,无疑具有十分重要的意义。

  高明的英文散文大师,有时会出于表达的目的以及抒发情感的需要,或用简单句,或用复杂句,或改变语序,或用长短句结合等手段,来调整文章的节奏。如此手法会产生意想不到的效果。如果翻译这样的散文,我们当惜墨如金,不管从其韵味,还是从句式安排,都要仔细对照研读,尽量使双语之间和谐统一。

例2   Today I have read The Tempest … Among the many reasons which make me glad to have been born in England, one of the first is that I read Shakespeare in my mother tongue. If I try to imagine myself as one who cannot know him face to face, who hears him only speaking from afar, and that in accents which only through the labouring intelligence can touch the living soul, there comes upon me a sense of chill discouragement, of dreary deprivation. I am wont to think that I can read Homer, assuredly, if any man enjoys him, it is I; but can I for a moment dream that Homer yields me all his music, that his word is to me as to him who walked by the Hellenic shore when Hellas lived ? I know that there reaches me across the vast of time no more than a faint and broken echo; I know that it would be fainter still, but for its blending with those memories of youth which are as a glimmer of the world's primeval glory. Let every land have joy of its poet; for the poet is the land itself, all its greatness and its sweetness, all that incommunicable heritage for which men live and die. As I close the book, love and reverence possess me, whether does my full heart turn to the great Enchanter, or to the Island upn which he has laid his spell? I know not. I cannot think of them apart. In the love and reverence awakened by that voice of voices, Shakespeare and England are but one.

今天我拜读了《暴风雨》……庆幸我能降生在英国的众多原因中,首要的原因是我能够以母语阅读莎士比亚。假如设想自己既不能与他当面相识,又不能聆听其诗篇,并且所用的言语还必须经过辛苦的思考才能触及心灵,那么,我会有心灰意冷、意气消沉之感觉。我一向自以为能读荷马,且深信不疑;如果说谁能欣赏荷马,那就是我。然而我几曾梦想荷马使我拥有了他全部和谐悦耳的诗篇;几曾梦想他的言辞对我而言与曾在希腊时期漫步在海滨的他竟如此地一致?我深知经过漫长岁月打动我的仅仅是那微弱破碎的回声;我也深知这个回声会变得更加微弱,倘若回声没有与远古世界昌盛之光的青春回忆融为一体的话。愿每个国家拥有诗人而拥有喜悦,因为诗人意味着国家本身;意味着国家的伟大和芳馨;意味着人们与之共生死的无法言表的传统。在我合上此书的那一刻,爱慕与崇敬之情便油然而生。全身心地崇敬这位伟大的诗人,还是爱恋他赋予了魅力的大不列颠呢?我不得而知。我无法把她们分开。在那绝伦无比的声音唤起的爱慕与崇敬之中,莎士比亚与大不列颠同在。

这是英国作家乔治·吉星(George Gissing,1857—1903)的一篇散文,短小精悍,其文体古雅考究,谨严冼炼,语言简洁,堪称散文精品。作者行文当中很注意长短句的变换。全文共11个句子。各句的字数顺序为6-27-49-52-46-31-10-21-3-6-17。文章开始句子较短,第4句为全文最长句,随即句子逐渐变短,这种安排产生的效果是不可低估的,它把文章所要陈述的背景逐渐集中于情感抒发者,并紧密地与之联系在一起。同时,第一人称代词I贯穿于文章始末,充分抒发了作者的真挚感情,这种感情随着句子的长短而起伏,随着句读节奏而跳跃,直到最后作者的情感达到了高潮。

我们看到,作者始终在变换使用长短句及不同句式来调节句读节奏。第2、3句都把从句或状语部分放置在前面,根据语言常识,读时需升调,为此两个句子读起来就会产生一扬一抑的节奏效果。尽管第4句是全文最长的句子,但是,作者在断句上处理得非常巧妙,前半部分采取了两个一长一短的句式,调节了节奏;后半部分是一个问句,又以that引导了两个从句,且为升调(因是一般问句),是整个文章节奏最缓慢的地方。第5句也是文中较长的一个句子,作者不惜笔墨用两个I know that…句式阐述了自己的深刻感受,节奏仍然不快。从第6句起,字数明显减少,并且在断句上有了较大的变化。第6句有31个单词,却划分成4部分,节奏明显加快,情感深厚。第7、8句与第2、3句在句读语调上相吻合,其共同点都把状语部分前置,使语调形成了变化,节奏强弱分明,抑扬顿挫,作者的情感通过语调和节奏充分地表现了出来。从整体看,文章在节奏上前呼后应,浑然一体。第9、10句,既是对前句的回答,又是对前两个长句的调节。最后一句又变为长句,不管从语义上还是句读节奏上都是对第2、3句的呼应和对称。

像这样读起来上口、内容感人的文章,句读节奏是起了一定作用的。那么,翻译时我们应该尽可能考虑这种节奏效果;尽可能使译文与原文达到"神似";尽可能使译文在句子节拍、停顿、节奏等方面间隔恰当,从而产生语言的节奏美。

4. 修辞

例1 High in a smooth ocean of sky floated a dazzling majestic sun: Fragments of powdery cloud, like spray flung from a wave crest, sprinkled the radiant, like blue heaven.

万里晴空,像水波不兴的大海,威严的烈日射出炫目的光芒。几片碎云,像从浪峰中喷出的火花,散落在蔚蓝色的天空,闪烁着银辉。(《英语世界》89.4)

此英文段落中的句式不是平铺直叙,而是以倒装句的修辞手段展开,由两个明喻排比而成。这样运笔,更使人感到"广阔无垠的天空"的绚丽壮观。译文注意了赖以存在的风格形式——语句的衔接,长短的搭配,节奏的变换,使行文流畅并与原文协调一致。此段如直译为"在广阔无垠的天空,高高地浮动着耀眼、神圣的太阳……"就很难体现此段的语言风格特色。

例2 Under water that was clear as glass the pool was carpeted with green sponge. Gray patches of sea squirts glistened on the ceiling and colonies of soft coral were a pale apricot color…The beauty of the reflected images and of the limpid pool itself was the poignant beauty of things that are ephemeral, existing only until the sea should return to fill the little cave.

在清明如镜的水下,潭底铺着一层碧绿的海绵。洞顶上一片片灰色的海螵蛸熠熠闪光,一堆堆软珊瑚披着淡淡的杏黄色衣裳……水中倒彩的美,清澈的水潭本身的美,这都是些生命短促的事物所体现的强烈而令人心醉的美——海水一旦漫过小洞,这种美便不复存在了。(《英语世界》86.2)

这是一个颇有诗意的美丽段落,文体的特点是言简意赅,采用明喻、暗喻、对比,堆砌的手法,渲染主题加强气势,使人印象深刻。

译文"水下"与"潭底"不仅汉语词语搭配得当,而且也表达了原文的情趣。"闪光"与"淡淡的杏黄色衣裳",表情贴切,音韵和谐,悦人耳目。两个of短语用汉语分句译出,前短后长,译成"水中倒影的美,清澈的水潭本身的美"。这样不但行文简洁,而且气韵十足,有一气呵成之感。读一读原文,看一看汉译,令人感到译文不但忠于原文风格,保持原句句意的完整和结构的紧凑,也合乎译入语的习惯。

需要强调的是,流畅是翻译散文的要求。流畅,就是译文通顺流利,语意贯通,脉理清晰,层次清楚,读起来朗朗上口。如果说小说是用形象翻译形象,那么散文则是注重层次结构,以生动简洁来打动读者的心。

众所周知,英文散文具有文笔流畅、意境清新、前后呼应、浑然一体的特点。在句子结构和表达形式上与汉语又大相径庭。如果翻译时拘泥于原文的形式,"对号入座",译文一定生硬、呆板,从而影响原文意思的完整表达。因此,译者首先对原文总的语言特点,例如全句的结构、修辞手段、气氛和感情效果吃透,然后用汉语加以融化、分解、重新组合,再创造,摆脱原文的约束,产生出贴切自然、流畅通顺的译文。上述译例均很好地体现了在流畅方面的追求。

二、小说的翻译

小说(novel)是四大文学体裁之一。它对社会生活进行艺术概括,它描绘生活事件,塑造人物形象,展开作品主题,表达作者思想感情,从而艺术地反映和表现社会生活。

小说的三要素是：生动的人物形象、完整的故事情节和具体的环境描写。小说一般描写人物故事，塑造多种多样的人物形象。小说中人物的对话是否具有鲜明的个性，每个人物是否有独特的语言风格，是衡量小说水平的一个重要标准。小说情节一般包括开端、发展、高潮、结局四部分，有的还包括序幕、尾声。环境包括自然环境和社会环境。

小说的主要特点（Features）有：①"虚构性"，是小说的本质。②"捕捉人物生活的感觉经验"，是小说竭力要挖掘的艺术内容。③难忘的典型人物。小说塑造人物，可以以某一真人为模特儿，综合其他人的一些事迹，如鲁迅所说："人物的模特儿，没有专用过一个人，往往嘴在浙江，脸在北京，衣服在山西，是一个拼凑起来的角色。"④小说的故事情节来源于生活，它是现实生活的提炼，但比现实生活更集中，更有代表性。

翻译汉语小说的时候，需要特别注意小说的以下几个特点：生动形象的语言、个性化的人物、广泛运用的修辞格、复杂多变的句式等。下面我们将选取几部中国名著的片段译文进行分析和探讨，着重讨论汉英小说翻译中的风格、词语及人物语言的传译等问题。

1. 生动形象的环境描写

小说在描绘环境或叙述故事情节时，往往都用生动形象的语言进行具体而细腻的描写，再现场景中的各种细节，渲染情绪，从而激发读者的兴趣，能给读者一种身临其境的感觉，使人读后印象深刻。在用词上，往往表现出用词准确，多形容词、副词，多修饰等特征。因此翻译小说时，要准确选择所用词语，提升表现力。

例1 The small locomotive engine, Number 4, came clanking, stumbling down from Salston with seven full wagons.（D.H.Lawrence, The Odor of Chrysanthemums）

译文：4号小火车的车头拖着7节装满货物的车厢，从赛尔斯顿方向跌跌撞撞地开了过来，一路上发出叮叮咣咣的声响。

这段文字用了small描写火车大小，用locomotive描写火车类别，用clanking, stumbling描写火车行进的声音动作，细致入微，惟妙惟肖，读者读之，如闻其声，如见其形。翻译的时候，也要仔细揣摩，尽力还原生动的场景。

例2 The fire began in the kitchen and spread to the hotel dining room. Without warning, or perhaps just the one muffled cry of alarm, a ball of fire (yes, actually a ball) rolled through the arched and shuttered doorway from the kitchen, a sphere of moving color so remarkable, it was as though it had life and menace, when, of course, it did not - when, of course, it was simply a fact of science or of nature and not of God. For a moment, I felt paralyzed, and I remember in the greatest detail the way the flame climbed the long vermilion drapes with a squirrel's speed and agility and how the fire actually leapt -from valance to valance, disintegrating the fabric and causing it to fall as pieces of ash onto the diners below. It was nearly impossible to witness such an event and not think a cataclysm had been visited upon the diners for their sins, past or future.（Anita Shreve, All He Ever Wanted）

大火从厨房开始，蔓延到宾馆的餐厅。毫无预兆，也许只有一声低沉的警告，一团火球，对，就是那么一团，从厨房开始沿着拱形的装有百叶窗的门口滚动过来；一团快速移动的颜色，那么鲜艳，仿佛具有生命，形成威胁。而事实上，它既无生命，也不吓人，也不是上帝之物，而是自然界中一个科学的事实而已。有一阵子，我动弹不得,现在我历历在目地记得,当时火苗像松鼠那样敏捷快速得爬上长长的朱红窗帘,在帷幔与帷幔之间跳跃,让织物窗帘布分崩离析,让片片灰烬落到下面的用餐者的身上。目睹这种事件,就会自然而然想到这场灾难之所以降临在用餐者头上,是因为他们过去所犯或将来会犯的罪过。(罗天译)

2.个性化的人物

个性化是小说的重要特性。小说往往从外貌、动作、语言、心理等方面对人物进行多层次的刻画,把人物的政治面貌、社会地位、人品性格和生活、语言习惯等描绘得惟妙惟肖。

(1)语言描写

例如,人物语言塑造人物形象及个性的一个重要手段。作家常常会让笔下的人物通过本人之口来表现自己的个性,所谓"只闻其声,便识其人"。不同的人物语言往往折射出人物迥异的身份、年龄、职业、地位、教养、性格等。尤其在角色众多的小说中,有的人物语言可能非常文雅,有的会十分浅显,有的则使用方言俚语,还有的十分粗俗。

翻译小说时,译者要揣摩人物各自的语言和对话特点,生动地展现人物的个性。在某种意义上说,原作的艺术风格能否在译作中得以体现,取决于译者对人物的语言处理是否得当。

例1 "I hate the whole house," continued Miss Sharp in a fury. "I hope I may never set eyes on it again. I wish it were in the bottom of the Thames, I do; and if Miss Pinkerton were there, I wouldn't pick her out, that I wouldn't. O how I should like to see her floating in the water yonder, turban and all, with her train streaming after her, and her nose like the beak of a wherry." (W.M.Thackeray, Vanity Fair)

夏泼小姐狠狠地说道:"我恨透了这整个儿的学校。但愿我一辈子也别再看见它,我恨不得叫它沉到泰晤士河里去。倘若平克顿小姐掉在河里,我也不高兴捞她起来。我才不干呢!哈!我就爱看她在水里泡着,头上包着包头布,后面拖着个大裙子,鼻子像个小船似的浮在水面上。"(杨必译)

例2 "Hello, Jim, have I been asleep? Why didn't you stir me up? "

"Goodness gracious, is dat you, Huck? En you ain' dead—you ain' drowned—you's back again? It's too good for true, honey, it is too good for true. Lemme look at you, chile, lemme feel o' you…"(the Adventures of Huckleberry)

译文 1.哎呀,我的天,是你吗,哈克?你原来没有死啊——你并没有淹死啊——你又回来了吗?这实在太好了,老弟,这实在太好了。让我来看看你,孩子,让我来摸摸你吧。啊呀,你并没有死啊!你又活蹦乱跳地、平平安安地回来啦,还是咱们原来的老哈克 还是原来的老哈克,真是谢天谢地啊!(张万里译)

译文 2.我的天,史(是)你吗,哈克?你没有自(死)吗——你没有落水盐(淹)自吗——你又回来啦?这太好啦,叫人布(不)敢相信,乖乖,叫人布敢相信哪。尚(让)我看看你,孩子,尚我摸摸你。布,你没有自!你又回来啦,活得好好耳(儿)的,还史原来那过(个)哈克——谢天谢地,还史原来那过哈克!(成时译)

在本例中,马克·吐温的小说 The Adventures of Huckleberry Finn,叙述部分即采用了经过锤炼的美国当代口语,书中的人物对话更是原原本本的生活语言的照录,此处为哈克与黑奴吉姆的对话。小说人物吉姆的语言充斥着讹读、吞音、不合语法、用词不妥(其中 dat=that, En=and, ain'=ain't=are not, drownded=drowned, you's=you are, chile=child, o'=of),这些极不规范的语言生动地展现了黑奴吉姆社会身份、受教育情况以及人物个性。

张万里的译文抹去了吉姆语言中的种种多无,而成时的译文采用了汉语讹读的方法,较好地保留了吉姆的语言特色。因此,从小说原著的语体色彩来看,成译比张译更加忠实地再现了这一修辞特色,达到了更好的修辞效果,更好地反映了人物的身份和性格。

(2)肖像描写

小说中人物形象塑造最常用的写作手法便是肖像描写,即通过描写人物的容貌、衣饰及姿态等外部特征来刻画人物形象,形神兼备地表现人物的思想性格。翻译时要特别注意这些起关键作用的细节描写,运用不同的翻译策略,精确再现人物形象。

例1 She was of a helpless, fleshy build, with a frank, open countenance and an innocent, diffident manner. Her eyes were large and patient, and in them dwelt such a shadow of distress as only those who have looked sympathetically into the countenances of the distraught and helpless poor know anything about. (Theodore Dreiser Jennie Gerhardt)

那妇人生着一副绵软多肉的体格,一张坦率开诚的面容,一种天真羞怯的神气,一双大落落的柔顺眼睛,里边隐藏着无穷的心事,只有那些对于凄惶无告的穷苦人面目作过同情观察的人才看得出来。(傅东华译)

例2 One day she was pink and flawless; another pale and tragical. When she was pink she was felling less than when pale; her more perfect beauty accorded with her less elevated mood; her more intense mood with her less perfect beauty. (Tomas Hardy Tess of the d'Urbervilles)

今天光艳照人,白玉无瑕;明天却又沮丧苍白,满面苍凉。鲜艳往往出自于无忧;而苍白,却总是由于多愁。胸中没了思虑她便魅力无暇,一旦烦愁涌起,便又容色憔悴。(孙法理译)

评析:孙译多处省略,简洁明快,使主人公的美更具感染。

(3)动作描写

人物形象刻画也离不开动作描写。小说作者常常使用精心挑选的动词,摹写人物在不同场景中的一系列动作、行为,折射出人物的性格特点。翻译时,需在译入语中找到等值的富有表现力的动词。

例如,英语表达"哭"这一动作时,有很多动词或词组可供选择:cry 大声哭,weep 默默地哭,sob 啜泣,whimper 呜咽,wail 号啕大哭,blubber 又哭又闹,lament 恸哭,mewl 低泣,snivel 啜泣,squall 大声哭喊,whine 发呜呜声,yammer 哭泣叹息,yowl 号叫,burst into tears, dissolve in tears, put on the weeps, shed bitter tears, turn on waterworks 等。

表达"笑"的动作时,除了 smile 微笑、laugh 出声地笑两个常用词之外,还有很多同义词、近义词供选择。例如:giggle 咯咯地笑、傻笑,grin 露齿而笑,chuckle 含笑、轻声笑,snicker 忍笑、暗笑;roar 哄笑、大笑,simper 假笑、痴笑、傻笑,give a soft smile 莞尔一笑,give a charming smile 嫣然一笑,give a faint smile 淡淡一笑,smile from ear to ear 满面笑容,be radiant with smile 笑容可掬,force a smile 苦笑,squeeze a smile 强颜欢笑,conjure up a smile 满脸堆笑等生

动形象的表达方式。

例1 Tom raved like a madman, beat his breast, tore his hair, stamped on the ground, and vowed the utmost vengeance on all who had been concerned. He then pulled off his coat, and buttoned it around it round her, put his hat upon her head, wiped the blood from her face as well as possible for a side-saddle, or a pillion, that he might carry her safe home. (Henry Fielding. Tom Jones)

汤姆像个疯子一样，咆哮叫骂，捶胸薅发，顿足震地，起誓呼天，要对所有一切参与其事的人，都极尽报仇雪恨之能事。于是他把自己的褂子，从身上剥下来，围在娟丽身上，把纽扣给她系好；把自己的帽子，戴在她头上；用手绢尽其所能，把她脸上的血给她擦掉；大声吩咐仆人，叫他尽力快快骑马，取一个偏鞍或后鞍来，以便她平平安安地送回家去。（张谷若译）

(4) 心理描写

心理描写通过对人物内心世界的直接叙述，反映人物的喜怒哀乐等情感状态和变化，展示人物的心灵和性格特征，也能对人物形象的塑造产生至关重要的影响。翻译时，需注意叙述主体的身份与个性，以适当的语气、语调来传递人物的心理状况，传达人物的心理情感，准确再现作者对人物的评价和情感。

例1 I didn't give a damn how I looked. Nobody was around anyway. Everybody was in the sack…If I am on a train at night I can usually even read one of those dumb stories in a magazine without. You know. One of those stories with a lot of phony, lean-jawed guys named Linda or Marcia that are always lighting all the goddam David's pipes for them.

我才不在乎什么不好看哩。可是路上没有一个人。谁都上床啦。……我要在晚上坐火车。有一大堆叫大卫的瘦下巴的假惺惺的家伙，还有一大堆叫林达或玛莎的假惺惺的姑娘，老是给大卫们点混账的烟斗。（施威荣译）

评析：本例节选自《麦田里的守望者》这是主人公 Holden 的第一人称内心独白，他是一个自嘲自讽、满口脏话的中学生，一个不满现实的小痞子。译文保留了俗语，再现了 Holden 的真实心理。

3. 修辞格的广泛运用

小说常常大量使用修辞格，如拟人、比喻、讽刺、夸张、双关等。这些修辞新颖独特、形象生动，往往给读者留下深刻印象。由于中西语言和文化的差异，修辞格的翻译往往比较困难。在翻译的过程中，译者要保证内容准确，力争表达形式妥当，尽量体现原文效果。

例1 Joe, a clumsy and timid horseman, did not look to advantage in the saddle, look at him, Amelia dear, driving in to the parlour windows. Such a bull in china shop, never saw. (William Thackeray, Vanity Fair)

译文：乔胆子小，骑术又拙，骑在鞍上老不像样。"爱米丽亚，亲爱的，快看，他骑到人家客厅的窗子里去了。我一辈子没见过这样儿，真是大公牛闯到瓷器店去了。"（杨必译）

综上所述，小说翻译时要注意"传神达意"，准确地再现原文小说的风格，需要特别关注叙述语言、人物形象、修辞方法等几方面。

Celebrated Jumping Frog of Calaveras County
Mark Twain

In compliance with the request of a friend of mine, who wrote me from the East, I called on good-natured, garrulous old Simon Wheeler, and inquired after my friend's friend, Leonidas W. Smiley, as requested to do, and I hereunto append the result.I have a lurking suspicion that Leonidas W.Smiley is a myth; and that my friend never knew such a personage; and that he only conjectured that if I asked old Wheeler about him, it would remind him of his infamous Jim Smiley, and he would go to work and bore me to death with some exasperating reminiscence of him as long and as tedious as it should be useless to me.If that was the design, it succeeded.

I found Simon Wheeler dozing comfortably by the barroom stove of the dilapidated tavern in the decayed mining camp of Angel's, and I noticed that he was fat and bald-headed, and had an expression of winning gentleness and simplicity upon his tranquil countenance.He roused up, and gave me good-day.I told him a friend had commissioned me to make some inquiries about a cherished companion of his boyhood named Leonidas W.Smiley—Rev.Leonidas W.Smiley, a young minister of the Gospel, who he had heard was at one time a resident of Angel's Camp.I added that if Mr.Wheeler could tell me anything about this Rev.Leonidas W.Smiley, I would feel under many obligations to him.

Simon Wheeler backed me into a corner and blockaded me there with his chair, and then sat down and reeled off the monotonous narrative which follows this paragraph.He never smiled, he never frowned, he never changed his voice from the gentle-flowing key to which he tuned his initial sentence, he never betrayed the slightest suspicion of enthusiasm; but all through the interminable narrative there ran a vein of impressive earnestness and sincerity, which showed me plainly that, so far from his imagining that there was anything ridiculous or funny about his story, he regarded it as a really important matter, and admired its two heroes as men of transcendent genius in finesse.I let him go on in his own way, and never interrupted him once.

"Rev.Leonidas W.H'm, Reverend Le-well, there was a feller here once by the name of Jim Smiley, in the winter of '49-or may be it was the spring of' 50-I Don't recollect exactly, somehow, though what makes me think it was one or the other is because I remember the big flume warn't finished when he first came to the camp; but any way, he was the curiousest man about always betting on anything that turned up you ever see, if he could get anybody to bet on the other side; and if he couldn't he'd change sides.Any way that suited the other man would suit him—any way just so's he got a bet, he was satisfied.But still he was lucky, uncommon lucky; he most always come out winner.He was always ready and laying for a chance; there couldn't be no solit'ry thing mentioned but that feller'd offer to bet on it, and take any side you please, as I was just telling you.If there was a horse-race, you'd find him flush or you'd find him busted at the end of it; if there was a dog-fight, he'd bet on it; if there was a cat-fight, he'd bet on it; if there was a chicken-fight, he'd bet on it; why, if there was two birds setting on a fence, he would bet you which one would fly first; or if there was a camp-meeting, he would be there reg'lar to bet on Parson Walker, which he judged to be the best exhorter about here, and he was, too, and a good man. If he even see a straddle-bug start to go anywheres, he would bet you how long it would take him to get to—to wherever he was going to, and if you took him up, he would foller that straddle-bug to Mexico but what he would find out where he was bound for and how long he was on the road.

Lots of the boys here has seen that Smiley and can tell you about him. Why, it never made no difference to him—he'd bet on any thing—the dangest feller. Parson Walker's wife laid very sick once, for a good while, and it seemed as if they warn't going to save her; but one morning he come in, and Smiley up and asked him how she was, and he said she was considerable better—thank the Lord for his inf'nit' mercy—and coming on so smart that with the blessing of Prov'dence she'd get well yet; and Smiley, before he thought, says, Well, I'll risk two-and-a-half she Don't anyway.'"

Thish-yer Smiley had a mare—the boys called her the fifteen-minute nag, but that was only in fun, you know, because, of course, she was faster than that—and he used to win money on that horse, for all she was so slow and always had the asthma, or the distemper, or the consumption, or something of that kind. They used to give her two or three hundred yards start, and then pass her under way; but always at the fag-end of the race she'd get excited and desperate-like, and come cavorting and straddling up, and scattering her legs around limber, sometimes in the air, and sometimes out to one side amongst the fences, and kicking up m-o-r-e dust and raising m-o-r-e racket with her coughing and sneezing and blowing her nose—and always fetch up at the stand just about a neck ahead, as near as you could cipher it down.

And he had a little small bull-pup, that to look at him you'd think he warn't worth a cent but to set around and look ornery and lay for a chance to steal something. But as soon as money was up on him he was a different dog; his under-jaw'd begin to stick out like the fo'-castle of a steamboat, and his teeth would uncover and shine like the furnaces. And a dog might tackle him and bully-rag him, and bite him, and throw him over his shoulder two or three times, and Andrew Jackson—which was the name of the pup—Andrew Jackson would never let on but what he was satisfied, and hadn't expected nothing else—and the bets being doubled and doubled on the other side all the time, till the money was all up; and then all of a sudden he would grab that other dog jest by the j'int of his hind leg and freeze to it—not chaw, you understand, but only just grip and hang on till they threwed up the sponge, if it was a year. Smiley always come out winner on that pup, till he harnessed a dog once that didn't have no hind legs, because they'd been sawed off in a circular saw, and when the thing had gone along far enough, and the money was all up, and he come to make a snatch for his pet holt, he see in a minute how he'd been imposed on, and how the other dog had him in the door, so to speak, and he 'peared surprised, and then he looked sorter discouraged-like, and didn't try no more to win the fight, and so he got shucked out bad. He gave Smiley a look, as much as to say his heart was broke, and it was his fault, for putting up a dog that hadn't no hind legs for him to take holt of, which was his main dependence in a fight, and then he limped off a piece and laid down and died. It was a good pup, was that Andrew Jackson, and would have made a name for hisself if he'd lived, for the stuff was in him and he had genius—I know it, because he hadn't no opportunities to speak of, and it Don't stand to reason that a dog could make such a fight as he could under them circumstances if he hadn't no talent. It always makes me feel sorry when I think of that last fight of his'n, and the way it turned out.

Well, thish-yer Smiley had rat-tarriers, and chicken cocks, and tom-cats and all of them kind of things, till you couldn't rest, and you couldn't fetch nothing for him to bet on but he'd match you. He ketched a frog one day, and took him home, and said he cal'lated to educate him; and so he never done nothing for three months but set in his back yard and learn that frog to jump. And you bet you he did learn him, too. He'd give him a little punch behind, and the next minute you'd see that frog whirling in the air like a doughnut—see him turn one summerset, or may be a couple, if he got a good start, and come down flat-footed and all right, like a cat.

He got him up so in the matter of ketching flies, and kep' him in practice so constant, that he'd nail a fly every time as fur as he could see him. Smiley said all a frog wanted was education, and he could do 'most anything—and I believe him. Why, I've seen him set Dan'l Webster down here on this floor—Dan'l Webster was the name of the frog—and sing out, "Flies, Dan'l, flies!" and quicker'n you could wink he'd spring straight up and snake a fly off'n the counter there, and flop down on the floor ag'in as solid as a gob of mud, and fall to scratching the side of his head with his hind foot as indifferent as if he hadn't no idea he'd been doin' any more'n any frog might do. You never see a frog so modest and straightfor'ard as he was, for all he was so gifted. And when it come to fair and square jumping on a dead level, he could get over more ground at one straddle than any animal of his breed you ever see. Jumping on a dead level was his strong suit, you understand; and when it come to that, Smiley would ante up money on him as long as he had a red. Smiley was monstrous proud of his frog, and well he might be, for fellers that had traveled and been everywheres, all said he laid over any frog that ever they see.

Well, Smiley kep' the beast in a little lattice box, and he used to fetch him downtown sometimes and lay for a bet. One day a feller—a stranger in the camp, he was—come acrost him with his box, and says:

"What might be that You've got in the box?"

And Smiley says, sorter indifferent-like, "It might be a parrot, or it might be a canary, maybe, but it ain't—it's only just a frog."

And the feller took it, and looked at it careful, and turned it round this way and that, and says, "H'm—so 'tis. Well, what's he good for?"

"Well," Smiley says, easy and careless, "he's good enough for one thing, I should judg-he can outjump any frog in Calaveras county."

The feller took the box again, and took another long, particular look, and give it back to Smiley, and says, very deliberate, "Well," he says, "I Don't see no p'ints about that frog that's any better'n any other frog."

"Maybe you Don't," Smiley says. "Maybe you understand frogs and maybe you Don't understand 'em; maybe You've had experience, and maybe you ain't only a amature, as it were. Anyways, I've got my opinion and I'll risk forty dollars that he can outjump any frog in Calaveras County."

And the feller studied a minute, and then says, kinder sad like, "Well, I'm only a stranger here, and I ain't got no frog; but if I had a frog, I'd bet you."

And then Smiley says, "That's all right—that's all right—if you'll hold my box a minute, I'll go and get you a frog." And so the feller took the box, and put up his forty dollars along with Smiley's, and set down to wait.

So he set there a good while thinking and thinking to his-self, and then he got the frog out and prized his mouth open and took a teaspoon and filled him full of quail shot-filled! him pretty near up to his chin—and set him on the floor. Smiley he went to the swamp and slopped around in the mud for a long time, and finally he ketched a frog, and fetched him in, and give him to this feller, and says:

"Now, if you're ready, set him alongside of Dan'l, with his forepaws just even with Dan'l's, and I'll give the word." Then he says, "One—two—three—git!" and him and the feller touched up the frogs from behind, and the new frog hopped off lively, but Dan'l give a heave, and hysted up his shoulders—so—like a Frenchman, but it warn't no use—he couldn't budge; he was planted as solid as a church, and he couldn't no more stir than if he was anchored out. Smiley was a good deal surprised, and he was disgusted too, but he didn't have no idea what the matter was, of course.

The feller took the money and started away; and when he was going out at the door, he sorter jerked his thumb over his shoulder—so—at Dan'l, and says again, very deliberate, "Well," he says, "I Don't see no p'ints about that frog that's any better'n any other frog."

Smiley he stood scratching his head and looking down at Dan'l a long time, and at last says, "I do wonder what in the nation that frog throwed off for—I wonder if there ain't something the matter with him—he 'pears to look mighty baggy, somehow." And he ketched Dan'l up by the nap of the neck, and hefted him, and says, "Why blame my cats if he Don't weigh five pounds!" and turned him upside down and he belched out a double handful of shot. And then he see how it was, and he was the maddest man—he set the frog down and took out after that feller, but he never ketched him. And—

(Here Simon Wheeler heard his name called from the front yard, and got up to see what was wanted.) And turning to me as he moved away, he said: "Just set where you are, stranger, and rest easy—I ain't going to be gone a second."

But, by your leave, I did not think that a continuation of the history of the enterprising vagabond Jim Smiley would be likely to afford me much information concerning the Rev. Leonidas W. Smiley, and so I started away.

At the door I met the sociable Wheeler returning, and he buttonholed me and recommenced:

"Well, thish-yer Smiley had a yaller, one-eyed cow that didn't have no tail, only jest a short stump like a bannanner, and—"

However, lacking both time and inclination, I did not wait to hear about the afflicted cow, but took my leave.

(2575 words)

第十一章

文学语篇的翻译(2)

The Charge of the Light Brigade

Alfred, Lord Tennyson (1809-1892)

1

Half a league, half a league,
Half a league onward,
All in the valley of Death
Rode the six hundred.
"Forward, the Light Brigade!
Charge for the guns!" he said:
Into the valley of Death
Rode the six hundred.

2

"Forward, the Light Brigade!"
Was there a man dismay'd?
Not tho' the soldier knew
Someone had blunder'd:
Theirs not to make reply,
Theirs not to reason why,
Theirs but to do and die:
Into the valley of Death
Rode the six hundred.

3

Cannon to right of them,
Cannon to left of them,
Cannon in front of them

　　　　Volley'd and thunder'd;
　　Storm'd at with shot and shell,
　　　Boldly they rode and well,
　　　　Into the jaws of Death,
　　　　Into the mouth of Hell
　　　　Rode the six hundred.
　　　　　　　4
　　　Flash'd all their sabres bare,
　　　Flash'd as they turn'd in air,
　　　Sabring the gunners there,
　　　Charging an army, while
　　　　All the world wonder'd:
　　　Plunged in the battery-smoke
　　Right thro' the line they broke;
　　　　Cossack and Russian
　　　Reel'd from the sabre stroke
　　　　Shatter'd and sunder'd.
　　Then they rode back, but not
　　　　Not the six hundred.
　　　　　　　5
　　　　Cannon to right of them,
　　　　Cannon to left of them,
　　　　Cannon behind them
　　　　Volley'd and thunder'd;
　　Storm'd at with shot and shell,
　　　While horse and hero fell,
　　　They that had fought so well
　　　Came thro' the jaws of Death
　　　Back from the mouth of Hell,
　　　　All that was left of them,
　　　　Left of six hundred.
　　　　　　　6
　　　When can their glory fade?
　　　O the wild charge they made!
　　　　All the world wondered.
　　　Honor the charge they made,
　　　　Honor the Light Brigade,
　　　　Noble six hundred.
　　　　　　(265 words)

佳译赏析

The Diverting History of John Gilpin

英 语 文 本	汉 语 文 本
The Diverting History of John Gilpin William Cowper（1731—1800）	痴汉骑马歌 辜鸿铭译❶
JOHN GILPIN was a citizen Of credit and renown, A train-band captain eke was he Of famous London town.	昔有富家翁，饶财且有名， 身为团练长，家居伦敦城。
John Gilpin's spouse said to her dear, 'Though wedded we have been These twice ten tedious years, yet we No holiday have seen.	妇对富翁言，结发同苦艰， 悠悠二十载，未得一日闲。
To-morrow is our wedding-day, And we will then repair Unto the Bell at Edmonton, All in a chaise and pair.	明日是良辰，城外好风景， 愿乘双马车，与君同游骋。
'My sister, and my sister's child, Myself, and children three, Will fill the chaise; so you must ride On horseback after we.'	阿姨与其女，妾偕三小儿， 一家盈车载，君当骑马随。
He soon replied, 'I do admire Of womankind but one, And you are she, my dearest dear, Therefore it shall be done.	富翁对妇言，相敬既如宾， 若不从汝言，相爱岂是真?
'I am a linen-draper bold, As all the world doth know, And my good friend the calender Will lend his horse to go.'	我是贩布客，声名驰寰区， 有友情更重，愿借千里驹。
Quoth Mrs. Gilpin, 'That's well said; And for that wine is dear, We will be furnished with our own, Which is both bright and clear.'	君言诚良是，还当载美酒， 沽市酒值昂，家醅旨且有。
John Gilpin kissed his loving wife; O'erjoyed was he to find, That though on pleasure she was bent, She had a frugal mind.	妇言良可钦，富翁喜不禁， 虽怀行乐志，犹存节俭心。

---

❶格尔宾(Gilpin, John)原著.痴汉骑马歌 华英合璧.北京:商务印书馆，1935.

The Merchant of Venice (Excerpt)

英语文本	汉语文本
Act IV 　　SCENE I. Venice. A court of justice. 　　William Shakespeare	第四幕 　　第一场 威尼斯法庭 　　朱生豪译❶
Enter the DUKE, the Magnificoes, ANTONIO, BASSANIO, GRATIANO, SALERIO, and others DUKE 　　What, is Antonio here? ANTONIO 　　Ready, so please your grace. DUKE 　　I am sorry for thee: thou art come to answer A stony adversary, an inhuman wretch uncapable of pity, void and empty From any dram of mercy. ANTONIO 　　I have heard Your grace hath ta'en great pains to qualify His rigorous course; but since he stands obdurate And that no lawful means can carry me Out of his envy's reach, I do oppose My patience to his fury, and am arm'd To suffer, with a quietness of spirit, 　　The very tyranny and rage of his. DUKE 　　Go one, and call the Jew into the court. SALERIO 　　He is ready at the door; he comes, my lord.	公爵,众绅士,安东尼奥,巴萨尼奥,葛莱西安诺,萨拉里诺,萨莱尼奥及余人等同上。 公爵 　　安东尼奥有没有来? 安东尼奥 　　有,殿下。 公爵 　　我很替你不快乐;你是来跟一个心如铁石的对手当庭质对,一个不懂得怜悯、没有一丝慈悲心的不近人情的恶汉。 安东尼奥 　　听说殿下曾经用尽力量劝他不要过为已甚,可是他一味坚持,不肯略作让步。既然没有合法的手段可以使我脱离他的怨毒的掌握,我只有用默忍迎受他的愤怒,安心等待着他的残暴的处置。 公爵 　　来人,传那犹太人到庭。 萨拉里诺 　　他在门口等着;他来了,殿下。
Enter SHYLOCK DUKE 　　Make room, and let him stand before our face. Shylock, the world thinks, and I think so too, 　　That thou but lead'st this fashion of thy malice To the last hour of act; and then 'tis thought Thou'lt show thy mercy and remorse more strange Than is thy strange apparent cruelty; 　　And where thou now exact'st the penalty, 　　Which is a pound of this poor merchant's flesh, Thou wilt not only loose the forfeiture, 　　But, touch'd with human gentleness and love, Forgive a moiety of the principal; 　　Glancing an eye of pity on his losses, 　　That have of late so huddled on his back, 　　Enow to press a royal merchant down And pluck commiseration of his state From brassy bosoms and rough hearts of flint, From stubborn Turks and Tartars, never train'd To offices of tender courtesy. 　　We all expect a gentle answer, Jew.	夏洛克上 公爵 　　大家让开些,让他站在我的面前。夏洛克,人家都以为你不过故意装出这一副凶恶的姿态,到了最后关头,就会显出你的仁慈恻隐来,比你现在这种表面上的残酷更加出人意料;现在你虽然坚持着照约处罚,一定要从这个不幸的商人身上割下一磅肉来,到了那时候,你不但愿意放弃这一种处罚,而且因为受到良心上的感动,说不定还会豁免他一部分的欠款。人家都是这样说,我也是这样猜想着。你看他最近接连遭逢的5大损失,足以使无论怎样富有的商人倾家荡产,即使铁石一样的心肠,从来不知道人类同情的野蛮人,也不能不对他的境遇发生怜悯。犹太人,我们都在等候你一句温和的回答。

---

❶莎士比亚戏剧选/(英)莎士比亚(Shakespeare, W.)著,朱生豪译.北京:光明日报出版社,2008:334-347.

续上表

英 语 文 本	汉 语 文 本
SHYLOCK 　　I have possess'd your grace of what I purpose; And by our holy Sabbath have I sworn To have the due and forfeit of my bond: 　　If you deny it, let the danger light Upon your charter and your city's freedom. 　　You'll ask me, why I rather choose to have A weight of carrion flesh than to receive Three thousand ducats: I'll not answer that: 　　But, say, it is my humour: is it answer'd? 　　What if my house be troubled with a rat And I be pleased to give ten thousand ducats To have it baned? What, are you answer'd yet? Some men there are love not a gaping pig; 　　Some, that are mad if they behold a cat; 　　And others, when the bagpipe sings i' the nose, Cannot contain their urine; for affection, 　　Mistress of passion, sways it to the mood Of what it likes or loathes. Now, for your answer As there is no firm reason to be render'd, 　　Why he cannot abide a gaping pig; 　　Why he, a harmless necessary cat; 　　Why he, a woollen bagpipe; but of force Must yield to such inevitable shame As to offend, himself being offended; 　　So can I give no reason, nor I will not, 　　More than a lodged hate and a certain loathing I bear Antonio, that I follow thus A losing suit against him. Are you answered?	夏洛克 　　我的意思已经向殿下告禀过了；我也已经指着我们的圣安息日起誓，一定要照约执行处罚；要是殿下不准许我的请求，那就是蔑视宪章，我要到京城里上告去，要求撤销贵邦的特权。您要是问我为什么不愿接受三千块钱，宁愿拿一块腐烂的臭肉，那我可没有什么理由可以回答您，我只能说我喜欢这样，这是不是一个回答？要是我的屋子里有了耗子，我高兴出一万块钱叫人把它们赶掉，谁管得了我？这不是回答了您吗？有的人不爱看张开嘴的猪，有的人瞧见一头猫就要发脾气，还有人听见人家吹风笛的声音，就忍不住要小便；因为一个人的感情完全受着喜恶的支配，谁也做不了自己的主。现在我就这样回答您：为什么有人受不住一只张开嘴的猪，有人受不住一只有益无害的猫，还有人受不住咿咿唔唔的风笛的声音，这些都是毫无充分的理由的，只是因为天生的癖性，使他们一受到刺激，就会情不自禁地现出丑相来；所以我不能举什么理由，也不愿举什么理由，除了因为我对于安东尼奥抱着久积的仇恨和深刻的反感，所以才会向他进行这一场对于我自己并没有好处的诉讼。现在您不是已经得到我的回答了吗？
BASSANIO 　　This is no answer, thou unfeeling man, 　　To excuse the current of thy cruelty. SHYLOCK 　　I am not bound to please thee with my answers. BASSANIO 　　Do all men kill the things they do not love? SHYLOCK 　　Hates any man the thing he would not kill? BASSANIO 　　Every offence is not a hate at first. SHYLOCK 　　What, wouldst thou have a serpent sting thee twice?	巴萨尼奥 　　你这冷酷无情的家伙，这样的回答可不能作为你的残忍的辩解。 夏洛克 　　我的回答本来不是为要讨你的欢喜。 巴萨尼奥 　　难道人们对于他们所不喜欢的东西，都一定要置之死地吗？ 夏洛克 　　哪一个人会恨他所不愿意杀死的东西？ 巴萨尼奥 　　初次的冒犯，不应该就引为仇恨。 夏洛克 　　什么！你愿意给毒蛇咬两次吗？
ANTONIO 　　I pray you, think you question with the Jew: 　　You may as well go stand upon the beach 　　And bid the main flood bate his usual height;	安东尼奥 　　请你想一想，你现在跟这个犹太人讲理，就像站在海滩上，叫那大海的怒涛减低它的奔腾的威力，责问豺狼为什么害母羊为了失去它的羔羊而哀啼，或是叫那山上的

续上表

英 语 文 本	汉 语 文 本

You may as well use question with the wolf Why he hath made the ewe bleat for the lamb;
 You may as well forbid the mountain pines To wag their high tops and to make no noise, When they are fretten with the gusts of heaven; You may as well do anything most hard;
 As seek to soften that-than which what's harder? —His Jewish heart: therefore, I do beseech you, Make no more offers, use no farther means;
 But with all brief and plain conveniency · Let me have judgment and the Jew his will.
 BASSANIO
     For thy three thousand ducats here is six.
 SHYLOCK
     What judgment shall I dread, doing Were in six parts and every part a ducat,
     I would not draw them; I would have my bond.
 DUKE
     How shalt thou hope for mercy, rendering none?
	松柏,在受到天风吹拂的时候,不要摇头摆脑,发出簌簌的声音。要是你能够叫这个犹太人的心变软——世上还存什么东西比它更硬呢?——那么还有什么难事不可以做到?所以我请你不用再跟他商量什么条件,也不用替我想什么办法,让我爽爽快快受到判决,满足这犹太人的心愿吧。
	巴萨尼奥
	    借了你三千块钱,现在拿六千块钱还你好不好?
	夏洛克
	    即使这六千块钱中间的每一块钱都可以分作六份,每一份都可以变成一块钱,我也不要它们,我只要照约处罚。
	公爵
	    你这样一点没有慈悲之心,将来怎么能够希望人家对你慈悲呢?

认知升级

一、诗歌的翻译

1.什么是诗歌

诗歌是用高度凝练的语言,形象表达作者丰富情感,集中反映社会生活并具有一定节奏和韵律的文学体裁。

我国现代诗人何其芳曾说:"诗是一种最集中地反映社会生活的文学样式,它饱含着丰富的想象和感情,常常以直接抒情的方式来表现,而且在精炼与和谐的程度上,特别是在节奏的鲜明上,它的语言有别于散文的语言。"柯尔律治(Coleridge)说:Prose is words in the best order; poetry is the best words in the best order.

诗歌具有四个特点:①诗歌的内容是社会生活的最集中的反映。②诗歌有丰富的感情与想象。③诗歌的语言具有精练、形象、音调和谐、节奏鲜明等特点。④诗歌在形式上,不是以句子为单位,而是以行为单位,且分行主要根据节奏,而不是以意思为主。

诗歌可以按照内容分为叙事诗和抒情诗。①叙事诗有比较完整的故事情节和人物形象。史诗、故事诗等都属于这一类,如古希腊荷马的《伊里亚特》和《奥德赛》,白居易的《长恨歌》。②抒情诗主要通过直接抒发诗人的思想感情来反映社会生活,不要求描述完整的故事情节和人物形象。包括情歌、颂歌、哀歌、挽歌和讽刺诗。比如,李白的《将进酒》、汪国真的《热爱生命》、舒婷的《致橡树》等。

诗歌又可以根据音韵格律和结构形式,大致分为格律诗、自由诗、散文诗和韵脚诗。①格律诗按照一定格式和规则写成,对诗的行数、诗句的字数(或音节)、声调音韵、词语对仗、句式排列等有严格规定,如,我国古代诗歌中的"律诗""绝句"和"词""曲",欧洲的"十四行诗"。②自由诗,不受格律限制,无固定格式,注重自然的、内在的节奏,押大致相近的韵或不押韵,字数、行数、句式、音调都比较自由,语言比较通俗。美国诗人惠特曼是欧美自由诗的创始人,《草叶集》是他的主要诗集。我国"五四"以来也流行这种诗体。③韵脚诗每一行诗的结尾均须押韵,读起来朗朗上口,如同歌谣。这里的韵脚诗指现代韵脚诗,属于一种新型诗体,如臧克家的《当炉女》。④散文诗是兼有散文和诗的特点。作品中有诗的意境和激情,常常富有哲理,注重自然的节奏感和音乐美,篇幅短小,像散文一样不分行、不押韵,如鲁迅的《野草》。

下面以格律诗为例,谈谈英汉诗歌的异同。

2.英语诗歌特点

英诗的主要特征有节奏(Rhythm)、音韵(Rhyme)和体例(form)。

(1)英诗的节奏

英语格律诗的一个显著特征就是节奏(Rhythm)。构成英诗节奏的基础是韵律(metre)和音步(Foot)。在希腊语,"metre"这个字是"尺度(标准)"的意思。英诗就是根据诗行中的音节和重读节奏作为"尺度(标准)"来计算韵律的。

音步(foot)就是重读(stressed)与非重读(unstressed)音节所组成的特殊性组合。一个音步的音节数量可能为两个或三个音节,但不能少于两个或多于三个音节,而且其中只有一个必须重读。分析英诗的格律就是将它划分成音步,并区分出是何种音步以及计算音步的数量。这种音步划分叫 scansion。

根据音步数量,英诗中,如果每一诗行一个音步称"单音步"(monometer);每一诗行有两个音步的,称"双音步"(dimeter);含有三个音步的,称"三音步"(trimeter);此外还有四音步(tetrameter)、五音步、(pentameter)、六音步(hexameter)、七音步(heptameter)、八音步(octometer)。下面的诗行中采用了双音步。

Is this | a fast,

to keep | the lard

or lean | and clean?

(Herrick)

(2)英诗的韵律

英诗的韵律是依据音步包含音节的数量及重读音节的位置而加以区分的。在每一个音节步调里,需要重读的称为扬,不需要重读的称为抑。传统英诗的音步有七种:抑扬格(Lambus)、扬抑格(Trochee)、抑抑扬格(Anapaest)、扬抑抑格(Dactyl)及抑扬抑格(Amphibrach)、扬抑抑格(Dactyl)及抑扬抑格(Amphibrach):

①抑扬格(轻重格)Iambus:是最常见的一种格式,每个音步由一个非重读音节加一个重读音节构成。下例中为四音步与三音步交叉。

My Luve Is like a Red, Red Rose

Robert Burns(1759—1796)

As fair / art thou / my bon/nie lass,

So deep / in luve / am I:

And I / will luve / thee still, / my dear,

Till a / the seas / gang dry.

注:art=are luve=love bonnie=beautiful a'=all gang=go

②扬抑格(重轻格)Trochee：

每个音步由一个重读音节加一个非重读音节构成。下例中为四音步扬抑格(少一个轻音节)。

The Tyger
(William Blake)

Tyger! / Tyger! / burning / bright
In the / forests / of the / night

③抑抑扬格(轻轻重格)Anapaestic：每个音步由两个非重读音节加一个重读音节构成。下例是三音步抑抑扬格。

Like a child / from the womb,
Like a ghost / from the tomb,
I arise / and unbuild / it again.

在同一首诗中常会出现不同的格律，格律解析对朗读诗歌有一定参考价值。现代诗中常不遵守规范的格律。

(3)英诗的押韵

押韵是指通过重复元音或辅音以达到一定音韵效果的诗歌写作手法。英语诗歌的行与行之间的押韵格式称作韵法(rhyming scheme)。

英语诗歌的押韵可以根据单词的内音素重复的部位不同而分成不同种类，最常见的有头韵(Alliteration)、谐元韵(Assonance)和尾韵(Rhyme)。一行诗中可能同时存在多种押韵形式。

①尾韵。尾韵则指词尾音素重复。尾韵是最常见，最重要的押韵方式。

联韵：aabb 型。

The Arrow and the Song
Henry Wadsworth Longfellow

I shot an arrow into the air,
It fell to earth, I knew not where;
For, so swiftly it flew, the sight
Could not follow it in its flight.

I breathed a song into the air,
It fell toearth, I knew not where;
For who has sight so keen and strong,
That it can follow the flight of song?

Long, long afterward, in an oak
I found the arrow, still unbroke;
And the song, from beginning to end,

I found again in the heart of a friend.

交叉韵:abab 型。

Crossing the Bar
Alfred Tennyson(1809—1892)

Sunset and evening star,
And one clear call for me!

And may there be no moaning of the bar,
When I put out to sea,
But such a tide as moving seems asleep,
Too full for sound and foam,
When that which drew from out the boundless deep
Turns again home.

Twilight and evening bell,
And after that the dark!
And may there be no sadness of farewell,
When I embark;

For tho' from out our bourne of Time and Place
The flood may bear me far,
I hope to see my Pilot face to face
When I havecrost the bar.

同韵:aaaa 型或 aaba 型。有的诗押韵,一韵到底,大多是在同一节诗中共用一个韵脚。如下例就共用/i /为韵脚。

Stopping by Woods on a Snowy Evening
Robert Frost (1874—1963)

Whose woods these are I think I know.
His house is in the village though;
He will not see me stopping here
To watch hiswoods fill up with snow.

My little horse must think it queer
To stop without a farmhouse near
Between the woods and frozen lake
The darkest evening of the year.

He gives his harness bells a shake
To ask if there is some mistake.
The only other sound's the sweep
Of easy wind and downy flake.

The woods are lovely, dark and deep,
But I have promises to keep,
And miles to go before I sleep,
And miles to go before I sleep.

②头韵(alliteration):是指一行(节)诗中几个词开头的辅音相同,形成押韵。下例中运用/f/、/b/与/s/头韵生动地写出了船在海上轻快航行的景象。

Rime of the Ancient Mariner (excerpt)
T.S. Coleridge
The fair breeze blew, the white foam flew,
The furrow followed free,
We were the first that ever burst
Into that silent sea.

③内韵(internal rhyme):指词与词之间语音的重复形成内部押韵。下面一节诗中/i/及/iŋ/重复照应,呈现出一派欢乐祥和的气氛。

Spring, the Sweet Spring (excerpt)
Thomas Nashe(1567-1601)

Spring, the sweet spring, is the year's pleasant king;
Then blooms each thing, then maids dance in a ring,
Cold dath not sting, the pretty birds do sing:
Cuckoo, jug-jug, pu-we, to-witta-woo!
The palm and may make country houses gay,
Lambs frisk and play, the shepherds pipe all day,
And we hear aye birds tune this merry lay:
Cuckoo, jug-jug, pu-we, to-witta-woo!

The fields breathe sweet, the daisies kiss our feet,
Young lovers meet, old wives a-sunning sit,
In every street these tunes our ears do greet:
Cuckoo, jug-jug, pu-we, to witta-woo!

(4)英诗的体例

英诗的特点之一是与其他文体不同的排列格式。各诗行不达到每页页边,每行开始词首大写。几行成为一节(stanza),不分段落。各行都要讲究一定的音节数量,行末押韵或不押韵,交错排列。

英诗有的诗分成几节(stanza),每节由若干诗行组成(每行诗均以大写字母开头);有的诗则不分节。目前我们常见的格律诗诗体有:十四行诗和打油诗。

①意大利十四行诗(sonnet):也称商籁体诗歌。源于中世纪民间抒情短诗,十三、十四世纪流行于意大利,意大利皮特拉克(Petrarch)为代表人物,每行十一个音节,全诗第一节八行(The Octave),由两个四行诗体(Quatrains)组成,第二节六行(The Sestet),韵脚用 abba, abba, cdcdcd (cdecde)。按严格的意大利十四行诗体,前八行提问,后六行回答,转入新的诗意。

②英国十四行诗:16 世纪,怀亚特(Thomas Wyatt,1503—1542)将十四行诗引入英国,为伊丽莎白(1558—1603)时代文人所喜爱。莎士比亚、斯宾塞及西德尼(Sidney)都写过著名的十四行诗。18 世纪十四行诗曾受到冷落。但后又被浪漫派诗人济慈、沃兹沃斯等人所复兴,以后许多诗人也多采用。格式为:五音步抑扬格,全诗前面三个四行加结尾一个二行,前三节提问,后一节结论。不过,韵脚使用上,诗人之间有所差别。斯宾塞用韵脚 abab, bcbc, cd, cd, ee。莎士比亚用韵脚 abab, cdcd, efef, gg,称莎士比亚式。莎士比亚式十四行诗中意境一气呵成,直到最后双行体,为全诗高潮。

SONNET 21 Shakespaere
So is not with me as with that Muse,
Stirr'd by a painted beauty to his verse,
Who heaven itself for ornament doth use
And every fair with his fair doth rehearse,

Making a couplement of proud compare,
With sun and moon, with earth and sea's rich gems.
With April's first-born flowers, and all things rare
That heaven's air in this huge rondure hems.

O, let metrue in love, but truly write,
And then believe me, my love is as fair
As any mother's child, though not so bright
As those gold candles fix'd in heaven's air.

Let them say more that like of hearsay well;
I will not praise that purpose not to sell.

③打油诗(Limericks):通常是小笑话甚至是胡诌,一般没有标题也无作者姓名,含有幽默讽刺性,常运用双关、内韵等手法。每首诗五个诗行,押韵为 aabba,格律以抑扬格和抑抑扬格为主。

There was a young lady of Nigger

  Who smiled as she rode on a tiger;
    They returned from the ride
     With the lady inside,
  And the smile on the face of the tiger.

(5)英诗的破格与变异

格律诗对形式的要求非常严格。可是有时形式的限制会导致诗歌内容情感表达的不便。此时,为了适应节奏格律的需要,诗人在语言运用方面享有一些特权(poetic license),即诗歌的破格。具体来说,诗人可以使用一些特殊的缩略形式(如 tis = it is, o'er = over),以减少音节数;他还可以灵活调整词序、主谓倒置、动宾倒置及对修饰词与被修饰词进行换位。

如果说破格还是有限的自由的话,那么变异(deviation)就是无拘无束的自由。变异是对语言常规的有意偏离,是诗人寻新求异的一种手法,是对语言的创造性的使用。变异在诗歌创作中早已有之,在现代和当代更是被发挥到极致。变异可以发生在诗歌语言的各个层面上,如语音、拼写、词汇、语法、句式等。诗在语音上的变异主要表现在单词的某些音节的省略、重音甚至整个发音的改变,如将 moan 读作[mei]而非[moun]以适应韵律的需要,便属于语音上的变异。

(6)英诗的用词

英诗与一般体裁的文章在用词上具有显著差别。就名词来说,常用词汇有:array (clothes), babe (baby), bane (poison, mischief), billow (wave), bliss (happiness), bower (dwelling), brine (ocean), brow (forehead), chanticleer (cock), charger (horse), dale (valley), foe, foeman (enemy), fere (friend), glebe (earth, field), goblet (cup), gore (blood), grot (cave), guile (deceit), ire (anger), maid (girl), main (sea or ocean), marge (margin), mart (market), mead (meadow), might (strength), morn (morning), nuptials (marriage), poesy (poetry), quest (search), scribe (writer), sire (father), steed (horse), swain (peasant), sward (grass), thrall (bondage), tilth (agriculture), troth (veracity or faithfulness), vale (valley), victor (conqueror), weal (welfare), woe (sorrow or misery), yeoman (peasant, farmer)等。

常用动词有:behold (see), brook (bear), cleave (cling), cumber (distress, trouble), deem (think), fare (walk), hearken (hear, attend), hie (hasten), ken (know), list (listen), methink (seem to me), quaff (drink), quoth (said), obscure (darken), slay (kill), smite (strike), sojorn (lodge or dwell), speed (hasten), tarry (remain), trow (believe), vanquish (conquer), wax (grow)等。

常用的形容词有:aweary (weary), baleful (pernicious), beauteous (beautiful), bootless (unprofitable), bosky (wooded), clamant (noisy), darksome (dark), dauntless (brave), dire (dreadful), dread (dreadful), drear (dreary), fair (beautiful), fond (foolish), forlorn (distressed), hallowed (holy), hapless (unhappy), ingrate (ungrateful), intrepid (brave), jocund (merry), joyless (unhappy), lone (lonesome, lonely), lovesome (lovely), lowly (low or humble), murky (grim), mute (silent), quenchless (inextinguishable), rapt (delighted), recreant (unfaithful), sequestered (retired, lonely), stilly (still), sylvan (woody), wrathful (angry)等。

3.汉语诗歌的特点

汉语诗歌有古体诗、近代诗和现代诗之分。古体诗,又称古风、古诗。名称始于唐,后人沿用唐人说法,将唐以前的乐府民歌文人诗以及唐以后文人仿作的诗,全称为"古体诗"。其特点是形式自由,如四言的曹操的《观沧海》,五言的孟郊"慈母手中线",七言的曹丕《燕歌行》,杂言的李白《梦游天姥吟离别》,押韵自由如《卖炭翁》。

近体诗,又称格律诗、今体诗,分为:①律诗(五律、七律、长律[排律])两句一联,八句,为首颔颈尾四联。②绝句(五绝、七绝)。汉语格律诗的标准是:"篇有定句,句有定字,字有定声,韵有定位,联有定对"。格律诗要从节奏、押韵、对仗、平仄等方面来分析和鉴赏。

(1)押韵

押韵,就是韵句之韵脚必须使用基本韵母相同的字。汉语格律诗也非常重视押韵。通常只有偶序句押韵,不能中途换韵,不用相同的字押韵(习惯1、2、4、6、8句末押韵)。但首句除外,也就是说,首句允许押韵。这样的诗,我们称之为"首句入韵诗"。

《春晓》
孟浩然
春眠不觉晓,处处闻啼鸟。
夜来风雨声,花落知多少?

此诗乃五言绝句。该诗第一句、第二句、第四句是韵句,押韵各句尾字的基本韵母是:晓、鸟、声、少。

(2)对仗

古诗中,一首诗从头起,往往每两诗句的意义相近或相关联。这样的两个诗句,我们称之为一联,亦称之为"诗联"。而律诗中间的两联,即颔联和颈联必须对仗工整。

诗歌中的队长又分工对(词性、词义严格对仗)和宽对(词性相近,词义大体相同)两种。例如,"向月穿针易,临风整线难"就是工对;"横眉冷对千夫指,俯首甘为孺子牛"则是宽对。

(3)节奏

汉语中一个字就是一个音节,在古代诗歌吟咏时往往出现两个音节作一停顿,我们将这样的两个音节叫作一个音步(亦称节拍)。但并非所有的音步都由两个音节构成,有时,一个音节亦构成一个音步,我们谓之单音步。由两个音节构成的音步,我们谓之双音步;此外还有三音节词,如"不倒翁",可视作三音步;亦可将其划分为一个双音步加一个单音步。

汉语诗歌的节奏通常有:四言,二二式两拍;五言,二二一式、二一二式,或一一三拍;七言,二二二一式四拍等几种。

《相思》
王维
红豆|生|南国,春来|发|几枝。
愿君|多|采撷,此物|最|相思。

(4)平仄

诗中每一个字都有一定的声调,平声字指一、二声调的字,仄声字指三、四声调的字,"平仄相间"会带来声音上的抑扬顿挫。

平仄的基本格式为"平平—仄仄"或"仄仄—平平"。五言绝句的平仄,可以看成是在格式基础上再加上一个声调形成。七言律诗不过是在五言基础上前面加上相反的平仄构成。综合起来,基本口诀是:"一三五不论,二四六分明",即七言诗们一、三五(五言则一、三)个字平仄可以不论,二四六(五言二、四)个字平仄必须分明。

例1　　　　　　　　仄起仄收(七言为平起仄收)
　　　　　　　　　　仄仄平平仄,平平仄仄平。
　　　　　　　　　　平平平仄仄,仄仄仄平平。
　　　　　　　　　　仄仄平平仄,平平仄仄平。
　　　　　　　　　　平平平仄仄,仄仄仄平平。

《旅夜书怀》
杜甫

细草微风岸,危樯独夜舟。
星垂平野阔,月涌大江流。
名岂文章著,官应老病休。
飘飘何所似,天地一沙鸥。

例2　　　　　　　　平起仄收式(七言为仄起仄收)
　　　　　　　　　　平平平仄仄,仄仄仄平平。
　　　　　　　　　　仄仄平平仄,平平仄仄平。
　　　　　　　　　　平平平仄仄,仄仄仄平平。
　　　　　　　　　　仄仄平平仄,平平仄仄平。

《山居秋暝》
王维

空山新雨后,天气晚来秋。
明月松间照,清泉石上流。
竹喧归浣女,莲动下渔舟。
随意春芳歇,王孙自可留。

4.英诗的翻译

诗歌翻译是一个众说纷纭的话题。很多人认为诗之不可译,例如罗伯特·弗洛斯特(Robert L.Frost)说:"诗就是在翻译中失去的那种东西"(Poetry is what is lost in translation)。当然,也有很多学者认为诗歌可译,而且强调要以诗译诗。例如,闻一多认为应该诗笔译诗。成仿吾认为"译诗也应当是诗,这是我们所最不能忘记的。译诗应当忠于原文"。许渊冲认为译诗要达到三美,即形美、音美、意美,译作甚至可以胜过原作。

如果说翻译难的话,那么最难莫过于译诗了,尤其是格律诗。原因主要在于诗味难译,诗的音韵美难译。诗歌各有千秋:有的明白畅晓,有的艰深晦涩,有的韵律严整,有的不受律法所限。译诗者也有水平高低之分、技艺优劣之别,所以诗难译但并非不可译。

请看下例:

That Time of Year

That time of year thou may'st in me behold
When yellow leaves, or none, or few, do hang
Upon those boughs which shake against the cold,
Bare ruined choirs where late the sweet birds sang,
In me thou see'st the twilight of such day
As after sunset fadeth in the west,
When by and by black night doth take away,

Death's second self, that seals up all in rest.
In me thou see'st the glowing of such fire,
That on the ashes of his youth doth lie.
As the deathbed whereon it must expire,
Consumed with that which it was nourished by.
This you perceivest, which makes thy love more strong,
To love that well which thou must leave ere long.

Notes:

(1) may'st: may; behold: see; late: no long ago; thou: you see'st: see

(2) fadeth: fades; doth: does; seals up all at rest: 彻底埋葬

(3) thy: your; perceivest: perceive; ere long: before long

此诗是莎士比亚(William Shakespeare, 1564—1616)的一首十四行诗。作为英国文学巨匠,他以37部剧作和154首十四行诗屹立于世界文坛。此诗为五音步抑扬格。全诗涉及衰老、死亡及爱情问题。前十二行:通过描写深秋的树枝黄叶凋零,曾是百鸟争鸣的歌坛,联想到自身青春会如夕阳消逝在远方,被黑夜吞没;自身的青春会如将尽的柴火奄奄一息,被曾滋养过它的火焰焚化。其中 choirs(歌坛),deathbed(灵床)使用暗喻手法,同时又用夕阳和柴火象征人的衰老死亡。最后两行:点题,人们对即将永别的东西会更珍惜。本文动词变化具有明显的伊丽莎白时代的特点。

译文:

十四行诗 第37

卞之琳 译

你在我身上会看见这种景致:
黄叶全无,或者是三三两两
牵系着那些迎风颤抖的枯枝——
唱诗廊废墟,再不见好鸟歌唱。
你在我身上会看见这样的黄昏:
夕阳在西天消退到不留痕迹,
黑夜逐渐来把暮色收拾干净——
死亡的影子把一切封进了安息。
你在我身上会看见炉火微红,
半明不灭的枕着它青春的死灰,
像躺在垂死的榻上,就只待送终,
滋养了它的也就在把它销毁。
你看出这一点,也就使你的爱更坚强,
好好的爱你不久要离开的对象。

另一个诗歌翻译的例子来自托马斯·格雷所写《墓园挽歌》。请看该诗第一个诗行的三个不同译本。

Elegy written in A Country Churchyard

Thomas Gray

The curfew tolls the knell of parting day,
The lowing herd wind slowly o'er the lea,

>The plowman homeward plods his weary way,
>And leaves the world to darkness and to me.

译文 1 （郭沫若译）

>暮钟鸣,昼已暝
>牛羊相呼,迂回草径
>农人荷锄归,蹒跚而行
>把全盘世界剩给我与黄昏

译文 2 （卞之琳译）

>晚钟响起来一阵阵给白昼报丧,
>牛群在草原上迂回,吼声起落。
>耕地人累了,回家走脚步踉跄,
>把整个世界给了黄昏与我。

译文 3 （丰华瞻译）

>晚钟殷殷响,夕阳已西沉,
>群牛呼叫归,迂回走草径,
>农人荷锄犁,倦倦回家门,
>惟我立旷野,独自对黄昏。

王东风[1]教授认为如果我们以原文为取向(source oriented),那么翻译诗歌时,对格律的处理,可以采用四种不同的方法,分别代表四个等级的难度。翻译的难度越大,星级越高;星级越高,诗学的保真度也越高。

诗歌翻译方法难度量表（原文取向）

诗歌翻译方法	难 度 等 级
平仄化	★★★★★
逗代化	★★★★
顿代化	★★★
自由化	★★

例如,以 The Isles of Greece(译名以《哀希腊》著称)第一节的翻译为例。原诗的节奏特征是抑扬格四音步。这首诗有诸多翻译版本。

>The Isles | of Greece | , the Isles | of Greece | !
>Where bur | ning Sa | ppho loved | and sung | ,
>Where grew | the arts | of war | and peace | ,
>Where De | los rose | , and Phoe | bus sprung | !
>Eter | nal su | mmer gilds | them yet | ,
>But all | , except | their sun | , is set | .

卞之琳的译文对于格律的处理方法就是"以顿代步",即以汉语的"顿"代替英语的"音步"以再现原诗的节奏。"顿"的特点是以自然词组为节奏单位,因此对音节数没有限制,可以是两个字一顿,也可以是三四个字一顿。

---

[1] 王东风.以平仄代抑扬 找回遗落的音美:英诗汉译声律对策研究[J].外国语,2019(1):72-82+110.

希腊|群岛啊|,希腊|群岛|！
从前有|火热的|萨福|唱情歌|,
从前长|文治|武功的|花草|
涌出过|德罗斯|,跳出过|阿波罗|,
夏天|来镀金|,还长久|灿烂|
除了|太阳|,什么都|落了山|！

——（卞之琳 1996:137）

卞之琳的译诗就采用了"以顿代步"：每顿或二或三。这种译法在音韵学和乐理上的缺陷很明显：各节奏单位之间的时值不一样,没有规律,节奏感不明显,这与原文一个抑扬格走到底的节奏特征和效果明显不同。

另一种格律转换方式是王东风 2014 年提出来的"以逗代步"式,该译法受闻一多"逗论"的启发而提出。闻一多认为,律诗的节奏单位是"逗",有"两字逗"和"三字逗"之分。根据汉语律诗的实际,律诗的基本节奏单位以二字逗为主。因此,"以逗代步"的基本原则就是以二字逗代原文的双音节音步、三字逗代三音节音步。

希腊|群岛|,希腊|群岛|！
萨福|如火|歌美|情浓|,
文治|卓越|兵法|精妙|,
提洛|昂立|飞布|神勇|！
长夏|无尽|群岛|煌煌|,
万般|皆沦|仅余|残阳|。

——（王东风译）

"以逗代步"解决了节奏的音节数或时值问题,但声律的调值问题仍悬而未决。为了解决节奏中的声律问题,王东风提出了"以平仄代抑扬"的方法。"以平仄代抑扬"是建立在"以逗代步"的基础之上的,与原诗的节奏对应模型是：

原诗：　　　　　抑扬|抑扬|抑扬|抑扬|
译诗：　　　　　平仄|平仄|平仄|平仄|

该诗改译为：

希腊群岛,希腊群岛！
莎馥如火歌美情重,
文治卓越兵法精妙,
提洛昂立飞布神勇！
长夏无尽群岛如曜,
浮世沉堕残日高照。

——（王东风,2014）

在这节译诗之中,每行有四逗,每逗两个字(音节),每逗的声律都是"平仄"组合,以对应原诗的抑扬格。

一首好诗,往往是"意中有境""境中寓言",读后沁人心脾、耐人寻味。译者在翻译时,应该充分发挥想象力和直觉的作用,对原作心领神会,而移情于自身,把原作的艺术美表现出来。

二、戏剧的翻译

戏剧是人类文明不可或缺的组成部分,在所有民族的文明史上俱皆存在。戏剧的内涵十分丰富,它运用了文学、导演、表演、音乐、美术等艺术手段来塑造人物和反映社会生活。多样化的戏剧不仅存在于各个国家和民族的历史,更存在于科技发达的当代社会。不仅有舞台剧,还包括以银幕、荧屏为载体,以胶片、电子声像为手段的电影故事片、动画片、广播剧、电视剧等。因此,研究戏剧翻译在今天有其现实意义。

1.戏剧基本知识

戏剧包括四要素,分别为演职员、观众、剧场(或其他现代载体)和剧本。戏剧翻译主要是指剧本的翻译。剧本是一种独特的文学体裁,融合了小说、诗歌、散文等文体特点。戏剧与其他文学体裁有着共同的特点:像小说一样,戏剧包含人物和情节;像诗歌一样,戏剧不仅需要读者去阅读,更需要他们去观赏和聆听;像论述一样,戏剧往往旨在探讨某些问题和传达某些观点。

然而,戏剧同时又是一种独特的文学样式。戏剧中人物的性格、情节的发展以及主题的表达都是通过人物自己的语言来表现。戏剧的语言特点主要表现在以下几方面:

(1)注重诗意

19 世纪末之前的西方戏剧大都是以诗歌写成的。剧作家十分讲究语言文字的精练优美,注重语言的韵律和节奏。例如莎士比亚的剧作《奥赛罗》中的一段:

> O balmy breath, that dost almost persuade
> Justice to break her sword! One more, one more!
> Be thus when thou art dead, and I will kill thee,
> And love thee after. One more, and that's the last!
> So sweet was ne'er so fatal. I must weep,
> But they are cruel tears. This sorrow's heavenly;
> It strikes where it doth love.

这一段台词是用无韵体诗写成的,短短的几行文字便细腻生动地刻画出奥赛罗在杀妻前爱恨交织的复杂情感,叩人心扉,感人至深。

(2)讲究修辞

艺术的创作既来源于生活,又高于生活,戏剧创作也不例外。戏剧语言是日常语言的提纯和精练。剧作者常常交织使用多种修辞手段来加强语言的艺术韵味。例如莎士比亚名剧《哈姆雷特》中的一段:

> King: But now, my cousin Hamlet, my son.
> Hamlet: (Aside) A little more than kin, and less than kind!
> King: How is it that the clouds still hang on you?
> Hamlet: Not so, my lord. I am too much in the sun.
>
> ——Hamlet, Act I, Scene II.

"kin"是"亲戚",谐音"kind"是"亲善""友爱"。kin 和 kind 是双声。此句音调工整,意味深长。后一句是双关暗讽,借 sun 和 son 同音,既反驳叔父的话,又表示不愿做他的儿子。

(3)还原真实,突出个性

西方戏剧从挪威剧作家易卜生时代起,日常生活语言开始进入了现代戏剧。有一部分剧作家摒弃了讲究修辞的传统,在剧本创作中以真实、自然为原则。在我国戏剧舞台上,直到 20 世纪初才出现了以日常生活的语言和服饰,并以对白为主来再现生活的话剧。话剧采用白话文来进行演出,摒弃了传统戏曲中诗歌舞不分家的习惯,演员完全在舞台上重现生活场景。因此,台词在戏剧中占有越来越重要的地位。

戏剧台词具体表现为三种形式：对白、独白及旁白，每一种形式各有其效用。台词对白多为散文体，语言通俗易懂，自然真实。话剧通过语言来塑造人物，人物的身份、背景、性格等多通过语言来表现，也就是说，语言体现了人物的个性。

例如，在曹禺的名作《日出》中人物众多，但无论是高洁自赏的交际花陈白露、小小年纪便被迫出卖肉体的小东西、忍辱含垢的妓女翠喜、主宰一切的大流氓金八、贪婪而凶恶的潘月亭，还是正直淳朴但却不谙世事的方达生、行尸走肉般的面首胡四和俗不可耐的顾八奶奶，每个人随着身份角色的不同而各有各的语言特点。

2. 戏剧翻译

戏剧翻译首先体现在剧本的翻译上。剧本翻译就是要体现出源语剧本的思想内涵和语言风格。无论是戏剧的译出或译入，这一点都是戏剧翻译者所应遵循的基本原则❶。在基本原则之下，根据不同的翻译目的可以采取不同的翻译途径。

剧本不仅是舞台演出的蓝本，同时，也可单独甚至专门作为文学作品来阅读。英语中的 closet drama（案头剧、书斋剧）就是指专供阅读而非演出的剧本。苏珊·巴斯耐特（Susan Bassnett）在 Still Trapped in the Labyrinth: Further Reflections on Translation and Theatre 一文中将剧本的阅读方式分为七类：①在课堂上仅仅当作文学作品阅读；②观众出于个人喜好对剧本的阅读；③导演对剧本的阅读，决定剧本是否适合上演；④演员对剧本的阅读，以便理解特定角色；⑤舞美对剧本的阅读，以便设计出舞台的可视空间和布景；⑥其他任何参演人员对剧本的阅读；⑦用于排练的剧本阅读，其中采用很多辅助语言学的符号，包括语气（tone）、曲折（inflexion）、音调（pitch）等，为演出做准备。

这七种阅读方式实际上不仅反映了剧本的两大功能：文学作品和演出蓝本；同时，也表明了剧本翻译的两大途径：单纯作为文学作品的剧本翻译和以舞台的演出为目的的剧本翻译。因此，戏剧翻译特别要注意可阅读性和可表演性，有时需要强调其一，有时需要两者相辅相成。

如果戏剧的翻译目的多样化，读者对象多样化，不同的译者就可以根据自身的情况，提供不同的译本。研究文学的译者可以将剧本翻译为文学作品以供学者研究或文学爱好者阅读，并标明是 standard edition（标准版），trade edition（普及版），school edition（学生版）或 abridged edition（缩写版）。戏剧译者可根据具体演出的要求对剧本进行翻译改写，给出适合演出的 performing edition（演出版）。

（1）作为文学作品的剧本翻译

苏珊·巴斯耐特提出了一个疑问："可表演性"（performability）是否可作为衡量戏剧译本优劣的标准？她指出：对于那些对戏剧表演没有经验的译者，可以不必太在意译本是否要一定适合舞台演出，只要将其作为文学作品来翻译即可，况且，有些剧本本来就不是为演出准备的（如 Closet Drama）或者很难直接搬上舞台，例如中国戏曲剧本的英译。中国的戏曲集诗歌舞为一体，唱词好学，歌舞难练，要将其搬上别国的舞台远非易事。要是硬用"可表演性"作为剧本翻译的唯一标准，确实强人所难。而将戏曲本子作为文学读本来翻译，所涉及的因素就单纯多了。

如果戏剧是作为文学作品被翻译，而读者对象又是文学专业的师生和外国文学爱好者，那么译本最好能最大限度地反映出原文的风格，包括源本的文体特色和语言特色。譬如莎士比亚戏剧的翻译。莎剧是用剧诗（素体诗和口语化散文）的形式写成，译者便可以诗译诗，

---

❶李基亚，冯伟年.论戏剧翻译的原则和途径[J].西北大学学报（哲学社会科学版），2004，34(4)：161-165.

而不必过多地考虑剧本的演出效果和观众对"诗剧"(一种新的戏剧形式)是否适应。当然,译文若是过于晦涩或注释过多,恐怕就无法获得他们的认同,从而丧失部分读者。有时,译者也要考虑市场,即如何迎合目标读者群的要求和喜好。

例如《哈姆雷特》的翻译:

Hamlet, Act I, Scene II.
King: But now, my cousin Hamlet, my son.
Hamlet: (Aside) A little more than kin, and less than kind!
King: How is it that the clouds still hang on you?
Hamlet: Not so, my lord. I am too much i' the sun.

哈姆雷特(卞之琳译)

王:得,哈姆雷特,我的侄儿,我的儿——
哈:(旁白)亲上加亲,越亲越不相亲!
王:你怎么还是让愁云惨雾罩着你?
哈:陛下,太阳大,受不了这个热劲"儿"。

哈姆雷特王子上场后第一句台词就是双关语。哈姆雷特暗示,虽然叔父和他是亲上加亲(既是叔父又是继父),实质上一点也不亲。后一句是双关暗讽,借 sun 和 son 同音,既反驳叔父的话,又表示不愿做他的儿子。同时,由于满厅的人都身着华服,只有哈姆雷特一人着黑装,形成了强烈对比,"太阳"也指满厅的光辉。可以说,朱生豪和卞之琳的译文都忠实地反映出了原文的双关含义,且表达流畅。卞之琳在此处还加了注释以方便读者理解。两位大家的译本都可作为标准版以供阅读。但对于观众而言,既没有足够的时间思考,又没有注释可看,双关的意思就不好理解了。

(2)作为演出蓝本的剧本翻译

如果剧本是用来舞台表演,那么翻译时所涉及的因素就更为复杂了。著名的戏剧艺术家英若诚先生在一次接受媒体的访问中,当被问及为什么要重新翻译已有中文译本的几部英文剧目时,答道:"我为什么要另起炉灶,再来一遍呢?这里面的难言之隐就是,这些现成的译本不适合演出,因为有经验的演员都会告诉你,演翻译过来的戏,要找到真正的'口语化'的本子多么困难。戏剧语言要求铿锵有力,切忌拖泥带水。莎士比亚在《哈姆雷特》中借大臣之口说:简练,才华之魂也。

因此,译者在翻译演出蓝本的戏剧时,不仅要注意文字(语言)的层面,更要注意到使用剧本的人的需求,也就是要特别强调可表演性。再以上面《哈姆雷特》的翻译为例。如果译者考虑到舞台表演的实际,不妨将译文适当扩充,在语言上稍加解释,或许双关语的含义会有所丧失,但剧中人的情绪却可以得到很好的表现,观众也不会有理解上的障碍。试译如下:

王:哈姆雷特,我的好侄子,过来吧。来,我的好儿子。现在,我们该更加亲近才是。
哈:(旁白)哼!我的好叔叔,我的继父大人,对您,我可亲近不起来。
王:你怎么还是满身丧气,没精打采,没半点喜气呢?
哈:不,陛下,我是沾了太多的喜气,这会儿倒提不起劲儿了。

(3)戏剧台词的翻译

在戏剧中,时间、地点、环境的描绘,事件的叙述,场景的变化,人物的介绍,心理活动的揭示等,这一切要必须由动作、对话或唱词来承担。戏剧的语言具有以下几个作用:叙述说明、场面连接、推动剧情发展、揭示人物性格、表达思想感情等。戏剧语言同时要达到几个目的。

剧本的台词是一种特殊的文学语言。首先,台词必须具有动作性。戏剧是行动的艺术,它必须在有限的舞台演出时间内迅速地展开人物的行动,并使之发生尖锐的冲突,以揭示人物的思想、性格、感情;其次,台词必须性格化。它必须根据人物的出身、年龄、职业、教养、经历、社会地位以及所处时代等条件,掌握人物的语言特征;再次,台词要精练、概括性强、容量大,力求用最简洁、最浓缩的词句来表达丰富的内容与深远的意境;最后,戏剧语言最好是通俗、浅近,易于被观众接受。台词、唱词要台词富于生活气息,亲切自然,使演员易说、易唱,观众易听、易懂。但绝不是内容含混、简单、贫乏,而是要深入浅出、言简意赅。

英若诚被称为著名表演艺术家、翻译家和艺术教育家。作为翻译家的英若诚,英文非常标准、地道、流利,对英语中的美国音、澳洲音、黑人音以及许多地方俚语都了如指掌。在翻译过程中,他非常注重语言对观众的直接效果,力求译文既忠实原著,又符合中国观众的审美习惯,使每个角色的语言都各具特点,达到良好的舞台效果。英若诚认为戏剧语言的翻译原则是:口语化与动作性的有机结合。

①口语化:戏剧语言的根本特征。

英先生认为,现在很多的戏剧译本的最大缺陷是不适合舞台表演,其原因就是"口语化"的本子太难找。究其原因,他分析道,"我们的很多译者,在处理译文的时候,考虑的不是舞台上的'直接效果',而是如何把原文中丰富的旁征博引、联想、内涵一点儿不漏地介绍过来。……本来,为了学术研究,这样做也无可厚非,有时甚至是必要的。但是舞台演出确实有它的特殊要求,观众希望听到的是'脆'的语言,巧妙而对仗工整的,有来有去的对白和反驳。这在一些语言大师,例如,王尔德或萧伯纳的作品中可以说俯拾皆是,作为译者,我们有责任将之介绍给我们的观众。"(英若诚,1999)

例如,英若诚的《推销员之死》译本是一个佳作。《推销员之死》(以下简称《推》)描写第二次世界大战后的美国社会,语言以纽约布鲁克林的方言为基础,为了表现这一语言特色,译者使用了北京天桥一带方言的某些词汇,赋予译文以老北京风味。请看以下译例。

例1 A word-sigh escapes his lips—it might be "Oh, boy, oh, boy."
    他情不自禁地长吁一口气,感叹地说了句话——可能是"够呛,真够呛"。(《推》P7)

例2 Biff:[steamed up] You know, with ten thousand bucks, boy!
    比夫:(兴奋起来)我告诉你,要有了一万块钱,你瞧着吧!(《推》P162)

例3 Willy:[stops short, looking at Biff] Glad to hear it, boy.
    威利:(一愣,看着比夫)很高兴听到你这么说,孩子。(《推》P164)

所以在以上三个例子当中,即便是同一个单词boy,在不同的场合也有不同的翻译方式。

例4 There's more people! That's what's ruining this country! Population is getting out of control. The competition is maddening!
    就是人多了!这个国家就要毁在这上头!人口失去控制了。竞争激烈得叫人发疯!(《推》P22)

例5 Happy: Sure, the guy's in line for the vice-presidency of the store. I Don't know what gets into me,...

哈比：真的，而且那个男人很快就要提拔成副经理了。我不知道我是犯了哪股劲儿，……（《推》P46）

例6 Biff: What the hell do you know about it?
比夫：你懂个屁！（《推》P132）

例7 Biff: [angered] Screw the business world!
比夫：（火了）去他妈的商业界！（slang）（《推》P146）

例8 Willy: [starting left for the stairs] Ah, you're counting your chickens again.
威利：（转身）嗨，又是八字没一撇儿就想发财。（《推》P152）

例4~例7中译者把英语中的口语翻译成大家耳熟能详的汉语口语，听起来大家一点也没有感到有翻译腔。而例8的翻译可谓是神来之笔，译者用汉语的口语准确地表达出原文的内涵。

②动作化：戏剧语言的表演基础。

关于戏剧语言的动作性，著名戏剧导演艺术家焦菊隐先生曾指出："有行动性的语言可以突出主题思想；突出人物性格；可以突出人物关系；可以引起观众丰富的联想。"（焦菊隐，1979，21）

英若诚提出的戏剧翻译中另一个非常重要的原则就是"语言的动作性"。他认为："'表演'不再只是做做样子，装扮一番，而是要'act'，也就是说，要'行动'，要'动作'。从这个意义上说，剧本中的台词不能只是发议论，抒情感，它往往掩盖着行动的要求或冲动，有的本身就是行动。例如挑衅、恐吓、争取、安抚、警告，以至于引为知己、欲擒故纵等等。"（英若诚，1999）。

例1 Biff: I sense it, you Don't give a good goddam about him. [He takes the rolled-up hose from his pocket and puts it on the table in front of Happy] Look what I found in the cellar, for Christ's sake. How can you bear to let it go on?
比夫：我觉得出来，他是死是活你压根儿不在乎。（他从衣袋里拿出卷起来的橡皮管子，放在桌上，哈皮面前）看吧，这是我在地窖子里找到的，天知道。你怎么能眼看着不管呢？（《推》P298）

例2 Howard: Sh, for God's sake!
霍华德：别出声，千万！（《推》P192）

例3 Biff: The thquare root of thixthy twee is...
比夫：山百山十山的平方根似……（《推》P308）

例4 The Woman: [enters, laughing. She lisps this] Can I come in? There's something in the bathtub, Willy, and it's moving!
妇人：（走进来，笑着，也学着大舌头）我也"掺"加行吗？威利，"找"盆里有个东西，还"债"那儿活动呢！

例5 Charley: Why must everybody like you? Who liked J.P.Morgan? Was he impressive?...（《推》P250）
查理：人家凭什么喜欢你？谁又喜欢银行大王摩根（补充说明）来着？他难道仪

表堂堂?……

例6 Stanley:…But I know you, you ain't from Hackensack. You know what I mean? (《推》P254)

斯坦利:……可我摸得着你的心思,您不是那号俗人。是不是这个意思?

戏剧深厚的文化底蕴和丰富的表现形式使其成为观众人数最多的艺术门类,因此,无论是向内介绍外来文化,还是向外传播我国的传统文化,戏剧(包括影视、广播剧)之功不可或缺。译者是戏剧的跨文化交流得以成功实现的关键。戏剧翻译途径的多样化有利于使译者放开手脚,发挥创造力,做到目标准确,不仅将国外优秀的剧目引入国内,也向全世界展现我国璀璨的戏剧艺术宝库。

Lord Ullin's Daughter

Thomas Campbell (1777-18-44)

1. A CHIEFTAIN to the Highlands bound
   Cries 'Boatman, do not tarry!
   And I'll give thee a silver pound
   To row us o''er the ferry!'
2. 'Now who be ye, would cross Lochgyle.
   This dark and stormy water?'
   'O I'm the chief of Ulva's isle,
   And this, Lord Ullin's daughter.
3. 'And fast before her father's men
   Three days we've fled together,
   For should he find us in the glen,
   My blood would stain the heather.
4. 'His horsemen hard behind us ride—
   Should they our steps discover,
   Then who will cheer my bonny bride,
   When they have slain her lover?'
5. Out spoke the hardy Highland wight,
   'I'll go, my chief, I'm ready:
   It is not for your silver bright,
   But for your winsome lady:—
6. 'And by my word! the bonny bird
   In danger shall not tarry;

So though the waves are raging white
　　I'll row you o'er the ferry.'
7. By this the storm grew loud apace,
　　The water-wraith was shrieking;
And in the scowl of heaven each face
　　Grew dark as they were speaking.
8. But still as wilder blew the wind,
　　And as the night grew drearer,
Adown the glen rodearmed men,
　　Their trampling sounded nearer.
9. "Oh, haste thee, haste!" the lady cries;
　　"Though tempests round us gather.
I'll meet the raging of the skies,
　　But not an angry father."
10. The boat has left a stormy land,
　　A stormy sea before her,—
When, oh! too strong for human hand
　　The tempest gathered o'er her!
11. And still they rowed amidst the roar
　　Of waters fast prevailing:
Lord Ullin reached that fatal shore—
　　His wrath was changed to wailing.
12. for, sore dismay'd through storm and shade,
　　His child he did discover:—
One lovely hand she stretch'd for aid,
　　And one was round her lover.
13. "Come back! come back!" he cried in grief,
　　Across this stormy water;
And I'll forgive your Highland chief,
　　My daughter—O my daughter!"
14. 'Twas vain: the loud waves lashed the shore,
　　Return or aid preventing;
The waters wild went o'er his child,
　　And he was left lamenting.

(343 words)

第十二章

应用语篇的翻译

Agreement

This Agreement is made this 8th day of August, 2018, by and between Victory Electronic Trading Co., Ltd. (hereinafter called "the Sellers"), a corporation duly organized and existing under the laws of Hong Kong, with its head office(principal place of business) at Kowloon, and Pan American Trading Co, Inc. (hereinafter called "the he Buyers"), a corporation duly organized and existing under the laws of California, the United States, with business at United States. its head office(principal place of Santa Barbara, California, the United States).

WHEREAS, the Sellers are desirous of exporting the under-mentioned products to the territory stipulated below; And

WHEREAS, the Buyers are desirous of importing the said products for sale in the said territory;

NOW, THEREFORE, it is hereby agreed and understood as follows:

…

Article 5. Seller warrants that all material, work product, and merchandise supplied under the Order(a) shall strictly conform to all specifications, drawings, samples, or other descriptions furnished to and approved by Buyer, (b) shall be fit and serviceable for the purpose intended, as agreed to by Buyer and Seller, (c) shall be of good quality and free from defects in materials and workmanship, (d) shall be new and not refurbished or reconditioned, unless expressly agreed in writing by Buyer, and (e) shall not infringe any patent, copyright, mask work, trademark, trade secret or other intellectual property, proprietary or contractual right of any third party. In addition, Seller warrants that Buyer shall have good and marketable title to all goods (including all components thereof) purchased by Buyer pursuant to the Order, free of all liens and encumbrances and that no licenses are required for Buyer to use such goods.

佳译赏析

The United Nations Charter (Excerpt)

英语文本	汉语文本
The UN Charter: The 70th anniversary 　　The Charter of the United Nations was signed on 26 June 1945, in San Francisco, at the conclusion of the United Nations Conference on International Organization, and came into force on 24 October 1945. The Statute of the International Court of Justice is an integral part of the Charter.	联合国宪章:70周年纪念版 　　联合国宪章是1945年6月26日联合国国际组织会议结束时在旧金山签字的,于1945年10月24日生效。国际法院规约是宪章的组成部分。
Preamble	序言
WE THE PEOPLES OF THE UNITED NATIONS DETERMINED 　　to save succeeding generations from the scourge of war, which twice in our lifetime has brought untold sorrow to mankind, and 　　to reaffirm faith in fundamental human rights, in the dignity and worth of the human person, in the equal rights of men and women and of nations large and small, and 　　to establish conditions under which justice and respect for the obligations arising from treaties and other sources of international law can be maintained, and 　　to promote social progress and better standards of life in larger freedom,	我联合国人民同兹决心 　　欲免后世再遭今代人类两度身历惨不堪言之战祸, 　　重申基本人权,人格尊严与价值,以及男女与大小各国平等权利之信念, 　　创造适当环境,俾克维持正义,尊重由条约与国际法其他渊源而起之义务,久而弗懈, 　　促成大自由中之社会进步及较善之民生,
AND FOR THESE ENDS 　　to practice tolerance and live together in peace with one another as good neighbours, and 　　to unite our strength to maintain international peace and security, and 　　to ensure, by the acceptance of principles and the institution of methods, that armed force shall not be used, save in the common interest, and 　　to employ international machinery for the promotion of the economic and social advancement of all peoples,	并为达此目的 　　力行容恕,彼此以善邻之道,和睦相处, 　　集中力量,以维持国际和平及安全, 　　接受原则,确立方法,以保证非为公共利益,不得使用武力, 　　运用国际机构,以促成全球人民经济及社会之进展,
HAVE RESOLVED TO COMBINE OUR EFFORTS TO ACCOMPLISH THESE AIMS 　　Accordingly, our respective Governments, through representatives assembled in the city of San Francisco, who have exhibited their full powers found to be in good and due form, have agreed to the present Charter of the United Nations and do hereby establish an international organization to be known as the United Nations.	用是发愤立志,务当同心协力,以竟厥功 　　爱由我各本国政府,经齐集金山市之代表各将所奉全权证书,互相校阅,均属妥善,议定本联合国宪章,并设立国际组织,定名联合国。
CHAPTER I PURPOSES AND PRINCIPLES	第一章　宗旨及原则

英 语 文 本	汉 语 文 本
Article 1 　　The Purposes of the United Nations are:	第一条 　　联合国之宗旨为:
1. To maintain international peace and security, and to that end: to take effective collective measures for the prevention and removal of threats to the peace, and for the suppression of acts of aggression or other breaches of the peace, and to bring about by peaceful means, and in conformity with the principles of justice and international law, adjustment or settlement of international disputes or situations which might lead to a breach of the peace;	一、维持国际和平及安全;并为此目的:采取有效集体办法,以防止且消除对于和平之威胁,制止侵略行为或其他和平之破坏;并以和平方法且依正义及国际法之原则,调整或解决足以破坏和平之国际争端或情势。
2. To develop friendly relations among nations based on respect for the principle of equal rights and self-determination of peoples, and to take other appropriate measures to strengthen universal peace;	二、发展国际间以尊重人民平等权利及自决原则为根据之友好关系,并采取其他适当办法,以增强普遍和平。
3. To achieve international co-operation in solving international problems of an economic, social, cultural, or humanitarian character, and in promoting and encouraging respect for human rights and for fundamental freedoms for all without distinction as to race, sex, language, or religion; and	三、促成国际合作,以解决国际间属于经济、社会、文化及人类福利性质之国际问题,且不分种族、性别、语言或宗教,增进并激励对于全体人类之人权及基本自由之尊重。
4. To be a centre for harmonizing the actions of nations in the attainment of these common ends.	四、构成一协调各国行动之中心,以达成上述共同目的。
Article 2 　　The Organization and its Members, in pursuit of the Purposes stated in Article 1, shall act in accordance with the following Principles.	第二条 　　为求实现第一条所述各宗旨起见,本组织及其会员国应遵行下列原则:
1. The Organization is based on the principle of the sovereign equality of all its Members.	一、本组织系基于各会员国主权平等之原则。
2. All Members, in order to ensure to all of them the rights and benefits resulting from membership, shall fulfill in good faith the obligations assumed by them in accordance with the present Charter.	二、各会员国应一秉善意,履行其依本宪章所担负之义务,以保证全体会员国由加入本组织而发生之权益。
3. All Members shall settle their international disputes by peaceful means in such a manner that international peace and security, and justice, are not endangered.	三、各会员国应以和平方法解决其国际争端,俾免危及国际和平、安全及正义。
4. All Members shall refrain in their international relations from the threat or use of force against the territorial integrity or political independence of any state, or in any other manner inconsistent with the Purposes of the United Nations.	四、各会员国在其国际关系上不得使用威胁或武力,或以与联合国宗旨不符之任何其他方法,侵害任何会员国或国家之领土完整或政治独立。
5. All Members shall give the United Nations every assistance in any action it takes in accordance with the present Charter, and shall refrain from giving assistance to any state against which the United Nations is taking preventive or enforcement action.	五、各会员国对于联合国依本宪章规定而采取之行动,应尽力予以协助,联合国对于任何国家正在采取防止或执行行动时,各会员国对该国不得给予协助。

续上表

英语文本	汉语文本
6. The Organization shall ensure that states which are not Members of the United Nations act in accordance with these Principles so far as may be necessary for the maintenance of international peace and security.	六、本组织在维持国际和平及安全之必要范围内，应保证非联合国会员国遵行上述原则。
7. Nothing contained in the present Charter shall authorize the United Nations to intervene in matters which are essentially within the domestic jurisdiction of any state or shall require the Members to submit such matters to settlement under the present Charter; but this principle shall not prejudice the application of enforcement measures under Chapter Vll.	七、本宪章不得认为授权联合国干涉在本质上属于任何国家国内管辖之事件，且并不要求会员国将该项事件依本宪章提请解决；但此项原则不妨碍第七章内执行办法之适用。

认知升级

应用翻译，或称实用翻译，不同于传达有较强情感意义和美学意义的文学翻译，应用翻译以传达信息为目的，同时考虑传递信息的效果，其题材范围几乎涵盖当今政治、经济、社会和文化生活的各个领域，可以说应用翻译在日常生活中起着举足轻重的作用。

本章探讨在当今社会应用性较强的语篇翻译，包括商务语篇翻译、科技语篇翻译、法律语篇翻译等，这些语篇在翻译时受到涉及应用领域特殊表达词汇、习语以及文化背景的限制，因此需要恰当使用相关的翻译技巧及表达形式。

一、商务语篇的翻译

随着国际商务的蓬勃发展，尤其是英语在全球化进程中的重要作用，商务语篇在国际经济贸易交流中越来越起着不可忽视的作用。商务语篇类型多样，包括备忘录（Memorandum）、会议纪要（Minutes）、广告（Commercials）、年度报告（Annual Report）、项目可行性研究报告（Project Feasibility Report）、通知（Notice）、说明书（Specification）、协议或合同（Agreement or Contract）等。

翻译商务语篇时，译者要有强烈的商务语境意识和对所翻译的文本的专业意识。这样，才能察觉到所译内容的特殊性，使译文在词语、语言规范、句子结构、文体等方面都符合行业表达习惯，译文最大限度地再现原文所要表达的内容，使译语读者的感受与原语读者的感受最大限度地接近或一致。

1. 商务语篇的文体特点

商务语篇以适应职场生活与商务领域交流的语言要求为主要目的，涉及商务活动的所有层面，包括技术引进、对外贸易、招商引资、海外投资、国际金融等。在长期的商务交流中，商务语篇逐渐形成了不同于日常语篇的诸多特征。这些文体特征表现在词汇层面、句式和文本层面。

（1）词汇特征

商务英语在词汇使用上最突出的特点是专业词汇的大量运用，其中既包括大量专业词汇、具有商务含义的普通词汇，也包括复合词以及缩略词等。此外，名词化程度高、新词层出不穷也是商务英语词汇的一个显著特征。

专业术语丰富。商务英语在词汇使用上最突出的特点是专业词汇的大量运用。专业术语是指使用于不同科学领域或专业的词,是用来精确表达专业概念的词汇,具有明确的内涵和清晰的外延。专业术语要求单一性,排斥多义性和歧义性,此外,专业术语具有较强的稳定性,即专业术语中的词汇和词序较为固定,不能随意替换或更改。

专业术语体现了明显的行业特点。国际贸易方面的术语有:free on board(离岸价)、sole license(排他性许可证)、standby letter of credit(备用信用证)、Exclusive license(独占性许可证)、Counter offer(还盘);经济学方面的词汇有:Gross National Product(国民生产总值)、demand curve(需求曲线);金融方面,如:fiscal deficit(财政赤字)、contract curve(契约曲线)、Insurance policy(保险单)、Clearance sale(清仓削价销售)等。

商务英语语言灵活且常见。不同的词序、介词以及单复数变化都会导致词义发生重大的变化,并给翻译带来一定的困难。例如:property in goods(货权)、property of goods(货物属性)、Appearance surface(外表)、surface appearance(表面状况)等。

商务英语使用一词多义现象也很丰富,例如下列词语中的 instrument 含义就不同:instrument of payment(支付工具)、instrument of pledge(抵押契据)、instrument of ratification(批准证书)、instrument of credit control(信用管制手段)、instrument of acquisition(购置凭证)等。

缩略语广泛运用。缩略语,具有言简意赅、快速捷达的特点,在国际商务活动中广泛使用。如:B/L 海运提单 Bill of Lading、DAF 边境交货 Delivered At Frontier、DES 目的港船上交货 Delivered Ex Ship、DEQ 目的港码头交货 Delivered Ex Quay、DDP 完税后交货 Delivered Duty Paid、D/P 付款交单 Document Against Payment、D/A 承兑交单 Document Against Acceptance、C&F 成本加海运费 Cost and Freight、C.Y.货柜场 Container Yard、C/(CNEE)收货人 Consignee 等。

名词化程度高。名词化是用名词来体现本来打算用动词或形容词所体现的"过程"或"特征"。商务英语语境下,名词化现象非常普遍。不同的商务文体,名词化分布各不一致。文体越正式,名词化程度越高。商务英语中,商务信函和合同中的名词化现象非常普遍,如在其他文体中常常使用动词 notify 的地方,商务英语更倾向于使用其名词形式 notification;其他文体使用形容词 careful 的地方,商务英语常常使用其名词 carefulness 等。

(2)句法特征

总的来说,商务英语句式复杂,具有较强的逻辑性;句法使用完整,多用被动语态;内容简洁,具有较强的时效性;社交礼貌用语广泛使用。

句式复杂、逻辑性强。商务语篇文体具有多样性,这决定了商务英语句式因问题的不同而不同。通常来说,商务英语中长句出现的频率较高,句子结构复杂、逻辑性强。如商务英语语境中常出现的合同用语,因其是具有法律效力的公文,在撰写合同时必须做到能够提供的信息完整、严密,不让读者产生曲解、误读。

结构完整、多用被动。因为其使用场合的正式性,商务英语中句子一般结构完整;被动句大量使用,而少用主动语态以凸显内容的客观性、原则性和效力性。商务英语追求内容的客观公正、准确无误和形式的简洁,因而常使用被动语态。被动句具有较高程度的礼貌性,能使句子衔接保持连贯,避免主观之嫌。尤其在商务信函中,为了使得请求听起来比较温和,从而变得礼貌得体,可以选择被动语态作为适当的语言形式。在商务谈判中,人们常用被动语态来避免直接批评对方。

社交礼貌语的使用。商务英语比较讲究客套,礼貌的商务写作表明友好的态度、公平交易、合作的心愿等。商务英语写作和交流往往注重语言的礼貌和友好,注意措辞婉转、诚恳、不卑不亢。如在信件开头,常用的固定表达有:We are pleased to inform/have pleasure in informing you that…;We have the pleasure to apprise/the honor to inform you of…;We take the liberty of announcing to you that…,We have to inform/advise you that(of)…等。

2.商务语篇的翻译原则和方法

商务语篇在词汇、句法、篇章等方面有其特殊之处,这种特殊性决定了商务英语应具有某些独特的翻译原则。商务语篇翻译应遵循至少四个原则,即专业性原则、准确性原则、礼貌原则及合作原则等。

(1)专业原则

专业原则指的是在商务语篇翻译中,针对某一专门行业,运用相关的专业知识和恰当的翻译策略和技巧,使译文的读者能获得对等的信息,尤其是在翻译中,应特别注意专业词汇的使用,具体包括正确使用专业术语,如 VAT(Value-added Tax)(增值税)、D/A(Documents Against Acceptance)(承兑交单);正确使用专业缩略词,如 GDP(国内生产总值)、IPO(首次公开发行)、正确使用专业新词汇。因为商务语篇翻译涉及经济、贸易、金融、财务等特定学科,所以要做好商务语篇翻译,一定要了解、熟悉相关的专业知识,才能最大限度地避免误译、错译,沟通双方也不会因为理解偏差造成不必要的损失和纠纷。

商务英语中存在大量专业术语,这也就决定了商务英语的翻译首先要求准确使用术语,符合学科要求,符合文本语境,符合目的语文本读者的要求,避免出现错译和误译。如商务谈判中的常见词 offer 和 counter offer,这两个词就不能按字面意思译为"提供"和"反提供",正确译法为"报盘"和"还盘",如果翻译为其他意思,则会引起行业内人士的误读。

(2)准确性原则

准确性原则指的是商务英语的翻译要忠实、准确地传递原文的信息,做到原文读者获得信息和译文读者获得信息内涵对等,即信息等值。这里所说的准确不是原文与译文在语言层面的相似或相同,而是指原文与译文在所承载的信息上一致。所以,商务英语翻译中的准确性原则主要强调信息的等值。

商务英语是实用文体,涉及的内容关乎相关方的切身利益。商务英语翻译更注重译文内容的忠实、准确,即所谓的"信"。无论是商务信函、经济合同、产品说明书、商业单据、涉外财务报表,还是经济案件的申诉、判决,都必须在翻译中把准确性原则放在第一位。

准确翻译数据　商务文本往往包含大量数据,这些数据常常关乎相关方面的切身利益,或者相关事项的正常运作,所以译文中的数据要准确无误,不然会引起不必要的麻烦或导致商家的损失。

计量单位也要翻译得准确无误,即使遇到英语中没有的单位也要换算成常用的公制单位,如中国文化中特有的计量单位亩、斛、斗等,如翻译成英语时,要根据语境进行相应的转换或说明。

例1 Multinational bank's services include issuing letter of credit, buying and selling foreign exchange, issuing banker's acceptances, accepting Eurocurrency deposits, making Eurocurrency loans, and assisting in the market of Eurobonds.

译文:跨国银行提供的服务包括开立信用证、买卖外汇、开立银行承兑,接受欧洲货币储存、提供欧洲货币贷款以及发行推销欧洲货币债券。

例2 Party B shall ship the goods within one month of the date of signing this Contract, i.e. not later than December 15.

译文：本合同签字之日一个月内，即不迟于12月25日，你方须将货物装船。

例3 Party A shall pay Party B a monthly salary of US＄500(SAY FIVE HUNDRED US DOLLARS ONLY).

译文：聘方须每月付给受聘方美元500元整。

(3) 礼貌原则

在国际商务活动中，一方如果语言不当，草率轻浮或者缺乏尊重，轻则会给贸易伙伴留下不好的印象，重则破坏商贸关系，阻碍有效沟通，可能导致交易的失败。由此可见，在商务翻译中使用得体的语言和相应的礼貌策略不容忽视。翻译时可以使用"敬希""恳请""贵方/贵公司""承蒙""冒昧""谨""收悉""祈谅""望……为盼""赐复"等。汉语公文中常用的客套委婉词语。有时，也采用典型的介词结构，使用"凡属…须于…""鉴于…"文言文句式，能使译文的语意更为确切、严密、周详和规范。

例1 You are kindly requested to act accordingly as soon as possible.

译文：敬希速遵照执行。

例2 Considering the friendly business relationship between our two banks, we decided not to charge you the overdue interests.

译文：鉴于贵我两行之间的友好业务关系，我行决定不收取贵行的过期利息。

以下是一些常见商务信函套语的双语句式。

We are pleased to inform you…特此奉告/函告……

In reply to your letter…兹复贵函……

We are writing concerning…兹去函关于……

We send you…兹寄上……

We are glad to answer…兹答复……

Enclosed we hand…随函附上……

Your kind reply will greatly oblige us.如蒙赐复，不胜……

We are looking forward to hearing from you soon.盼早日赐复。

Hoping you will favor me with an early reply.敬祈早日赐复为盼。

We shall appreciate it(be grateful)if you could…如蒙……不胜感激。

Thank you in advance for…承蒙……谨先致谢。

We regret to inform you that…/We greatly regret that…非常遗憾，今致函奉告……

We are very sorry to hear/know…获悉……我方甚感遗憾。

(4) 合体原则

翻译商务语篇是一定要遵从相应的格式要求的，不可随意而为。例如，商务信函在格式上通常包括以下部分：reference number(编号，引证号，文档号)，subject(事由，主题)，attention(收件人，经办人)，CC—carbon copy(抄送)，from(发信人)date(日期)，inside address(信内地址)，salutation(称呼)，body(正文)，complimentary closing(结尾套语)，enclosure(附件)，signature(签名)，P.S.—postscript(又及)等。这些内容，可以按照汉语信函的排版格式准确译出，不可随意增减。

其中 salutation 中的 Dear 商务信函和其他公函中通常译作"尊敬的",这样不确定对象的称呼 Dear Sir(s)/Madam 可译成"尊敬的阁下(先生)/女士"或"敬启者"等。

结尾套语 complimentary dosing 中,Best wishes 通常译作"祝好!""此致……敬礼!",Yours sincerely/Yours faithfully 之类则常译成"敬上"或"谨上"等。

二、科技语篇的翻译

"科技文体是随着科学技术的发展而形成的独立的文体形式,包括科学专著、科学论文、科学报道、试验报告、技术规范、工程技术说明、科技文献以及科普读物等,涉及自然科学各个专业的题材。由于科技文本种类繁杂,信息最丰富,科技翻译以准确传递信息,再现原文信息功能为最终目标。"[1]

科技语篇是一种重要的英语文体。科技语篇泛指一切论及或谈及科学和技术的文本,其中包括:一、科技著述、科技论文和科学报道、实验报告和方案;二、各类科技情报和文字资料;三、科技实用手册的结构描述和操作规程;四、有关科技问题的会谈、会议、交谈;五、有关科技的影片、录像、光盘等有声资料。

科技语篇是最有信息功能的文本,以客观陈述为主,以传达信息为根本目的,要求客观性、准确性和严密性,注重叙事逻辑上的连贯及表达上的明晰与畅达,避免行文晦涩。科技语篇力求平易和精确,避免使用旨在加强语言感染力和宣传效果的各种修辞格,以免使读者产生行文浮华、内容虚饰之感。

在科技翻译的过程中,要注意保持对原文信息的忠实,还要注重保持科技语篇专业、准确、客观、严谨、简明等特点。

1.词汇特点与翻译

科技英语大量使用专业词汇和半专业词汇。专业词汇是指仅用于某一学科或专业的词汇或术语。每门学科或专业都有自己的一套含义精确而狭窄的术语。从词源角度来分析,专业词汇有两个主要的来源,一方面是来自英语日常词汇,另一方面是来自拉丁语和希腊语词根及词缀的词汇。

科技语篇中绝大多数专业词汇,尤其是名词术语则是由拉丁语和希腊语的词根和词缀构成的。现以前缀 hyper(超出,过度,在……上)和后缀-asis,-osis(或(表示疾病)分别举例如下:

hyperacid 胃酸过多的;酸过多的, hypercharge 超荷, hyperextension 伸展过度, hyperfine structure 超精细结构, hyperfocal distance 超焦距, hyperkinesia 肌肉运动过度、痉挛, hypermorph 超等位基因, hyperplane 超平面, hyperspace 超空间, dermatosis 皮肤病, filariasis 丝虫病, lithiaais 结石病, nephrosis 背病, schistosomiasis 血吸虫病, silicosis 砂肺等。

日常词汇用于某一专业科技领域便成为专业技术用语,具有严格的科学含义。例如,splash 这个词在日常生活中表示"(水等)飞溅",被医学借用后表示"苯丙胺,安非他命";growth 在日常生活中表示"生长,成长,发育",被医学借用后表示"赘生物、肿瘤"。"imitative"在日常生活中表示"模仿的、模拟的",被生物学借用后表示"拟态的"。现代英语中,新兴科学在传统科学的影响下,尽量利用常用旧词,赋予新义于旧词。例如,近年来遗传工程学的发展给旧词 template(刻印模板)带来了新义"遗传密码载体分子"。

在翻译时,要注意术语译名的规范化。各专业的科技术语,都由有关学会的名词委员会

---

[1] 陈宏薇,李亚丹.新编汉英翻译教程[M].上海:上海外语教育出版社,2004:242.

审定过,其译法都已有规定,译者不能根据自己理解任意翻译。如机制专业中,feed 必须译成"进给",而不能译成"喂料"。恰当运用本专业或行业的术语和习惯用语,是科技翻译中极其重要的一环。

科技语篇专业术语多,且同一词语在不同专业领域中的意义不尽相同。我们在翻译时首先要在本专业的概念体系中弄清术语所表达的意义、概念范畴和概念关系,然后进行两种语言的术语概念的对比。要特别注意一个词在某一特定的专业领域中的特有词义,勿将科技词语误认为不具有特殊专业含义的普通词语;同时应严格遵循某一专业技术领域的用语习惯,某一词语一经译出,即应保持一贯性,不应在上下文中随意改动,引起概念上的混乱。在科技英语翻译中,特别需要恪守严谨的作风,不容丝毫的主观随意性。

翻译中特别要注意半专业词汇的使用。半专业词汇是指那些既用于日常英语,同时又是科技语篇中常用的词汇。半专业词汇与专业词汇的主要区别在于半专业词汇一般不专用于某一学科,而是为各学科所通用。这些词汇用在不同学科中虽然基本含义不变,但其确切含义则存在较大差别。例如,power 一词在日常英语中表示"力量,权力"等意思,用于体育专业表示"爆发力",用于机械专业表示"动力",用于电力专业表示"电力",用于物理专业表示"功率";pencil 一词,在日常英语中表示"铅笔",在物理学中表示"光线束""光线锥",而在数学中则表示"线束""面束"及"圆束"等意思;plate 在日常英语中表示"盘子",在摄影技术中表示"感光板",在动物学中表示"板形器官",在医学中表示"假牙托",在电子学中表示"阳极",在地质学中表示"板块",在采矿业中表示"碟形粉末",在建筑业中表示"横木"。

专业术语应该根据约定俗成的表达方式进行翻译。例如 printing 一词,在电子计算机专业中,printing telegraphy 译成"电传打字电报",printing keyboard perforator 译成"印字键盘打孔机";在摄像专业中,printing speed 译成"印像速度";在纺织业中,printing hydro 译成"雕白粉"。值得注意的是,同一个词即使在不同专业领域出现,译文也不一定相同。如 spectroscopy 指代光谱理论的研究时译为"光谱学",当指光谱分析的实验时可译为"光谱术"。

英语科技语篇具有较强的名词化特点。名词化指将动词或形容词转换为抽象名词使用。这些名词,常伴有修饰成分或附加成分,构成短语,称为名词化结构。例如 possible possibility, available availability, clean cleanness 等。名词化结构的组合方式多,意义容量大,适宜于表达精细复杂的思想,使文章具有庄重感和严肃感。

由于汉语科技语篇中动词的使用比较频繁,因此在翻译时,往往能够将这些抽象的名词或名词化结构,转换成汉语的动词或动宾短语。例如:

例1 The operation of a machine needs some knowledge of its performance.
操作机器需要懂得机器的一些性能。

例2 Recent developments in the utilization of salinity power by reverse electrodialysis and other methods are discussed.
本文讨论采用逆电渗法和别的方法来利用盐动力的最新进展。

句中,名词化结构 the utilization of salinity power by reverse electrodialysis and other methods 已从物体的行为过程抽象出来,形成一个复杂的整体概念,与介词 in 构成短语,来修饰 developments。具有整体概念和抽象的特点。翻译时,将其转换成动宾结构"利用盐动力"。

特别需要注意的是,名词修饰语与形容词修饰语有时在语义方面也有着显著的区别。一般说来,名词定语侧重于职能方面的修饰或限制另一方面,而形容词修饰名词只在属性方面起修饰作用。有时名词修饰名词,但其中一个名词更具动词属性。翻译时对此需要特别注意。

efficiency expert 研究提高工作效率的专家
efficient expert 工作效率高的专家
obesity specialist 肥胖病专家
obese specialist 胖专家
riot police 防暴警察
riotous police 暴乱的警察

2.句法特点与翻译

科技语篇是科学技术的载体,用来客观表达科技的实质。因此,科技语篇的句法特点有:①多用一般现在时;②多用情态动词 can 和 may;③广泛使用非人称主语;④大量使用被动语态;⑤长句的使用频率较高。

(1)科技英语中多用动词的现在时,尤其是多用一般现在时来表示"无时间性"的"一般叙述",即叙述事实或真理,客观地表述定义、定理、方程式、公式、图表等。当然,也会使用到一般进行时,现在完成时等。在翻译时,注意区分时态,用不同的汉语副词来表达。

例1 There is general acknowledgment that the characteristics of an individual are a result of an interaction of genetics and environment.
众所周知,某一个体的特性是遗传和环境相互作用的结果。

例2 Action is equal to reaction but it acts in a contrary direction.
作用力和反作用力大小相等,方向相反。

例3 The length of the runway restricts the landing speed of aircraft.
跑道长度限制飞机的着陆速度。

例4 E-mail is starting to edge out the fax, the telephone, overnight mail and land mail.
电子邮件正在取代传真、电话、快速邮递和陆地邮递。

(2)科技英语中 can 和 may 比其他情态动词使用的频率要高些。这是因为这两个情态动词可用来表示客观可能性,而其他则多突出主观性。翻译时,需要加以体现。

例1 You cannot get AIDS by working or attending school with some-one who has the disease.
与艾滋病患者一起工作或上学不会传染上艾滋病。

例2 There is no doubt that animal viruses can jump into humans.
毫无疑问,动物病毒能进入人体。

例3 Anyone with a personal computer, a modem and the necessary software to link computers over telephone lines can sign on.
任何人只要有一台个人电脑,再有一个调制解调器和必要的软件,就可以把电脑连接到电话线上,然后就能申请上网。

(3)科技语篇在句法上的另一个显著的特点就是大量使用非人称主语,很少使用有人称的句子。原因在于科技文章所描述和所讨论的重点是科学发现或科技事实,而不是报告这些结果或自然规律是由谁发现或完成的,因此,科技文章大多数情况不使用人称主语。在翻译时,可以处理成汉语的无主句等。

例1 When a copper plate is put into the sulfuric acid electrolyte, very few of its atoms dissolve.
当将铜片置于硫酸电解液中时,几乎没有铜原子溶解。

例2 Evaporation emphasis is placed on concentrating a solution rather than forming and building crystals.

蒸发着重于将溶液浓缩,而不是生成和析出晶体。

例3 Up to now, sulfur dioxide has been regarded as one of the most serious of these pollutants.

到目前为止,二氧化硫一直被看作是这些污染物中最严重的一种。

(4)科技英语倾向于使用被动语态。这是因为科技英语注重对事实和方法、性能和特征做出客观表述。与主动语态相比,被动语态表达更为客观,有助于将读者的注意力集中在叙述中的事物、现实或过程上。在翻译时,可以根据具体语境,灵活处理,将被动语态句转换成汉语的隐性被动句、主动句,或者无主句等。

例1 Noise is transmitted from a source to a receiver.

噪声从噪声源传递到接收者。

例2 Nuclear power plants are said to be under preparation for construction.

据说,核电站正在筹建中。

例3 Not only hearts and kidney, but also other parts, which are even more delicate, are exchanged.

不仅心脏和背,即使其他更复杂的器官也能被移植。

例4 Atoms can be thought of as miniature solar systems, with a nucleus at the center and electrons orbiting at specific distances from it.

原子可被看作是一个微型的太阳系,原子核在其中心,而电子以一定的距离绕核做圆周运动。

(5)科技英语中复杂的长句使用较多,这是由于科技文章要求叙述准确,而且推理严密。在翻译时,可以将英语长句分成几个汉语短句,再根据逻辑次序,重新安排句子;采用顺译、倒译、分译、重组等翻译方法。例如:

例1 Each chemical element had its number and fixed position in the table, and from this it became possible to predict its behavior: how it would react with other elements, what kind of compounds it would form, and what sort of physical properties it would have.

每个化学元素在周期表中都有一定的原子数和位置,可以据此来推测它所具有的特点:如何同其他元素发生反应,形成什么样的化合物以及其物理属性。

例2 Often cheaper and less disruptive than traditional cleanup methods, this natural approach to remediating hazardous wastes in the soil, water, and air is capturing the attention of government regulators, industries, landowners, and researchers interested in finding better and less expensive ways to clean up the world's toxic waste.

与传统清除方法相比,采用这种自然清除方法清除土壤、水以及空气中的污染费用低、破坏性小,正日益受到各政府首脑、企业、土地所有者、研究人员们的关注,因为他们正在寻求更加有效、经济的方法来清除世界上的有毒废品。

例3 Protection against complete structural failure is achieved in three different ways: first, by proper selection of material, especially in high load areas, to provide a consistent slow rate of crack propagation, and high residual strength; second, by providing such multipath structure on the airplane that the loss of any one segment would not endanger the airplane; and third, by providing readily accessible structure which can be inspected and maintained properly.

用三种方法来防止整个结构的损坏：一、适当选用材料，特别是在高荷载区的材料，要具有一致的、迟缓的裂痕扩散速率特性以及高剩余强度；二、采用多路传力结构，使某一局部损坏不危及整个飞机；三、使结构具有易卸性，便于检查与维修。

例 4 We learn that sodium or any of its compounds produces a spectrum having a bright yellow double line by noticing that there is no such line in the spectrum of light when sodium is not present, but that if the smallest quantity of sodium be thrown into the flame or other sources of light, the bright yellow line instantly appears.

我们注意到，如果把非常少的钠投入火焰或其他光源中时，立即出现亮黄色的双线，当钠不存在时，光谱中就没有这样的双线。由此，我们知道钠或者钠的任何化合物都能产生带有一条亮黄色双线的光谱。（分译+重组）

例 5 Aluminum, the richest metallic element in nature, remained unknown until the nineteenth century, because no where in nature is it found free, owing to its always being combined with other element most commonly with oxygen, for which it has a strong affinity.

铝是自然界储藏量最丰富的元素，它总是和其他元素化合。与氧化合的情况最为普遍，因为这种元素对氧具有很强的亲和力。由于这个原因，在自然界任何地方都找不到处于游离状态的铝，所以直到19世纪才被人们知道。

(6)句式格式化。科技语篇中，许多固定句式出现频率颇高，若能熟练掌握这些句式的翻译规律，既可保证译文的准确性和可读性，又可提高翻译的效率。例如，科技论文摘要中的常用句型和译文有：

the principle of…is outlined 本文概述……原则
the apparatus for…is described 本文描述……装置
automation of…is discussed 本文讨论……自动化
the use of…is addressed 本文论述……的应用
the mechanism…is examined 本文探讨……机理
the dependence of…was established 本文确定……关系
an analysis of…was carried out 本文进行了……分析

在技术标准文献中，对某标准的使用范围要做明确的规定，常用语句如：

This standard(This specification) deals with / relates to / is concerned with…
本标准(本规范)涉及，论及，有关……
specifies…/prescribes… 本标准(本规范)规定……
This standard(This specification) covers /is for/applies to… 本标准(本规范)适用于……

3.科技语篇特点与翻译

在文本层面，科技语篇的特点有：重视衔接，强调逻辑；结构程式化；文风质朴、少用修辞格，语体正式、客观准确。

(1)由于科技语篇正式程度高，逻辑严密、层次分明、条理清晰，非常注重衔接等语篇手段。在词汇衔接(lexical cohesion)方面，专用科技文体以同词重述为多，也用上义词替代。衔接在逻辑连接词(logical connectives)或称过渡性词语(transitional words and phrases)方面，由于专用科技文章逻辑性强，论证严密，需要经常表达逻辑思维的各种模式，例如时间与空间、列举与例证、原因与结果、强调与增补、比较与限定、推论与总结等，因此各种逻辑连接词大量使用，其词频之高，是因为表达复杂思想和铺陈文章逻辑关系的必然结果。

这就要求我们在翻译时，必须尽量避免将原文进行字面意义的串联、拼凑或主观臆断，而要透彻地分析句子的深层结构，积极了解相关的专业知识，使译文既要有逻辑性与科学性，又要符合专业要求，力求做到文理通顺，准确地、有效地表达出原文的内容。

例1 The specimen can be inserted between pieces of similar hardness; the sample can be plated; when using casting resins, a slurry of resin and alumina made for just this purpose can be poured around the specimen; the specimen can be surrounded by short, small revetments, rings, etc., of about the same hardness.

试样可夹在具有同样硬度的工件之间，可镀层。当用充填料时，可将树脂与矾土的浆料注入试样周围，使试样被短小的护壁、环状填料（硬度差不多）等所包围。

句中，主题词 specimen 简单重复三次，the sample 是上义词替代。概念重述是概念的继续。原文不用一个代词，译成汉语时同样不用代词，重复出现"试样"。

例2 The environmental conditions' variable, (c), has at least three dimensions, in relation to time period of effects. These can be roughly characterized as short-run, medium-term, and long-run effects. The first is exemplified by responses of ecosystems and human activities to storms producing runoff from urban and non-urban areas. Therefore, runoff of nutrients in the spring may result in excessive algae growth (i.e., eutrophication) in the midsummer. Suspended sediment discharges during and following storms can impinge adversely on some types of activities in the 1CZM area, such as beach activities, including swimming. Medium-term effects are exemplified by the effects of a major storm resulting in very high fresh water inflow to an estuary, that changes the salinity profile of the estuary.

环境条件 c 是个变量，至少在三种时间尺度上造成效应：近期、中期和远期效应。风暴带来的城乡径流对生态系统和人类活动的影响可视为近期效应。因此，春季富养径流可能在仲夏引起水华（即富营养化）。风暴期间及其后所带来的悬浮泥沙会对海岸带综合管理区内游泳等海滨活动产生不利影响。大风暴引起大量淡水流入河口区，致使河口盐度分布发生变化，从而导致贝类生态环境发生变化以及产量下降，这被视为中期效应。

（2）科技语篇还有程式化的特点。程式化是指同类语篇大致相同的体例和表达方式。例如，科技论文的体例按次为：1. Title（标题）；2. Abstract（摘要）；3. Introduction（引言）；4. Materials and methods（材料与方法），或 Equipment and test/experiment procedure（设备与试验/实验过程）；5. Result（结果）；6. Discussion（讨论）；7. Conclusion（结论）；8. Acknowledgments（致谢）；9. References（参考文献）。

这些科技论文在翻译时也需要严格保持其格式体例，不能轻易变更。

（3）科技语篇的文体风格正式、质朴、陈述客观、准确。这是因为科技活动本身是一种十分严肃的事情，来不得半点马虎，在语气上比较正式。科技文章是反映客观事物的，文章中不能掺杂作者个人的主观意识，对客观事物的陈述必须客观、准确。这既是科技文章的特征，也是对科技文章作者的基本要求。在修辞手段上，科技文章少用修辞，文理清晰，描述准确,不像文学文体那样富于美学修辞(Aesthetic rhetoric)手段和艺术色彩。科技语篇主要强调语言的统一性(Unity)和连贯性(Coherence)强,语句平衡匀密,简洁而不单调,语句长而不累赘、迂回等。翻译时,要注意保持译文的风格特点。

例1 A gas may be defined as a substance which remains homogeneous, and of which the volume increases without limit, when the pressure on it is continuously reduced, the temperature being maintained constant.

所谓气体就是一种始终处于均匀状态的物质;当温度保持不变,而对其施加的压力不断降低时,气体的体积可以无限增大。

例2 Dies are usually made of cast iron. The dies should be split so that the cores and the casting can be readily removed, the cores preferably upwards so as not to interfere with gas heating of the die assembly from below. Where the die will not be tilted, sprues should be inclined, narrow, constricted at the bottom in front of the gate and arranged to fan out into the latter at an angle of 45 so as to avoid sharp corners. Several gates connected by a horizontal runner may be useful.

模具通常由铸铁制成。模具应制成可拆卸型,以确保方便地取出型芯和铸件,型芯最好朝上,以保证其不受在模具组件下方进行气体加热的影响。模具在使用过程中不倾斜时,应在浇口前方底部设置倾斜、狭窄且缢缩的注入口,并使注入口以45°角展入模具底部,以避免出现急弯。有时可能用到由一条横浇道连起来的几个浇口。

三、法律语篇的翻译

广义而言,法律语篇通常包括宪法、法律、行政法规、条令、条例、条约、合同书、协议书、契约、遗嘱、文凭、各类证书、规程等。在法制社会里,作为一个翻译工作者,无时无刻不与这些法律语篇打交道。

法律文本的翻译应遵循以下几个原则:语言明确;条理清晰;行文严谨;符合规范格式。

1.法律语篇的特点

(1)词汇特征

法律英语词语的另一个特征是专业性。因为专业术语具有国际通用性,意义明确,无歧义,不带个人感情色彩,使用范围明确。如 imputed negligence(转嫁的过失责任),特指可向与行为人有利害关系的人或有合同关系的另一方追究责任的过失。广义的法律术语则包括在法律文件中被赋予特定法律意义的现象,如 action(诉讼),party(当事人),decision(裁决),final(终局裁决)等。在翻译中,一定要注意法律语言术语译文的统一性和准确性。不能在同一篇译文中出现同一术语的不同对应译文,因为术语在不同的语境中有不同的语义。

法律专业术语多。法律文本中有相当一部分词汇是法律专业术语,它们使用频繁,地位稳定,最具有法律语言的特征,如"法人""无行为能力人""defendant(被告)""estoppel(禁止翻供)"等。它们仅出现在法律语体中,并使法律语体与其他语体如文学作品、科技作品和新闻报道等有十分明显的区别。

每一个法律术语只能表达一个特定的法律概念。法律术语的词义必须单一而固定。任何人在任何情况下必须对其有同一的解释。不仅法律专门术语要求词义单一,由民族共同语转化而来的法律词汇也必须表达单一的法律概念。有些民族共同语属于多义词,但是其中一个义项在法律语境中有特定的法律含义,这种法律词汇也被称为人工法律术语。例如"assignment"在法律语境下表示"权利或财产的转让",而不表示在日常用语中的"任务"的含义;"deed"不是日常所说的"行为",而是指法律中的"契约"。

法律语言具有权威性,它排斥多义与歧义。一些日常生活中使用的普通用语在法律文体中有了更为明确的概念含义。例如 infant 一词,在日常语言中一般指"婴儿""幼儿",但在法律上是指 21 岁或 18 岁以下的人。Demise 一词在日常英语中有许多意思,如死亡、终止、失败、职位的丧失等,但在法律上,它专指财产的转让,或称让渡,或遗赠,如指死亡亦是专指引起财产或权力转让的死亡。

常 用 单 词	一般文体含义	法律文体含义
action	行动	诉讼
alienation	疏远	转让
consideration	考虑	对价
counterpart	对方、对手	有同等效力的副本
satisfaction	满意	清偿、补偿
execution	执行	签署、签订
avoidance	逃避	宣告无效
hand	手	签名
instrument	工具	法律文件
limitation	限制	时效
prejudice	偏见	损害
presents	呈现,礼物	本法律文件
save	节省,救	除了

用词庄重。除了专门术语外,法律语言的一个显著特征是用词庄重,多用大词,吕俊、侯向群先生对此做了系统的分析和比较。下面是英语中日常用语词汇和法律文体词汇的比较:

日常用语词汇	法律用语词汇	日常用语词汇	法律用语词汇
make	render	by itself	in isolation
imagine	visualise	show	evince
place	locality	give	denote
tell	acquaint	begin	commence

常用古体词和外来词。这些古体词多为复合副词,大多是由 here,there 和 where 分别加上 after,at,by,from,in,to,under,upon,with 等一个或几个介词构成的复合副词。明白了这些词语在法律语言中的用法,就会使得翻译比较顺利。如:herewith(与此一道),therein(在其中),thereinafter(在下文中),thereof(其),thereto(附随),whereas(鉴于)等,不过这类副词实际翻译起来还是比较困难的。因此,必须首先掌握这类词的结构和语义之间的联系。这类复合词中的 here 指的是 this,即"本文件(合同,协定等)";there 指的是 that,即"另外的文件(合同,协定等)";where 指的是 what 或 which,即"那个文件(合同,协定等)"。如:hereafter,hereinafter,hereunder,含义和用法大体相同,一般可以互换,汉译时都有"自此以后""此后下

文中""以下"等意思。Herein,hereof,herewith 都可译为"在……中"。Hereby 意为"by the"(据此,特此),hereto 意为"relating to this"(与此有关)。以 there 为词根的旧体词,在汉语翻译时一般都有"那""该""其""之"的意思。以 where 为词根的旧体词,如 whereas 意为"鉴于""有鉴于";whereby 意为"凭""据"。

以 here 开头的词有:

hereupon	于是	hereunder	下文
hereto	至此	hereof	在本文中
herewith	与此一道	herein	于此
hereafter	今后	hereat	由此

以 there 开头的词有:

thereupon	在其上	thereunder	在其下
thereto	此外	thereof	由此
therewith	随即	therein	在那里

此外,还有一些以 where 开头的关系副词型的复合词,如:

whereupon	据此	whereby	借以
wherefore	为此	wherewith	用以
wherein	在那种情况下	whereof	关于那人(事,物)

这些词用来确指法律文本中的某一方或合同双方,使行文准确,从而提高法律文书的正式性。如下例:

例1 Whereas the contract between the two parties stipulated that either party may withdraw at six months' notice.

有鉴于双方之间合同规定,无论哪一方都不能提前6个月发通知来撤销合同。

这些古体词语的使用除了体现其庄重、严肃以外,还可避免不必要的重复,使意义更加清楚、简明。例如:"依照本合同相关规定",在英文商务合同中几乎见不到 according to relevant terms and conditions in the contract 这种表达方式,常见的表达方式是 pursuant to provisions contained herein 或 as provided herein 等。

词语的叠用。法律英语词语还常常使用外来词,或同义、相关词并列结构,共同来表达意思,以显示法律语言的精确性和严密性。词汇并列现象有:同义词或近义词并列,相关词并列,反义词并列以及固定模式。

terms and conditions(条件)

null and void(无效)

free and clear of(无)

made and signed(由……签订)

able and willing(能够并愿意)

purchase and sell(购买和销售)

have and hold 持有

agent or collector(代理或收款人)

covenants and agreements(契约和协议)

goods and chattels(货物与动产)

due and payable(到期应付的)

breaking and entering 闯入
will and testament 遗嘱
by and between(由……并在……之间)
and/or(和/或)
on and after(在……和在……之后)

这种词汇并列的使用可以达到两个目的：一是通过两个或多个词语的共同含义来限定其词义的唯一性，从而排除了由于一词多义可能产生的歧义，这正是法律语言必须表达严谨、杜绝语义歧义或漏洞的需要；二是通过两个或多个词语的并列来体现法律英语的历史渊源特征和正式特征。这种词汇叠用的目的是追求词义的准确性和内容的完整性，体现出法律英语的复杂性和保守性，因此在使用和翻译时是不可以随意拆开或割裂的。

例1 This contract is made by and between the Buyers and the Sellers, whereby the Buyers agree to buy and the Sellers agree to sell the under—mentioned commodity in accordance with the terms and conditions stipulated below.

句中若单独使用 by，则仅表明合同是由谁来达成的，单用 between 也只对合同签约当事人的范围进行了限定，而并列结构 by and between 的含义则比单独使用 by 或 between 更加明确，表明参与合同谈判全过程并最终签约的都是 the Buyers and the sellers，并无其他当事人。同时，并列结构 terms and conditions 表示"(合同、协议、谈判等的)条款"，其词义具有唯一性，没有任何语义歧义；属于合同用语的固定模式，体现了法律英语的正式性。

例2 The contents of a contract shall be agreed upon by the parties thereto, and shall in general, cover and include the following causes…
合同的内容由当事人约定，一般包括以下条款……

例3 The property acquired by either party as a result of a contract shall be returned to the other party after the contract is confined to be null and void or has been rescinded.
合同无效或者被撤销后，因该合同取得的财产，应当予以返还。

固定用语和套语多这是法律英语词语最明显的特征。这些固定用语中常用的是正式的古词语或拉丁词以及古体语法形式。套语在很大程度上保持了法律语言特征的稳定性、规范性和严紧性。如：Hereafter called(以下称为)；Hereafter referred to as(以下称为)；According to the terms and conditions stipulated below(根据以下所订条款)；we hereby certify/declare/guarantee(兹证实/宣布/保证)；should be taken as valid and binding(应以……为准)；are final and binding on both parties(是终局性的，对双方均有约束力)；In witness there of(特此为证)；shall have equal status in law(具有同等法律效力)等。这些套语在一定程度上使得语言准确而不易使人产生误解。

例1 Without prejudice to section 5, the following shall be treated as properly executed…
在不违背第 5 条规定的原则下，以下所言须视为正式签立……

对代词严格限制。法律英语中，指人或物的词往往重复，而不使用代词，以避免代词指代不明而引起不同的理解与解释。例如：

The Author should bear the cost of any necessary fees for textual and illustrative permissions but the Publishers agree to pay such fees on the Author's behalf up to an agreed maximum amount and may deduct the same from my sums that may become due to the Author under this Agreement.

情态动词的频繁使用。由于法律文件的权威性和约束性,其用词通常带有命令语气,因此,在法律英语中,情态动词(Modal Auxiliary)shall,may,must,should,ought to 等使用非常频繁。

"may"表示"可以做什么"(用于规定当事人的义务和责任)。

"must"表示"必须做什么"(用于规定强制性义务)。

"may not"表示"不得做什么"(用于规定禁止性义务)。

"shall"则是法律英语中最常见的情态动词,表示"应该、必须做什么",带有指令性和强制性。

"should"在法律问题中,不表示法律义务,只表示一般义务或道义上的义务,一般译为应该或应当。

"shall"在法律英语中的重要性不可忽视。它是构成现代英文法律文体特征的一个主要词汇。当 shall 作为情态动词主要与第三人称(如今有主见扩充到第二人称的趋势)一起使用时,它主要表示命令、义务、职责等强制性的语用功能。在汉语中通常被译成"须""应",有时被译成"必须",有时则译成"当""可"等。例如:

例1 Shipment:The Date of the Bill of Lading shall be accepted as a conclusive evidence of the date of shipment.

付运:提货单的日期须被承认为付运日期的确实证据。(薛华业编,1989:12-13)

例2 The Purchaser shall, upon receipt of Corporation's respective invoices therefore, pay to Corporation all amounts which become due by the Purchaser to Corporation hereunder, including without limitation an amount equal to the taxes and duties.

收到公司的各种发票后,买方必须立刻付给公司业已到期应付的所有款项,包括各种税收费用在内,不得有例外。(薛华业编,1989:60)

例3 In the event the Buyers' such appointment does not arrive in time, the Sellers' system of inspection shall be final and binding upon the parties concerned.

万一买方这种委托未能及时到达,卖方的检查制度将是决定性的并对有关各方有约束力。(薛华业编,1989:14)

(2)句法特征

长句是法律英语的最大特征。法律英语的句法特点是和法律英语的文体特征密切相连的,正式的法律条规和文本中由于对中心词的限定过多,对某一法律概念成立的条件限定很多,所以法律英语的长句居多、短句少。很多法律文书的制定者都倾向于使用远远超出英语句子的平均长度的句子,往往一个句子就是一个段落,长达数十上百个字的长句比比皆是。

长句结构复杂,能负载的含义多,包含的信息量也大,可以用来表达复杂的思想,叙事具体,说理严密,层次分明。法律英语中的长句主要指多重复合句,除主谓结构外,还有许多修饰成分,如从句、短语等,其主从关系有各种连接词贯通以表示逻辑关系,句子结构严谨。

例1 Any controversy or claim arising out of or relating to this agreement, or any breach hereof, must be settled by confidential binding arbitration in ×××(city), ×××(state) in accordance with the Commercial Arbitration Rules of the American Arbitration Association, and judgment upon the award rendered by the arbitrator may be entered in any court having jurisdiction thereof.

由本协议或违反本协议条款而产生或者与此相关的争议或索赔,必须根据《美国仲裁协会商务仲裁规定》在×××州以机密的有拘束力的仲裁方式加以解决。

例2 Each Party hereby agrees to identify, hold harmless and defend the other party from and against any and all claims, suits, losses, damages and disbursements (including legal and management costs) arising out of any alleged or actual breach of failure to comply with the terms and condition hereof including but not limit to any infringement of the other Party's intellectual property or other rights occurring as a result of the offending Party's fault, omission or activities in connection with the Project.

各方谨此同意,如另一方被指控所谓违反或实际违反与项目有关的本协议的条款,包括但不限于其知识产权或其他权利受到侵犯,是违约方的过错、不作为或活动引起的,那么,该违约方须向另一方赔偿因他引起的所有索赔、诉讼、损害和支出(包括律师费和管理费),使另一方免受损害,并为其进行抗辩。

大量使用被动句,表意较客观。在英语中,尤其在法律英语中,一般而言,在无必要说出动作发出者,或者无法说出动作发出者时,都用被动语态来表示。在将法律英语翻译成中文时,应根据汉语的理解习惯,可适当将英语被动句翻译成汉语的主动句。例如:

例1 The formation of this Contract, its The forma, interpretation, execution and settlement of disputes in connection herewith shall be governed by the laws of the People's Republic of China.

本合同的订立、效力、解释、执行及合同争议的解决,均受中华人民共和国法律管辖。

例2 Any case which involves preferring of or exemption from a public charge shall be examined and decided on by the People's procuratorate.

任何案件,不论是否需要提起公诉,均由人民检察院审查决定。

例3 Civil actions are generally brought for breach of a contract, or for a wrong or tort.

民事诉讼通常是指因违反合同、民事犯罪或侵权所提起的诉讼。

(3) 特殊句型

英语法律文本中的一些句式、短语频繁出现在,但其他文类,尤其是日常英语中极少使用。这类句型,使得英语法律文本晦涩难懂。了解和掌握这类句式的特点和含义对法律翻译者来说十分必要。

在此我们总结了几种法律语篇的特有句式,分别是:①含有 subject to 的句式;②含有 provided that/ provided...that 的句式;③含有 where 的句式;④含有 notwithstanding 的句式;⑤含有 otherwise 的句式。

含有 subject to 的句式　句式中的 subject to 在法律英语中一般都跟 agreement、section、contract 等法律文件名或文件中特定条款名配合使用。其含义是"以……为条件""根据……规定""在符合……的情况下""除……另有规定外"以及"在不抵触……下"等。例如:

例1 This condition applies if the property is sold subject to any tenancy...

如该财产是连同任何租约出售,则本条件适用……

例2 Subject to this section, an appeal shall be brought in such manner and shall be subject to such conditions as are prescribed by rules made under subsection(5).

在符合本条的规定下,上诉须按根据(5)款订立的规则内订明的方式提出,并须受该规则所订明的条件规限。

含有 where 的句式。在普通英语中,用 where 引导的从句为地点状语从句。但在英语法律文本中,where 引导的是法律条款中的条件状语从句,相当于 in the case where。通常可以用中文表达为"凡……"或"如果……"。例如:

例1 Where a defendant is fined and the same is not forthwith paid, the magistrate may order the defendant to be searched.

凡被告人被判处罚款,但没有随即缴付罚款,地方法官可命令搜查被告人。

含有 notwithstanding 的句式 介词 notwithstanding 在普通英语中已不多见,属于古旧废词之列。但在英语法律文本中该词常常被使用,其作用和 although/though/even if 等引导的状语从句基本相同,意思是"尽管……""即使……",表示一种让步。但该词所引导的并非是一个让步状语从句,因为该词后面不跟从句,而是跟一个名词性短语。例如:

例1 Notwithstanding any other agreements, the Parties shall enter into a new contract with respect to the subject matter.

尽管有任何其他协议,双方仍应就标的物签订新合同。

含有 otherwise 的句式 Otherwise 在法律英语中的用法:①跟 unless 引导的句子(让步状语从句)连用;②置放在连词 or 之后使用;③与 than 一起,通常用来否定句子的主语。

例1 In this Ordinance, unless the context otherwise requires, "state" means a territory or group of territories having its own law of nationality. (Laws of Hong Kong, Cap. 30, Wills Ordinance, Art. 2)

在本条例中,除文意另有所指外,"国家"指拥有本身国籍法的领域或一组领域。

例2 A notice under subjection (1) shall, unless it otherwise provides, apply to the income from any property specified therein as it applies to the property itself.

根据第①款发出的通知书,除其中另有订定外,亦适用于通知书内指明的财产的收入,一如适用于该项财产本身。

例3 Any person who by threats, persuasion or otherwise induces a witness or a party not to give evidence in any hearing before the Board commits an offence.

任何人借恐吓、怂恿或以其他手段诱使证人或一方当事人不在仲裁处聆讯中作证,即属犯罪。

含有 save 的句式。在法律英文中,它是一个与 except(for) 相同的介词。词源上这是一个法文词,由于历史的原因,法国人统治英国达相当长一段时间。自然而然,相当数量的、反映法国统治者意志的法语词进入了法律英语的范畴。Save 便是其中最典型的、至今仍然保留使用的一个。不管是 save 还是 except(for),之后都可跟一个名词性短语,也可以跟一个从句或另一个介词短语。save/except as(is) provided/stipulated 可以用另一个法律上常用的句式去取代:unless otherwise provided/stipulated 功能与其相同,可以是一个标准的替代。汉语的译文为"除……外"。

例1 Save as is provided in this Ordinance, no claim within the jurisdiction of the Board shall be actionable in any court.

除非本条例另有规定,否则凡属仲裁处司法管辖权范围内的申索,不得在任何法庭进行诉讼。

例2 Save under and in accordance with the provisions of this section no action shall lie in any civil court against a magistrate for any act done in a matter over which by law he has no jurisdiction or in which he has exceeded his jurisdiction.

除根据及按照本条的条文外,不得就裁判官在一项他在法律上并无司法管辖权或超越其司法管辖权的事项上所作的任何作为,在民事法庭提出针对裁判官的诉讼。

2. 法律语篇的翻译原则

(1) 专业化与精确性

法律文本翻译要求的准确性比任何文本翻译的要求都高。法律文体通常规定或隐含相关当事人的权利及相应法律后果,因此,要求译文词义确切,表达清晰,意思高度完整。如果译文译者没有做到准确翻译,那么,译文不仅无法有效传递原文信息,而且还容易被一方曲解而导致法律纠纷,或者被不法商贩故意利用文字漏洞以逃避法律责任。

在正确理解了法律文件原文含义的基础上,译者应尽量使用在本国法律中与原词对等或接近对等的专门术语来解释。对于无对等的翻译,对原文意义做正确理解后可以将之译为非法律专业用语的中性词。总之,一定要在正确理解原文的基础上正确地给出最接近的译文。

法律翻译要遵循专业化与精确性原则。强调这一原则旨在提醒译者在翻译法律文件时切记使用专业术语。

如某法律英语书中的"motion"一词被翻译成"动议"。虽然"motion"在一般英语中的意思是会议中的"动议",但在此却是诉讼程序上的专门术语。*Black's Law Dictionary* 的定义是:A written or oral application requesting a court to make a specified ruling or order. 所以"申请"是比"动议"更适合而正确的译法。《简明英汉法律辞典》将 motion 译为"申请(指诉讼人向法院提出的以求作出有利于申请人的裁决)、动议;提议;发议(议会法用语)",可见申请和动议是不能混用的。另外,如"target"在法律上为"标的"(不译"目标"),"subject matter"为"标的物"(不译"主题"),"cause of action"为"案由"(不译"行为原因")。

例1 The seller shall present the following documents required for negotiation to the banks.

原译:卖方应将下列洽谈所需资料递交银行。

改译:卖方必须将下列单据提交银行进行议付。

该例文中 negotiation 一词作为法律专业词汇,应该译为"议付"。由于译者对法律专业词汇不熟悉,所以误把其理解为"谈判、洽谈之意"。这里的错误在于译者没有找到目的语中与原文意思最接近的术语。

例2 The burden of proof rests with the defendant.

原译:证明的负担应由防守者提出。

改译:举证责任由被告承担。

例中,"burden of proof"是法律英语中的专门术语,指"举证责任",另一个表达是"onus of proof",原译"证明的负担"显然译得太不专业了,不符合法律英语的行文规范。

例3 The Vendor shall procure that the Purchaser acquires good title to the Shares free from all charges, lines, encumbrances and claims whatsoever.

原译:卖方应保证买方获得良好的股份所有权,且该股份不带任何责任、线条、负担、权益和主张。

改译:卖方应保证买方获得不容置疑的股份所有权,且该股份不带任何押记、留置、负担、权益和主张。

上述例文的原文中的"good"一词,不能翻译成普通词汇"好"。"good"一词在法律文件中的意思各种各样。在此例中,"good title"是指法律上有效的所有权,或无可争辩的所有权。

法律文本翻译专业化原则不仅涉及法律词汇的翻译,而且涉及法律文件中常用句法、句型等的翻译。如果译文具有很高的法律专业水准,自然有利于各方更有效地解决法律事务。准确和精确对法律翻译来说有着特别重要的意义,是法律翻译的最基本原则。对于正式程度较高、涉及面广或责任重大的法律文件,其译文不仅要准确,还必须达到精确的程度,否则很可能造成差之毫厘、谬之千里的严重后果。

(2) 一致性与同一性

法律翻译的一致性与同一性原则,是指在法律翻译的过程中用同一法律术语表示同一法律概念的原则,即:①在法律翻译的过程中,我们应自始至终地坚持用同一术语表示同一概念,那些看似同义或近义的词语,都有可能表示不同的概念,因此应严格禁止使用;②在法律翻译的过程中如果碰到两个或两个以上看似同义或近义的法律术语,我们应该清楚地认识到它们并非同义术语,而应尽我们的最大努力分辨它们之间存在的语义差别,运用确切的词语将它们准确地表达出来。例如在保险单中多次出现的"insured"一词,可译作"被保险人""受保人"或"投保人",但在同一份法律文件中,译者只能任择其一,连贯使用,不能三者交替。法律文件中用词讲究统一,目的就是避免各词语的意思发生相互抵触。

再如"agreement"一词通常有两种译法,即"协定"和"协议"。在1995年我国出版的《乌拉圭多边贸易谈判结果最后文件》(中英文对照)中,"General Agreement on Tariffs and Trade"(GATT)译为《关税与贸易总协定》,"General Agreement on Trade in Service"(GATS)译为《服务贸易总协定》,"Agreement on Trade-Related Aspects of Intellectual Property Rights"(TRIPS)译为《与贸易有关的知识产权协定》,其他"agreement"均译为"协议",如"Agreement on Textiles and Clothing"译为《纺织品与服装协议》。这种在一套法律文件中不一致的译法在2000年出版的《乌拉圭回合多边贸易谈判结果》中得到彻底纠正,"agreement"作为具体法律文本的名称一律译成"协定",以免给人造成"协定"的法律地位比"协议"的法律地位高的错误印象。但是动词词组"reach agreement"这一表述根据汉语习惯,译为"达成协议"或"达成一致",而不是"达成协定"。

在整个法律文件的翻译中要始终保持关键词在表述上的前后一致性,概念上始终同一,这样就能避免法律解释上的麻烦,避免因为法律文件翻译不当所引发的官司。

(3) 清晰性与简明性

现代法律文体主张简练、平实,提倡在法律文件中尽量使用易于理解的语言,避免不必要的冗词赘语的简明(法律)语言运动。在可有可无的情况下,法律原文不必逐字翻译,只选其一即可,应力求清晰简明;在必不可少的情况下,要逐一译出,汉语中不一定有对应词的情况下还要格外慎重推敲,必要的情况下可能还得新造词,但是不管属于那种情况,用词都要力求清晰简明。例如:

例1 The packing and wrapping expenses shall be borne by the Buyer.
包装费应由买方负担。

例2 If the contractor shall duly perform and observe all the terms, provisions, conditions and stipulations of the said contract, this obligation shall be null and void.
如果承包人切实履行并遵守上述合同的所有条款,本报证书所承担的义务即告无效。

例3 Taxation shall comprise all forms of taxes, including without limitation income tax, capital gains tax, stamp duty, tariffs, import and export duties, impositions, and all fines, fees and rates collected by the taxation authority and other competent authorities.

税收包括各种形式的税项,包括但不限于税务局和其他主管部门征收的所得税、印花税、资本税、关税、进出口税、各种征税,及一切罚金、收税和税款。

例4 If any person over the age of 16 years who has the custody, charge or care of any child or young person under that age willfully assaults, ill-treats, neglects, abandons or exposes such child or young person... such person shall be guilty of an offence...

任何超过16岁而对不足该年岁的儿童或少年负有管养、看管及照顾责任的人,如故意袭击、虐待、忽略、抛弃或遗弃该儿童或少年……也属犯罪。

例1中的"packing and wrapping"纯属可有可无的赘语,因为两个同义词的意思完全相同,只要翻译成一个词就可以了。例2中的"null and void"也是一样。但是例3中的税名表示性质各不相同的税收,所以得逐一译出,并且用词清晰简明。例4中"custody、charge、care"三个词概念略有不同,"custody"指"法律上的抚养权","charge"含有"带领、负责"之意,"care"是"照顾"。汉语里没有这么多对应词,译文中的"管养"就是一个新造的词,力图达到与英文的对应。

法律文本中平行结构使用很多,包括单词、词组、从句、段落以及其他多层次的平行结构。这种结构不仅看上去一目了然,更重要的是具有同等效果或起类似作用的法律效果。Richard K. Neumann(2001:223)指出,要表达一组类似的事物或思想必须要用一致的结构和同样的语法构造,即法律文本的句式往往包含多个短语,每个短语的语法结构都应该相同或平行。翻译时尽量保留平行结构、保持语法一致也是使句式保持简明的手段之一。例如:

例1 Producers of toxic chemicals have the following options: (1) <u>require</u> purchasers to assume responsibility for subsequent spills, (2) <u>deposit</u> money in a damages escrow fund, (3) <u>terminate</u> production, or (4) <u>post</u> a conspicuous disclaimer of liability on every container.

有毒化学品的生产者具有下列选择:(1)要求买方承担由泄漏而造成的责任;(2)<u>交纳赔偿保证金</u>;(3)<u>停止生产</u>;(4)在每只集装箱上贴明显的免责标签。

例句原文将4个可供选择的选项用数字表明,各选项都采用动词词组形式,构成平行结构,内容表达清晰明了,译文同样很好地保留了动词的平行结构。

简明清晰也是法律翻译的一种必要原则。译者可采取灵活的手法,尽量将译文的意思用简洁、精练的词语和句式表达出来,以便准确地传递相关信息。

英语法律文书中绝大多数句子都是长句,可以先将长句化繁为简、化整为零,以得出句子的主干成分。然后将各成分译出后根据其在句中的作用还原到特定位置,或经过语序调整,以形成最终译文。翻译时既要考虑行文的层次性和先后顺序,又不能生搬硬套,忽略了句子的逻辑性和前后关联性。例如:

例1 Both Parties their servants agents representatives or advisors will treat as confidential this Agreement and any agreements supplemental thereto and all its terms and conditions and shall not at any time unless required by law disclose the same or any part thereof to any other person or body without the consent of the other Party!

协议双方当事人、工作人员代理人、代表或顾问应将该协议、补充协议和所有条款和条件视为机密，不论何时，不经另一方同意，均不得将它们或其中一部分向其他任何人或任何团体公开。

该句包含若干个从句及许多短语，较为复杂，翻译时适当调整了部分成分的顺序和结构，处置得当，既不违背原意，又符合汉语的语言习惯，较为流畅准确。

The BMW 7 Series

SOMETIMES SOMETHING HAPPENS THAT MAKES US LOOK AT THINGS IN A COMPLETELY NEW LIGHT. SOMETHING THAT SETS STANDARDS WITHOUT COMPROMISING CORE PRINCIPLES.

IT'S TIME FOR A NEW DEFINITION.

STYLE

Inner values, outwardly expressed.

The BMW 7 Series. True visionaries are impossible to categorise because true vision is always unique. Pioneers do not tread well-worn paths because new routes lead to new perspectives. And virtuosos do not set things in stone because free thinking means full creative expression. The results are often beyond compare and this car is the perfect example. The BMW 7 Series-style redefined.

Some encounters make a particularly captivating impression-as demonstrated by the BMW 7 Series Saloon. Even the rear profile impresses the beholder: a dynamic design perfected with the utmost elegance. Its horizontal contouring, emphasised by the distinctive chrome strips, accentuates the visual impression of width. And the rear lights, set within a contrasting double L-shaped design, round off an exclusive overall picture with their striking night-time presence. Even in the dark, the BMW 7 Series is unmistakably unique.

ENERGY

Turning vision into advantage: the dynamics of the BMW 7 Series.

When great passion and outstanding innovative power meet, an energy arises that is hard to resist. As you will discover when driving the BMW 7 Series. The combination of comfort, dynamics and efficiency at the highest level is without equal. Advanced engines with BMW Twin Power Turbo technology emphasise the car's leadership position when it comes to the balance of impressive performance and efficient fuel consumption. The intelligent BMW xDrive all-wheel system transfers engine power optimally to every road, whether on tight bends, slippery surfaces or you're making a hill-start and thus ensures an even greater feeling of safety in every driving situation. Technology like this not only provides typical BMW agility, but also superior driving comfort. And that gives drivers of the BMW 7 Series one thing above all: energy.

RESPECT

Gives everything, misses nothing. BMW EfficientDynamicsin the BMW 7 Series.

Bring contrasts into perfect harmony, equate responsibility with excitement, make less more-turning the impossible into the standard deserves recognition. With BMW EfficientDynamics, the

BMW 7 Series is equipped with one of the newest and most comprehensive technology packages to reduce fuel consumption and increase driving dynamics-from intelligent lightweight construction via BMW TwinPower Turbo technology through to ECO PRO mode. In this way, it even further enhances its role model status in its class. Not because it makes compromises, but because it takes a firm stance: for more efficiency and more driving pleasure.

Driving pleasure is a core competence of every BMW. As is low fuel consumption. This apparent contradiction is resolved, among other ways, by the innovative drive concepts of the BMW 7 Series. To illustrate the point, here are just two examples from the impressive engine range. The BMW 750d xDrive1 with TwinPower Turbo technology sets new standards for driving enjoyment, low fuel consumption and reduced emissions. And the BMW Active Hybrid 7, with its hybrid technology and intelligent energy management, takes the combination of efficiency, low emissions and dynamics to unprecedented heights.

CONVINCING, RESPONSIBLE, FORWARD-LOOKING-THE BMW 7 SERIES WITH ECO PRO MODE

More performance with less emissions-the aim of BMW EfficientDynamics. To this end, the innovative technology package optimises the interplay between the driver and the environment. The best example of this is ECO PRO mode1, which always finds the most efficient route to driving pleasure with a multitude of possibilities. Its integration into the Driving Experience button is proof enough. As impressive as the Comfort+, Comfort, Sport and Sport+ modes, ECO PRO not only gears the whole vehicle towards maximum efficiency, it also, with ECO PRO tips, supports an efficient driving style. Fuel savings can reach up to 20% 2 depending on individual driving behaviour.

ECO PRO mode offers special advantages through the intelligent fusion of the latest technologies. Preview Assistant 3, for instance, uses navigation data and informs the driver in good time when to lift off the accelerator due to upcoming speed restrictions. There's also the Coasting function, which enables you to glide along the road without power and, therefore, minimum fuel consumption. This is intelligence that pays dividends-with every kilometre.

CLARITY

All you need to know. BMW ConnectedDrive in the BMW 7 Series. Wherever we go, we are always surrounded by information-vasts amount of it. The skill is to filter out what matters and make it accessible at the right place and at the right time. Which is where BMW ConnectedDrive-a wealth of technology for more safety, convenience and infotainment-comes in. These are innovations that improve visibility in the dark and warn in good time of fatigue.

They ensure that driver focus always remains on the road and they practically do away with blind spots. The BMW 7 Series always knows in advance what to expect, with safety and convenience remaining the focus at all times thanks to clear, self-explanatory menus. Essentially, the whole world is present inside this vehicle. To be more accurate, the part you need to know about at any given moment.

EQUALS

As rare as it is significant: meeting someone who shares the same goals, who speaks the same language and on whom you can rely one hundred per cent. The BMW 7 Series is such a companion-and your equal at the highest level. Every detail in the cockpit has been created with the driver in mind, from the iDrive Controller to the optional full-colour BMW Head-Up Display from BMW ConnectedDrive *. The latter projects all driving-relevant information into your immediate field of vision, so your eyes are always focused on the road. Not only is this safer, but it also significantly increases driving comfort. Because this is what defines the perfect partner: they always make you feel good.

The interior of the BMW 7 Series not only convinces with its high-quality, luxurious character, but also with its functionality. One central reason for this is that all cockpit controls are geared towards the needs of the driver. One, not immediately obvious, feature is particularly impressive: the optional Multifunctional Instrument Display from BMW ConnectedDrive. Only the chrome rings indicate what to expect once the start button is pressed. You soon see, however, a completely new set of display functions that clearly demonstrate the prowess of the BMW 7 Series. All important information is presented in the Multifunctional Instrument Display according to the driver's exact requirements. The zoom function, with its various size options, is just one of many examples and ensures even greater driving comfort.

(1101 words)

参考文献

[1] Baker, Mona. In Other Words: A Coursebook on Translation. Beijing: Foreign Language Teaching and Research Press, 2000.

[2] Munday, Jeremy. Introducing Translation Studies: Theories and Applications. Routledge. 2016.

[3] Newmark, Peter. A Textbook of Translation. Shanghai: Shanghai Foreign Language Education Press, 2001.

[4] Nida, Eugene A. & Charles R. Taber. The Theory and Practice of Translation. Leiden: E. J. Brill, 1969/1982.

[5] Nord, Christiane. Text Analysis in Translation. Amsterdam: Rodopi, 1991.

[6] Venuti, Lawrence. The Translator's Invisibility: A History of Translation. London & New York: Routledge, 1995.

[7] 陈文伯.译艺　英汉汉英双向笔译[M].北京:世界知识出版社,2004.

[8] 方梦之,毛忠明.英汉—汉英应用翻译综合教程[M].上海:上海外语教育出版社,2014.

[9] 冯庆华.文体翻译论[M].上海:上海外语教育出版社,2008.

[10] 冯庆华.实用翻译教程　英汉互译[M].3版.上海:上海外语教育出版社,2010.

[11] 胡安江.新编应用语篇翻译教程[M].上海:上海交通大学出版社,2016.

[12] 胡显耀,李力.高级文学翻译[M].北京:外语教学与研究出版社,2009.

[13] 黄忠廉,等.译文观止例话篇[M].北京:语文出版社,2009.

[14] 黄忠廉.翻译变体研究[M].北京:中国对外翻译出版公司,2000.

[15] 金圣华.齐向译道行[M].北京:商务印书馆,2011.

[16] 李基亚,冯伟年.论戏剧翻译的原则和途径[J].西北大学学报(哲学社会科学版),2004(04):161-165.

[17] 连淑能.英汉对比研究[M].北京:高等教育出版社,1993.

[18] 廖七一.胡适诗歌翻译研究[M].北京:清华大学出版社,2006.

[19] 刘宓庆.英汉翻译技能指引[M].北京:中国对外翻译出版公司,2006.

[20] 马红军.翻译批评散论[M].北京:中国对外翻译出版公司,2000.

[21] 毛荣贵,廖晟.译谐译趣[M].北京:中国对外翻译出版公司,2005.

[22] 毛荣贵,张琦.译文比读分析　译然自得[M].北京:中国对外翻译出版公司,2005.

[23] 邵志洪,邵惟韺.新编英汉语研究与对比[M].上海:华东理工大学出版社,2013.

[24] 邵志洪.英汉对比翻译导论[M].上海:华东理工大学出版社,2010.

[25] 孙致礼.新编英汉翻译教程[M].上海:上海外语教育出版社,2011.

[26] 王东风.英汉名译赏析[M].北京:外语教学与研究出版社,2014.

[27] 王东风.以平仄代抑扬　找回遗落的音美:英诗汉译声律对策研究[J].外国语,2019(1):72-82+110.

[28] 肖开容,罗天.汉英翻译教程[M].北京:中国人民大学出版社,2018.

[29] 胥瑾.英汉对比与翻译教程[M].北京:化学工业出版社,2010.

[30] 杨全红.高级翻译十二讲[M].武汉:武汉大学出版社,2009.
[31] 张经浩,陈可培.名家 名论 名译[M].上海:复旦大学出版社,2005.
[32] 张美芳.功能途径论翻译:以英汉翻译为例[M].北京:外文出版社,2015.
[33] 张威.戏剧翻译的理论与实践——英若诚戏剧翻译评析[J].广东外语外贸大学学报,2014,24(02):68-71.
[34] 张彦.科学术语翻译概论[M].杭州:浙江大学出版社,2008.

附录 1 英汉译音表

国际音标	辅音																						
元音	单音读法	b	p	d	t	g	k	v	f	z dz	s	ʃ	dʒ	tʃ	θ ð	h	m	n	l	r	w	hw	kw	j	ts
a, aː, æː, ʌ	阿	布	普	德	特	格	克	弗[夫]	弗[夫]	兹	斯	什	吉	奇	思	赫	姆	恩	尔	尔	伍			伊	茨
ai	艾	巴[芭]	帕	达	塔	加	卡	瓦[娃]	法	扎	萨	沙	贾	查	撒	哈	马[玛]	纳[娜]	拉	拉	瓦		夸	亚	茨
ei, e	埃	拜	派	代[戴]	泰	盖	凯	瓦伊	法伊	扎伊	赛	沙伊	贾伊	蔡	赛	海	迈	奈	莱	赖	怀	怀	夸伊		蔡
e, ə	厄	伯	佩	代[戴]	泰	盖	凯	维	法	泽	塞	谢	贾伊	蔡	塞	黑	迈	内	莱	赖	韦	惠	奎	耶	蔡
i, iː	伊	比	珀	德	特	格	克	弗	弗	泽	塞	舍	杰	切	瑟	赫	梅	纳	勒	雷	沃		夸	耶	策
u, uː	乌	布	皮	迪	蒂	吉	基	维	菲	齐	西[锡]	希	吉	彻	西[锡]	希	默	尼	利[莉]	里[丽]	威	惠	奎	伊	齐
ɔ, ɔː	奥	博	波	多	图	古	库	武	富	朱	苏	舒	朱	奇	苏	胡	米	努	卢	鲁	伍	霍	库	尤	楚
əu, ou	奥	保	波	道	托	戈	科	沃	弗	佐	索	肖	乔	乔	索	霍	莫	诺	洛	罗	沃			约	佐
au	奥	鲍	保	陶	陶	高	考	沃	福	佐	索	肖	乔	乔	索	蒙	毛	瑙	劳	劳	沃	霍		姚	
juː, ju	尤	比尤	皮尤	迪尤	蒂尤	久	丘	维尤	菲尤	齐尤	休	休	久	丘	休	休	米尤	纽						尤	
æm, aːm æn, aːn	安	班	潘	丹	坦	甘	坎	范	范	赞	桑	香	詹	钱	桑	汉	曼	南[楠]	兰	兰	万		夸	扬	
ain	艾因	拜因	派因	戴因	泰因	盖因	凯因	瓦因	法因	扎因	赛因	沙因	贾因	查因	赛因	海因	迈因	奈因	莱因	赖因	瓦因	怀因			茨因

· 240 ·

续上表

国际音标	辅音	b	p	d	t	g	k	v	f	z dz	s	ʃ	dʒ	tʃ	θ ð	h	m	n	l	r	w	hw	kw	j	ts
ən, əm en, em	恩	本	彭	登	坦	根	肯	文	芬	增	森	申	詹	琴	森	亨	门	南[楠]	伦	伦	温		昆	延	岑
in, im	因	宾	平	丁	廷	金	金	文	芬	津	辛	欣	津	钦	辛	欣	明	宁	林	林	温		昆	英	青
aun, ɔːn, ɔːm, ɔm	昂	邦	庞	唐	汤	冈	康	冯	方	藏	桑	肖 恩	琼	琼	桑	杭	芒	农	朗	朗	旺		匡	扬	仓
uːn, un, uŋ, uːm, um	翁	本	蓬	东[栋]	通	贡	孔	冯	丰	宗	松	雄	琼	琼	松	洪	蒙	农	隆	龙	温		孔	荣	聪
ʌn, ʌm	昂	邦	庞	邓	滕	冈	孔	文	丰	增	森	申	琼	琼	森	亨	芒	南[楠]	伦	朗	旺		昆	扬	岑

附录2 英汉标点符号对照表

标点符号是书面语言的有机组成部分,是书面语言不可缺少的辅助工具。它帮助人们确切地表达思想感情和理解书面语言。标点符号的正确使用和转换也是译者必须掌握的技能。

NO.	中文标点		English punctuations	
1	句号	。	Period, Full stop	.
2	逗号	,	Comma	,
3	问号	?	Question mark	?
4	感叹号	!	Exclamation mark	!
5	分号	;	semicolon	;
6	引号	" " ' ' 〝 〞	Quotation Mark	" " ' '
7	括号	( ) { }	Parenthesis	( )
8	方括号	[ ]	Brackets	[ ]
9	冒号	:	Colon	:
10	省略号	……	Ellipsis	…
11	破折号	——	Dash	—
12	斜线号	/	Slash	/
13	间隔号	·(用于人名等)		
14	顿号	、		
15	书名号	《 》		
16	着重号	.		
17			Apostrophe	'(省略/所有格)
18			hyphen	-
19			Underlining	_____

附录3 语料库与翻译

语料库通常指为语言研究收集的、用电子形式保存的语言材料,由自然出现的书面语或口语的样本汇集而成,用来代表特定的语言或语言变体。经过科学选材和标注、具有适当规模的语料库能够反映和记录语言的实际使用情况。

与词典的主要功能(提供词语用法、搭配、同义词等)相比,语料库功能更为强大。语料库可为翻译提供如下帮助:①语料库提供的都是真实的语例,具有现实指导意义。因为凭空臆造的翻译文本很容易误导读者,或造成理解困难。②语料库可以使清楚地看到自己平时没有留意但却是经常使用的语言形式,拓展译者的语言技能。③语料库可以提供词语使用的语境,通过条件检索,确定译文的可接受程度、可读性。④语料库提供大量语言使用的变体以及新鲜而有创意的形式,体现出语言的最新发展和变化,使译者能够紧跟时代变换。

下面推荐一些优质的英语语料库资源,以应翻译之需。

一、英语语料库资源

1.杨百翰大学语料库

https://corpus.byu.edu/

杨百翰大学的 Mark Davies 教授开发的语料库统一检索平台,整合了美国当代英语语料库、美国历史英语语料库、美国时代杂志语料库、英国英语国家语料库、西班牙语料库、葡萄牙语料库等15个语料库的资源。是目前世界上最广泛使用的网络语料库。

2.美国当代英语语料库(COCA)

http://www.americancorpus.org

该语料库由美国 Brigham Young University 的 Mark Davies 教授开发,高达3.6亿词汇的美国最新当代英语语料,是当今世界上最大的英语平衡语料库。与其他语料库不同的是它是免费在线,供大家使用的,给全世界英语学习者带来了福音,是不可多得的一个英语学习宝库,也是观察美国英语使用和变化的一个绝佳窗口。

3.英国国家语料库(The British National Corpus online)

http://www.natcorp.ox.ac.uk/

英国国家语料库(British National Corpus,简称BNC)是目前网络可直接使用的最大的语料库之一,也是目前世界上最具代表性的当代英语语料库之一。由英国牛津出版社、朗文出版公司、牛津大学计算机服务中心、兰卡斯特大学英语计算机中心以及大英图书馆等联合开发建立,于1994年完成。英国国家语料库词容量超过一亿,由4124篇现代英式英语文本构成。其中书面语占90%,口语占10%。

4.国际英语语料库(ICE)

https://www.ucl.ac.uk/english-usage/projects/ice-gb/

CE-GB is the British component of the International Corpus of English (ICE). It began in 1990 with the primary aim of providing material for comparative studies of varieties of English throughout the world. More than twenty centres around the world are preparing corpora of their own national or regional variety of English. These include Australia, Cameroon, Canada, East Africa (Kenya, Malawi, Tanzania), Fiji, Great Britain(parsed), Hong Kong, India, Ireland, Jamaica,

Kenya, etc. ICE-GB is fully grammatically analysed. Like all the ICE corpora, ICE-GB consists of a million words of spoken and written English and adheres to the common corpus design. 200 written and 300 spoken texts make up the million words. Every text is grammatically annotated, permitting complex and detailed searches across the whole corpus. ICE-GB contains 83,394 parse trees, including 59,640 in the spoken part of the corpus. This is the biggest collection of parsed spoken material anywhere with the exception of DCPSE(which only contains spoken material). The picture below shows ICECUP 3.1 displaying a single tree from the spoken part of the corpus.

5. 美国公开国家语料库(ANC) The Open American National Corpus

http://www.anc.org/

It is a massive electronic collection of American English, including texts of all genres and transcripts of spoken data produced from 1990 onward. All data and annotations are fully open and unrestricted for any use. Available Data and Annotations includes: (1) OANC: 15 million words of contemporary American English with automatically-produced annotations for a variety of linguistic phenomena; (2) MASC: 500,000 words of OANC data equally distributed over 19 genres of American English, with manually produced or validated annotations for several layers of linguistic phenomena.

6. A collection of English corpora(University of Leeds)

http://corpus.leeds.ac.uk/protected/query.html

The corpora listed above: 1. BNC, a classic 100MW corpus, 2. A corpus of British News, a collection of news stories from 2004 from each of the four major British newspapers: Guardian/Observer, Independent, Telegraph and Times, 200 million words. 3. I-EN, a 150MW Internet corpus collected by Serge Sharoff using random queries to Google; 4. the Reuters corpus, a collection of newswires from Reuters for one year from 1996-08-20 to 1997-08-19, 90 million words. 5. UK-WAC, a 2GW corpus of English UK webpages collected by Marco Baroni and his colleagues(it's huge; handle this corpus with care), 6. BASE, British Academic Spoken English, collected by Hilary Nesi and colleagues at Coventry University The interface has been designed by Serge Sharoff, University of Leeds. The source code is hosted under the GPL open source license on http://csar.sourceforge.net

7. Michigan Corpus of Academic Spoken English

http://quod.lib.umich.edu/m/micase/

An on-line, searchable part of our collection of transcripts of academic speech events recorded at the University of Michigan. There are currently 152 transcripts(totaling 1,848,364 words) available at this site.

8. SkELL

http://skell.sketchengine.co.uk

SkELL(Sketch Engine for Language Learning) is a simple tool for students and teachers of English to easily check whether or how a particular phrase or a word is used by real speakers of English. No registration or payment required. Just type a word and click a button. All examples, collocations and synonyms were identified automatically by ingenious algorithms and state-of-the-art software analysing large multi-billion samples of text. No manual work was involved. It is the ultimate tool to explore how language works. Its algorithms analyze authentic texts of billions of words(text corpora)to identify instantly what is typical in language and what is rare, unusual or emerging usage. It is also designed for text analysis or text mining applications. Sketch Engine is used by linguists, lexicographers, translators, students and teachers. It is a first choice solution for publishers, universities, translation agencies and national language institutes throughout the world. It contains 500 ready-to-use corpora in 90+ languages, each having a size of up to 30 billion words to provide a truly representative sample of language.

9.Stringnet

http://nav4.stringnet.org/index.php

StringNet is an English lexico-grammatical knowledgebase consisting of multiword patterns of word behavior. These are represented by what we call hybrid n-grams and their relations to each other. Currently, StringNet contains about two billion hybrid n-grams extracted from the British National Corpus(BNC), each hybrid n-gram linked to all tokens attested in BNC. The design and motivation of(an earlier version of)StringNet are described in Wible and Tsao(2010).

10.JustTheWord

http://www.just-the-word.com/

JustTheWord is a completely new kind of aid to help you with writing English and choosing just the word. If English is your first language, it can help you express that elusive idea with le mot juste. If you're learning English, it can justify your choice of words or suggest improvements - and it knows about some common errors made by speakers of your mother tongue. When we write, we search our knowledge of words in two ways. We choose between words that mean similar things. A thesaurus gives us access to this sort of knowledge. But our choice constrains and is constrained by the other words in the sentence. We know, or need to know, which word combinations sound natural. A dictionary gives us access to some of this sort of knowledge. By analysing a huge amount of English text, we've built up a highly detailed knowledge base of the word combinations whose mastery is at the heart of fluent English.

二、汉语语料库资源

1.国家语委现代汉语语料库

http://www.cncorpus.org/CnCindex.aspx

大规模的平衡语料库,语料选材类别广泛,时间跨度大。现代汉语语料库在线提供免费检索的语料约2000万字,为分词和词性标注语料。可以网络查询,检索速度更快,功能强,同时提供检索结果下载。

2.国家语委古代汉语语料库

http://www.cncorpus.org/ACindex.aspx

网站现在还增加了一亿字的古代汉语生语料,研究古代汉语的也可以去查询和下载。含四库全书中的大部分古籍资料。部分书目如下:诗经、尚书、周易、老子、论语、孟子、左传、楚辞、礼记、大学、中庸、吕氏春秋、史记、战国策、三国志、文心雕龙、全唐诗、朱子语类、封神演义、三国演义、水浒传、西游记、红楼梦、儒林外史等。同时,还提供了分词、词性标注软件、词频统计、字频统计软件,基于国家语委语料库的字频词频统计结果和发布的词表等,以供学习研究语言文字的老师同学使用。

3. 新词语语料库

http://ling.cuc.edu.cn/newword/

"新词语研究资源库"是中国传媒大学国家语言资源监测与研究有声媒体中心承担建设,它包括以下四个部分:新词语词库,收集了编年本词条约10150条;研究文献库,收集了新词语词典(160余部)、期刊论文(353篇)、会议论文(29篇)、硕士论文(98篇)、博士论文(24篇)和专著(29部);传媒语料库,包括传媒语言生语料(约1亿字)和传媒语言熟语料;词汇变化图,可以查看某个词语在传媒语料库中的历时变化图表。

4. 现代汉语语料库

http://ncl.xmu.edu.cn/shj/jcfccorpus?id=3

厦门大学国家语言资源监测与研究教育教材中心"现代汉语语料库"含报纸、博客、网站新闻、文学作品、杂志、口语材料、教材语料等内容,规模近2亿字。提供在线按字符串和分词单位检索的检索功能,支持"正则表达式"。"现代汉语语料库"在国家社科基金项目"基于国家语委'通用语料库'之上的汉语义频词库的开发"及厦门大学国家语言资源监测与研究教育教材中心其他课题中得到应用并不断完善。

5. 全球华语语料库

https://huayu.jnu.edu.cn/source.aspx

暨南大学华文学院海外华语研究中心建设,主要包括四个子库:①东南亚主要华文媒体语料库来源以新加坡、马来西亚和泰国等主流媒体为主,语料时间跨度为2005年到2008年,总共文本数为343978个,约3亿字。已经分词和标注词性。②东南亚小学华文教材语料库以新加坡、马来西亚、菲律宾、印尼、越南的小学华文教材为主。选取了20套、约240本小学华文教材,已经输入电脑,总共约300万字。已经进行自动分词,并标注了词性。③东南亚华裔留学生作文语料库收集了2001—2010年的留学生作文,大约400万字。④东南亚华裔留学生口语语料库收集了2001—2010年的留学生口语,大约20万字。

6. 泛华语地区汉语共时语料库

http://www.livac.org/

LIVAC汉语共时语料库(Linguistic Variation in Chinese Speech Communities)来源权威、语料广泛,数据量庞大。直至2016年,LIVAC已累计过滤25亿汉字语料,已处理6.0亿多字,持续提炼出200多万词条。采用"共时性"窗口模式,显示内容丰富。此外,语料库又兼顾了"历时性",方便有意者以专词搜索(KWIC),以便客观地观察与研究视窗内20多年来有代表性的语用发展全面动态。语料库在1995—2018年持续更新。全时段地区分布、实际例句、分词标注等。

7. 兰开斯特汉语语料库(LCMC)

http://ota.oucs.ox.ac.uk/scripts/download.php?otaid=2474

由兰开斯特大学语言学系承担的并得到英国经社研究委员会资助(项目代号:RES-000-220135)的研究项目。LCMC语料库是与Freiburg-LOB Corpus of British English(即FLOB)平行对应的汉语语料库,它有助于我们从事汉语的单语和英汉双语的对比研究。通过上述网址可以免费索取LCMC语料用于研究之用。

三、英汉对照或多语料库

1. Jukuu（句酷）

http://www.jukuu.com/

句酷,2004年初创立于北京邮电大学的双语例句搜索引擎。依靠中文词语处理、信息抽取、智能挖掘等技术,经过近4年的不断发展,已经积累了上千万的双语例句,拥有中英、中日、日英三种语言对和覆盖全国的广大用户群,其中又以白领、译员和大学生居多。句酷的双语例句库具备语料量大、覆盖面广、真实地道的特点,可以部分地解决两个问题:（1）说（写）出来的英语对不对？（2）说（写）出来的英语是否符合外国人的习惯？

2. BCC 语料库

http://bcc.blcu.edu.cn/

北京语言大学大数据与语言教育研究建 BCC 汉语语料库,总字数约150亿字,包括：报刊(20亿字)、文学(30亿字)、微博(30亿字)、科技(30亿字)、综合(10亿字)和古汉语(20亿字)等多领域语料,是可以全面反映当今社会语言生活的大规模语料库。其中,还包括法语和英语语料。英语语料主要由华尔街日报(Wall Street Journal)的语言资源构成。

3. 中国汉英平行语料大世界（绍兴文理学院）

http://corpus.usx.edu.cn/

中国汉英平行语料库由绍兴文理学院创建,收录了大量中国经典文学作品的双语语料,并提供免费的检索功能。分为传统典籍、四大名著、其他名著、鲁迅小说、伟人作品以及全国（包括港澳台）法律法规等子库。其中,传统典籍子库中还包括了《楚辞》《大学》《老子》《庄子》《孟子》《论语》《孙子兵法》《墨子》《易经》等古典典籍。

4. "中国特色话语对外翻译标准化术语库"

http://210.72.20.108/index/index.jsp

中国特色话语对外翻译标准化术语库是中国外文局、中国翻译研究院主持建设的首个国家级多语种权威专业术语库,是服务国家话语体系建设和中国文化国际交流的基础性工程。目前,平台发布了中国最新政治话语、马克思主义中国化成果、改革开放以来党政文献、敦煌文化等多语种专业术语库的5万余条专业术语,并已陆续开展少数民族文化、佛教文化、中医、非物质文化遗产等领域的术语编译工作。该术语库平台以语种的多样性、内容的权威性为突出特色,提供中文与英、法、俄、德、意、日、韩、西、阿等多种语言的术语对译查询服务。

5. 哈工大信息检索研究室对外共享语料库资源

http://ir.hit.edu.cn/demo/ltp/Sharing_Plan.htm

该语料库为汉英双语语料库,10万对齐双语句对,同义词词林扩展版。77343条词语,秉承《同义词词林》的编撰风格,同时采用五级编码体系,多文档自动文摘语料库。40个主题,同一主题下是同一事件的不同报道。汉语依存树库,不带关系5万句,带关系1万句,LTML 化,分词、词性、句法部分人工标注,可以图形化查看。问答系统问题集,6264句,已标注问题类型,LTML 化,分词、词性、句法、词义、浅层语义等程序处理得到。单文档自动文摘语料库,211篇,分不同体裁,LTML 化,文摘句标注,分词、词性、句法、词义、浅层语义、文本分类、指代消解等程序处理得到。

6.联合国文件数据库

https://documents.un.org/prod/ods.nsf/home.xsp

本文件系统包括了 1993 年以来联合国印发的所有正式文件。不过,联合国的早期文件也逐日添加到本系统。本文件系统也提供从 1946 年以来联合国大会、安全理事会、经济及社会理事会和托管理事会通过的所有决议。本系统不提供新闻稿、联合国出版物、联合国条约汇编或新闻部印发的新闻材料。由日本捐赠的 3 万多份数字化文件已被增添进正式文件系统。

附录4 计算机辅助翻译

当今社会,信息技术迅猛发展,全球化程加快,全球信息爆炸式增长,对翻译行业产生了巨大的影响,翻译迅速转变为一种产业。在这样的新形式和背景下,职业译员不仅要有过硬的语言功底、较强的翻译能力,还要掌握现代翻译技术,运用一些机辅翻译软件,完成数量巨大的翻译任务时。借助当代计算机技术,运用恰当的翻译软件,可以提高翻译工作效率,保障翻译质量。

目前,市场上流行的翻译软件主要有三种:电子词典、机器翻译软件及计算机辅助翻译软件。

一是电子词典。相比纸质词典,电子词典使用方便快捷,输入一个英文单词后便可以找到该单词的中文解释、音标,有的产品还可以进行实际的发声演示。现在也有桌面电子词典,如金山词霸、babylon、灵格斯词霸、有道桌面词典等,优势在于可以实现双向查询,词义收录较全,例句丰富。

二是机器翻译软件。机器翻译(Machine Translation),就是用电脑代替人工做翻译,一般是把一门语言转换为另外一门语言,而且是全文翻译。与传统的人工翻译相比,机器翻译的反馈速度更快、成本更低,能同时处理大数量的翻译要求。当然,机器翻译也存在一些劣势。目前软件在翻译时只是句法结构和词汇的机械对应,不会从上下文语境对单词、句法等进行分析,所以译文质量很难让人满意,机器翻译在很长一段时间内还是无法达到人工翻译的质量水平。常见的全文翻译的软件,有google的全文翻译、百度翻译、金山快译、东方快车等。

三是计算机辅助翻译(CAT,Computer-Aided Translation)软件。要解决译文质量和翻译效率这对矛盾,目前而言,也许唯一的答案就是机辅翻译。它把计算机的高速能力(查找、替换、提示等)与翻译人员的丰富经验和最终裁决结合在一起,是基于历史语料回收的一种记忆软件。历史语料库越大,效率越高。机辅翻译软件是大项目或长期项目客户的最佳选择。从相关问卷调查的结果可见,Trados,Deja Vu,Wordfast和雅信是国内外比较常见的四种CAT软件。

机辅翻译透过人工智能搜寻及比对技术,运用参考数据库和翻译记忆程式,记录译员所完成的译文,遇到相同与重复的句型、词组或专业术语时,能给译员提供建议和解决方案,有效节省翻译时间及成本,同时确保翻译品质与风格的一致性。因此,它能够帮助翻译者优质、高效、轻松地完成翻译工作。

机辅翻译软件技术的核心是翻译记忆(Translation Memory)技术。科学研究表明,翻译中重复的工作量高达30%,许多企业的这个数字更高。如欧盟的许多资料翻译重复率接近100%,微软的许多项目重复率也高达60%。在翻译过程中,如此大量重复或相似的句子和片段,哪怕是最简单的句子,译者也需要书写一遍,因此十分耗时费力。使用机辅翻译软件进行翻译,译者在不停地工作时,软件则在后台忙于建立语言数据库,存储译者翻译的内容,这就是所谓的翻译记忆。翻译记忆是译者运用计算机程序部分参与翻译过程的一种翻译策略(Shuttleworth & Cowie,2004:98)。

除了记忆功能,翻译记忆技术还有提示功能。译者使用软件翻译到某个句子时,系统自动搜索用户已经翻译过的句子,如果当前翻译的句子曾经翻译过,会自动给出以前的翻译结果;对于相似的句子,也会给出翻译参考和建议,译者可以根据自己的需要,采用、舍弃或编辑重复出现的文本。

机辅翻译软件是一个不断积累翻译资源的工具,它会在翻译过程中为用户不断积累翻译的句子和新的短语,以原文和译文句子一一对应的方式存储下来;还可以将用户曾经翻译过的资料转换为可以重复使用的记忆库。这样,用户就无需重复以前的劳动,从而提高翻译速度和准确性。

因此,翻译记忆技术有两个主要优势:一是重复的内容可以循环利用,因此可以提高翻译效率,缩短翻译项目周期,节省花费。二是翻译风格更加统一,翻译质量得到保证,相同的句子不会有不同的译文。

除了翻译记忆技术,机辅翻译软件还有其他的辅助功能,具体而言主要有以下三种:

第一种,术语管理(Terminology Database Management)功能。一般来说,机辅翻译软件都有术语库,术语库是存储术语的地方。术语库不仅可以保存术语的文字释义,还能保存与该术语相关的图片、音频、视频等材料,以便译者更详细地了解该术语的意义和用法。使用软件翻译时,如果译者挂载术语库,翻译时就可以在术语库里查找相关术语的释义;术语库还能在翻译时主动识别术语,提示用户该术语的释义,译者还能选择将新的术语存入记忆库,以备将来使用。

第二种,辅助功能,也叫作翻译对齐(Alignment)功能。这种功能主要用于整理以前的翻译资源,译者可以利用软件的这个功能,把以前翻译过的文字材料做成记忆库。广义上说,翻译中出现的任何词汇,如果有重复使用的必要,都可以作为术语进行保存,保存的术语集合则成为术语库。术语库也可以为某个客户或产品存储特定的术语,这些术语在一般的词典上可能难以找到。术语库还可以重复利用,不仅是本次翻译,还可以在以后的项目或其他人的翻译工作中重复使用,不但提高工作效率,更重要的是解决了翻译一致性问题。

明确了机辅翻译软件的核心技术和主要辅助功能,其工作流程也不难理解了。一般来说,翻译项目在翻译公司的流程大致为:订单确认→技术分析→实施计划→技术交流→文件准备→文件翻译→文件审核→编辑排版→文件通读→文件后处理→文件交付→项目总结→项目反馈。而翻译软件参与的步骤为:技术分析→文件准备→文件翻译→文件审核→项目总结。

Trados(塔多思)翻译软件是由德国 TradosGmbH 公司开发的,已经成为全球专业翻译领域的标准工具,Trados 系列工具是业界的标准。目前已成为世界上领先的专业翻译领域的技术。该软件支持 57 种语言之间的双向互译,大大提高了工作效率,降低了成本,提高了质量。实践证明,应用塔多思解决方案后,用户的翻译工作效率提高了 30%~80%,翻译成本降低 30%~60%。软件的后台是一个非常强大的神经网络数据库,保证系统及信息安全;软件支持所有流行文档格式(DOC,RTF,HTML 等),翻译后无需再排版。它还具有完善的辅助功能,如时间、度量、表格、固定格式的自动替换等能够帮助客户大大提高工作效率。目前,Trados 是国内所有的外企、国内大型公司和专业翻译人员的首选。

Déjà Vu 翻译软件由法国 Atril 公司开发,被许多职业译者誉为 CAT 工具中的后起之秀。它可以在自己的独立界面中完成创建术语库和翻译记忆库、创建项目文件、预翻译、校对和质量控制以及导出翻译结果等功能。

Trados 2011 版主页视图

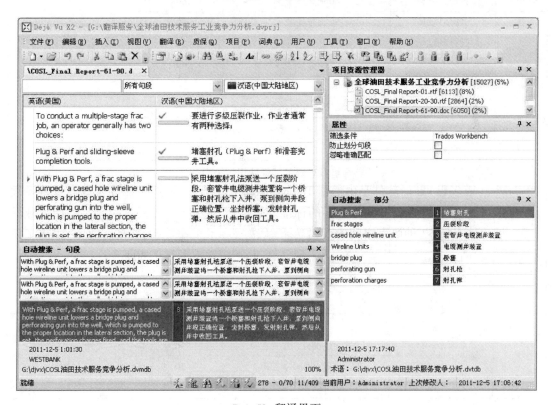

Deja Vu 翻译界面

附录5　全国翻译专业资格(水平)考试

全国翻译专业资格(水平)考试,英文名称为:China Aptitude Test for Translators and Interpreters(英文缩写为CAT TI),是为适应社会主义市场经济和我国加入世界贸易组织的需要,加强我国外语翻译专业人才队伍建设,科学、客观、公正地评价翻译专业人才水平和能力,更好地为我国对外开放和国际交流与合作服务,根据建立国家职业资格证书制度的精神,在全国实行统一的、面向社会的、国内最具权威的翻译专业资格(水平)认证,是对参试人员口译或笔译方面的双语互译能力和水平的认定。

全国翻译专业资格(水平)考试,分为四个等级,即资深翻译;一级口译、笔译翻译;二级口译、笔译翻译;三级口译、笔译翻译。各级别翻译专业资格(水平)考试均设英、日、俄、德、法、西、阿等语种。各语种、各级别均设口译和笔译考试。

各级别笔译考试均设《笔译综合能力》和《笔译实务》2个科目。下面介绍英语笔译二、三级模块设置情况。更多信息可查阅官方网站 http://www.catti.net.cn/。

英语笔译三级考试模块设置一览表

序　号	题　型		题　量	分　值	时间(分钟)
笔译综合能力					
1	词汇和语法		60道选择题	60	120
2	阅读理解		30道选择题	30	
3	完形填空		20道填空题	10	
总计				100	
笔译实务					
1	翻译	英译汉	两段或一篇文章,600个单词左右	50	180
		汉译英	一篇文章,400字左右	50	
总计				100	

英语笔译二级考试模块设置一览表

序　号	题　型		题　量	分　值	时间(分钟)
笔译综合能力					
1	词汇和语法		60道选择题	60	120
2	阅读理解		30道选择题	30	
3	完形填空		20道填空题	10	
总计				100	
笔译实务					
1	翻译	英译汉	两段文章共900个单词左右	50	180
		汉译英	两段文章共600字左右	50	
总计				100	

附录6 翻译竞赛简介

随着全球化进程的加速、一带一路倡议的大力推进,中外交流日趋频繁。翻译已经作为独立的专业学科,在高校开设。翻译作为沟通中外交流的桥梁,将会发挥越来越重要的作用。而众多高等院校、社会院所、学术机构等,纷纷举办翻译大赛,搭建了众多发现、培养、输送翻译人才的平台。

名　　称	主办单位	发布时间
《中国翻译》韩素音青年翻译奖	《中国翻译》 http://www.tac-online.org.cn/	每年2—5月
《英语世界》杯翻译竞赛	《英语世界》杂志社	每年5—10月
全国大学生"海伦·斯诺翻译奖"竞赛	陕西翻译协会 http://www.chsta.org	每年8—10月
"华政杯"全国法律翻译大赛	华东政法大学、全国翻译专业学位研究生教育指导委员会、教育部高等学校翻译专业教学协作组	每年4—7月
世界中医翻译大赛	国家中医药管理局国际合作司、中国翻译协会、中国翻译研究院	每年1—5月
许渊冲翻译大赛	山西大同大学许渊冲翻译与比较文化研究院、《外语学刊》编辑部	每年2—6月
新纪元全球华文青年文学奖(创作组、翻译组)	香港中文大学	每两年一次,1—7月
梁实秋文学奖(创作组、翻译组)	台湾师范大学图书馆出版中心	每年7—8月
"沪江"杯翻译竞赛	上海市文学艺术界联合会上海世纪出版(集团)有限公司	每年6—8月
全国科技翻译大赛	上海市科技翻译学会	每年7—9月